KB166293

Easy Way to Learn Korean in 2weeks
  by Jinho Kim
with designs by Heungseok Choi /
  Euiryoung Hwang / Jihoon Yun
supervisioned by Taesseo Kim

e-mail : jnenglish@naver.com

 jinho7846

ISBN 979-11-979409-0-3

If you have a question about Korean,
send a massage to jnenglish@naver.com

EASY WAY TO LEARN KOREAN IN 2WEEKS

**EASY! FAST!
LONG - LASTING!**

하

가 나 다 라

마 바 사

거 너

아 자

머리말

당신은 어떻게 당신의 모국어를 말하게 되었나요?

여러분 주위의 사람들로부터 말을 듣고 따라 하다 보면 말하게 되었을 겁니다.

물론 단어부터 말하게 되었겠지요.

한국에는 많은 외국인이 있습니다. 그중에 대부분의 사람이 한국어를 꽤 잘 말합니다.

어떻게 한국어를 배웠을까요? 체계적인 교육에 의해서였을까요?

아닙니다.

처음에는 한국어가 어려웠지만 그저 주변 사람들이 하는 말을 듣고 따라 하다가 할 수 있게

되었습니다.

여기 여러분이 모국어를 말하듯, 한국에 있는 외국인들이 한국말을 하듯,

한국어를 짧은 시간에 배울 수 있는 방법이 있습니다.

많은 연구 끝에 그 방법을 이 책에 담았습니다.

이 책에서 제시한 대로 따라 하다 보면, 불과 2주 만에 여러분도 한국어를 말할 수 있게 됩니다.

한국 사람들이 가장 많이 사용하는 900단어와 가장 많이 사용하는 문장으로,

아주 쉽게, 빠른 시간 안에 한국어를 배울 수 있는 방법이 들어 있는 이 책으로

한국어를 자유롭게 말할 수 있기를 바랍니다.

이 책이 나오기까지 애써주신 김태서 형제님, 김경은 자매님, 부모님과 형제자매들,

멘토 안상원님, 이진수 사장님과 진호 언어연구소 직원들에게 감사드리며,

특히 이 모든 것을 가능케 해주신 예수님께 감사드립니다.

※ 주의: 반드시 교재에서 제시한 순서대로 학습하시기 바랍니다.

PREFACE

How did you come to speak your native language?

You may have come to speak it listening to and speaking what people around you say.

Of course, you must have spoken the words at the very beginning.

There are many foreigners in Korea. Most of them speak Korean pretty well.

How did they come to speak Korean? Was it by systematic education?

No.

At first, Korean was difficult, but they were able to speak Korean after just listening to what people around them said and copying them.

Here is a way to learn Korean in a short time, just as foreigners in Korea speak Korean, as you speak your native language.

After a lot of research, I put the method in this book.

If you follow what this book suggests, you will be able to speak Korean in just 2 weeks.

With 900 words and sentences that Koreans use the most, you can speak Korean easily with this book, which contains a very easy and quick way to learn Korean.

I would like to thank Kim Tae-seo, and Jinho Language Research Institute staff for their hard work until this book came out. Thanks for my parents, brothers, Kim Kyeong-Eun, mentor Ahn Sang-Won and Lee Jun-Su.

※ Caution: Be sure to learn in the order presented in the book.

Table of Contents

Korean Consonants and Vowels

K- consonant	Roman		K- vowel	Roman	
ㄱ (gi-yeok)	g/k	game	ㅏ	a	father
ㄴ (ni-eun)	n	name	ㅑ	ya	yard
ㄷ (di-geud)	d/t	dog	ㅓ	eo	onion
ㄹ (ri-eul)	r/l	road	ㅕ	yeo	young
ㅁ (mi-eum)	m	moon	ㅗ	o	origin
ㅂ (bi-eub)	b/p	boy	ㅛ	yo	yoga
ㅅ (si-os)	s	sky	ㅜ	u	do
ㅇ (i-eung)	ng	young	ㅠ	yu	cute
ㅈ (ji-euj)	j	just	ㅡ	eu	face
ㅊ (chi-eucc)	ch(cc)	chair	ㅣ	i	kill
ㅋ (ki-euk)	k	key	ㅐ	ae	apple
ㅌ (ti-eut)	t	tea	ㅒ	yae	Yale Naim
ㅍ (pi-eub)	p	pin	ㅔ	e	bed
ㅎ (hi-euh)	h	hat	ㅖ	ye	yes
ㄲ (ssang-gi-yeok)	kk	sky	ㅚ	oe	
ㄸ (ssang-di-geud)	tt	style	ㅟ	wi	quick
ㅃ (ssang-bi-eub)	pp	spoon	ㅢ	ui	
ㅆ (ssang-si-os)	ss	cycle	ㅘ	wa	quiet
ㅉ (ssang-ji-euj)	jj	pretzel	ㅝ	wo	one
			ㅙ	wae	
			ㅞ	we	Wednesday

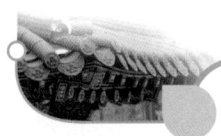

Korean Pronunciation Checklist (1)

	ㅏ (a)	ㅑ (ya)	ㅓ (eo)	ㅕ (yeo)	ㅗ (o)	ㅛ (yo)	ㅜ (u)	ㅠ (yu)	ㅡ (eu)	ㅣ (i)
ㄱ	가	갸	거	겨	고	교	구	규	그	기
(g)	ga	gya	geo	gyeo	go	gyo	gu	gyu	geu	gi
ㄴ	나	냐	너	녀	노	뇨	누	뉴	느	니
(n)	na	nya	neo	nyeo	no	nyo	nu	nyu	neu	ni
ㄷ	다	댜	더	뎌	도	됴	두	듀	드	디
(d)	da	dya	deo	dyeo	do	dyo	du	dyu	deu	di
ㄹ	라	랴	러	려	로	료	루	류	르	리
(r)	ra	rya	reo	ryeo	ro	ryo	ru	ryu	reu	ri
ㅁ	마	먀	머	며	모	묘	무	뮤	므	미
(m)	ma	mya	meo	myeo	mo	myo	mu	myu	meu	mi
ㅂ	바	뱌	버	벼	보	뵤	부	뷰	브	비
(b)	ba	bya	beo	byeo	bo	byo	bu	byu	beu	bi
ㅅ	사	샤	서	셔	소	쇼	수	슈	스	시
(s)	sa	sya	seo	syeo	so	syo	su	syu	seu	si
ㅇ	아	야	어	여	오	요	우	유	으	이
(-)	a	ya	eo	yeo	o	yo	u	yu	eu	i
ㅈ	자	쟈	저	져	조	죠	주	쥬	즈	지
(j)	ja	jya	jeo	jyeo	jo	jyo	ju	jyu	jeu	ji
ㅊ	차	챠	처	쳐	초	쵸	추	츄	츠	치
(ch)	cha	chya	cheo	chyeo	cho	chyo	chu	chyu	cheu	chi
ㅋ	카	캬	커	켜	코	쿄	쿠	큐	크	키
(k)	ka	kya	keo	kyeo	ko	kyo	ku	kyu	keu	ki
ㅌ	타	탸	터	텨	토	툐	투	튜	트	티
(t)	ta	tya	teo	tyeo	to	tyo	tu	tyu	teu	ti
ㅍ	파	퍄	퍼	펴	포	표	푸	퓨	프	피
(p)	pa	pya	peo	pyeo	po	pyo	pu	pyu	peu	pi
ㅎ	하	햐	허	혀	호	효	후	휴	흐	히
(h)	ha	hya	heo	hyeo	ho	hyo	hu	hyu	heu	hi

Korean Pronunciation Checklist (2)

	ㅏ (a)	ㅑ (ya)	ㅓ (eo)	ㅕ (yeo)	ㅗ (o)	ㅛ (yo)	ㅜ (u)	ㅠ (yu)	ㅡ (eu)	ㅣ (i)
ㄲ	까	꺄	꺼	껴	꼬	꾜	꾸	뀨	끄	끼
(kk)	kka	kkya	kkeo	kkyeo	kko	kkyo	kku	kkyu	kkeu	kki
ㄸ	따	땨	떠	뗘	또	뚀	뚜	뜌	뜨	띠
(tt)	tta	ttya	tteo	ttyeo	tto	ttyo	ttu	ttyu	tteu	tti
ㅃ	빠	뺘	뻐	뼈	뽀	뾰	뿌	쀼	쁘	삐
(pp)	ppa	ppya	ppeo	ppyeo	ppo	ppyo	ppu	ppyu	ppeu	ppi
ㅆ	싸	쌰	써	쎠	쏘	쑈	쑤	쓔	쓰	씨
(ss)	ssa	ssya	sseo	ssyeo	sso	ssyo	ssu	ssyu	sseu	ssi
ㅉ	짜	쨔	쩌	쪄	쪼	쬬	쭈	쮸	쯔	찌
(jj)	jja	jjya	jjeo	jjyeo	jjo	jjyo	jju	jjyu	jjeu	jji

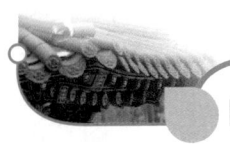

Korean Pronunciation Checklist (3)

가									
ga									
각	간	갈	감	갑	갓	강	개	객	거
gak	gan	gal	gam	gap(b)	gat(s)	gang	gae	gaek	geo
건	걸	검	겁	게	겨	격	견	결	겸
geon	geol	geom	geop(b)	ge	gyeo	gyeok	gyeon	gyeol	gyeom
겹	경	계	고	곡	곤	골	곳	공	곶
gyeop(b)	gyeong	gye	go	gok	gon	gol	got(s)	gong	got(j)
과	곽	관	괄	광	괘	괴	굉	교	구
gwa	gwak	gwan	gwal	gwang	gwae	goe	goeng	gyo	gu
국	군	굴	굿	궁	권	궐	귀	규	균
guk	gun	gul	gut(s)	gung	gwon	gwol	gwi	gyu	gyun
귤	그	극	근	글	금	급	긍	기	긴
gyul	geu	geuk	geun	geul	geum	geup(b)	geung	gi	gin
길	김	까	깨	꼬	꼭	꽃	꾀	꾸	꿈
gil	gim	kka	kkae	kko	kkok	kkot(cc)	kkoe	kku	kkum
끝	끼								
kkeut	kki								

나									
na									
낙	난	날	남	납	낭	내	냉	너	널
nak	nan	nal	nam	nap(b)	nang	nae	naeng	neo	neol
네	녀	녁	년	념	녕	노	녹	논	놀
ne	nyeo	nyeok	nyeon	nyeom	nyeong	no	nok	non	nol
농	뇌	누	눈	눌	느	늑	늠	능	늬
nong	noe	nu	nun	nul	neu	neuk	neum	neung	nui
니	닉	닌	닐	님					
ni	nik	nin	nil	nim					

다									
da									
단	달	담	답	당	대	댁	더	덕	도
dan	dal	dam	dap(b)	dang	dae	daek	deo	deok	do
독	돈	돌	동	돼	되	된	두	둑	둔
dok	don	dol	dong	dwae	doe	doen	du	duk	dun
뒤	드	득	들	등	디	따	땅	때	또
dwi	deu	deuk	deul	deung	di	tta	ttang	ttae	tto
뚜	뚝	뜨	띠						
ttu	ttuk	tteu	tti						
라									
ra									
락	란	람	랑	래	랭	량	렁	레	려
rak	ran	ram	rang	rae	raeng	ryang	reong	re	ryeo
력	련	렬	렴	렵	령	례	로	록	론
ryeok	ryeon	ryeol	ryeom	ryeop(b)	ryeong	rye	ro	rok	ron
롱	뢰	료	롱	루	류	륙	륜	률	륭
rong	roe	ryo	ryong	ru	ryu	ryuk	ryun	ryul	ryung
르	륵	른	름	릉	리	린	림	립	
reu	reuk	reun	reum	reung	ri	rin	rim	rip(b)	
마									
ma									
막	만	말	망	매	맥	맨	맹	머	먹
mak	man	mal	mang	mae	maek	maen	maeng	meo	meok
메	며	멱	면	멸	명	모	목	몰	못
me	myeo	myeok	myeon	myeol	myeong	mo	mok	mol	mot(s)
몽	뫼	묘	무	묵	밀				
mong	moe	myo	mu	muk	mil				
문	물	므	미	민					
mun	mul	meu	mi	min					

바
ba

박	반	발	밥	방	배	백	뱀	버	번
bak	ban	bal	bap(b)	bang	bae	baek	baem	beo	beon
벌	범	법	벼	벽	변	별	병	보	복
beol	beom	beop(b)	byeo	byeok	byeon	byeol	byeong	bo	bok
본	봉	부	북	분	불	붕	비	빈	빌
bon	bong	bu	buk	bun	bul	bung	bi	bin	bil
빔	빙	빠	빼	뻐	뽀	뿌	쁘	삐	
bim	bing	ppa	ppae	ppeo	ppo	ppu	ppeu	ppi	

사
sa

삭	산	살	삼	삽	상	샅	새	색	생
sak	san	sal	sam	sap(b)	sang	sat	sae	saek	saeng
서	석	선	설	섬	섭	성	세	셔	소
seo	seok	seon	seol	seom	seop(b)	seong	se	syeo	so
속	손	솔	솟	송	쇄	쇠	수	숙	순
sok	son	sol	sot(s)	song	swae	soe	su	suk	sun
술	숨	숭	쉬	스	슬	슴	습	승	시
sul	sum	sung	swi	seu	seul	seum	seup(b)	seung	si
식	신	실	심	십	싱	싸	쌍	쌔	쏘
sik	sin	sil	sim	sip(b)	sing	ssa	ssang	ssae	sso
쑥	씨								
ssuk	ssi								

아									
a									
악	안	알	암	압	앙	앞	애	액	앵
ak	an	al	am	ap(b)	ang	ap	ae	aek	aeng
야	약	얀	양	어	억	언	얼	엄	업
ya	yak	yan	yang	eo	eok	eon	eol	eom	eop(b)
에	여	역	연	열	염	엽	영	예	오
e	yeo	yeok	yeon	yeol	yeom	yeop(b)	yeong	ye	o
옥	온	올	옴	옹	와	완	왈	왕	왜
ok	on	ol	om	ong	wa	wan	wal	wang	wae
외	왼	요	욕	용	우	욱	운	울	움
oe	oen	yo	yok	yong	u	uk	un	ul	um
웅	워	원	월	위	유	육	윤	율	융
ung	wo	won	wol	wi	yu	yuk	yun	yul	yung
윳	으	은	을	음	읍	응	의	이	익
yut(cc)	eu	eun	eul	eum	eup(b)	eung	ui	i	ik
인	일	임	입	잉					
in	il	im	ip(b)	ing					

자									
ja									
작	잔	잠	잡	장	재	쟁	저	적	전
jak	jan	jam	jap(b)	jang	jae	jaeng	jeo	jeok	jeon
절	점	접	정	제	조	족	존	졸	종
jeol	jeom	jeop(b)	jeong	je	jo	jok	jon	jol	jong
좌	죄	주	죽	준	줄	중	쥐	즈	즉
jwa	joe	ju	juk	jun	jul	jung	jwi	jeu	jeuk
즐	즘	즙	증	지	직	진	질	짐	집
jeul	jeum	jeup(b)	jeung	ji	jik	jin	jil	jim	jip(b)
징	짜	째	쪼	찌					
jing	jja	jjae	jjo	jji					

차 cha									
착	찬	찰	참	창	채	책	처	척	천
chak	chan	chal	cham	chang	chae	chaek	cheo	cheok	cheon
철	첨	첩	청	체	초	촉	촌	총	최
cheol	cheom	cheop(b)	cheong	che	cho	chok	chon	chong	choe
추	축	춘	출	춤	충	측	층	치	칙
chu	chuk	chun	chul	chum	chung	cheuk	cheung	chi	chik
친	칠	침	칩	칭					
chin	chil	chim	chip(b)	ching					

카 ka									
코	쾌	크	큰	키					
ko	kwae	keu	keun	ki					

타 ta									
탁	탄	탈	탐	탑	탕	태	택	탱	터
tak	tan	tal	tam	tap(b)	tang	tae	taek	taeng	teo
테	토	톤	톨	통	퇴	투	퉁	튀	트
te	to	ton	tol	tong	toe	tu	tung	twi	teu
특	틈	티							
teuk	teum	ti							

파 pa									
판	팔	패	팽	퍼	페	펴	편	폄	평
pan	pal	pae	paeng	peo	pe	pyeo	pyeon	pyeom	pyeong
폐	포	폭	표	푸	품	풍	프	피	픽
pye	po	pok	pyo	pu	pum	pung	peu	pi	pik
필	핍								
pil	pip(b)								

하									
ha									
학	한	할	함	합	항	해	핵	행	향
hak	han	hal	ham	hap(b)	hang	hae	haek	haeng	hyang
허	헌	험	헤	혀	혁	현	혈	혐	협
heo	heon	heom	he	hyeo	hyeok	hyeon	hyeol	hyeom	hyeop(b)
형	혜	호	혹	혼	홀	홉	홍	화	확
hyeong	hye	ho	hok	hon	hol	hop(b)	hong	hwa	hwak
환	활	황	홰	횃	회	획	횡	효	후
hwan	hwal	hwang	hwae	hwaet(s)	hoe	hoek	hoeng	hyo	hu
훈	원	훼	휘	휴	휼	흉	흐	흑	흔
hun	hwon	hwe	hwi	hyu	hyul	hyung	heu	heuk	heun
흘	흠	흡	흥	희	흰	히	힘		
heul	heum	heup(b)	heung	hui	huin	hi	him		

"Easy Way to Learn Korean in 2 weeks"

How to learn Day (　)

1. Listen and speak the K-words(meaning and pronunciation) three times.

2. Cover the K-words and write the K-words in K-word ①.

3. Write not-filled K-words of ①, in K-word ② from the top in a row.

4. Write English words in English ③.

5. Read K-word ② and English ③ three times.

6. Cover K-word ② and write K-words in K-word ④.

7. Write not-filled K-words of ④, in K-word ⑤ and English words in English ⑥.

8. Read K-word ⑤ and English ⑥ three times.

9. Cover K-word ⑤ and write the K-words in K-word ⑦.

10. Write not-filled K-words of ⑦, in K-word ⑧ and English words in English ⑨ in Final check.

11. Read and speak K-word ⑧ and English ⑨ three times.

How to learn Day Review

12. Read Day (1)-Day (5) Final check K-word ⑧ and English ⑨ three times.

13. Write the meaning of 100 K-words in English blank ＿＿＿＿＿ of Day (　) Review.

14. Write not-filled K-words of Day Review in K-word ⑩ and English words in English ⑪.

15. Read K-word ⑩ and English ⑪ three times.

16. Cover K-word ⑩ and write K-words in K-word ⑫.

17. Write not-filled K-words of ⑫, in K-word ⑬ and English words in English ⑭.

18. Read K-word ⑬ and English ⑭ three times.

19. Cover K-word ⑬ and write K-words in K-word ⑮.

20. Write not-filled K-words of ⑮, in K-word ⑯ and English words in English ⑰ in Final check.

How to learn Day Sentence ( )

21. Read Final check K-word ⑯ and English ⑰ three times.

22. Speak the K-words of Sentence Words while listening to them.

23. Write K-words in _____ of Day Sentence( ), referring to Sentence Words.

24. Write not-filled K-words of _____, in K-word ⑱ and English words in English ⑲.

25. Read K-word ⑱ and English ⑲ three times.

26. Cover K-word ⑱ and write K-words in K-word ⑳.

27. Write not-filled K-words of ⑳, in K-word ㉑ and English words in English ㉒.

28. Read K-word ㉑ and English ㉒ three times.

29. Cover K-word ㉑ and write K-words in K-word ㉓.

30. Write not-filled K-words of ㉓, in K-word ㉔ and English words in English ㉕ in Final check.

How to learn Day List (　)

31. Mark ✓ in the □(☑), if you can't think of the K-word meaning.

32. Write ☑ K-words, in K-word ㉖ and English words in English ㉗ of Day List Study

33. Read K-word ㉖ and English ㉗ three times.

34. Cover K-word ㉖ and write K-words in K-word ㉘.

35. Write not-filled K-words of ㉘, in K-word ㉙ and English words in English ㉚.

36. Read K-word ㉙ and English ㉚ three times.

37. Cover K-word ㉙ and write K-words in K-word ㉛.

38. Write not-filled K-words of ㉛, in Final check K-word ㉜ and English words in English ㉝.

You must learn in order.

How to Learn Day ( )

1) Listen and speak the K-words three times.

	K-word	Pronounce	English	K-word ❶	Sentence example
1	것	geos	thing		You did a good thing.
2	한다	han-da	do		They do works happily.
3	된다	doen-da	become		They become nervous.
4	수	su	number		Number 7 means good luck.
5	수	su	way		I have a good way.
6	길	gil	way		Could you tell me the way?
7	쪽	jjok	way		Come this way.
.	.	.	.		.
.	.	.	.		.
20	국민	guk-min	people		Korean people love peace.

2) Cover the K-words and write the K-words in K-word ①.

	K-word	Pronounce	English	K-word ❶	Sentence example
1		geos	thing	것	You did a good thing.
2		han-da	do		They do works happily.
3		doen-da	become		They become nervous.
4		su	number		Number 7 means good luck.
5		su	way	수	I have a good way.
6		gil	way	길	Could you tell me the way?
7		jjok	way	쪽	Come this way.
8		bang-sik	way		I like his way of thinking.
9		jeom	way	점	It's a success in every way.
10		jeom	store		He went to the convenience store.
11		na	I		I always try.
.		.	.		

3) Write not-filled K-words of ① in K-word ② from the top in a row.

Final	K-word ❽				
check	English ❾				

K-word ❷	English ❸	K-word ❹	K-word ❺	English ❻	K-word ❼
한다					
된다					
수					
방식					
점					
나					

4) Write English words in English ③.

Final	K-word ❽				
check	English ❾				

K-word ❷	English ❸	K-word ❹	K-word ❺	English ❻	K-word ❼
한다	do				
된다	become				
수	number				
방식	way				
점	store				
나	I				

5) Read K-word ② and English ③ three times.

6) Cover K-word ② and write K-words in K-word ④.

Final	K-word ❽				
check	English ❾				

K-word ❷	English ❸	K-word ❹	K-word ❺	English ❻	K-word ❼
	do	한다			
	become				
	number	수			
	way				
	store				
	I	나			

7) Write not-filled K-words of ④, in K-word ⑤ and English words in English ⑥.

Final	K-word ❽				
check	English ❾				

K-word ❷	English ❸	K-word ❹	K-word ❺	English ❻	K-word ❼
한다	do	한다	된다	*become*	
된다	become		방식	*way*	
수	number	수	점	*store*	
방식	way				
점	store				
나	I	나			

8) Read K-word ⑤ and English ⑥ three times.

9) Cover K-word ⑤ and write the K-words in K-word ⑦.

Final	K-word ❽				
check	English ❾				

K-word ❷	English ❸	K-word ❹	K-word ❺	English ❻	K-word ❼
한다	do	한다		become	된다
된다	become			way	
수	number	수		store	점
방식	way				
점	store				
나	I	나			

10) Write not-filled K-words of ⑦, in K-word ⑧ and English words in English ⑨
in Final check.

Final	K-word ❽	방식			
check	English ❾	way			

K-word ❷	English ❸	K-word ❹	K-word ❺	English ❻	K-word ❼
한다	do	한다	된다	become	된다
된다	become		방식	way	
수	number	수	점	store	점
방식	way				
점	store				
나	I	나			

11) Read and speak K-word ⑧ and English ⑨ three times.

12) Read Day(1)-Day(5) Final check K-word ⑧ and English ⑨ three times.

Final	K-word ❽	방식			
check	English ❾	way			

13) Write the meanings of 100 K-words in English blank ....

Day Review

	K-word	English		K-word	English
1	것	You did a good _thing._	21	우리	.... succeeded!
2	한다	They _do_ works happily.	22	이	This _tooth_ is loose.
3	된다	They _become_ nervous.	23	이	_This_ book is mine.
4	수	_Number_ 7 means good luck.	24	이런	I like _this_ kind of person.
5	수	I have a good _way._	25	이것	_This_ is mine.
6	길	Could you tell me the ....?	26	이거	How much is ....?
7	쪽	Come this _way._	27	보다	Better _than_ nothing.
8	방식	I like his _way_ of thinking.	28	본다	I _see_ the result.
9	점	It's a success in every _way._	29	같다	Our hometown is the _same._
10	점	He went to the convenience _store._	30	준다	They .... examples.
11	나	_I_ always try.	31	드린다	I _give_ a car to my father today.
12	내	_I_ 'll do it.	32	대한다	I .... people kindly.
13	그	_He_ laughed.	33	간다	They _go_ to America today.
14	없다	I .... money.	34	다닌다	I .... to a temple.
.	.		.	.	.
.	.		.	.	.
.	.		.	.	.
.	.		100	다른	Paint a _different_ color.

14) Write not-filled K-words of Day Review, in K-word ⑩ and English words in English ⑪ in Day Review Study.

Day Review Study

Final	K-word ⑯				
check	English ⑰				

K-word ⑩	English ⑪	K-word ⑫	K-word ⑬	English ⑭	K-word ⑮
길	way				
없다	not have				
우리	we				
이거	this				
준다	give				
대한다	treat				
다닌다	go				

15) Read K-word ⑩ and English ⑪ three times.

16) Cover K-word ⑩ and write K-words in K-word ⑫.

Final	K-word ⑯			
check	English ⑰			

K-word ⑩	English ⑪	K-word ⑫	K-word ⑬	English ⑭	K-word ⑮
	way	길			
	not have	없다			
	we				
	this	이거			
	give				
	treat	대한다			
	go				

17) Write not-filled K-words of ⑫, in K-word ⑬ and English
   words in English ⑭.

Final	K-word ⑯				
check	English ⑰				

K-word ⑩	English ⑪	K-word ⑫	K-word ⑬	English ⑭	K-word ⑮
길	way	길	우리	we	
없다	not have	없다	준다	give	
우리	we		다닌다	go	
이거	this	이거			
준다	give				
대한다	treat	대한다			
다닌다	go				

18) Read K-word ⑬ and English ⑭ three times.

19) Cover K-word ⑬ and write K-words in K-word ⑮.

Final	K-word ⑯				
check	English ⑰				

K-word ⑩	English ⑪	K-word ⑫	K-word ⑬	English ⑭	K-word ⑮
길	way	길		we	
없다	not have	없다		give	준다
우리	we			go	다닌다
이거	this	이거			
준다	give				
대한다	treat	대한다			
다닌다	go				

20) Write not-filled K-words of ⑮, in K-word ⑯ and English words in English ⑰ in Final check.

Final	K-word ⑯	우리			
check	English ⑰	*we*			

K-word ⑩	English ⑪	K-word ⑫	K-word ⑬	English ⑭	K-word ⑮
길	way	길	우리	we	
없다	not have	없다	준다	give	준다
우리	we		다닌다	go	다닌다
이거	this	이거			
준다	give				
대한다	treat	대한다			
다닌다	go				

21) Read Final check K-word ⑯ and English ⑰ three times.

Final	K-word ⑯	우리			
check	English ⑰	we			

K-word ⑩	English ⑪	K-word ⑫	K-word ⑬	English ⑭	K-word ⑮

22) Listen and speak the K-words of Sentence Words(　).

Sentence Words(　)

	K-word	pronounce	English		K-word	pronounce	English
1	너는	neo-neun	you	13	그는	geu-neun	he
	좋은	joh-eun	good		웃었다	us-eoss-da	laughed
	것을	geos-eul	thing	14	나는	na-neun	I
	했다	haess-da	did		돈이	don-i	money
2	그들은	geu-deul-eun	they		없다	eobs-da	don't have
	행복하게	haeng-bok-ha-ge	happily	15	오늘은	o-neul-eun	today
	일을	il-eul	works		날씨가	nal-ssi-ga	the weather
	한다	han-da	do		좋지않다	joh-ji-anh-da	is not fine
3	그들은	geu-deul-eun	they	16	이것	i-geos	this
	긴장하게	gin-jang-ha-ge	nervous		말고	mal-go	not
	된다	doen-da	become		저것	jeo-geos	that
	.	.	.		.	.	.
	.	.	.		.	.	.
	.	.	.		.	.	.

23) Write K-words in .... of Day Sentence( ), referring to
Sentence Words.

Day Sentence( )

	Write K-word in		Write K-word in ....
1	You did a good thing. 너는 좋은 _것_ 을 했다.	14	I don't have money. 나는 돈이 _없다_ .
2	They do works happily. 그들은 행복하게 일을 _한다_ .	15	It' not fine today. 오늘은 날씨가 좋지 _____.
3	They become nervous. 그들은 긴장하게 _된다_ .	16	Please give me not this but that. 이 것 _말고_ 저 것 주세요.
4	Number7 means good luck. 7 이라는 _수_ 는 행운을 의미한다.	17	He is not a doctor. 그는 의사가 _아니다_ .
5	I have a good way. 나에게 좋은 _수_ 가 있어.	18	I don't go to church. 나는 교회에 가지 _않는다_ .
6	Could you tell me the way? 나에게 _길_ 을 말씀해주시겠어요?	19	People love freedom. _사람_ 들은 자유를 사랑한다.
7	Come this way. 이 _____으로 와.	20	Korean people love peace.. 대한민국 _국민_ 들은 평화를 사랑한다.
8	I like his way of thinking. 나는 그의 생각하는 _____이 좋다.	21	We succeeded! _____는 성공했다!
9	It's a success in every way. 그것은 모든 _점_ 에서 성공이다.	22	This tooth is loose. 이 _이_ 가 헐렁하다.
10	He went to the convenience store. 그는 편의 _점_ 에 갔다.	23	This book is mine. _이_ 책은 나의 것이다.
	·		·
	·		·
	·		·
	·		·
	·	100	·
	·		·

24) Write not-filled K-words of .... , in K-word ⑱ and English words in English ⑲.

Day Sentence Study

	Final	K-word ㉔				
	check	English ㉕				

K-word ⑱	English ⑲	K-word ⑳	K-word ㉑	English ㉒	K-word ㉓
쪽	way				
방식	way				
않다	not				
우리	we				

25) Read K-word ⑱ and English ⑲ three times.

26) Cover K-word ⑱ and write K-words in K-word ⑳.

	Final	K-word ㉔				
	check	English ㉕				

K-word ⑱	English ⑲	K-word ⑳	K-word ㉑	English ㉒	K-word ㉓
	way				
	way	방식			
	not				
	we				

27) Write not-filled K-words of ⑳, in K-word ㉑ and English words in English ㉒.

Final	K-word ㉔				
check	English ㉕				

K-word ⑱	English ⑲	K-word ⑳	K-word ㉑	English ㉒	K-word ㉓
쪽	way		쪽	*way*	
방식	way	방식	않다	*not*	
않다	not		우리	*we*	
우리	we				

28) Read K-word ㉑ and English ㉒ three times.

29) Cover K-word ㉑ and write K-words in K-word ㉓.

Final	K-word ㉔				
check	English ㉕				

K-word ⑱	English ⑲	K-word ⑳	K-word ㉑	English ㉒	K-word ㉓
쪽	way			way	쪽
방식	way	방식		not	않다
않다	not			we	
우리	we				

30) Write not-filled K-words of ㉓, in K-word ㉔ and English words in English ㉕ in Final check.

Final	K-word ㉔	우리			
check	English ㉕	*we*			

K-word ⑱	English ⑲	K-word ⑳	K-word ㉑	English ㉒	K-word ㉓
쪽	way		쪽	way	쪽
방식	way	방식	않다	not	않다
않다	not		우리	we	
우리	we				

How to learn Day List (   )

31) Mark ✓ in the □(☑), if you can't think of the K-word meaning.

Day1 List (1)

1-100				
□ 1) 것	□ 31) 드린다	□ 61) 집	□ 91) 파악하고 있다	
□ 2) 한다	□ 32) 대한다	□ 62) 나온다	□ 92) 자신	
☑ 3) 된다	□ 33) 간다	□ 63) 따른다	□ 93) 문화	
□ 4) 수	□ 34) 다닌다	□ 64) 그리고	□ 94) 원	
□ 5) 수	☑ 35) 년	□ 65) 및	□ 95) 생각	
□ 6) 길	□ 36) 한	□ 66) 그때	□ 96) 명	
□ 7) 쪽	□ 37) 말	□ 67) 그럼	□ 97) 통한다	
□ 8) 방식	□ 38) 일	□ 68) 문제	□ 98) 소리	
□ 9) 점	□ 39) 일	□ 69) 그런	□ 99) 다시	
□ 10) 점	□ 40) 일 한다	☑ 70) 산다	☑ 100) 다른	
□ 11) 나	□ 41) 작품	□ 71) 산다		
□ 12) 내	□ 42) 작업	□ 72) 지낸다		
.	.			

32) Write ☑ K-words in K-word ㉖ and English words in English ㉗ of Day List Study.

Day List Study

Final	K-word ㉜				
check	English ㉝				

K-word ㉖	English ㉗	K-word ㉘	K-word ㉙	English ㉚	K-word ㉛
된다	*become*				
년	*year*				
산다	*live*				
다른	*different*				
.	.				

33) Read K-word ㉖ and English ㉗ three times.

34) Cover K-word ㉖ and write K-words, in K-word ㉘.

Day List Study

Final	K-word ㉜				
check	English ㉝				

K-word ㉖	English ㉗	K-word ㉘	K-word ㉙	English ㉚	K-word ㉛
	become	된다			
	year				
	live	산다			
	different				

35) Write not-filled K-words of ㉘, in K-word ㉙ and English words in English ㉚.

Day List Study

Final	K-word ㉜				
check	English ㉝				

K-word ㉖	English ㉗	K-word ㉘	K-word ㉙	English ㉚	K-word ㉛
된다	become	된다	년	*year*	
년	year		다른	*different*	
산다	live	산다			
다른	different				

36) Read K-word ㉙ and English ㉚ three times.

37) Cover K-word ㉙ and write K-words, in K-word ㉛.

Final	K-word ㉜			
check	English ㉝			

K-word ㉖	English ㉗	K-word ㉘	K-word ㉙	English ㉚	K-word ㉛
된다	become	된다		year	
년	year			different	다른
산다	live	산다			
다른	different				

38) Write not-filled K-words of ㉛, in K-word ㉜ and English words in English ㉝ in Final check.

Final	K-word ㉜	년			
check	English ㉝	year			

K-word ㉖	English ㉗	K-word ㉘	K-word ㉙	English ㉚	K-word ㉛
된다	become	된다	년	year	
년	year		다른	different	다른
산다	live	산다			
다른	different				

	K-word	Pronounce	English	K-word ❶	Sentence example
1	것	geos	thing		You did a good thing.
2	한다	han-da	do		They do works happily.
3	된다	doen-da	become		They become nervous.
4	수	su	number		Number 7 means good luck.
5	수	su	way		I have a good way.
6	길	gil	way		Could you tell me the way?
7	쪽	jjok	way		Come this way.
8	방식	bang-sik	way		I like his way of thinking.
9	점	jeom	way		It's a success in every way.
10	점	jeom	store		He went to the convenience store.
11	나	na	I		I always try.
12	내	nae	I		I'll do it.
13	그	geu	he		He laughed.
14	없다	eobs-da	not have		I don't have money.
15	않다	anh-da	not		It' not fine today.
16	말고	mal-go	not		Please give me not this but that.
17	아니다	a-ni-da	not		He is not a doctor.
18	않는다	anh-neun-da	do not		I don't go to church.
19	사람	sa-ram	people		People love freedom.
20	국민	guk-min	people		Korean people love peace.

Final	K-word ❽				
check	English ❾				

K-word ❷	English ❸	K-word ❹	K-word ❺	English ❻	K-word ❼

	K-word	Pronounce	English	K-word ❶	Sentence example
21	우리	u-ri	we		We succeeded!
22	이	i	tooth		This tooth is loose.
23	이	i	this		This book is mine.
24	이런	i-reon	this		I like this kind of person.
25	이것	i-geos	this		This is mine.
26	이거	i-geo	this		How much is this?
27	보다	bo-da	than		Better than nothing.
28	본다	bon-da	see		I see the result.
29	같다	gat-da	same		Our hometown is the same.
30	준다	jun-da	give		They give examples.
31	드린다	deu-rin-da	give		I give a car to my father today.
32	대한다	dae-han-da	treat		I treat people kindly.
33	간다	gan-da	go		They go to America today.
34	다닌다	da-nin-da	go		I go to a temple.
35	년	nyeon	year		What year is it?
36	한	han	one		I need one person.
37	말	mal	word		I understand your words.
38	일	il	day		He works 4 days a week.
39	일	il	work		This is a hard work.
40	일한다	il-han-da	work		He works hard everyday.

Final	K-word ❽				
check	English ❾				

K-word ❷	English ❸	K-word ❹	K-word ❺	English ❻	K-word ❼

	K-word	Pronounce	English	K-word ❶	Sentence example
41	작품	jak-pum	work		This painting is his work.
42	작업	jak-eob	work		He is resting after hard work.
43	직장	jik-jang	job		Job is precious.
44	때문	ttae-mun	because of		It's because of you.
45	말한다	mal-han-da	speak		You speak so fast.
46	위하여	wi-ha-yeo	for		I did it for you.
47	그러나	geu-reo-na	but		Sad but true.
48	온다	on-da	come		They come today.
49	안다	an-da	know		I know you.
50	씨	ssi	family name		I can't see Kim these days.
51	그렇다	geu-reoh-da	right		That's right!
52	큰	keun	big		He has a big nose.
53	크다	keu-da	big		The moon is big.
54	또	tto	once again		He is late once again.
55	사회	sa-hoe	society		The society won't accept me.
56	안에	an-e	in		I'm in a cave.
57	좋은	joh-eun	good		He is a good man.
58	더	deo	more		I want more.
59	받는다	bad-neun-da	receive		I receive an award tomorrow.
60	그것	geu-geos	it		Forget it.

Final	K-word ❽				
check	English ❾				

K-word ❷	English ❸	K-word ❹	K-word ❺	English ❻	K-word ❼

	K-word	Pronounce	English	K-word ❶	Sentence example
61	집	jib	house		Leave my house.
62	나온다	na-on-da	come out		He comes out of prison today.
63	따른다	tta-reun-da	obey		People obey his order.
64	그리고	geu-ri-go	and		And it was my turn.
65	및	micc	and		Be careful home and school.
66	그때	geu-ttae	then		We woke up by then.
67	그럼	geu-reom	then		Then, I'll see you there.
68	문제	mun-je	problem		Is there a problem?
69	그런	geu-reon	such		I love such a thing.
70	산다	san-da	buy		I buy a car today.
71	산다	san-da	live		I live in Seoul.
72	지낸다	ji-naen-da	live		I live well.
73	저	jeo	um		Um, do I know you?
74	생각한다	saeng-gak-han-da	think		He always thinks deeply.
75	모른다	mo-reun-da	don't know		I don't know you.
76	속	sok	inside		The inside of the box is empty.
77	만든다	man-deun-da	make		My mother makes cakes.
78	삼는다	sam-neun-da	make		I make him my brother today.
79	시킨다	si-kin-da	make		He makes them work.
80	두	du	two		There are two people.

Final	K-word ❽				
check	English ❾				

K-word ❷	English ❸	K-word ❹	K-word ❺	English ❻	K-word ❼

	K-word	Pronounce	English	K-word ❶	Sentence example
81	둘	dul	two		You two, come here.
82	앞	ap	front		It stopped in front of me.
83	경우	gyeong-u	case		In case of fire, dial 119.
84	중	jung	monk		She is a monk.
85	중	jung	during		It rained during the night.
86	동안에	dong-an-e	during		It rained during the night.
87	어떤	eo-tteon	any		Any questions?
88	잘	jal	well		She swims well.
89	그녀	geu-nyeo	she		She smiled.
90	먹는다	meok-neun-da	eat		Monks eat vegetables.
91	파악하고 있다	pa-ak-ha-go iss-da	grasp		They grasp the situation.
92	자신	ja-sin	self		I love myself.
93	문화	mun-hwa	culture		Culture destroys language.
94	원	won	₩		Give me ₩500.
95	생각	saeng-gak	thought		Let you know my thought.
96	명	myeong	famous		He is a famous lecturer.
97	통한다	tong-han-da	make sense		This sentence makes sense.
98	소리	sori	sound		He heard the sound.
99	다시	da-si	again		Once again.
100	다른	da-reun	different		Paint a different color.

Final	K-word ❽				
check	English ❾				

K-word ❷	English ❸	K-word ❹	K-word ❺	English ❻	K-word ❼

	K-word	English		K-word	English
1	것	You did a good	21	우리	.... succeeded!
2	한다	They .... works happily.	22	이	This .... is loose.
3	된다	They .... nervous.	23	이	.... book is mine.
4	수	.... 7 means good luck.	24	이런	I like .... kind of person.
5	수	I have a good	25	이것	.... is mine.
6	길	Could you tell me the ....?	26	이거	How much is ....?
7	쪽	Come this	27	보다	Better .... nothing.
8	방식	I like his .... of thinking.	28	본다	I .... the result.
9	점	It's a success in every	29	같다	Our hometown is the ....
10	점	He went to the convenience	30	준다	They .... examples.
11	나	.... always try.	31	드린다	I .... a car to my father today.
12	내	.... 'll do it.	32	대한다	I .... people kindly.
13	그	.... laughed.	33	간다	They .... to America today.
14	없다	I do .... money.	34	다닌다	I .... to a temple.
15	않다	It's .... fine today.	35	년	What .... is it?
16	말고	Please give me .... this but that.	36	한	I need .... person.
17	아니다	He is .... a doctor.	37	말	I understand your ....
18	않는다	I .... go to church.	38	일	He works 4 .... a week.
19	사람	.... love freedom.	39	일	This is a hard ....
20	국민	Korean .... love peace.	40	일한다	He .... hard everyday.

1) thing　　2) do　　3) become　　4) Number
5) way　　6) way　　7) way　　8) way
9) way　　10) store　　11) I　　12) I　　13) He　　14) not have　　15) not　　16) not
17) not　　18) do not　　19) People　　20) people　　21) We　　22) tooth　　23) This　　24) this
25) This　　26) this　　27) than　　28) see　　29) same　　30) give　　31) give　　32) treat
33) go　　34) go　　35) year　　36) one　　37) words　　38) days　　39) work　　40) works

	K-word	English		K-word	English
41	작품	This painting is his _____.	61	집	Leave my _____.
42	작업	He is resting after hard _____.	62	나온다	He _____ of prison today.
43	직장	_____ is precious.	63	따른다	People _____ his order.
44	때문	It's _____ you.	64	그리고	_____ it was my turn.
45	말한다	You _____ so fast.	65	및	Be careful home _____ school.
46	위하여	I did it _____ you.	66	그때	We woke up by _____.
47	그러나	Sad _____ true.	67	그럼	_____, I'll see you there.
48	온다	They _____ today.	68	문제	Is there a _____?
49	안다	I _____ you.	69	그런	I love _____ a thing.
50	씨	I can't see _____ these days.	70	산다	I _____ a car today.
51	그렇다	That's _____!	71	산다	I _____ in Seoul.
52	큰	He has a _____ nose.	72	지낸다	I _____ well.
53	크다	The moon is _____.	73	저	_____, do I know you?
54	또	He is late _____.	74	생각한다	He always _____ deeply.
55	사회	The _____ won't accept me.	75	모른다	I _____ you.
56	안에	I'm _____ a cave.	76	속	The _____ of the box is empty.
57	좋은	He is a _____ man.	77	만든다	My mother _____ cakes.
58	더	I want _____.	78	삼는다	I _____ him my brother today.
59	받는다	I _____ an award tomorrow.	79	시킨다	He _____ them work.
60	그것	Forget _____.	80	두	There are _____ people.

41) work　　42) work　　43) Job　　44) because of　　45) speak　　46) for　　47) but　　48) come
49) know　　50) Kim　　51) right　　52) big　　53) big　　54) once again　　55) society　　56) in
57) good　　58) more　　59) receive　　60) it　　61) house　　62) comes out　　63) obey　　64) And
65) and　　66) then　　67) Then　　68) problem　　69) such　　70) buy　　71) live　　72) live
73) Um　　74) thinks　　75) don't know　　76) inside　　77) makes　　78) make　　79) makes　　80) two

	K-word	English
81	둘	You ...., come here.
82	앞	It stopped in .... of me.
83	경우	In .... of fire, dial 119.
84	중	She is a ....
85	중	It rained .... the night.
86	동안에	It rained .... the night.
87	어떤	.... questions?
88	잘	She swims ....
89	그녀	.... smiled.
90	먹는다	Monks .... vegetables.
91	파악하고 있다	They .... the situation.
92	자신	I love my ....
93	문화	.... destroys language.
94	원	Give me .... 500.
95	생각	Let you know my ....
96	명	He is a .... lecturer.
97	통한다	This sentence ....
98	소리	He heard the ....
99	다시	Once ....
100	다른	Paint a .... color.

King Sejong

– The 4th king of Joseon Dynasty

King Sejong was born in 1397.
His 32 year reign marked great achievements.
Hangeul, created by King Sejong,
has been used as a common script for
the Republic of Korea and North Korea.

81) two   82) front   83) case   84) monk
85) during   86) during   87) Any   88) well
89) She   90) eat   91) grasp   92) self
93) Culture   94) ₩   95) thought   96) famous
97) makes sense 98) sound   99) again   100) different

Day1 Review Study

Final	K-word ⑯				
check	English ⑰				

K-word ⑩	English ⑪	K-word ⑫	K-word ⑬	English ⑭	K-word ⑮

Day1 Sentence(1)

	Write K-word in		Write K-word in ....
1	You did a good thing. 너는 좋은 ....을 했다.	14	I don't have money. 나는 돈이 ....
2	They do works happily. 그들은 행복하게 일을	15	The weather is not fine today. 오늘은 날씨가 좋지 ....
3	They become nervous. 그들은 긴장하게	16	Please give me not this but that. 이것 .... 저것 주세요.
4	Number 7 means good luck. 7 이라는 ....는 행운을 의미한다.	17	He is not a doctor. 그는 의사가 ....
5	I have a good way. 나는 좋은 ......가 있어.	18	I don't go to church. 나는 교회에 가지 ....
6	Could you tell me the way? 나에게 ....을 말씀해주시겠어요?	19	People love freedom. ....들은 자유를 사랑한다.
7	Come this way. 이 ......으로 와.	20	Korean people love peace.. 대한민국 ....들은 평화를 사랑한다.
8	I like his way of thinking. 나는 그의 생각하는 ......이 좋다.	21	We succeeded! ....는 성공했다!
9	It's a success in every way. 그것은 모든 ......에서 성공이다.	22	This tooth is loose. 이 ......가 헐렁하다.
10	He went to the convenience store. 그는 편의......에 갔다.	23	This book is mine. .... 책은 나의 것이다.
11	I always try. ....는 항상 노력한다.	24	I like this kind of person. 나는 .... 종류의 사람을 좋아한다.
12	I'll do it. ....가 그것을 할게.	25	This is mine. ....은 나의 것이다.
13	He laughed. ....는 웃었다.		

1) 것 2) 한다 3) 된다 4) 수 5) 수 6) 길 7) 쪽 8) 방식 9) 점
10) 점 11) 나 12) 내 13) 그 14) 없다 15) 않다 16) 말고 17) 아니다 18) 않는다
19) 사람 20) 국민 21) 우리 22) 이 23) 이 24) 이런 25) 이것

	K-word	pronounce	English		K-word	pronounce	English
1	너는	neo-neun	you	13	그는	geu-neun	he
	좋은	joh-eun	good		웃었다	us-eoss-da	laughed
	것을	geos-eul	thing	14	나는	na-neun	I
	했다	haess-da	did		돈이	don-i	money
2	그들은	geu-deul-eun	they		없다	eobs-da	don't have
	행복하게	haeng-bok-ha-ge	happily	15	오늘은	o-neul-eun	today
	일을	il-eul	works		날씨가	nal-ssi-ga	the weather
	한다	han-da	do		좋지 않다	joh-ji anh-da	is not fine
3	그들은	geu-deul-eun	they	16	이것	i-geos	this
	긴장하게	gin-jang-ha-ge	nervous		말고	mal-go	not
	된다	doen-da	become		저것	jeo-geos	that
4	칠 이라는 수는	chil-i-ra-neun su-neun	number 7		주세요	ju-se-yo	please give me
	행운을	haeng-un-eul	good luck	17	그는	geu-neun	he
	의미한다	ui-mi-han-da	mean		의사가	ui-sa-ga	doctor
5	나는	na-neun	I		아니다	a-ni-da	is not
	좋은	joh-eun	good	18	나는	na-neun	I
	수가	su-ga	way		교회에	gyo-hoe-e	to church
	있어	iss-eo	have		가지 않는다	ga-ji anh-neun-da	don't go
6	나에게	na-e-ge	me	19	사람들은	sa-ram-deul-eun	people
	길을	gil-eul	the way		자유를	ja-yu-reul	freedom
	말씀해주시겠어요?	mal-sseum-hae-ju-si-gess-eo-yo?	could you tell?		사랑한다	sa-rang-han-da	love
7	이쪽으로	i-jjok-eu-ro	this way	20	대한민국	dae-han-min-guk	Korean
	와	wa	come		국민들은	guk-min-deul-eun	people
8	나는	na-neun	I		평화를	pyeong-hwa-reul	peace
	그의	geu-ui	his		사랑한다	sa-rang-han-da	love
	생각하는	saeng-gak-ha-neun	thinking	21	우리는	u-ri neun	we
	방식이	bang-sik-i	way		성공했다	seong-gong-haess-da	succeeded
	좋다	joh-da	like	22	이	i	this
9	그것은	geu-geos-eun	it		이가	i-ga	tooth
	모든	mo-deun	every		헐렁하다	heol-leong-ha-da	is loose
	점에서	jeom-e-seo	in way	23	이	i	this
	성공이다	seong-gong-i-da	is a success		책은	chaek-eun	book
10	그는	geu-neun	he		나의 것	na-ui geos	mine
	편의점에	pyeon-ui-jeom-e	to the convenience store		이다	i-da	is
	갔다	gass-da	went	24	나는	na-neun	I
11	나는	na-neun	I		이런 종류의	i-reon jong-ryu-ui	this kind of
	항상	hang-sang	always		사람을	sa-ram-eul	person
	노력한다	no-ryeok-han-da	try		좋아한다	joh-a-han-da	like
12	내가	nae-ga	I	25	이것은	i-geos-eun	this
	그것을	geu-geos-eul	it		나의 것	na-ui geos	mine
	할게	hal-ge	will do		이다	i-da	is

Day1 Sentence(2)

	Write K-word in		Write K-word in ....
26	How much is this? .... 얼마 인가요?	39	This is a hard work. 이것은 힘든 .... 이다.
27	Better than nothing. 없는 것 .... 낫다.	40	He works hard everyday. 그는 매일 열심히 ....
28	I see the result. 나는 결과를	41	This painting is his work. 이 그림은 그의 .... 이다.
29	Our hometown is the same. 우리의 고향은	42	He is resting after hard work. 그는 힘든 .... 후에 쉬고 있다.
30	They give examples. 그들이 예시를	43	Job is precious. .... 은 소중하다.
31	I give a car to my father today. 나는 오늘 아버지에게 차를	44	It's because of you. 그것은 너 .... 이다.
32	I treat people kindly. 나는 사람들을 친절하게	45	You speak so fast. 너는 너무 빠르게 ....
33	They go to America today. 그들은 오늘 미국으로	46	I did it for you. 나는 너를 .... 그것을 했다.
34	I go to a temple. 나는 절에	47	Sad but true. 슬프다 .... 사실이다.
35	What year is it? 몇 .... 입니까?	48	They come today. 그들이 오늘 ....
36	I need one person. 나는 .... 사람이 필요하다.	49	I know you. 나는 너를 ....
37	I understand your words. 나는 너의 .... 을 이해한다.	50	I can't see Kim these days. 나는 요즘 김 .... 를 볼 수 없다.
38	He works 4 days a week. 그는 일주일에 4 .... 일한다.		

26) 이거 27) 보다 28) 본다 29) 같다 30) 준다 31) 드린다 32) 대한다 33) 간다 34) 다닌다
35) 년 36) 한 37) 말 38) 일 39) 일 40) 일한다 41) 작품 42) 작업 43) 직장
44) 때문 45) 말한다 46) 위하여 47) 그러나 48) 온다 49) 안다 50) 씨

Sentence Words(2)

	K-word	pronounce	English		K-word	pronounce	English
26	이거	i-geo	this		힘든	him-deun	hard
	얼마	eol-ma	how much		일	il	work
	인가요?	in-ga-yo?	is?		이다	i-da	is
27	없는 것보다	eobs-neun geos-bo-da	than nothing	40	그는	geu-neun	he
	낫다	nas-da	better		매일	mae-il	everyday
28	나는	na-neun	I		열심히	yeol-sim-hi	hard
	결과를	gyeol-gwa-reul	result		일한다	il han-da	work
	본다	bon-da	see	41	이	i	this
29	우리의	u-ri-ui	our		그림은	geu-rim-eun	painting
	고향은	go-hyang-eun	hometown		그의	geu-ui	his
	같다	gat-da	is the same		작품	jak-pum	work
30	그들이	geu-deul-i	they		이다	i-da	is
	예시를	ye-si-reul	example	42	그는	geu-neun	he
	준다	jun-da	give		힘든	him-deun	hard
31	나는	na-neun	I		작업 후에	jak-eob hu-e	after work
	오늘	o-neul	today		쉬고 있다	swi-go-iss-da	is resting
	아버지에게	a-beo-ji-e-ge	to my father	43	직장은	jik-jang-eun	job
	차를	cha-reul	a car		소중하다	so-jung-ha-da	is precious
	드린다	deu-rin-da	give	44	그것은	geu-geos-eun	it
32	나는	na-neun	I		너	neo	you
	사람들을	sa-ram-deul-eul	people		때문	ttae-mun	because of
	친절하게	chin-jeol-ha-ge	kindly		이다	i-da	is
	대한다	dae-han-da	treat	45	너는	neo-neun	you
33	그들은	geu-deul-eun	they		너무	neo-mu	so
	오늘	o-neul	today		빠르게	ppa-reu-ge	fast
	미국으로	mi-guk-eu-ro	to America		말한다	mal-han-da	speak
	간다	gan-da	go	46	나는	na-neun	I
34	나는	na-neun	I		너를	neo-reul	you
	절에	jeol-e	to a temple		위하여	wi-ha-yeo	for
	다닌다	da-nin-da	go		그것을	geu-geos-eul	it
35	몇 년	myeocc-nyeon	what year		했다	haess-da	did
	입니까?	ib-ni-kka?	is it?	47	슬프다	seul-peu-da	sad
36	나는	na-neun	I		그러나	geu-reo-na	but
	한 사람이	han sa-ram-i	one person		사실이다	sa-sil-i-da	true
	필요하다	pil-yo-ha-da	need	48	그들이	geu-deul-i	they
37	나는	na-neun	I		오늘	o-neul	today
	너의	neo-ui	your		온다	on-da	come
	말을	mal-eul	words	49	나는	na-neun	I
	이해한다	i-hae-han-da	understand		너를	neo-reul	you
38	그는	geu-neun	he		안다	an-da	know
	일주일에	il-ju-il-e	a week	50	나는	na-neun	I
	4일	sa-il	4 days		요즘	yo-jeum	these days
	일 한다	il han-da	work		김씨를	gim-ssi-reul	Kim
39	이것은	i-geos-eun	this		볼 수 없다	bol su eobs-da	can't see

	Write K-word in			Write K-word in ....
51	That's right! .... !	64	And it was my turn. .... 나의 차례였다.
52	He has a big nose. 그는 .... 코를 가지고 있다.	65	Be careful home and school. 가정 .... 학교에서 조심해.
53	The moon is big. 달이	66	We woke up by then. 우리는 .... 쯤에 일어났다.
54	He is late once again. 그는 .... 늦었다.	67	Then, I'll see you there. ...., 거기서 봐.
55	The society won't accept me. .... 는 날 받아주지 않는다.	68	Is there a problem? .... 가 있나요 ?
56	I'm in a cave. 나는 동굴 .... 에 있다.	69	I love such a thing. 나는 .... 것을 좋아한다.
57	He is a good man. 그는 .... 사람이다.	70	I buy a car today. 나는 오늘 차를 ....
58	I want more. 나는 .... 원한다.	71	I live in Seoul. 나는 서울에 ....
59	I receive an award tomorrow. 나는 내일 상을	72	I live well. 나는 잘 ....
60	Forget it. .... 을 잊어 버려라!	73	Um, do I know you? ...., 제가 당신을 아나요?
61	Leave my house. 내 .... 에서 떠나라.	74	He always thinks deeply. 그는 항상 깊게 ....
62	He comes out of prison today. 그가 오늘 교도소에서	75	I don't know you. 나는 너를 ....
63	People obey his order. 사람들이 그의 명령을		

51) 그렇다　　52) 큰　　53) 크다　　54) 또　　55) 사회　　56) 안에　　57) 좋은　　58) 더　　59) 받는다
60) 그것　　61) 집　　62) 나온다　　63) 따른다　　64) 그리고　　65) 및　　66) 그때　　67) 그럼　　68) 문제
69) 그런　　70) 산다　　71) 산다　　72) 지낸다　　73) 저　　74) 생각한다　　75) 모른다

Sentence Words(3)

	K-word	pronounce	English		K-word	pronounce	English
51	그렇다	geu-reoh-da	That's right!	64	그리고	geu-ri-go	and
52	그는	geu-neun	he		나의	na-ui	my
	큰	keun	big		차례	cha-rye	turn
	코를	ko-reul	nose		였다	yeoss-da	was
	가지고 있다	ga-ji-go iss-da	has	65	가정	ga-jeong	home
53	달이	dal-i	the moon		및	micc	and
	크다	keu-da	is big		학교에서	hak-gyo-e-seo	school
54	그는	geu-neun	he		조심해	jo-sim-hae	be careful
	또	tto	once again	66	우리는	u-ri-neun	we
	늦었다	neuj-eoss-da	is late		그때쯤에	geu-ttae-jjeum-e	by then
55	사회는	sa-hoe-neun	the society		일어났다	il-eo-nass-da	woke up
	날	nal	me	67	그럼	geu-reom	then
	받아주지 않는다	bad-a-ju-ji-anh-neun-da	won't accept		거기서	geo-gi-seo	there
56	나는	na-neun	I		봐	bwa	I'll see you
	동굴	dong-gul	cave	68	문제가	mun-je-ga	a problem
	안에	an-e	in		있나요?	iss-na-yo?	is there?
	있다	iss-da	am	69	나는	na-neun	I
57	그는	geu-neun	he		그런 것을	geu-reon geos-eul	such a thing
	좋은	joh-eun	good		좋아한다	joh-a-han-da	love
	사람	sa-ram	man	70	나는	na-neun	I
	이다	i-da	is		오늘	o-neul	today
58	나는	na-neun	I		차를	cha-reul	car
	더	deo	more		산다	san-da	buy
	원한다	won-han-da	want	71	나는	na-neun	I
59	나는	na-neun	I		서울에	seo-ul-e	in Seoul
	내일	nae-il	tomorrow		산다	san-da	live
	상을	sang-eul	award	72	나는	na-neun	I
60	받는다	bad-neun-da	receive		잘	jal	well
	그것을	geu-geos-eul	it		지낸다	ji-naen-da	live
	잊어버려	ij-eo-beo-ryeo	forget	73	저	jeo	um
61	내	nae	my		제가	je-ga	I
	집에서	jib-e-seo	house		당신을	dang-sin-eul	you
	떠나라	tteo-na-ra	leave		아나요?	a-na-yo?	do know?
62	그가	geu-ga	he	74	그는	geu-neun	he
	오늘	o-neul	today		항상	hang-sang	always
	교도소에서	gyo-do-so-e-seo	of prison		깊게	gip-ge	deeply
	나온다	na-on-da	come out		생각한다	saeng-gak-han-da	think
63	사람들이	sa-ram-deul-i	people	75	나는	na-neun	I
	그의	geu-ui	his		너를	neo-reul	you
	명령을	myeong-ryeong-eul	order		모른다	mo-reun-da	don't know
	따른다	tta-reun-da	obey				

	Write K-word in			Write K-word in ....
76	The inside of the box is empty. 그 상자의 .... 은 비어있다.	89	She smiled. .... 가 미소 지었다.
77	My mother makes cakes. 엄마는 케이크를	90	Monks eat vegetables. 수도승은 채소를 ....
78	I make him my brother today. 나는 오늘 그를 형제로	91	They grasp the situation. 그들은 그 상황을 ....
79	He makes them work. 그는 그들이 일하게	92	I love myself. 나는 나 .... 을 사랑한다.
80	There are two people. .... 사람이 있다.	93	Culture destroys language. .... 는 언어를 파괴한다.
81	You two, come here. 너희 .... , 이리 와.	94	Give me ₩500. 나에게 500 .... 을 줘.
82	It stopped in front of me. 그것은 내 .... 에서 멈추었다.	95	Let you know my thought. 내 .... 을 알려줄게.
83	In case of fire, dial 119. 불이 난 .... , 119로 전화하시오.	96	He is a famous lecturer. 그는 .... 강사이다.
84	She is a monk. 그녀는 .... 이다.	97	This sentence makes sense. 이 문장은 뜻이 ....
85	It rained during the night. 밤 .... 에 비가 왔다.	98	He heard the sound. 그는 그 .... 를 들었다.
86	It rained during the night. 밤 .... 비가 왔다.	99	Once again. .... 한 번.
87	Any questions? .... 질문 있나요?	100	Paint a different color. .... 색깔을 칠해라.
88	She swims well. 그녀는 수영을 .... 한다.		

76) 속   77) 만든다   78) 삼는다   79) 시킨다   80) 두   81) 둘   82) 앞   83) 경우   84) 중
85) 중   86) 동안에   87) 어떤   88) 잘   89) 그녀   90) 먹는다   91) 파악하고 있다   92) 자신   93) 문화
94) 원   95) 생각   96) 명   97) 통한다   98) 소리   99) 다시   100) 다른

Sentence Words(4)

	K-word	pronounce	English		K-word	pronounce	English
76	그 상자	geu sang-ja	the box	87	어떤	eo-tteon	any
	의	ui	of		질문 있나요?	jil-mun iss-na-yo?	questions?
	속은	sok-eun	the inside	88	그녀는	geu-nyeo-neun	she
	비어있다	bi-eo-iss-da	is empty		수영을 잘 한다	su-yeong-eul jal han-da	swim well
77	엄마는	eom-ma-neun	my mother	89	그녀가	geu-nyeo-ga	she
	케이크를	ke-i-keu-reul	cakes		미소 지었다	mi-so ji-eoss-da	smiled
	만든다	man-deun-da	make	90	수도승은	su-do-seung-eun	monk
78	나는	na-neun	I		채소를	chae-so-reul	vegetables
	오늘	o-neul	today		먹는다	meok-neun-da	eat
	그를	geu-reul	him	91	그들은	geu-deul-eun	they
	형제로	hyeong-je-ro	my brother		그 상황을	geu sang-hwang-eul	the situation
	삼는다	sam-neun-da	make		파악하고 있다	pa-ak-ha-go iss-da	grasp
79	그는	geu-neun	he	92	나는	na-neun	I
	그들이	geu-deul-i	them		내 자신을	nae ja-sin-eul	myself
	일하게	il-ha-ge	work		사랑한다	sa-rang-han-da	love
	시킨다	si-kin-da	makes	93	문화는	mun-hwa-neun	culture
80	두	du	two		언어를	eon-eo-reul	language
	사람이	sa-ram-i	people		파괴 시킨다	pa-goe-si-kin-da	destroy
	있다	iss-da	there are	94	나에게	na-e-ge	me
81	너희 둘	neo-hui dul	you two		500원을	o-baek-won-eul	₩500
	이리 와	i-ri wa	come here		줘	jwo	give
82	그것은	geu-geos-eun	it	95	내	nae	my
	내	nae	me		생각을	saeng-gak-eul	thought
	앞에서	ap-e-seo	in front of		알려줄게	al-lyeo-jul-ge	let you know
	멈추었다	meo-mchu-eoss-da	stopped	96	그는	geu-neun	he
83	불이 난	bul-i nan	fire		명	myeong	famous
	경우에	gyeong-u-e	in case of		강사	gang-sa	lecturer
	119로	il-il-gu-ro	119		이다	i-da	is
	전화하시오	jeon-hwa-ha-si-o	dial	97	이	i	this
84	그녀는	geu-nyeo-neun	she		문장은	mun-jang-eun	sentence
	중	jung	monk		뜻이 통한다	tteus-i tong-han-da	make sense
	이다	i-da	is	98	그는	geu-neun	he
85	밤	bam	night		그 소리를	geu so-ri-reul	the sound
	중에	jung-e	during		들었다	deul-eoss-da	heard
	비가 왔다	bi-ga wass-da	it rained	99	다시 한 번	da-si han beon	once again
86	밤	bam	night	100	다른	da-reun	different
	동안에	dong-an-e	during		색깔을	saek-kkal-eul	color
	비가 왔다	bi-ga wass-da	it rained		칠해라	chil-hae-ra	paint

Final	K-word ㉔				
check	English ㉕				

K-word ⑱	English ⑲	K-word ⑳	K-word ㉑	English ㉒	K-word ㉓

1-100				
☐ 1) 것	☐ 31) 드린다	☐ 61) 집	☐ 91) 파악하고 있다	
☐ 2) 한다	☐ 32) 대한다	☐ 62) 나온다	☐ 92) 자신	
☐ 3) 된다	☐ 33) 간다	☐ 63) 따른다	☐ 93) 문화	
☐ 4) 수	☐ 34) 다닌다	☐ 64) 그리고	☐ 94) 원	
☐ 5) 수	☐ 35) 년	☐ 65) 및	☐ 95) 생각	
☐ 6) 길	☐ 36) 한	☐ 66) 그때	☐ 96) 명	
☐ 7) 쪽	☐ 37) 말	☐ 67) 그럼	☐ 97) 통한다	
☐ 8) 방식	☐ 38) 일	☐ 68) 문제	☐ 98) 소리	
☐ 9) 점	☐ 39) 일	☐ 69) 그런	☐ 99) 다시	
☐ 10) 점	☐ 40) 일 한다	☐ 70) 산다	☐ 100) 다른	
☐ 11) 나	☐ 41) 작품	☐ 71) 산다		
☐ 12) 내	☐ 42) 작업	☐ 72) 지낸다		
☐ 13) 그	☐ 43) 직장	☐ 73) 저		
☐ 14) 없다	☐ 44) 때문	☐ 74) 생각한다		
☐ 15) 않다	☐ 45) 말한다	☐ 75) 모른다		
☐ 16) 말고	☐ 46) 위하여	☐ 76) 속		
☐ 17) 아니다	☐ 47) 그러나	☐ 77) 만든다		
☐ 18) 않는다	☐ 48) 온다	☐ 78) 삼는다		
☐ 19) 사람	☐ 49) 안다	☐ 79) 시킨다		
☐ 20) 국민	☐ 50) 씨	☐ 80) 두		
☐ 21) 우리	☐ 51) 그렇다	☐ 81) 둘		
☐ 22) 이	☐ 52) 큰	☐ 82) 앞		
☐ 23) 이	☐ 53) 크다	☐ 83) 경우		
☐ 24) 이런	☐ 54) 또	☐ 84) 중		
☐ 25) 이것	☐ 55) 사회	☐ 85) 중		
☐ 26) 이거	☐ 56) 안에	☐ 86) 동안에		
☐ 27) 보다	☐ 57) 좋은	☐ 87) 어떤		
☐ 28) 본다	☐ 58) 더	☐ 88) 잘		
☐ 29) 같다	☐ 59) 받는다	☐ 89) 그녀		
☐ 30) 준다	☐ 60) 그것	☐ 90) 먹는다		

1-100			
1) thing	31) give	61) house	91) grasp
2) do	32) treat	62) come out	92) self
3) become	33) go	63) obey	93) culture
4) number	34) go	64) and	94) ₩
5) way	35) year	65) and	95) thought
6) way	36) one	66) then	96) famous
7) way	37) word	67) then	97) make sense
8) way	38) day	68) problem	98) sound
9) way	39) work	69) such	99) again
10) store	40) work	70) buy	100) different
11) I	41) work	71) live	
12) I	42) work	72) live	
13) he	43) job	73) um	
14) not have	44) because of	74) think	
15) not	45) speak	75) don't know	
16) not	46) for	76) inside	
17) not	47) but	77) make	
18) do not	48) come	78) make	
19) people	49) know	79) make	
20) people	50) family name	80) two	
21) we	51) right	81) two	
22) tooth	52) big	82) front	
23) this	53) big	83) case	
24) this	54) once again	84) monk	
25) this	55) society	85) during	
26) this	56) in	86) during	
27) than	57) good	87) any	
28) see	58) more	88) well	
29) same	59) receive	89) she	
30) give	60) it	90) eat	

Day1 List Study

Final	K-word ㉜				
check	English ㉝				

K-word ㉖	English ㉗	K-word ㉘	K-word ㉙	English ㉚	K-word ㉛

	K-word	Pronounce	English	K-word ❶	Sentence example
101	다르다	da-reu-da	different		We are different.
102	여자	yeo-ja	girl		The girl is beautiful.
103	소녀	so-nyeo	girl		Girl, come forward!
104	개	gae	dog		Dogs bark.
105	그 정도	geu-jeong-do	that much		I like that much.
106	뒤	dwi	back		I saw it at the back.
107	듣는다	deud-neun-da	hear		I hear music every morning.
108	다	da	all		All is here.
109	좀	jom	a little		Call me a little later.
110	조금	jo-geum	a little		We're a little late.
111	든다	deun-da	pick up		He picks up the knife.
112	키운다	ki-un-da	raise		Tom raises three dogs.
113	올린다	ol-lin-da	raise		He raises the gun.
114	기른다	gi-reun-da	raise		He raises cattle on his farm.
115	싶다	sip-da	want		I want to go home.
116	보인다	bo-in-da	look		He looks happy.
117	표정	pyo-jeong	look		What's that look for?
118	모습	mo-seub	appearance		Your appearance is ideal.
119	가지고 있다	ga-ji-go-iss-da	have		I have $10,000.
120	갖고 있다	gaj-go-iss-da	have		He has a good heart.

Final	K-word ❽				
check	English ❾				

K-word ❷	English ❸	K-word ❹	K-word ❺	English ❻	K-word ❼

Day2 (2)

	K-word	Pronounce	English	K-word ❶	Sentence example
121	지닌다	ji-nin-da	have		I always have $1,000.
122	가진다	ga-jin-da	have		You'll have $20,000.
123	갖추고 있다	gaj-chu-go-iss-da	have		This factory has a lot of tools.
124	당한다	dang-han-da	get p.p		I often get scammed.
125	함께	ham-kke	with		I'll go with you.
126	아이	a-i	kid		Kids, listen!
127	지나간다	ji-na-gan-da	pass by		He passes by quickly.
128	많이	manh-i	much		I ate much.
129	훨씬	hwol-ssin	much ~er		This is much better than that.
130	시간	si-gan	time		It is time for dinner.
131	너	neo	you		Are you busy?
132	당신	dang-sin	you		You were busy.
133	인간	in-gan	human		You are human.
134	사실	sa-sil	in fact		In fact, it's true.
135	과연	gwa-yeon	indeed		Indeed, will she succeed?
136	난다	nan-da	grow		Hair grows on the chest.
137	자란다	ja-ran-da	grow		Plants grow on fertile grounds.
138	어머니	eo-meo-ni	mother		Where is Mother?
139	엄마	eom-ma	mom		Where is Mom?
140	눈	nun	eye		Open your eyes.

Final	K-word ❽				
check	English ❾				

K-word ❷	English ❸	K-word ❹	K-word ❺	English ❻	K-word ❼

	K-word	Pronounce	English	K-word ❶	Sentence example
141	눈	nun	snow		The snow is melting.
142	뭐	mwo	what		What will I say?
143	무엇	mu-eos	what		What are you doing?
144	무슨	mu-seun	what		What book is this?
145	시대	si-dae	era		We live in the nuclear era.
146	다음	da-eum	next		Next person, please.
147	이러하다	i-reo-ha-da	like this		The truth is like this.
148	누구	nu-gu	who		Who are they?
149	전	jeon	all		This includes all areas.
150	곳	gos	place		I like this place.
151	자리	ja-ri	place		I remember this place.
152	여러	yeo-reo	several		I met several people.
153	많은	manh-eun	many		Many fish died.
154	하나	ha-na	one		I have one.
155	세계	se-gye	world		The world is unfair.
156	세상	se-sang	world		He knows much of the world.
157	버린다	beo-rin-da	dump		People dump much waste.
158	위	wi	up		He jumped up.
159	운동	un-dong	exercise		Running is a good exercise.
160	학교	hak-gyo	school		How's school?

Final	K-word ❽							
check	English ❾							

K-word ❷	English ❸	K-word ❹	K-word ❺	English ❻	K-word ❼

	K-word	Pronounce	English	K-word ❶	Sentence example
161	자기	ja-gi	darling		How are you, darling?
162	가장	ga-jang	~est		I did it the fastest.
163	제일	je-il	~est		I did it the fastest.
164	대부분	dae-bu-bun	most		Most of them are women.
165	대통령	dae-tong-ryeong	president		Obama was the president.
166	가지	ga-ji	kinds		There are three kinds of cakes.
167	시작한다	si-jak-han-da	start		He starts again.
168	바로	ba-ro	right away		He will come right away.
169	어느	eo-neu	which		Which one is heavier?
170	그래서	geu-rae-seo	so		So, I love him.
171	그러니까	geu-reo-ni-kka	so		So, you mean Sunday?
172	정부	jeong-bu	government		The government imposes taxes.
173	모든	mo-deun	every		Every person is equal.
174	번	beon	times		I've met her three times.
175	그거	geu-geo	it		It is good.
176	돈	don	money		He needs money.
177	국가	guk-ga	nation		The flag means a nation.
178	나라	na-ra	nation		The flag means a nation.
179	그런데	geu-reon-de	by the way		By the way, I found that book.
180	근데	geun-de	by the way		By the way, where do you live?

Final	K-word ❽				
check	English ❾				

K-word ❷	English ❸	K-word ❹	K-word ❺	English ❻	K-word ❼

	K-word	Pronounce	English	K-word ❶	Sentence example
181	날	nal	day		It's a bad day.
182	여기	yeo-gi	here		He is not here.
183	여성	yeo-seong	female		Only female is allowed.
184	친구	chin-gu	friend		We were friends.
185	마음	ma-eum	mind		Keep that in mind.
186	관계	gwan-gye	relationship		They ended their relationship.
187	아버지	a-beo-ji	father		My father walks everyday.
188	남자	nam-ja	male		He heard a male voice.
189	남성	nam-seong	male		Is that a male?
190	어디	eo-di	where		Where are you?
191	몸	mom	body		My whole body aches.
192	얼굴	eol-gul	face		Wash your face.
193	들어간다	deul-eo-gan-da	go into		He goes into the room.
194	들어온다	deul-eo-on-da	come in		Customers come in my shop.
195	왜	wae	why		Why are you crying?
196	나타난다	na-ta-nan-da	emerge		She emerges out of nowhere.
197	말아라	mal-a-ra	don't		Don't worry.
198	지역	ji-yeok	area		Clear the area.
199	물	mul	water		Water is important.
200	만난다	man-nan-da	meet		I meet Mary everyday.

Final	K-word ❽				
check	English ❾				

K-word ❷	English ❸	K-word ❹	K-word ❺	English ❻	K-word ❼

	K-word	English		K-word	English
101	다르다	We are _____.	121	지닌다	I always _____ $1,000.
102	여자	The _____ is beautiful.	122	가진다	You'll _____ $20,000.
103	소녀	_____, come forward!	123	갖추고 있다	This factory _____ a lot of tools.
104	개	_____ bark.	124	당한다	I often _____ scamm_____.
105	그 정도	I like _____.	125	함께	I'll go _____ you.
106	뒤	I saw it at the _____.	126	아이	_____, listen!
107	듣는다	I _____ music every morning.	127	지나간다	He _____ quickly.
108	다	_____ is here.	128	많이	I ate _____.
109	좀	Call me _____ later.	129	훨씬	This is _____ better than that.
110	조금	We're _____ late.	130	시간	It is _____ for dinner.
111	든다	He _____ the knife.	131	너	Are _____ busy?
112	키운다	Tom _____ three dogs.	132	당신	_____ were busy.
113	올린다	He _____ the gun.	133	인간	You are _____.
114	기른다	He _____ cattle on his farm.	134	사실	_____, it's true.
115	싶다	I _____ to go home.	135	과연	_____, will she succeed?
116	보인다	He _____ happy.	136	난다	Hair _____ on the chest.
117	표정	What's that _____ for?	137	자란다	Plants _____ on fertile grounds.
118	모습	Your _____ is ideal.	138	어머니	Where is _____?
119	가지고 있다	I _____ $10,000.	139	엄마	Where is _____?
120	갖고있다	He _____ a good heart.	140	눈	Open your _____.

101) different 102) girl 103) Girl 104) Dogs 105) that much 106) back 107) hear 108) All
109) a little 110) a little 111) picks up 112) raises 113) raises 114) raises 115) want 116) looks
117) look 118) appearance 119) have 120) has 121) have 122) have 123) has 124) get, ed
125) with 126) Kids 127) passes by 128) much 129) much 130) time 131) you 132) You
133) human 134) In fact 135) Indeed 136) grows 137) grow 138) Mother 139) Mom 140) eyes

	K-word	English		K-word	English
141	눈	The _____ is melting.	161	자기	How are you, _____?
142	뭐	_____ will I say?	162	가장	I did it the fast _____.
143	무엇	_____ are you doing?	163	제일	I did it the fast _____.
144	무슨	_____ book is this?	164	대부분	_____ of them are women.
145	시대	We live in the nuclear _____.	165	대통령	Obama was the _____.
146	다음	_____ person, please.	166	가지	There are three _____ of cakes.
147	이러하다	The truth is _____.	167	시작한다	He _____ again.
148	누구	_____ are they?	168	바로	He will come _____.
149	전	This includes _____ areas.	169	어느	_____ one is heavier?
150	곳	I like this _____.	170	그래서	_____, I love him.
151	자리	I remember this _____.	171	그러니까	_____, you mean Sunday?
152	여러	I met _____ people.	172	정부	The _____ imposes taxes.
153	많은	_____ fish died.	173	모든	_____ person is equal.
154	하나	I have _____.	174	번	I've met her three _____.
155	세계	The _____ is unfair.	175	그거	_____ is good.
156	세상	He knows much of the _____.	176	돈	He needs _____.
157	버린다	People _____ much waste.	177	국가	The flag means a _____.
158	위	He jumped _____.	178	나라	The flag means a _____.
159	운동	Running is a good _____.	179	그런데	_____, I found that book.
160	학교	How's _____?	180	근데	_____, where do you live?

141) snow   142) What   143) What   144) What   145) era   146) Next   147) like this   148) Who
149) all   150) place   151) place   152) several   153) Many   154) one   155) world   156) world
157) dump   158) up   159) exercise   160) school   161) darling   162) est   163) est   164) Most
165) president   166) kinds   167) starts   168) right away   169) Which   170) So   171) So   172) government
173) Every   174) times   175) It   176) money   177) nation   178) nation   179) By the way   180) By the way

	K-word	English
181	날	It's a bad ....
182	여기	He is not ....
183	여성	Only .... is allowed.
184	친구	We were ....
185	마음	Keep that in ....
186	관계	They ended their ....
187	아버지	My .... walks everyday.
188	남자	He heard a .... voice.
189	남성	Is that a .... ?
190	어디	.... are you?
191	몸	My whole .... aches.
192	얼굴	Wash your ....
193	들어간다	He .... the room.
194	들어온다	Customers .... my shop.
195	왜	.... are you crying?
196	나타난다	She .... out of nowhere.
197	말아라	.... worry.
198	지역	Clear the ....
199	물	.... is important.
200	만난다	I .... Mary everyday.

King Sejong

– The 4th king of Joseon Dynasty

King Sejong was born in 1397.
His 32 year reign marked great achievements.
Hangeul, created by King Sejong,
has been used as a common script for
the Republic of Korea and North Korea.

181) day   182) here   183) female   184) friends
185) mind   186) relationship   187) father   188) male
189) male   190) Where   191) body   192) face
193) goes into   194) come in   195) Why   196) emerges
197) Don't   198) area   199) Water   200) meet

Final	K-word ⑯				
check	English ⑰				

K-word ⑩	English ⑪	K-word ⑫	K-word ⑬	English ⑭	K-word ⑮

	Write K-word in		Write K-word in ....
101	We are different. 우리는	114	He raises cattle on his farm. 그는 농장에서 소를 ....
102	The girl is beautiful. 그 .... 는 아름답다.	115	I want to go home. 나는 집에 가고 ....
103	Girl, come forward! .... 야, 앞으로 나오너라!	116	He looks happy. 그는 행복하게 ....
104	Dogs bark. .... 들이 짖는다.	117	What's that look for? .... 이 왜 그래?
105	I like that much. 나는 .... 가 좋다.	118	Your appearance is ideal. 너의 .... 은 이상적이다.
106	I saw it at the back. 나는 .... 에서 그것을 보았다.	119	I have $10,000. 나는 만 달러를 ....
107	I hear music every morning. 나는 매일 아침 음악을	120	He has a good heart. 그는 좋은 마음을 ....
108	All is here. .... 여기 있다.	121	I always have $1,000. 나는 항상 천 달러를 ....
109	Call me a little later. .... 있다가 전화해.	122	You'll have $20,000. 당신이 20,000 달러를 ....
110	We're a little late. 우리는 .... 늦었다.	123	This factory has a lot of tools. 이 공장은 많은 도구를 ....
111	He picks up the knife. 그가 칼을	124	I often get scammed. 나는 종종 사기 ....
112	Tom raises three dogs. 톰은 세 마리의 개를	125	I'll go with you. 나는 너와 .... 갈 것이다.
113	He raises the gun. 그는 총을		

101) 다르다　　102) 여자　　103) 소녀　　104) 개　　105) 그 정도　　106) 뒤　　107) 듣는다　　108) 다　　109) 좀
110) 조금　　111) 든다　　112) 키운다　　113) 올린다　　114) 기른다　　115) 싶다　　116) 보인다　　117) 표정　　118) 모습
119) 가지고 있다　　120) 갖고있다　　121) 지닌다　　122) 가진다　　123) 갖추고 있다　　124) 당한다　　125) 함께

	K-word	pronounce	English		K-word	pronounce	English
101	우리는	u-ri-neun	we		기른다	gi-reun-da	raise
	다르다	da-reu-da	are different	115	나는	na-neun	I
102	그 여자는	geu yeo-ja-neun	the girl		집에	jib-e	home
	아름답다	a-reum-dab-da	is beautiful		가고 싶다	ga-go sip-da	want to go
103	소녀야	so-nyeo-ya	girl	116	그는	geu-neun	he
	앞으로	ap-eu-ro	forward		행복하게	haeng-bok-ha-ge	happy
	나오너라	na-o-neo-ra	come		보인다	bo-in-da	look
104	개들이	gae-deul-i	dogs	117	표정이	pyo-jeong-i	that look
	짖는다	jij-neun-da	bark		왜 그래?	wae geu-rae?	what's for?
105	나는	na-neun	I	118	너의	neo-ui	your
	그 정도가	geu jeong-do-ga	that much		모습은	mo-seub-eun	appearance
	좋다	joh-da	like		이상적이다	i-sang-jeok-i-da	is ideal
106	나는	na-neun	I	119	나는	na-neun	I
	뒤에서	dwi-e-seo	at the back		만 달러를	man dal-leo-reul	$10,000
	그것을	geu-geos-eul	it		가지고 있다	ga-ji-go iss-da	have
	보았다	bo-ass-da	saw	120	그는	geu-neun	he
107	나는	na-neun	I		좋은	joh-eun	good
	매일 아침	mae-il a-chim	every morning		마음을	ma-eum-eul	heart
	음악을	eum-ak-eul	music		갖고 있다	gaj-go iss-da	has
	듣는다	deud-neun-da	hear	121	나는	na-neun	I
108	다	da	all		항상	hang-sang	always
	여기	yeo-gi	here		천 달러를	cheon dal-leo-reul	$1,000
	있다	iss-da	is		지닌다	ji-nin-da	have
109	좀 있다가	jom iss-da-ga	a little later	122	당신이	dang-sin-i	you
	전화해	jeon-hwa-hae	call		20,000달러를	i-man dal-leo-reul	$20,000
110	우리는	u-ri-neun	we		가진다	ga-jin-da	have
	조금	jo-geum	a little	123	이	i	this
	늦었다	neuj-eoss-da	are late		공장은	gong-jang-eun	factory
111	그가	geu-ga	he		많은	manh-eun	a lot of
	칼을	kal-eul	the knife		도구를	do-gu-reul	tool
	든다	deun-da	pick up		갖추고 있다	gaj-chu-go iss-da	has
112	톰은	tom-eun	Tom	124	나는	na-neun	I
	세 마리의	se ma-ri-ui	three		종종	jong-jong	often
	개를	gae-reul	dogs		사기당한다	sa-gi-dang-han-da	get scammed
	키운다	ki-un-da	raise	125	나는	na-neun	I
113	그는	geu-neun	he		너와 함께	neo-wa ham-kke	with you
	총을	chong-eul	the gun		갈 것이다	gal geos-i-da	will go
	올린다	ol-lin-da	raise				
114	그는	geu-neun	he				
	농장에서	nong-jang-e-seo	on his farm				
	소를	so-reul	cattle				

Day2 Sentence(2)

	Write K-word in		Write K-word in ....
126	Kids, listen! 　　　　　들아, 들어봐!	139	Where is Mom? 　　　　　는 어디 계시니?
127	He passes by quickly. 그가 빠르게 　　　　　.	140	Open your eyes. 　　　　　을 뜨시오.
128	I ate much. 나는 　　　　　먹었다.	141	The snow is melting. 　　　　　이 녹고 있다.
129	This is much better than that. 이것이 저것보다 　　　　　좋다.	142	What will I say? 나 　　　　　라고 말하지?
130	It is time for dinner. 저녁 먹을 　　　　　이다.	143	What are you doing? 너는 　　　　　을 하고 있니?
131	Are you busy? 　　　　　바쁘니?	144	What book is this? 이것은 　　　　　책인가요?
132	You were busy. 　　　　　은 바빴었다.	145	We live in the nuclear era. 우리는 핵　　　　　에 살고 있다.
133	You are human. 너는 　　　　　이다.	146	Next person, please. 　　　　　분이요.
134	In fact, it's true. 　　　　　그것은 진실이다.	147	The truth is like this. 진실은 　　　　　.
135	Indeed, will she succeed? 　　　　　, 그녀가 성공할까?	148	Who are they? 그들은 　　　　　니?
136	Hair grows on the chest. 가슴에 털이 　　　　　.	149	This includes all areas. 이것은 　　　　　영역을 포함한다.
137	Plants grow on fertile grounds. 식물은 비옥한 땅에서 　　　　　.	150	I like this place. 나는 이 　　　　　이 좋다.
138	Where is Mother? 　　　　　는 어디 계시니?		

126) 아이　　127) 지나간다　　128) 많이　　129) 훨씬　　130) 시간　　131) 너　　132) 당신　　133) 인간　　134) 사실
135) 과연　　136) 난다　　137) 자란다　　138) 어머니　　139) 엄마　　140) 눈　　141) 눈　　142) 뭐　　143) 무엇
144) 무슨　　145) 시대　　146) 다음　　147) 이러하다　　148) 누구　　149) 전　　150) 곳

Sentence Words(2)

	K-word	pronounce	English		K-word	pronounce	English
126	아이들아	a-i-deul-a	kids	139	엄마는	eom-ma-neun	mom
	들어봐	deul-eo-bwa	listen		어디	eo-di	where
127	그가	geu-ga	he		계시니?	gye-si-ni?	is?
	빠르게	ppa-reu-ge	quickly	140	눈을	nun-eul	your eyes
	지나간다	ji-na-gan-da	pass by		뜨시오	tteu-si-o	open
128	나는	na-neun	I	141	눈이	nun-i	the snow
	많이	manh-i	much		녹고 있다	nok-go iss-da	is melting
	먹었다	meok-eoss-da	ate	142	나는	na-neun	I
129	이것이	i-geos-i	this		뭐라고	mwo-ra-go	what
	저것	jeo-geos	that		말하지?	mal-ha-ji?	will say?
	보다	bo-da	than	143	너는	neo-neun	you
	훨씬 좋다	hwol-ssin joh-da	is much better		무엇을	mu-eos-eul	what
130	저녁 먹을	jeo-nyeok meok-eul	for dinner		하고 있니?	ha-go iss-ni?	are doing?
	시간이다	si-gan-i-da	it is time	144	이것은	i-geos-eun	this
131	너	neo	you		무슨	mu-seun	what
	바쁘니?	ba-ppeu-ni?	are busy?		책	chaek	book
132	당신은	dang-sin-eun	you		인가요?	in-ga-yo?	is?
	바빴었다	ba-ppass-eoss-da	were busy	145	우리는	u-ri-neun	we
133	너는	neo-neun	you		핵	haek	nuclear
	인간	in-gan	human		시대에	si-dae-e	in the era
	이다	i-da	are		살고 있다	sal-go iss-da	live
134	사실	sa-sil	in fact	146	다음	da-eum	next
	그것은	geu-geos-eun	it		분이요	bun-i-yo	person, please
	진실이다	jin-sil-i-da	is true	147	진실은	jin-sil-eun	the truth
135	과연	gwa-yeon	indeed		이러하다	i-reo-ha-da	is like this
	그녀가	geu-nyeo-ga	she	148	그들은	geu-deul-eun	they
	성공할까?	seong-gong-hal-kka?	will succeed?		누구니?	nu-gu-ni?	who are?
136	가슴에	ga-seum-e	on the chest	149	이것은	i-geos-eun	this
	털이	teol-i	hair		전	jeon	all
	난다	nan-da	grow		영역을	yeong-yeok-eul	areas
137	식물은	sik-mul-eun	plants		포함한다	po-ham-han-da	include
	비옥한	bi-ok-han	fertile	150	나는	na-neun	I
	땅에서	ttang-e-seo	on grounds		이곳이	i-gos-i	this place
	자란다	ja-ran-da	grow		좋다	joh-da	like
138	어머니는	eo-meo-ni-neun	mother				
	어디	eo-di	where				
	계시니?	gye-si-ni?	is?				

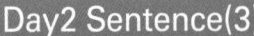

	Write K-word in		Write K-word in ....
151	I remember this place. 나는 이 .... 를 기억한다.	164	Most of them are women. 그들 .... 이 여자다.
152	I met several people. 나는 .... 사람을 만났다.	165	Obama was the president. 오바마는 .... 이었다.
153	Many fish died. .... 물고기들이 죽었다.	166	There are three kinds of cakes. 세 .... 의 케이크가 있다.
154	I have one. 나는 .... 가지고 있다.	167	He starts again. 그는 다시 ....
155	The world is unfair. .... 는 불공평하다.	168	He will come right away. 그가 .... 올 것이다.
156	He knows much of the world. 그는 .... 에 대해 많이 안다.	169	Which one is heavier? .... 것이 더 무겁습니까?
157	People dump much waste. 사람들이 많은 쓰레기를	170	So, I love him. .... , 나는 그를 사랑한다.
158	He jumped up. 그는 .... 로 뛰었다.	171	So, you mean Sunday? .... , 일요일을 의미하니?
159	Running is a good exercise. 달리기는 좋은 .... 이다.	172	The government imposes taxes. .... 는 세금을 부과한다.
160	How's school? .... 는 어때?	173	Every person is equal. .... 사람은 평등하다.
161	How are you, darling? 잘 지내고 있어, ... 야?	174	I've met her three times. 나는 그녀를 세 .... 만났다.
162	I did it the fastest. 나는 .... 빨리 그것을 했다.	175	It is good. .... 좋다.
163	I did it the fastest. 나는 .... 빨리 그것을 했다.		

151) 자리　　152) 여러　　153) 많은　　154) 하나　　155) 세계　　156) 세상　　157) 버린다　　158) 위　　159) 운동
160) 학교　　161) 자기　　162) 가장　　163) 제일　　164) 대부분　　165) 대통령　　166) 가지　　167) 시작한다　　168) 바로
169) 어느　　170) 그래서　　171) 그러니까　　172) 정부　　173) 모든　　174) 번　　175) 그거

	K-word	pronounce	English		K-word	pronounce	English
151	나는	na-neun	I		제일 빨리	je-il ppal-li	the fastest
	이	i	this		그것을	geu-geos-eul	it
	자리를	ja-ri-reul	place		했다	haess-da	did
	기억 한다	gi-eok han-da	remember	164	그들	geu-deul	them
152	나는	na-neun	I		대부분이	dae-bu-bun-i	most of
	여러	yeo-reo	several		여자다	yeo-ja-da	are women
	사람을	sa-ram-eul	people	165	오바마는	o-ba-ma-neun	Obama
	만났다	man-nass-da	met		대통령	dae-tong-ryeong	the present
153	많은	manh-eun	many		이었다	i-eoss-da	was
	물고기들이	mul-go-gi-deul-i	fish	166	세 가지의	se ga-ji-ui	three kinds of
	죽었다	juk-eoss-da	died		케이크가	ke-i-keu-ga	cakes
154	나는	na-neun	I		있다	iss-da	there are
	하나	ha-na	one	167	그는	geu-neun	he
	가지고 있다	ga-ji-go iss-da	have		다시	da-si	again
155	세계는	se-gye-neun	the world		시작한다	si-jak-han-da	start
	불공평하다	bul-gong-pyeong-ha-da	is unfair	168	그가	geu-ga	he
156	그는	geu-neun	he		바로	ba-ro	right away
	세상에 대해	se-sang-e dae-hae	of the world		올 것이다	ol geos-i-da	will come
	많이	manh-i	much	169	어느 것이	eo-neu geos-i	which one
	안다	an-da	know		더 무겁습니까?	deo mu-geob-seub-ni-kka?	is heavier?
157	사람들이	sa-ram-deul-i	people	170	그래서	geu-rae-seo	so
	많은	manh-eun	much		나는	na-neun	I
	쓰레기를	sseu-re-gi-reul	waste		그를	geu-reul	him
	버린다	beo-rin-da	dump		사랑한다	sa-rang-han-da	love
158	그는	geu-neun	he	171	그러니까	geu-reo-ni-kka	so
	위로	wi-ro	up		일요일을	il-yo-il-eul	Sunday
	뛰었다	ttwi-eoss-da	jumped		의미하니?	ui-mi-ha-ni?	you mean?
159	달리기는	dal-li-gi-neun	running	172	정부는	jeong-bu-neun	government
	좋은	joh-eun	good		세금을	se-geum-eul	taxes
	운동	un-dong	exercise		부과한다	bu-gwa-han-da	impose
	이다	i-da	is	173	모든	mo-deun	every
160	학교는	hak-gyo-neun	school		사람은	sa-ram-eun	person
	어때?	eo-ttae?	how's?		평등하다	pyeong-deung-ha-da	is equal
161	잘 지내고 있어	jal ji-nae-go iss-eo	how are you	174	나는	na-neun	I
	자기야	ja-gi-ya	darling		그녀를	geu-nyeo-reul	her
162	나는	na-neun	I		세 번	se beon	three times
	가장 빨리	ga-jang ppal-li	the fastest		만났다	man-nass-da	have met
	그것을	geu-geos-eul	it	175	그거	geu-geo	it
	했다	haess-da	did		좋다	joh-da	is good
163	나는	na-neun	I				

	Write K-word in			Write K-word in ....
176	He needs money. 그는 .... 이 필요하다.	189	Is that a male? 저 사람은 .... 이니?
177	The flag means a nation. 국기는 .... 를 의미한다.	190	Where are you? 너는 .... 있니?
178	The flag means a nation. 국기는 .... 를 의미한다.	191	My whole body aches. 온 .... 이 아프다.
179	By the way, I found that book. .... , 나는 그 책을 찾았어.	192	Wash your face. 당신의 .... 을 씻으시오.
180	By the way, where do you live? .... , 너 어디 사니?	193	He goes into the room. 그가 방에 ....
181	It's a bad day. 안 좋은 .... 이다.	194	Customers come in my shop. 손님들이 나의 가게에 ....
182	He is not here. 그는 .... 없다.	195	Why are you crying? .... 너는 울고 있니?
183	Only female is allowed. 오직 .... 만 허락된다.	196	She emerges out of nowhere. 그녀가 갑자기 ....
184	We were friends. 우리는 .... 였다.	197	Don't worry. 걱정 ....
185	Keep that in mind. 그것을 .... 에 새기세요.	198	Clear the area. 그 .... 을 청소해라.
186	They ended their relationship. 그들은 그들의 .... 를 끝냈다.	199	Water is important. .... 은 중요하다.
187	My father walks everyday. 나의 .... 는 매일 걷는다.	200	I meet Mary everyday. 나는 매일 메리를 ....
188	He heard a male voice. 그는 .... 목소리를 들었다.		

176) 돈   177) 국가   178) 나라   179) 그런데   180) 근데   181) 날   182) 여기   183) 여성   184) 친구
185) 마음   186) 관계   187) 아버지   188) 남자   189) 남성   190) 어디   191) 몸   192) 얼굴   193) 들어간다
194) 들어온다   195) 왜   196) 나타난다   197) 말아라   198) 지역   199) 물   200) 만난다

	K-word	pronounce	English		K-word	pronounce	English
176	그는	geu-neun	he	188	그는	geu-neun	he
	돈이	don-i	money		남자	nam-ja	male
	필요하다	pil-yo-ha-da	need		목소리를	mok-so-ri-reul	voice
177	국기는	guk-gi-neun	the flag		들었다	deul-eoss-da	heard
	국가를	guk-ga-reul	nation	189	저 사람은	jeo sa-ram-eun	that
	의미한다	ui-mihan-da	means		남성이니?	nam-seong-i-ni?	is a male?
178	국기는	guk-gi-neun	the flag	190	너는	neo-neun	you
	나라를	na-ra-reul	nation		어디	eo-di	where
	의미한다	ui-mi-han-da	means		있니?	iss-ni?	are
179	그런데	geu-reon-de	by the way	191	온 몸이	on mom-i	my whole body
	나는	na-neun	I		아프다	a-peu-da	ache
	그	geu	that	192	당신의	dang-sin-ui	your
	책을	chaek-eul	book		얼굴을	eol-gul-eul	face
	찾았어	chaj-ass-eo	found		씻으시오	ssis-eu-si-o	wash
180	근데	geun-de	by the way	193	그가	geu-ga	he
	너	neo	you		방에	bang-e	the room
	어디	eo-di	where		들어간다	deul-eo-gan-da	go into
	사니?	sa-ni?	live?	194	손님들이	son-nim-deul-i	customers
181	안 좋은	an joh-eun	bad		나의	na-ui	my
	날	nal	day		가게에	ga-ge-e	shop
	이다	i-da	it is		들어온다	deul-eo-on-da	come in
182	그는	geu-neun	he	195	왜	wae	why
	여기	yeo-gi	here		너는	neo-neun	you
	없다	eobs-da	is not		울고 있니?	ul-go iss-ni?	are crying?
183	오직	o-jik	only	196	그녀가	geu-nyeo-ga	she
	여성만	yeo-seong-man	female		갑자기	gab-ja-gi	out of nowhere
	허락 된다	heo-rak doen-da	is allowed		나타난다	na-ta-nan-da	emerge
184	우리는	u-ri-neun	we	197	걱정	geok-jeong	worry
	친구	chin-gu	friends		말아라	mal-a-ra	don't
	였다	yeoss-da	were	198	그 지역을	geu ji-yeok-eul	the area
185	그것을	geu-geos-eul	that		청소해라	cheong-so-hae-ra	clear
	마음에	ma-eum-e	in mind	199	물은	mul-eun	water
	새기세요	sae-gi-se-yo	keep		중요하다	jung-yo-ha-da	is important
186	그들은	geu-deul-eun	they	200	나는	na-neun	I
	그들의	geu-deul-ui	their		매일	mae-il	everyday
	관계를	gwan-gye-reul	relationship		메리를	me-ri-reul	Mary
	끝냈다	kkeut-naess-da	ended		만난다	man-nan-da	meet
187	나의	na-ui	my				
	아버지는	a-beo-ji-neun	father				
	매일	mae-il	everyday				
	걷는다	geod-neun-da	walk				

Final	K-word ㉔				
check	English ㉕				

K-word ⑱	English ⑲	K-word ⑳	K-word ㉑	English ㉒	K-word ㉓

1-150				
☐ 1) 것	☐ 31) 드린다	☐ 61) 집	☐ 91) 파악하고 있다	☐ 121) 지닌다
☐ 2) 한다	☐ 32) 대한다	☐ 62) 나온다	☐ 92) 자신	☐ 122) 가진다
☐ 3) 된다	☐ 33) 간다	☐ 63) 따른다	☐ 93) 문화	☐ 123) 갖추고 있다
☐ 4) 수	☐ 34) 다닌다	☐ 64) 그리고	☐ 94) 원	☐ 124) 당한다
☐ 5) 수	☐ 35) 년	☐ 65) 및	☐ 95) 생각	☐ 125) 함께
☐ 6) 길	☐ 36) 한	☐ 66) 그때	☐ 96) 명	☐ 126) 아이
☐ 7) 쪽	☐ 37) 말	☐ 67) 그럼	☐ 97) 통한다	☐ 127) 지나간다
☐ 8) 방식	☐ 38) 일	☐ 68) 문제	☐ 98) 소리	☐ 128) 많이
☐ 9) 점	☐ 39) 일	☐ 69) 그런	☐ 99) 다시	☐ 129) 훨씬
☐ 10) 점	☐ 40) 일 한다	☐ 70) 산다	☐ 100) 다른	☐ 130) 시간
☐ 11) 나	☐ 41) 작품	☐ 71) 산다	☐ 101) 다르다	☐ 131) 너
☐ 12) 내	☐ 42) 작업	☐ 72) 지낸다	☐ 102) 여자	☐ 132) 당신
☐ 13) 그	☐ 43) 직장	☐ 73) 저	☐ 103) 소녀	☐ 133) 인간
☐ 14) 없다	☐ 44) 때문	☐ 74) 생각한다	☐ 104) 개	☐ 134) 사실
☐ 15) 않다	☐ 45) 말한다	☐ 75) 모른다	☐ 105) 그 정도	☐ 135) 과연
☐ 16) 말고	☐ 46) 위하여	☐ 76) 속	☐ 106) 뒤	☐ 136) 난다
☐ 17) 아니다	☐ 47) 그러나	☐ 77) 만든다	☐ 107) 듣는다	☐ 137) 자란다
☐ 18) 않는다	☐ 48) 온다	☐ 78) 삼는다	☐ 108) 다	☐ 138) 어머니
☐ 19) 사람	☐ 49) 안다	☐ 79) 시킨다	☐ 109) 좀	☐ 139) 엄마
☐ 20) 국민	☐ 50) 씨	☐ 80) 두	☐ 110) 조금	☐ 140) 눈
☐ 21) 우리	☐ 51) 그렇다	☐ 81) 둘	☐ 111) 든다	☐ 141) 눈
☐ 22) 이	☐ 52) 큰	☐ 82) 앞	☐ 112) 키운다	☐ 142) 뭐
☐ 23) 이	☐ 53) 크다	☐ 83) 경우	☐ 113) 올린다	☐ 143) 무엇
☐ 24) 이런	☐ 54) 또	☐ 84) 중	☐ 114) 기른다	☐ 144) 무슨
☐ 25) 이것	☐ 55) 사회	☐ 85) 중	☐ 115) 싶다	☐ 145) 시대
☐ 26) 이거	☐ 56) 안에	☐ 86) 동안에	☐ 116) 보인다	☐ 146) 다음
☐ 27) 보다	☐ 57) 좋은	☐ 87) 어떤	☐ 117) 표정	☐ 147) 이러하다
☐ 28) 본다	☐ 58) 더	☐ 88) 잘	☐ 118) 모습	☐ 148) 누구
☐ 29) 같다	☐ 59) 받는다	☐ 89) 그녀	☐ 119) 가지고 있다	☐ 149) 전
☐ 30) 준다	☐ 60) 그것	☐ 90) 먹는다	☐ 120) 갖고있다	☐ 150) 곳

1-150				
1) thing	31) give	61) house	91) grasp	121) have
2) do	32) treat	62) come out	92) self	122) have
3) become	33) go	63) obey	93) culture	123) have
4) number	34) go	64) and	94) ₩	124) get p.p
5) way	35) year	65) and	95) thought	125) with
6) way	36) one	66) then	96) famous	126) kid
7) way	37) word	67) then	97) make sense	127) pass by
8) way	38) day	68) problem	98) sound	128) much
9) way	39) work	69) such	99) again	129) much ~er
10) store	40) work	70) buy	100) different	130) time
11) I	41) work	71) live	101) different	131) you
12) I	42) work	72) live	102) girl	132) you
13) he	43) job	73) um	103) girl	133) human
14) not have	44) because of	74) think	104) dog	134) in fact
15) not	45) speak	75) don't know	105) that much	135) indeed
16) not	46) for	76) inside	106) back	136) grow
17) not	47) but	77) make	107) hear	137) grow
18) do not	48) come	78) make	108) all	138) mother
19) people	49) know	79) make	109) a little	139) mom
20) people	50) family name	80) two	110) a little	140) eye
21) we	51) right	81) two	111) pick up	141) snow
22) tooth	52) big	82) front	112) raise	142) what
23) this	53) big	83) case	113) raise	143) what
24) this	54) once again	84) monk	114) raise	144) what
25) this	55) society	85) during	115) want	145) era
26) this	56) in	86) during	116) look	146) next
27) than	57) good	87) any	117) look	147) like this
28) see	58) more	88) well	118) appearance	148) who
29) same	59) receive	89) she	119) have	149) all
30) give	60) it	90) eat	120) have	150) place

151-200				
□ 151) 자리	□ 181) 날			
□ 152) 여러	□ 182) 여기			
□ 153) 많은	□ 183) 여성			
□ 154) 하나	□ 184) 친구			
□ 155) 세계	□ 185) 마음			
□ 156) 세상	□ 186) 관계			
□ 157) 버린다	□ 187) 아버지			
□ 158) 위	□ 188) 남자			
□ 159) 운동	□ 189) 남성			
□ 160) 학교	□ 190) 어디			
□ 161) 자기	□ 191) 몸			
□ 162) 가장	□ 192) 얼굴			
□ 163) 제일	□ 193) 들어간다			
□ 164) 대부분	□ 194) 들어온다			
□ 165) 대통령	□ 195) 왜			
□ 166) 가지	□ 196) 나타난다			
□ 167) 시작한다	□ 197) 말아라			
□ 168) 바로	□ 198) 지역			
□ 169) 어느	□ 199) 물			
□ 170) 그래서	□ 200) 만난다			
□ 171) 그러니까				
□ 172) 정부				
□ 173) 모든				
□ 174) 번				
□ 175) 그거				
□ 176) 돈				
□ 177) 국가				
□ 178) 나라				
□ 179) 그런데				
□ 180) 근데				

Day1~2 English (2)

151-200				
151) place	181) day			
152) several	182) here			
153) many	183) female			
154) one	184) friend			
155) world	185) mind			
156) world	186) relationship			
157) dump	187) father			
158) up	188) male			
159) exercise	189) male			
160) school	190) where			
161) darling	191) body			
162) ~est	192) face			
163) ~est	193) go into			
164) most	194) come in			
165) president	195) why			
166) kinds	196) emerge			
167) start	197) don't			
168) right away	198) area			
169) which	199) water			
170) so	200) meet			
171) so				
172) government				
173) every				
174) times				
175) it				
176) money				
177) nation				
178) nation				
179) by the way				
180) by the way				

Day1~2 List Study

Final	K-word ㉜					
check	English ㉝					

K-word ㉖	English ㉗	K-word ㉘	K-word ㉙	English ㉚	K-word ㉛

Day1~2 List Study

Final	K-word ㉜				
check	English ㉝				

K-word ㉖	English ㉗	K-word ㉘	K-word ㉙	English ㉚	K-word ㉛

Day1~2 List Study

Final	K-word ㉜				
check	English ㉝				

K-word ㉖	English ㉗	K-word ㉘	K-word ㉙	English ㉚	K-word ㉛

	K-word	Pronounce	English	K-word ❶	Sentence example
201	낸다	naen-da	pay		He always pays for the meal.
202	쓴다	sseun-da	write		He writes books.
203	쓴다	sseun-da	use		He uses much water.
204	사용한다	sa-yong-han-da	use		I use a lot of water.
205	없이	eobs-i	without		We went on a trip without her.
206	이번	i-beon	this time		I will win this time.
207	이때	i-ttae	at this time		At this time, he appeared.
208	생활	saeng-hwal	life		I don't like a city life.
209	삶	salm	life		Life and Death.
210	생명	saeng-myeong	life		Life is precious.
211	인생	in-saeng	life		Life is a game.
212	지금	ji-geum	now		Leave now.
213	뿐	ppun	only		He only laughs.
214	다만	da-man	only		I only do my work.
215	만	man	only		I love only you.
216	사이에	sa-i-e	between		There was a silence between us.
217	방법	bang-beob	manner		Do it in this manner.
218	새롭다	sae-rob-da	new		That's new.
219	새	sae	new		Which is new?
220	우리나라	u-ri-na-ra	our country		I love our country.

Final	K-word ❽				
check	English ❾				

K-word ❷	English ❸	K-word ❹	K-word ❺	English ❻	K-word ❼

	K-word	Pronounce	English	K-word ❶	Sentence example
221	앉는다	anj-neun-da	sit down		He comes and sit down.
222	처음의	cheo-eum-ui	initial		That was my initial thought.
223	초기	cho-gi	initial		The initial cost is high.
224	손	son	hand		Hands up!
225	몇	myeocc	a few		I see you a few weeks later.
226	과정	gwa-jeong	course		It is a complicated course.
227	찾는다	chaj-neun-da	search		I often search goods online.
228	특히	teuk-hi	especially		It is especially hot today.
229	도시	do-si	city		I don't like big cities.
230	이상	i-sang	more than		I want more than ₩20,000.
231	이야기	i-ya-gi	story		He told me about the story.
232	얘기	yae-gi	story		Your story is interesting.
233	교육	gyo-yuk	education		Education is important.
234	경제	gyeong-je	economy		The economy is improving.
235	아직	a-jik	yet		He hasn't arrived yet.
236	잡는다	jab-neun-da	catch		Tom catches thieves.
237	같이	gat-i	together		We study together.
238	선생님	seon-saeng-nim	teacher		He is a math teacher.
239	예술	ye-sul	art		Tom loves art.
240	일어선다	il-eo-seon-da	stand up		He stans up silently.

Final	K-word ❽				
check	English ❾				

K-word ❷	English ❸	K-word ❹	K-word ❺	English ❻	K-word ❼

	K-word	Pronounce	English	K-word ❶	Sentence example
241	못	mos	nail		She hammered the nail in.
242	못	mos	can't		I can't play tennis.
243	못한다	mos-han-da	can't do		I can't do the work.
244	읽는다	ilk-neun-da	read		I always read classics.
245	이제	i-je	now		It's time to go now.
246	결과	gyeol-gwa	result		What was the result?
247	내용	nae-yong	content		The content is important.
248	물론	mul-lon	of course		Of course, I can.
249	책	chaek	book		Read this book.
250	일어난다	il-eo-nan-da	happen		Accidents happen.
251	시장	si-jang	market		He went to the market.
252	넣는다	neoh-neun-da	insert		He inserts the key in the lock.
253	중요한	jung-yo-han	important		I have an important meeting.
254	느낀다	neu-kkin-da	feel		I feel faint.
255	어려운	eo-ryeo-un	difficult		This is a difficult question.
256	힘	him	power		Information is power.
257	너무	neo-mu	too		It's too hot.
258	부른다	bu-reun-da	call		She calls the police!
259	의미	ui-mi	meaning		I know the meaning.
260	뜻	tteus	meaning		What's the meaning of this word?

Final	K-word ❽				
check	English ❾				

K-word ❷	English ❸	K-word ❹	K-word ❺	English ❻	K-word ❼

	K-word	Pronounce	English	K-word ❶	Sentence example
261	밝힌다	balk-hin-da	reveal		The detective reveals the truth.
262	죽는다	juk-neun-da	die		Everyone dies.
263	이미	i-mi	already		Die already!
264	정치	jeong-chi	politics		I hate politics.
265	학생	hak-saeng	student		You are new students.
266	연구	yeon-gu	research		The research takes a long time.
267	이름	i-reum	name		I know your name.
268	내린다	nae-rin-da	get off		I get off at this station.
269	사건	sa-geon	incident		I'll explain the incident.
270	쉬운	swi-un	easy		He had an easy test.
271	짓는다	jis-neun-da	build		Birds build nests.
272	또한	tto-han	also		I also went.
273	까닭	kka-dalk	reason		What is the reason you love me?
274	이유	i-yu	reason		What is the reason you love me?
275	또는	tto-neun	or		He can't read or write
276	혹은	hok-eun	or		Window or aisle?
277	필요하다	pil-yo-ha-da	need		I need your help.
278	글	geul	writing		Your writing is logical.
279	생긴다	saeng-gin-da	arise		Difficulties arise.
280	남편	nam-pyeon	husband		Call my husband.

Final	K-word ❽				
check	English ❾				

K-word ❷	English ❸	K-word ❹	K-word ❺	English ❻	K-word ❼

	K-word	Pronounce	English	K-word ❶	Sentence example
281	밖	bakk	outside		Wait outside the room.
282	작은	jak-eun	small		I gave her a small gift.
283	탄다	tan-da	burn		My skin burns easily.
284	대학	dae-hak	university		Seoul has many universities.
285	상황	sang-hwang	situation		It is a fun situation.
286	가운데	ga-un-de	among		Tom is the tallest among them.
287	보낸다	bo-naen-da	send		He often sends us flowers.
288	즉	jeuk	namely		Two boys, namely, Peter and Tom.
289	따라서	tta-ra-seo	thus		Thus, it is crucial to speak English.
290	상태	sang-tae	state		I'm in a confused state of mind.
291	이후	i-hu	since		I have loved him since then.
292	당시	dang-si	at the time		I was 16 at the time.
293	문학	mun-hak	literature		She majors in French literature.
294	더욱	deo-uk	~er		The day is getting shorter.
295	아주	a-ju	very		This problem is very easy.
296	매우	mae-u	very		Thanks very much.
297	지방	ji-bang	fat		You should cut down on fat.
298	밤	bam	night		It's night.
299	높은	nop-eun	high		He lives in a high hill.
300	최근	choe-geun	recent		Please bring recent photos.

Final	K-word ❽				
check	English ❾				

K-word ❷	English ❸	K-word ❹	K-word ❺	English ❻	K-word ❼

	K-word	English		K-word	English
201	낸다	He always _____ for the meal.	221	앉는다	He comes and _____.
202	쓴다	He _____ books.	222	처음의	That was my _____ thought.
203	쓴다	He _____ much water.	223	초기	The _____ cost is high.
204	사용한다	I _____ a lot of water.	224	손	_____ s up!
205	없이	We went on a trip _____ her.	225	몇	I see you _____ weeks later.
206	이번	I will win _____.	226	과정	It is a complicated _____.
207	이때	_____, he appeared.	227	찾는다	I often _____ goods online.
208	생활	I don't like a city _____.	228	특히	It is _____ hot today.
209	삶	_____ and Death.	229	도시	I don't like big _____.
210	생명	_____ is precious.	230	이상	I want _____ ₩20,000.
211	인생	_____ is a game.	231	이야기	He told me about the _____.
212	지금	Leave _____.	232	얘기	Your _____ is interesting.
213	뿐	He _____ laughs.	233	교육	_____ is important.
214	다만	I _____ do my work.	234	경제	The _____ is improving.
215	만	I love _____ you.	235	아직	He hasn't arrived _____.
216	사이에	There was a silence _____ us.	236	잡는다	Tom _____ thieves.
217	방법	Do it in this _____.	237	같이	We study _____.
218	새롭다	That's _____.	238	선생님	He is a math _____.
219	새	Which is _____?	239	예술	Tom loves _____.
220	우리나라	I love _____.	240	일어선다	He _____ silently.

201) pays 202) writes 203) uses 204) use 205) without 206) this time 207) At this time 208) life
209) Life 210) Life 211) Life 212) now 213) only 214) only 215) only 216) between
217) manner 218) new 219) new 220) our country 221) sits down 222) initial 223) initial 224) Hand
225) a few 226) course 227) search 228) especially 229) cities 230) more than 231) story 232) story
233) Education 234) economy 235) yet 236) catches 237) together 238) teacher 239) art 240) stands up

	K-word	English		K-word	English
241	못	She hammered the _____ in.	261	밝힌다	The detective _____ the truth.
242	못	I _____ play tennis.	262	죽는다	Everyone _____ .
243	못한다	I _____ the work.	263	이미	Die _____ !
244	읽는다	I always _____ classics.	264	정치	I hate _____ .
245	이제	It's time to go _____ .	265	학생	You are new _____ .
246	결과	What was the _____ ?	266	연구	The _____ takes a long time.
247	내용	The _____ is important.	267	이름	I know your _____ .
248	물론	_____ , I can.	268	내린다	I _____ at this station.
249	책	Read this _____ .	269	사건	I'll explain the _____ .
250	일어난다	Accidents _____ .	270	쉬운	He had an _____ test.
251	시장	He went to the _____ .	271	짓는다	Birds _____ nests.
252	넣는다	He _____ the key in the lock.	272	또한	I _____ went.
253	중요한	I have an _____ meeting.	273	까닭	What is the _____ you love me?
254	느낀다	I _____ faint.	274	이유	What is the _____ you love me?
255	어려운	This is a _____ question.	275	또는	He can't read _____ write
256	힘	Information is _____ .	276	혹은	Window _____ aisle?
257	너무	It's _____ hot.	277	필요하다	I _____ your help.
258	부른다	She _____ the police!	278	글	Your _____ is logical.
259	의미	I know the _____ .	279	생긴다	Difficulties _____ .
260	뜻	What's the _____ of this word?	280	남편	Call my _____ .

241) nail   242) can't   243) can't do   244) read   245) now   246) result   247) content   248) Of course
249) book   250) happen   251) market   252) inserts   253) important   254) feel   255) difficult   256) power
257) too   258) calls   259) meaning   260) meaning   261) reveals   262) dies   263) already   264) politics
265) students   266) research   267) name   268) get off   269) incident   270) easy   271) build   272) also
273) reason   274) reason   275) or   276) or   277) need   278) writing   279) arise   280) husband

	K-word	English
281	밖	Wait .... the room.
282	작은	I gave her a .... gift.
283	탄다	My skin .... easily.
284	대학	Seoul has many ....
285	상황	It is a fun ....
286	가운데	Tom is the tallest .... them.
287	보낸다	He often .... us flowers.
288	즉	Two boys, ..., Peter and Tom.
289	따라서	.................., it is crucial to speak English.
290	상태	I'm in a confused .... of mind.
291	이후	I have loved him .... then.
292	당시	I was 16 ....
293	문학	She majors in French ....
294	더욱	The day is getting short ....
295	아주	This problem is .... easy.
296	매우	Thanks .... much.
297	지방	You should cut down on ....
298	밤	It's ....
299	높은	He lives in a .... hill.
300	최근	Please bring .... photos.

King Sejong

– The 4th king of Joseon Dynasty

King Sejong was born in 1397.
His 32 year reign marked great achievements.
Hangeul, created by King Sejong,
has been used as a common script for
the Republic of Korea and North Korea.

281) outside   282) small   283) burns   284) universities
285) situation   286) among   287) sends   288) namely
289) Thus   290) state   291) since   292) at the time
293) literature   294) er   295) very   296) very
297) fat   298) night   299) high   300) recent

Day3 Review Study

Final	K-word ⑯				
check	English ⑰				

K-word ⑩	English ⑪	K-word ⑫	K-word ⑬	English ⑭	K-word ⑮

Day3 Sentence(1)

	Write K-word in		Write K-word in ....
201	He always pays for the meal. 그는 항상 밥값을	214	I only do my work. 나는 .... 나의 일을 한다.
202	He writes books. 그는 책을	215	I love only you. 나는 너 .... 사랑한다.
203	He uses much water. 그는 많은 물을	216	There was a silence between us. 우리 .... 침묵이 있었다.
204	I use a lot of water. 나는 많은 물을	217	Do it in this manner. 이런 .... 으로 하세요.
205	We went on a trip without her. 우리는 그녀 .... 여행을 갔다.	218	That's new. 그건 ....
206	I will win this time. 나는 .... 에는 이길 것이다.	219	Which is new? 어떤 것이 .... 것이니?
207	At this time, he appeared. .... 그가 나타났다.	220	I love our country. 나는 .... 를 사랑한다.
208	I don't like a city life. 나는 도시 .... 이 싫다.	221	He comes and sit down. 그가 와서 ....
209	Life and Death. .... 과 죽음.	222	That was my initial thought. 그것은 내 .... 생각이었다.
210	Life is precious. .... 은 소중하다.	223	The initial cost is high. .... 비용이 높다.
211	Life is a game. .... 은 게임이다.	224	Hands up! .... 들어!
212	Leave now. .... 떠나라.	225	I see you a few weeks later. 나는 너를 .... 주 후에 볼 것이다.
213	He only laughs. 그는 웃을 .... 이다.		

201) 낸다　　202) 쓴다　　203) 쓴다　　204) 사용한다　　205) 없이　　206) 이번　　207) 이때　　208) 생활　　209) 삶
210) 생명　　211) 인생　　212) 지금　　213) 뿐　　214) 다만　　215) 만　　216) 사이에　　217) 방법　　218) 새롭다
219) 새　　220) 우리나라　　221) 앉는다　　222) 처음의　　223) 초기　　224) 손　　225) 몇

Sentence Words(1)

	K-word	pronounce	English		K-word	pronounce	English
201	그는	geu-neun	he	214	나는	na-neun	I
	항상	hang-sang	always		다만	da-man	only
	밥	bab	the meal		나의	na-ui	my
	값을 낸다	gaps-eul naen-da	pay for		일을	il-eul	work
202	그는	geu-neun	he		한다	han-da	do
	책을	chaek-eul	book	215	나는	na-neun	I
	쓴다	sseun-da	write		너만	neo-man	only you
203	그는	geu-neun	he		사랑한다	sa-rang-han-da	love
	많은	manh-eun	much	216	우리	u-ri	us
	물을	mul-eul	water		사이에	sa-i-e	between
	쓴다	sseun-da	use		침묵이	chim-muk-i	silence
204	나는	na-neun	I		있었다	iss-eoss-da	there was
	많은	manh-eun	a lot of	217	이런	i-reon	this
	물을	mul-eul	water		방법으로	bang-beob-eu-ro	in manner
	사용한다	sa-yong-han-da	use		하세요	ha-se-yo	do
205	우리는	u-ri-neun	we	218	그건	geu-geon	that
	그녀	geu-nyeo	her		새롭다	sae-rob-da	is new
	없이	eobs-i	without	219	어떤 것이	eo-tteon geos-i	which
	여행을	yeo-haeng-eul	trip		새 것이니?	sae geos-i-ni?	is new?
	갔다	gass-da	went on	220	나는	na-neun	I
206	나는	na-neun	I		우리나라를	u-ri-na-ra-reul	our country
	이번에는	i-beon-e-neun	this time		사랑한다	sa-rang-han-da	love
	이길 것이다	i-gil geos-i-da	will win	221	그가	geu-ga	he
207	이때	i-ttae	at this time		와서	wa-seo	comes and
	그가	geu-ga	he		앉는다	anj-neun-da	sit down
	나타났다	na-ta-nass-da	appeared	222	그것은	geu-geos-eun	that
208	나는	na-neun	I		내	nae	my
	도시	do-si	city		처음의	cheo-eum-ui	initial
	생활이	saeng-hwal-i	life		생각	saeng-gak	thought
	싫다	silh-da	don't like		이었다	i-eoss-da	was
209	삶	salm	life	223	초기	cho-gi	initial
	과	gwa	and		비용이	bi-yong-i	cost
	죽음	juk-eum	death		높다	nop-da	is high
210	생명은	saeng-myeong-eun	life	224	손	son	hand
	소중하다	so-jung-ha-da	is precious		들어	deul-eo	up
211	인생은	in-saeng-eun	life	225	나는	na-neun	I
	게임	ge-im	game		너를	neo-reul	you
	이다	i-da	is		몇	myeocc	a few
212	지금	ji-geum	now		주	ju	week
	떠나라	tteo-na-ra	leave		후에	hu-e	later
213	그는	geu-neun	he		볼 것이다	bol geos-i-da	see
	웃을 뿐이다	us-eul ppun-i-da	only laugh				

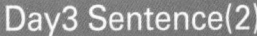

	Write K-word in		Write K-word in ....
226	It is a complicated course. 이건 복잡한 .... 이다.	239	Tom loves art. 톰은 .... 을 사랑한다.
227	I often search goods online. 나는 종종 상품을 온라인에서	240	He stans up silently. 그는 조용히 ....
228	It is especially hot today. 오늘은 .... 덥다.	241	She hammered the nail in. 그녀가 .... 을 박았다.
229	I don't like big cities. 나는 대 .... 를 좋아하지 않는다.	242	I can't play tennis. 나는 테니스를 .... 친다.
230	I want more than ₩20,000. 나는 이만 원 .... 을 원한다.	243	I can't do the work. 나는 그 일을 ....
231	He told me about the story. 그는 나에게 그 .... 에 대해 말했다.	244	I always read classics. 나는 항상 고전을 ....
232	Your story is interesting. 너의 .... 는 재미있다.	245	It's time to go now. .... 갈 시간이다.
233	Education is important. .... 은 중요하다.	246	What was the result? .... 가 어떻습니까?
234	The economy is improving. .... 가 개선되고 있다.	247	The content is important. .... 이 중요하다.
235	He hasn't arrived yet. 그는 .... 도착하지 않았다.	248	Of course, I can. .... , 내가 할 수 있다.
236	Tom catches thieves. 톰은 도둑을	249	Read this book. 이 .... 을 읽어라.
237	We study together. 우리는 .... 공부한다.	250	Accidents happen. 사고는 ....
238	He is a math teacher. 그는 수학 .... 이다.		

226) 과정   227) 찾는다   228) 특히   229) 도시   230) 이상   231) 이야기   232) 얘기   233) 교육   234) 경제
235) 아직   236) 잡는다   237) 같이   238) 선생님   239) 예술   240) 일어선다   241) 못   242) 못   243) 못한다
244) 읽는다   245) 이제   246) 결과   247) 내용   248) 물론   249) 책   250) 일어난다

Sentence Words(2)

	K-word	pronounce	English		K-word	pronounce	English
226	이건	i-geon	it	238	그는	geu-neun	he
	복잡한	bok-jab-han	complicated		수학	su-hak	math
	과정	gwa-jeong	course		선생님	seon-saeng-nim	teacher
	이다	i-da	is		이다	i-da	is
227	나는	na-neun	I	239	톰은	tom-eun	Tom
	종종	jong-jong	often		예술을	ye-sul-eul	art
	상품을	sang-pum-eul	goods		사랑한다	sa-rang-han-da	love
	온라인에서	on-ra-in-e-seo	online	240	그는	geu-neun	he
	찾는다	chaj-neun-da	search		조용히	jo-yong-hi	silently
228	오늘은	o-neul-eun	today		일어선다	il-eo-seon-da	stand up
	특히	teuk-hi	especially	241	그녀가	geu-nyeo-ga	she
	덥다	deob-da	is hot		못을	mos-eul	the nail
229	나는	na-neun	I		박았다	bak-ass-da	hammered in
	대	dae	big	242	나는	na-neun	I
	도시를	do-si-reul	city		테니스를	te-ni-seu-reul	tennis
	좋아하지 않는다	joh-a-ha-ji anh-neun-da	don't like		못 친다	mos chin-da	can't play
230	나는	na-neun	I	243	나는	na-neun	I
	이만 원	i-man won	₩20,000		그 일을	geu il-eul	the work
	이상을	i-sang-eul	more than		못한다	mos-han-da	can' do
	원한다	won-han-da	want	244	나는	na-neun	I
231	그는	geu-neun	he		항상	hang-sang	always
	나에게	na-e-ge	me		고전을	go-jeon-eul	classics
	그 이야기	geu i-ya-gi	the story		읽는다	ilk-neun-da	read
	에 대해	e dae-hae	about	245	이제	i-je	now
	말했다	mal-haess-da	told		갈	gal	to go
232	너의	neo-ui	your		시간이다	si-gan-i-da	it's time
	얘기는	yae-gi-neun	story	246	결과가	gyeol-gwa-ga	the result
	재미있다	jae-mi-iss-da	is interesting		어떻습니까?	eo-tteoh-seub-ni-kka?	what was?
233	교육은	gyo-yuk-eun	education	247	내용이	nae-yong-i	the content
	중요하다	jung-yo-ha-da	is important		중요하다	jung-yo-ha-da	is important
234	경제가	gyeong-je-ga	the economy	248	물론	mul-lon	of course
	개선되고 있다	gae-seon-doe-go iss-da	is improving		내가	nae-ga	I
235	그는	geu-neun	he		할 수 있다	hal su iss-da	can
	아직	a-jik	yet	249	이	i	this
	도착하지 않았다	do-chak-ha-ji anh-ass-da	hasn't arrived		책을	chaek-eul	book
236	톰은	tom-eun	Tom		읽어라	ilk-eo-ra	read
	도둑을	do-duk-eul	thieves	250	사고는	sa-go-neun	accidents
	잡는다	jab-neun-da	catch		일어난다	il-eo-nan-da	happen
237	우리는	u-ri-neun	we				
	같이	gat-i	together				
	공부한다	gong-bu-han-da	study				

	Write K-word in		Write K-word in ....
251	He went to the market. 그는 .... 에 갔다.	264	I hate politics. 나는 .... 가 싫다 .
252	He inserts the key in the lock. 그는 자물쇠에 열쇠를	265	You are new students. 너희들은 새로운 .... 들이다.
253	I have an important meeting. 나는 .... 회의가 있다.	266	The research takes a long time. 그 .... 는 오랜 시간이 걸린다.
254	I feel faint. 나는 현기증을	267	I know your name. 나는 당신의 .... 을 안다.
255	This is a difficult question. 이것은 .... 질문이다.	268	I get off at this station. 나는 이번 역에서 ....
256	Information is power. 정보는 .... 이다.	269	I'll explain the incident. 나는 그 .... 을 설명할 것이다.
257	It's too hot. .... 덥다.	270	He had an easy test. 그는 .... 시험을 보았다.
258	She calls the police! 그녀가 경찰을 .... !	271	Birds build nests. 새는 둥지를 ....
259	I know the meaning. 나는 그 .... 를 안다.	272	I also went. 나 .... 갔다.
260	What's the meaning of this word? 이 단어의 .... 이 무엇인가요?	273	What is the reason you love me? 당신이 나를 좋아하는 .... 이 뭐야?
261	The detective reveals the truth. 탐정이 진실을	274	What is the reason you love me? 당신이 나를 좋아하는 .... 가 뭐야?
262	Everyone dies. 모두가	275	He can't read or write 그는 읽거나 .... 쓸 수 없다.
263	Die already! .... 죽었다!		

251) 시장   252) 넣는다   253) 중요한   254) 느낀다   255) 어려운   256) 힘   257) 너무   258) 부른다   259) 의미
260) 뜻   261) 밝힌다   262) 죽는다   263) 이미   264) 정치   265) 학생   266) 연구   267) 이름   268) 내린다
269) 사건   270) 쉬운   271) 짓는다   272) 또한   273) 까닭   274) 이유   275) 또는

	K-word	pronounce	English		K-word	pronounce	English
251	그는	geu-neun	he	265	너희들은	neo-hui-deul-eun	you
	시장에	si-jang-e	to the market		새로운	sae-ro-un	new
	갔다	gass-da	went		학생들	hak-saeng-deul	students
252	그는	geu-neun	he		이다	i-da	are
	자물쇠에	ja-mul-soe-e	in the lock	266	그 연구는	geu yeon-gu-neun	the research
	열쇠를	yeol-soe-reul	the key		오랜	o-raen	long
	넣는다	neoh-neun-da	insert		시간이	si-gan-i	time
253	나는	na-neun	I		걸린다	geol-lin-da	take
	중요한	jung-yo-han	important	267	나는	na-neun	I
	회의가	hoe-ui-ga	meeting		당신의	dang-sin-ui	your
	있다	iss-da	have		이름을	i-reum-eul	name
254	나는	na-neun	I		안다	an-da	know
	현기증을	hyeon-gi-jeung-eul	faint	268	나는	na-neun	I
	느낀다	neu-kkin-da	feel		이번 역	i-beon yeok	this station
255	이것은	i-geos-eun	this		에서	e-seo	at
	어려운	eo-ryeo-un	difficult		내린다	nae-rin-da	get off
	질문	jil-mun	question	269	나는	na-neun	I
	이다	i-da	is		그 사건을	geu sa-geon-eul	the incident
256	정보는	jeong-bo-neun	information		설명할 것이다	seol-myeong-hal geos-i-da	will explain
	힘	him	power	270	그는	geu-neun	he
	이다	i-da	is		쉬운	swi-un	easy
257	너무	neo-mu	too		시험을	si-heom-eul	test
	덥다	deob-da	it's hot		보았다	bo-ass-da	had
258	그녀가	geu-nyeo-ga	she	271	새는	sae-neun	bird
	경찰을	gyeong-chal-eul	the police		둥지를	dung-ji-leul	nest
	부른다	bu-reun-da	call		짓는다	jis-neun-da	build
259	나는	na-neun	I	272	나	na	I
	그 의미를	geu ui-mi-reul	the meaning		또한	tto-han	also
	안다	an-da	know		갔다	gass-da	went
260	이	i	this	273	당신이	dang-sin-i	you
	단어	dan-eo	word		나를	na-reul	me
	의	ui	of		좋아하는	joh-a-ha-neun	love
	뜻이	tteus-i	the meaning		까닭이	kka-talk-i	the reason
	무엇인가요?	mu-eos-in-ga-yo?	what is?		뭐야?	mwo-ya?	what is?
261	탐정이	tam-jeong-i	the detective	274	당신이	dang-sin-i	you
	진실을	jin-sil-eul	the truth		나를	na-reul	me
	밝힌다	balk-hin-da	reveal		좋아하는	joh-a-ha-neun	love
262	모두가	mo-du-ga	everyone		이유가	i-yu-ga	the reason
	죽는다	juk-neun-da	die		뭐야?	mwo-ya?	what is?
263	이미	i-mi	already	275	그는	geu-neun	he
	죽었다	juk-eoss-da	die		읽거나 또는	ilk-geo-na tto-neun	read or
264	나는	na-neun	I		쓸 수 없다	sseul su eobs-da	can't write
	정치가	jeong-chi-ga	politics				
	싫다	silh-da	hate				

	Write K-word in			Write K-word in ....
276	Window or aisle? 창가 .... 통로?	289	Thus, it is crucial to speak English. ...., 영어를 말하는 것은 중요하다.
277	I need your help. 나는 너의 도움이	290	I'm in a confused state of mind. 나는 마음이 혼란한 .... 에 있다.
278	Your writing is logical. 너의 .... 은 논리적이다.	291	I have loved him since then. 나는 그때 .... 그를 좋아했다.
279	Difficulties arise. 어려운 일들은	292	I was 16 at the time. 나는 .... 열여섯 이었다.
280	Call my husband. 나의 .... 에게 전화해라.	293	She majors in French literature. 그녀는 프랑스 .... 을 전공한다.
281	Wait outside the room. 방 .... 에서 기다려.	294	The day is getting shorter. 날이 .... 짧아지고 있다.
282	I gave her a small gift. 나는 그녀에게 .... 선물을 주었다.	295	This problem is very easy. 이 문제는 .... 쉽다.
283	My skin burns easily. 내 피부는 쉽게	296	Thanks very much. .... 감사합니다.
284	Seoul has many universities. 서울은 많은 .... 을 가지고 있다.	297	You should cut down on fat. 너는 .... 을 줄여야 한다.
285	It is a fun situation. 그것은 웃긴 .... 이다.	298	It's night. .... 이다.
286	Tom is the tallest among them. 그들 .... Tom이 가장 크다.	299	He lives in a high hill. 그는 .... 언덕에서 산다.
287	He often sends us flowers. 그는 종종 우리에게 꽃을	300	Please bring recent photos. .... 사진을 가져 오세요.
288	Two boys, namely, Peter and Tom. 두 소년, ..., 피터와 톰.		

276) 혹은   277) 필요하다   278) 글   279) 생긴다   280) 남편   281) 밖   282) 작은   283) 탄다   284) 대학
285) 상황   286) 가운데   287) 보낸다   288) 즉   289) 따라서   290) 상태   291) 이후   292) 당시   293) 문학
294) 더욱   295) 아주   296) 매우   297) 지방   298) 밤   299) 높은   300) 최근

	K-word	pronounce	English		K-word	pronounce	English
276	창가	chang-ga	window		즉	jeuk	namely
	혹은	hok-eun	or		피터와 톰	piteo-wa tom	Peter and Tom
	통로	tong-ro	aisle	289	따라서	tta-ra-seo	thus
277	나는	na-neun	I		영어를	yeong-eo-reul	English
	너의	neo-ui	your		말하는 것은	mal-ha-neun geos-eun	to speak
	도움이	do-um-i	help		중요하다	jung-yo-ha-da	is crucial
	필요하다	pil-yo-ha-da	need	290	나는	na-neun	I
278	너의	neo-ui	your		마음이	ma-eum-i	mind
	글은	geul-eun	writing		혼란한	hon-ran-han	confused
	논리적이다	non-ri-jeok-i-da	is logical		상태에	sang-tae-e	in a state
279	어려운 일들은	eo-ryeo-un il-deul-eun	difficulties		있다	iss-da	am
	생긴다	saeng-gin-da	arise	291	나는	na-neun	I
280	나의	na-ui	my		그때	geu-ttae	then
	남편에게	nam-pyeon-e-ge	husband		이후	i-hu	since
	전화해라	jeon-hwa-hae-ra	call		그를	geu-reul	him
281	방	bang	the room		좋아했다	joh-a-haess-da	have loved
	밖에서	bakk-e-seo	outside	292	나는	na-neun	I
	기다려	gi-da-ryeo	wait		당시	dang-si	at the time
282	나는	na-neun	I		열여섯	yeol-yeo-seos	16
	그녀에게	geu-nyeo-e-ge	her		이었다	i-eoss-da	was
	작은	jak-eun	small	293	그녀는	geu-nyeo-neun	she
	선물을	seon-mul-eul	gift		프랑스	peu-rang-seu	French
	주었다	ju-eoss-da	gave		문학을	mun-hak-eul	literature
283	내	nae	my		전공한다	jeon-gong-han-da	major
	피부는	pi-bu-neun	skin	294	날이	nal-i	the day
	쉽게	swib-ge	easily		더욱 짧아지고	deo-uk jjalb-a-ji-go	shorter
	탄다	tan-da	burn		있다	iss-da	is getting
284	서울은	seo-ul-eun	Seoul	295	이	i	this
	많은	manh-eun	many		문제는	mun-je-neun	problem
	대학을	dae-hak-eul	university		아주 쉽다	a-ju swib-da	is very easy
	가지고 있다	ga-ji-go-iss-da	has	296	매우	mae-u	very much
285	그것은	geu-geos-eun	it		감사합니다	gam-sa-hab-ni-da	thanks
	웃긴	us-gin	fun	297	너는	neo-neun	you
	상황이다	sang-hwang-i-da	is a situation		지방을	ji-bang-eul	fat
286	그들	geu-deul	them		줄여야 한다	jul-yeo-ya han-da	should cut down on
	가운데	ga-un-de	among	298	밤	bam	night
	Tom이	tom-i	Tom		이다	i-da	it is
	가장 크다	ga-jang keu-da	is the tallest	299	그는	geu-neun	he
287	그는	geu-neun	he		높은	nop-eun	high
	종종	jong-jong	often		언덕에서	eon-deok-e-seo	in a hill
	우리에게	u-ri-e-ge	us		산다	san-da	live
	꽃을	kkocc-eul	flowers	300	최근	choe-geun	recent
	보낸다	bo-naen-da	send		사진을	sa-jin-eul	photos
288	두 소년	du so-nyeon	two boys		가져오세요	ga-jyeo-o-se-yo	please bring

Day3 Sentence Study

Final	K-word ㉔				
check	English ㉕				

K-word ⑱	English ⑲	K-word ⑳	K-word ㉑	English ㉒	K-word ㉓

1-150				
□ 1) 것	□ 31) 드린다	□ 61) 집	□ 91) 파악하고 있다	□ 121) 지닌다
□ 2) 한다	□ 32) 대한다	□ 62) 나온다	□ 92) 자신	□ 122) 가진다
□ 3) 된다	□ 33) 간다	□ 63) 따른다	□ 93) 문화	□ 123) 갖추고 있다
□ 4) 수	□ 34) 다닌다	□ 64) 그리고	□ 94) 원	□ 124) 당한다
□ 5) 수	□ 35) 년	□ 65) 및	□ 95) 생각	□ 125) 함께
□ 6) 길	□ 36) 한	□ 66) 그때	□ 96) 명	□ 126) 아이
□ 7) 쪽	□ 37) 말	□ 67) 그럼	□ 97) 통한다	□ 127) 지나간다
□ 8) 방식	□ 38) 일	□ 68) 문제	□ 98) 소리	□ 128) 많이
□ 9) 점	□ 39) 일	□ 69) 그런	□ 99) 다시	□ 129) 훨씬
□ 10) 점	□ 40) 일 한다	□ 70) 산다	□ 100) 다른	□ 130) 시간
□ 11) 나	□ 41) 작품	□ 71) 산다	□ 101) 다르다	□ 131) 너
□ 12) 내	□ 42) 작업	□ 72) 지낸다	□ 102) 여자	□ 132) 당신
□ 13) 그	□ 43) 직장	□ 73) 저	□ 103) 소녀	□ 133) 인간
□ 14) 없다	□ 44) 때문	□ 74) 생각한다	□ 104) 개	□ 134) 사실
□ 15) 않다	□ 45) 말한다	□ 75) 모른다	□ 105) 그 정도	□ 135) 과연
□ 16) 말고	□ 46) 위하여	□ 76) 속	□ 106) 뒤	□ 136) 난다
□ 17) 아니다	□ 47) 그러나	□ 77) 만든다	□ 107) 듣는다	□ 137) 자란다
□ 18) 않는다	□ 48) 온다	□ 78) 삼는다	□ 108) 다	□ 138) 어머니
□ 19) 사람	□ 49) 안다	□ 79) 시킨다	□ 109) 좀	□ 139) 엄마
□ 20) 국민	□ 50) 씨	□ 80) 두	□ 110) 조금	□ 140) 눈
□ 21) 우리	□ 51) 그렇다	□ 81) 둘	□ 111) 든다	□ 141) 눈
□ 22) 이	□ 52) 큰	□ 82) 앞	□ 112) 키운다	□ 142) 뭐
□ 23) 이	□ 53) 크다	□ 83) 경우	□ 113) 올린다	□ 143) 무엇
□ 24) 이런	□ 54) 또	□ 84) 중	□ 114) 기른다	□ 144) 무슨
□ 25) 이것	□ 55) 사회	□ 85) 중	□ 115) 싶다	□ 145) 시대
□ 26) 이거	□ 56) 안에	□ 86) 동안에	□ 116) 보인다	□ 146) 다음
□ 27) 보다	□ 57) 좋은	□ 87) 어떤	□ 117) 표정	□ 147) 이러하다
□ 28) 본다	□ 58) 더	□ 88) 잘	□ 118) 모습	□ 148) 누구
□ 29) 같다	□ 59) 받는다	□ 89) 그녀	□ 119) 가지고 있다	□ 149) 전
□ 30) 준다	□ 60) 그것	□ 90) 먹는다	□ 120) 갖고있다	□ 150) 곳

1-150				
1) thing	31) give	61) house	91) grasp	121) have
2) do	32) treat	62) come out	92) self	122) have
3) become	33) go	63) obey	93) culture	123) have
4) number	34) go	64) and	94) ₩	124) get p.p
5) way	35) year	65) and	95) thought	125) with
6) way	36) one	66) then	96) famous	126) kid
7) way	37) word	67) then	97) make sense	127) pass by
8) way	38) day	68) problem	98) sound	128) much
9) way	39) work	69) such	99) again	129) much ~er
10) store	40) work	70) buy	100) different	130) time
11) I	41) work	71) live	101) different	131) you
12) I	42) work	72) live	102) girl	132) you
13) he	43) job	73) um	103) girl	133) human
14) not have	44) because of	74) think	104) dog	134) in fact
15) not	45) speak	75) don't know	105) that much	135) indeed
16) not	46) for	76) inside	106) back	136) grow
17) not	47) but	77) make	107) hear	137) grow
18) do not	48) come	78) make	108) all	138) mother
19) people	49) know	79) make	109) a little	139) mom
20) people	50) family name	80) two	110) a little	140) eye
21) we	51) right	81) two	111) pick up	141) snow
22) tooth	52) big	82) front	112) raise	142) what
23) this	53) big	83) case	113) raise	143) what
24) this	54) once again	84) monk	114) raise	144) what
25) this	55) society	85) during	115) want	145) era
26) this	56) in	86) during	116) look	146) next
27) than	57) good	87) any	117) look	147) like this
28) see	58) more	88) well	118) appearance	148) who
29) same	59) receive	89) she	119) have	149) all
30) give	60) it	90) eat	120) have	150) place

151–300				
☐ 151) 자리	☐ 181) 날	☐ 211) 인생	☐ 241) 못	☐ 271) 짓는다
☐ 152) 여러	☐ 182) 여기	☐ 212) 지금	☐ 242) 못	☐ 272) 또한
☐ 153) 많은	☐ 183) 여성	☐ 213) 뿐	☐ 243) 못한다	☐ 273) 까닭
☐ 154) 하나	☐ 184) 친구	☐ 214) 다만	☐ 244) 읽는다	☐ 274) 이유
☐ 155) 세계	☐ 185) 마음	☐ 215) 만	☐ 245) 이제	☐ 275) 또는
☐ 156) 세상	☐ 186) 관계	☐ 216) 사이에	☐ 246) 결과	☐ 276) 혹은
☐ 157) 버린다	☐ 187) 아버지	☐ 217) 방법	☐ 247) 내용	☐ 277) 필요하다
☐ 158) 위	☐ 188) 남자	☐ 218) 새롭다	☐ 248) 물론	☐ 278) 글
☐ 159) 운동	☐ 189) 남성	☐ 219) 새	☐ 249) 책	☐ 279) 생긴다
☐ 160) 학교	☐ 190) 어디	☐ 220) 우리나라	☐ 250) 일어난다	☐ 280) 남편
☐ 161) 자기	☐ 191) 몸	☐ 221) 앉는다	☐ 251) 시장	☐ 281) 밖
☐ 162) 가장	☐ 192) 얼굴	☐ 222) 처음의	☐ 252) 넣는다	☐ 282) 작은
☐ 163) 제일	☐ 193) 들어간다	☐ 223) 초기	☐ 253) 중요한	☐ 283) 탄다
☐ 164) 대부분	☐ 194) 들어온다	☐ 224) 손	☐ 254) 느낀다	☐ 284) 대학
☐ 165) 대통령	☐ 195) 왜	☐ 225) 몇	☐ 255) 어려운	☐ 285) 상황
☐ 166) 가지	☐ 196) 나타난다	☐ 226) 과정	☐ 256) 힘	☐ 286) 가운데
☐ 167) 시작한다	☐ 197) 말아라	☐ 227) 찾는다	☐ 257) 너무	☐ 287) 보낸다
☐ 168) 바로	☐ 198) 지역	☐ 228) 특히	☐ 258) 부른다	☐ 288) 즉
☐ 169) 어느	☐ 199) 물	☐ 229) 도시	☐ 259) 의미	☐ 289) 따라서
☐ 170) 그래서	☐ 200) 만난다	☐ 230) 이상	☐ 260) 뜻	☐ 290) 상태
☐ 171) 그러니까	☐ 201) 낸다	☐ 231) 이야기	☐ 261) 밝힌다	☐ 291) 이후
☐ 172) 정부	☐ 202) 쓴다	☐ 232) 얘기	☐ 262) 죽는다	☐ 292) 당시
☐ 173) 모든	☐ 203) 쓴다	☐ 233) 교육	☐ 263) 이미	☐ 293) 문학
☐ 174) 번	☐ 204) 사용한다	☐ 234) 경제	☐ 264) 정치	☐ 294) 더욱
☐ 175) 그거	☐ 205) 없이	☐ 235) 아직	☐ 265) 학생	☐ 295) 아주
☐ 176) 돈	☐ 206) 이번	☐ 236) 잡는다	☐ 266) 연구	☐ 296) 매우
☐ 177) 국가	☐ 207) 이때	☐ 237) 같이	☐ 267) 이름	☐ 297) 지방
☐ 178) 나라	☐ 208) 생활	☐ 238) 선생님	☐ 268) 내린다	☐ 298) 밤
☐ 179) 그런데	☐ 209) 삶	☐ 239) 예술	☐ 269) 사건	☐ 299) 높은
☐ 180) 근데	☐ 210) 생명	☐ 240) 일어선다	☐ 270) 쉬운	☐ 300) 최근

		151-300		
151) place	181) day	211) life	241) nail	271) build
152) several	182) here	212) now	242) can't	272) also
153) many	183) female	213) only	243) can't do	273) reason
154) one	184) friend	214) only	244) read	274) reason
155) world	185) mind	215) only	245) now	275) or
156) world	186) relationship	216) between	246) result	276) or
157) dump	187) father	217) manner	247) content	277) need
158) up	188) male	218) new	248) of course	278) writing
159) exercise	189) male	219) new	249) book	279) arise
160) school	190) where	220) our country	250) happen	280) husband
161) darling	191) body	221) sit down	251) market	281) outside
162) ~est	192) face	222) initial	252) insert	282) small
163) ~est	193) go into	223) initial	253) important	283) burn
164) most	194) come in	224) hand	254) feel	284) university
165) president	195) why	225) a few	255) difficult	285) situation
166) kinds	196) emerge	226) course	256) power	286) among
167) start	197) don't	227) search	257) too	287) send
168) right away	198) area	228) especially	258) call	288) namely
169) which	199) water	229) city	259) meaning	289) thus
170) so	200) meet	230) more than	260) meaning	290) state
171) so	201) pay	231) story	261) reveal	291) since
172) government	202) write	232) story	262) die	292) at the time
173) every	203) use	233) education	263) already	293) literature
174) times	204) use	234) economy	264) politics	294) ~er
175) it	205) without	235) yet	265) student	295) very
176) money	206) this time	236) catch	266) research	296) very
177) nation	207) at this time	237) together	267) name	297) fat
178) nation	208) life	238) teacher	268) get off	298) night
179) by the way	209) life	239) art	269) incident	299) high
180) by the way	210) life	240) stand up	270) easy	300) recent

Day1~3 List Study

Final	K-word ㉜				
check	English ㉝				

K-word ㉖	English ㉗	K-word ㉘	K-word ㉙	English ㉚	K-word ㉛

Day1~3 List Study

Final	K-word ㉜				
check	English ㉝				

K-word ㉖	English ㉗	K-word ㉘	K-word ㉙	English ㉚	K-word ㉛

Day1~3 List Study

Final	K-word ㉜				
check	English ㉝				

K-word ㉖	English ㉗	K-word ㉘	K-word ㉙	English ㉚	K-word ㉛

	K-word	Pronounce	English	K-word ❶	Sentence example
301	만큼	man-keum	as~as		I am as tall as you.
302	채	chae	as		He was found as dead.
303	대로	dae-ro	as		I did it as you said.
304	현실	hyeon-sil	reality		He refuses to face reality.
305	환경	hwan-gyeong	environment		We influence our environment.
306	먼저	meon-jeo	first		You go first.
307	첫	cheos	first		Mary is his first wife.
308	일단	il-dan	first		Do the work first.
309	얼마나	eol-ma-na	how		How long have you been here?
310	어쩌다	eo-jjeo-da	how		How did you get hurt?
311	어떠하니	eo-tteo-ha-ni	how?		How's your body condition?
312	자체	ja-che	in ~self		It's good in itself.
313	연다	yeon-da	open		The store opens at 12.
314	열린다	yeol-lin-da	open		The door opens automatically.
315	머리	meo-ri	head		My head aches.
316	고개	go-gae	head		Raise your head.
317	묻는다	mud-neun-da	ask		I ask your name.
318	남는다	nam-neun-da	remain		I remain here.
319	부분	bu-bun	part		I love this part.
320	일부	il-bu	part		A part of the bridge collapsed.

Final	K-word ❽				
check	English ❾				

K-word ❷	English ❸	K-word ❹	K-word ❺	English ❻	K-word ❼

	K-word	Pronounce	English	K-word ❶	Sentence example
321	기업	gi-eob	corporation		I set up a corporation.
322	사업	sa-eob	business		He began his business.
323	거기에	geo-gi-e	there		Go there.
324	변화	byeon-hwa	change		Change comes.
325	변한다	byeon-han-da	change		Leaves change colours in autumn.
326	바뀐다	ba-kkwin-da	change		Seats change everyday.
327	달라졌다	dal-la-jyeoss-da	change		Rick changed.
328	바꾼다	ba-kkun-da	change		She often changes her seats.
329	아들	a-deul	son		He has three sons.
330	의지	ui-ji	will		Where there's a will, there's a way.
331	아	a	ah		Ah, there you are.
332	기다린다	gi-da-rin-da	await		We awaits your answer.
333	떨어진다	tteol-eo-jin-da	fall		Leaves fall in autumn.
334	선거	seon-geo	election		Presidential election is important.
335	관하여	gwan-ha-yeo	about		Do you know about it?
336	그냥	geu-nyang	just		Just a wild guess.
337	나눈다	na-nun-da	divide		They divide their money in half.
338	이용한다	i-yong-han-da	utilize		People utilize resources.
339	거의	geo-ui	almost		I am almost dead.
340	곧	god	soon		See you soon!

Final	K-word ❽					
check	English ❾					

K-word ❷	English ❸	K-word ❹	K-word ❺	English ❻	K-word ❼

	K-word	Pronounce	English	K-word ❶	Sentence example
341	중심	jung-sim	center		The city is the center of world trade.
342	중앙	jung-ang	center		Shoot the center.
343	활동	hwal-dong	activity		There are many classroom activities.
344	오늘	o-neul	today		Today is my birthday.
345	오늘날	o-neul-nal	today		Today, Korea is in a turning point.
346	서로	seo-ro	each other		We really loved each other.
347	관심	gwan-sim	interest		He shows interest in her.
348	역시	yeok-si	as well		I didn't see her as well.
349	광고	gwang-go	advertise-ment		Put an advertisement in the paper.
350	아무런	a-mu-reon	no		I've received no goods.
351	아니	a-ni	no		No, I can't go.
352	방	bang	room		Is that your room?
353	정신	jeong-sin	spirit		We have the tribe spirit.
354	이른다	i-reun-da	reach		They reach the border today.
355	땅	ttang	land		He owns this land.
356	이룬다	i-run-da	achieve		He always achieves his goal.
357	아침	a-chim	morning		Good morning, everybody.
358	웃는다	us-neun-da	laugh		They laugh loudly.
359	웃음	us-eum	laugh		She showed a little laugh.
360	현상	hyeon-sang	phenomenon		A typhoon is a natural phenomenon.

Final	K-word ❽				
check	English ❾				

K-word ❷	English ❸	K-word ❹	K-word ❺	English ❻	K-word ❼

	K-word	Pronounce	English	K-word ❶	Sentence example
361	둔다	dun-da	put		He puts money under the bed.
362	놓는다	noh-neun-da	put		He puts the gun down.
363	떠난다	tteo-nan-da	leave		I leave today.
364	기술	gi-sul	skill		I have a good skill.
365	전체	jeon-che	total		How much in total?
366	그래	geu-rae	yes		Yes, you are right.
367	네	ne	yes		Are you happy? Yes.
368	예	ye	yes		He said, 'Yes.'
369	예	ye	example		This is a good example.
370	얻는다	eod-neun-da	get		I get energy from exercise.
371	분	bun	anger		He's full of anger.
372	아름다운	a-reum-da-un	beautiful		Mary is a beautiful girl.
373	끝	kkeut	end		This is the end.
374	민족	min-jok	race		He is a German by race.
375	간	gan	seasoning		The seasoning is good.
376	조사한다	jo-sa-han-da	survey		We often survey smokers.
377	듯하다	deus-ha-da	seem		He seems to have gone home.
378	입	ib	mouth		Open your mouth!
379	그대로	geu-dae-ro	as it is		Leave it as it is.
380	영화	yeong-hwa	movie		The movie starts soon.

Final	K-word ❽				
check	English ❾	-			

K-word ❷	English ❸	K-word ❹	K-word ❺	English ❻	K-word ❼

	K-word	Pronounce	English	K-word ❶	Sentence example
381	필요	pil-yo	need		There's no need to hurry.
382	줄	jul	row		Fall in a row!
383	하늘	ha-neul	sky		The sky is clear.
384	과학	gwa-hak	science		Science is fun.
385	자연	ja-yeon	nature		I love nature.
386	정말	jeong-mal	really		It was really fun.
387	구조	gu-jo	structure		The structure of it is strong.
388	결국	gyeol-guk	eventually		Everyone dies eventually.
389	밥	bab	meal		Have your meal.
390	식사	sik-sa	meal		Enjoy your meal!
391	입는다	ib-neun-da	wear		He wears thick coats.
392	오히려	o-hi-ryeo	rather		Rather, he did it bad.
393	이루어진다	i-ru-eo-jin-da	come true		Dreams come true.
394	남	nam	stranger		He's a stranger.
395	하루	ha-ru	one day		One day is a short time.
396	그림	geu-rim	picture		Look at this picture.
397	적	jeok	enemy		She has no enemies.
398	터	teo	site		The site is nice.
399	마신다	ma-sin-da	drink		Animals also drink water.
400	친다	chin-da	hit		She hits the ball too hard.

Final	K-word ❽				
check	English ❾				

K-word ❷	English ❸	K-word ❹	K-word ❺	English ❻	K-word ❼

	K-word	English		K-word	English
301	만큼	I am .... tall .... you.	321	기업	I set up a ....
302	채	He was found .... dead.	322	사업	He began his ....
303	대로	I did it .... you said.	323	거기에	Go ....
304	현실	He refuses to face	324	변화	.... comes.
305	환경	We influence our	325	변한다	Leaves .... colours in autumn.
306	먼저	You go	326	바뀐다	Seats .... everyday.
307	첫	Mary is his .... wife.	327	달라졌다	Rick ....
308	일단	Do the work	328	바꾼다	She often .... her seats.
309	얼마나	.... long have you been here?	329	아들	He has three ....
310	어쩌다	.... did you get hurt?	330	의지	Where there's a .... , there's a way.
311	어떠하니	.... 's your body condition?	331	아	.... , there you are.
312	자체	It's good in	332	기다린다	We .... your answer.
313	연다	The store .... at 12.	333	떨어진다	Leaves .... in autumn.
314	열린다	The door .... automatically.	334	선거	Presidential .... is important.
315	머리	My .... aches.	335	관하여	Do you know .... it?
316	고개	Raise your	336	그냥	.... a wild guess.
317	묻는다	I .... your name.	337	나눈다	They .... their money in half.
318	남는다	I .... here.	338	이용한다	People .... resources.
319	부분	I love this	339	거의	I am .... dead.
320	일부	A .... of the bridge collapsed.	340	곧	See you .... !

301) as~as   302) as   303) as   304) reality   305) environment 306) first   307) first   308) first
309) How   310) How   311) How   312) itself   313) opens   314) opens   315) head   316) head
317) ask   318) remain   319) part   320) part   321) corporation   322) business   323) there   324) Change
325) change   326) change   327) changed   328) changes   329) sons   330) will   331) Ah   332) await
333) fall   334) election   335) about   336) Just   337) divide   338) utilize   339) almost   340) soon

	K-word	English		K-word	English
341	중심	The city is the _____ of world trade.	361	둔다	He _____ money under the bed.
342	중앙	Shoot the _____.	362	놓는다	He _____ the gun down.
343	활동	There are many classroom _____.	363	떠난다	I _____ today.
344	오늘	_____ is my birthday.	364	기술	I have a good _____.
345	오늘날	_____, Korea is in a turning point.	365	전체	How much in _____?
346	서로	We really loved _____.	366	그래	_____, you are right.
347	관심	He shows _____ in her.	367	네	Are you happy? _____.
348	역시	I didn't see her _____.	368	예	He said, '_____.'
349	광고	Put an _____ in the paper.	369	예	This is a good _____.
350	아무런	I've received _____ goods.	370	얻는다	I _____ energy from exercise.
351	아니	_____, I can't go.	371	분	He's full of _____.
352	방	Is that your _____?	372	아름다운	Mary is a _____ girl.
353	정신	We have the tribe _____.	373	끝	This is the _____.
354	이른다	They _____ the border today.	374	민족	He is a German by _____.
355	땅	He owns this _____.	375	간	The _____ is good.
356	이룬다	He always _____ his goal.	376	조사한다	We often _____ smokers.
357	아침	Good _____, everybody.	377	듯하다	He _____ to have gone home.
358	웃는다	They _____ loudly.	378	입	Open your _____!
359	웃음	She showed a little _____.	379	그대로	Leave it _____.
360	현상	A typhoon is a natural _____.	380	영화	The _____ starts soon.

341) center   342) center   343) activities   344) Today   345) Today   346) each other   347) interest   348) as well
349) advertisement   350) no   351) No   352) room   353) spirit   354) reach   355) land   356) achieves
357) morning   358) laugh   359) laugh   360) phenomenon   361) puts   362) puts   363) leave   364) skill
365) total   366) Yes   367) Yes   368) Yes   369) example   370) get   371) anger   372) beautiful
373) end   374) race   375) seasoning   376) survey   377) seems   378) mouth   379) as it is   380) movie

	K-word	English
381	필요	There's no .... to hurry.
382	줄	Fall in a ....!
383	하늘	The .... is clear.
384	과학	.... is fun.
385	자연	I love ....
386	정말	It was .... fun.
387	구조	The .... of it is strong.
388	결국	Everyone dies ....
389	밥	Have your ....
390	식사	Enjoy your ....!
391	입는다	He .... thick coats.
392	오히려	...................., he did it bad.
393	이루어진다	Dreams ....
394	남	He's a ....
395	하루	.... is a short time.
396	그림	Look at this ....
397	적	She has no ....
398	터	The .... is nice.
399	마신다	Animals also .... water.
400	친다	She .... the ball too hard.

King Sejong

– The 4th king of Joseon Dynasty

King Sejong was born in 1397.
His 32 year reign marked great achievements.
Hangeul, created by King Sejong,
has been used as a common script for
the Republic of Korea and North Korea.

381) need	382) row	383) sky	384) Science
385) nature	386) really	387) structure	388) eventually
389) meal	390) meal	391) wears	392) Rather
393) come true	394) stranger	395) One day	396) picture
397) enemies	398) site	399) drink	400) hits

Day4 Review Study

Final	K-word ⑯				
check	English ⑰				

K-word ⑩	English ⑪	K-word ⑫	K-word ⑬	English ⑭	K-word ⑮

	Write K-word in			Write K-word in ....
301	I am as tall as you. 나는 너 .... 크다.	314	The door opens automatically. 문이 자동으로 ....
302	He was found as dead. 그는 죽은 .... 발견되었다.	315	My head aches. .... 가 아프다.
303	I did it as you said. 네가 말한 .... 나는 그것을 했다.	316	Raise your head. .... 를 들어.
304	He refuses to face reality. 그는 .... 에 직면하기를 거부한다.	317	I ask your name. 나는 너의 이름을 ....
305	We influence our environment. 우리는 .... 에 영향을 끼친다.	318	I remain here. 나는 여기에 ....
306	You go first. 당신이 .... 하세요.	319	I love this part. 나는 이 .... 을 사랑한다.
307	Mary is his first wife. 메리는 그의 .... 아내이다.	320	A part of the bridge collapsed. 다리의 .... 가 붕괴됐다.
308	Do the work first. .... 그 일을 해라.	321	I set up a corporation. 나는 .... 을 세웠다.
309	How long have you been here? 너는 .... 오래 여기에 있었니?	322	He began his business. 그는 그의 .... 을 시작했다.
310	How did you get hurt? .... 다쳤니?	323	Go there. .... 가라.
311	How's your body condition? 몸 상태가 .... ?	324	Change comes. .... 는 온다.
312	It's good in itself. 그것은 그 .... 로 좋다.	325	Leaves change colors in autumn. 가을에는 나뭇잎들의 색깔이 ....
313	The store opens at 12. 그 가게는 12시에		

301) 만큼　　302) 채　　303) 대로　　304) 현실　　305) 환경　　306) 먼저　　307) 첫　　308) 일단　　309) 얼마나
310) 어쩌다　311) 어떠하니　312) 자체　313) 연다　314) 열린다　315) 머리　316) 고개　317) 묻는다　318) 남는다
319) 부분　320) 일부　321) 기업　322) 사업　323) 거기에　324) 변화　325) 변한다

Sentence Words(1)

	K-word	pronounce	English		K-word	pronounce	English
301	나는	na-neun	I		좋다	joh-da	is good
	너	neo	you	313	그 가게는	geu ga-ge-neun	the store
	만큼	man-keum	as as		12시에	yeol-du-si-e	at 12
	크다	keu-da	am tall		연다	yeon-da	open
302	그는	geu-neun	he	314	문이	mun-i	the door
	죽은 채	juk-eun chae	as dead		자동으로	ja-dong-eu-ro	automatically
	발견되었다	bal-gyeon-doe-eoss-da	was found		열린다	yeol-lin-da	open
303	니가	ni-ga	you	315	머리가	meo-ri-ga	my head
	말한 대로	mal-han-dae-ro	as said		아프다	a-peu-da	ache
	나는	na-neun	I	316	고개를	go-gae-reul	your head
	그것을	geu-geos-eul	it		들어	deul-eo	raise
	했다	haess-da	did	317	나는	na-neun	I
304	그는	geu-neun	he		너의	neo-ui	your
	현실에	hyeon-sil-e	reality		이름을	i-reum-eul	name
	직면하기를	jik-myeon-ha-gi-reul	to face		묻는다	mud-neun-da	ask
	거부한다	geo-bu-han-da	refuse	318	나는	na-neun	I
305	우리는	u-ri-neun	we		여기에	yeo-gi-e	here
	환경에	hwan-gyeong-e	our environment		남는다	nam-neun-da	remain
	영향을 끼친다	yeong-hyang-eul kki-chin-da	influence	319	나는	na-neun	I
306	당신이	dang-sin-i	you		이	i	this
	먼저 하세요	meon-jeo ha-se-yo	go first		부분을	bu-bun-eul	part
307	메리는	me-ri-neun	Mary		사랑한다	sa-rang-han-da	love
	그의	geu-ui	his	320	다리의	da-ri-ui	of the bridge
	첫	cheos	first		일부가	il-bu-ga	a part
	아내	a-nae	wife		붕괴됐다	bung-goe-dwaess-da	collapsed
	이다	i-da	is	321	나는	na-neun	I
308	일단	il-dan	first		기업을	gi-eob-eul	a corporation
	그 일을	geu il-eul	the work		세웠다	se-woss-da	set up
	해라	hae-ra	do	322	그는	geu-neun	he
309	너는	neo-neun	you		그의	geu-ui	his
	얼마나 오래	eol-ma-na o-rae	how long		사업을	sa-eob-eul	business
	여기에	yeo-gi-e	here		시작했다	si-jak-haess-da	began
	있었니?	iss-eoss-ni?	have been?	323	거기에	geo-gi-e	there
310	어쩌다	eo-jjeo-da	how		가라	ga-ra	go
	다쳤니?	da-chyeoss-ni?	did you get hurt?	324	변화는	byeon-hwa-neun	change
311	몸	mom	your body		온다	on-da	come
	상태가	sang-tae-ga	condition	325	가을에는	ga-eul-e-neun	in autumn
	어떠하니?	eo-tteo-ha-ni?	how is?		나뭇잎들의	na-mus-ip-deul-ui	leaves
312	그것은	geu-geos-eun	it		색깔이	saek-kkal-i	colours
	그 자체로	geu ja-che-ro	in itself		변한다	byeon-han-da	change

	Write K-word in			Write K-word in ....
326	Seats change everyday. 자리가 매일		339	I am almost dead. 나는 .... 죽은 거다.
327	Rick changed. 릭은		340	See you soon! .... 만나!
328	She often changes her seats. 그녀는 종종 자리를		341	The city is the center of world trade. 그 도시는 세계 무역의 .... 이다.
329	He has three sons. 그는 .... 이 셋 있다.		342	Shoot the center. .... 을 쏴라.
330	Where there's a will, there's a way. .... 가 있는 곳에 길이 있다.		343	There are many classroom activities. 많은 교실 .... 들이 있다.
331	Ah, there you are. .... , 너 거기 있구나.		344	Today is my birthday. .... 은 나의 생일이다.
332	We awaits your answer. 우리는 당신의 답을		345	Today, Korea is in a turning point. .... , 한국은 전환기에 있다.
333	Leaves fall in autumn. 잎들이 가을에		346	We really loved each other. 우리는 .... 정말 사랑했다.
334	Presidential election is important. 대통령 .... 는 중요하다.		347	He shows interest in her. 그는 그녀에게 .... 을 보인다.
335	Do you know about it? 너는 그것에 .... 알고 있니?		348	I didn't see her as well. 나도 .... 그녀를 보지 못했다.
336	Just a wild guess. .... 추측 한 거야.		349	Put an advertisement in the paper. 신문에 .... 를 내라.
337	They divide their money in half. 그들은 돈을 반으로		350	I've received no goods. 나는 .... 물건도 받지 않았다.
338	People utilize resources. 사람들은 자원을			

326) 바뀐다   327) 달라졌다   328) 바꾼다   329) 아들   330) 의지   331) 아   332) 기다린다   333) 떨어진다   334) 선거
335) 관하여   336) 그냥   337) 나눈다   338) 이용한다   339) 거의   340) 곧   341) 중심   342) 중앙   343) 활동
344) 오늘   345) 오늘날   346) 서로   347) 관심   348) 역시   349) 광고   350) 아무런

Sentence Words(2)

	K-word	pronounce	English		K-word	pronounce	English
326	자리가	ja-ri-ga	seats	339	나는	na-neun	I
	매일	mae-il	everyday		거의	geo-ui	almost
	바뀐다	ba-kkwin-da	change		죽은 거다	juk-eun geo-da	is dead
327	릭은	rik-eun	Rick	340	곧	god	soon
	달라졌다	dal-la-jyeoss-da	changed		만나	man-na	see you
328	그녀는	geu-nyeo-neun	she	341	그	geu	the
	종종	jong-jong	often		도시는	do-si-neun	city
	자리를	ja-ri-reul	her seat		세계	se-gye	world
	바꾼다	ba-kkun-da	change		무역의	mu-yeok-ui	of trade
329	그는	geu-neun	he		중심	jung-sim	the center
	아들이	a-deul-i	sons		이다	i-da	is
	셋	ses	three	342	중앙을	jung-ang-eul	the center
	있다	iss-da	has		쏴라	sswa-ra	shoot
330	의지가	ui-ji-ga	a will	343	많은	manh-eun	many
	있는 곳에	iss-neun-gos-e	where there's		교실	gyo-sil	classroom
	길이	gil-i	a way		활동들이	hwal-dong-deul-i	activities
	있다	iss-da	there's		있다	iss-da	there are
331	아	a	ah	344	오늘은	o-neul-eun	today
	너	neo	you		나의	na-ui	my
	거기	geo-gi	there		생일	saeng-il	birthday
	있구나	iss-gu-na	are		이다	i-da	is
332	우리는	u-ri-neun	we	345	오늘날	o-neul-nal	today
	당신의	dang-sin-ui	your		한국은	han-guk-eun	Korea
	답을	dab-eul	answer		전환기에	jeon-hwan-gi-e	in a turning point
	기다린다	gi-da-rin-da	await		있다	iss-da	is
333	잎들이	ip-deul-i	leaves	346	우리는	u-ri-neun	we
	가을에	ga-eul-e	in autumn		서로	seo-ro	each other
	떨어진다	ttel-eo-jin-da	fall		정말	jeong-mal	really
334	대통령	dae-tong-ryeong	presidential		사랑했다	sa-rang-haess-da	loved
	선거는	seon-geo-neun	election	347	그는	geu-neun	he
	중요하다	jung-yo-ha-da	is important		그녀에게	geu-nyeo-e-ge	in her
335	너는	neo-neun	you		관심을	gwan-sim-eul	interest
	그것에	geu-geos-e	it		보인다	bo-in-da	show
	관하여	gwan-ha-yeo	about	348	나도	na-do	I
	알고 있니?	al-go iss-ni?	do you know?		역시	yeok-si	as well
336	그냥	geu-nyang	just		그녀를	geu-nyeo-reul	her
	추측 한 거야	chu-cheuk han geo-ya	a wild guess		보지 못했다	bo-ji mos-haess-da	didn't see
337	그들은	geu-deul-eun	they	349	신문에	sin-mun-e	in the paper
	돈을	don-eul	their money		광고를	gwang-go-reul	an advertisement
	반으로	ban-eu-ro	in half		내라	nae-ra	put
	나눈다	na-nun-da	divide	350	나는	na-neun	I
338	사람들은	sa-ram-deul-eun	people		아무런 물건도	a-mu-reon mul-geon-do	goods
	자원을	ja-won-eul	resources		받지 않았다	bad-ji anh-ass-da	have received no
	이용한다	i-yong-han-da	utilize				

	Write K-word in		Write K-word in ....
351	No, I can't go. ...., 나는 갈 수 없다.	364	I have a good skill. 나는 좋은 .... 을 가지고 있다.
352	Is that your room? 저것이 네 .... 이니?	365	How much in total? .... 얼마에요?
353	We have the tribe spirit. 우리는 부족 .... 을 가지고 있다.	366	Yes, you are right. ...., 네가 맞아.
354	They reach the border today. 그들은 오늘 국경에	367	Are you happy? Yes. 너 행복하니? ....
355	He owns this land. 그가 이 .... 을 소유하고 있다.	368	He said, "Yes." 그가 '..........'라고 말했다.
356	He always achieves his goal. 그는 항상 목표를	369	This is a good example. 이것이 좋은 .... 이다.
357	Good morning, everybody. 좋은 .... 입니다 여러분.	370	I get energy from exercise. 나는 운동으로부터 에너지를 ....
358	They laugh loudly. 그들은 크게	371	He's full of anger. 그는 .... 에 차있다.
359	She showed a little laugh. 그녀가 작은 .... 을 보였다.	372	Mary is a beautiful girl. 메리는 .... 여자다.
360	A typhoon is a natural phenomenon. 태풍은 자연 .... 이다.	373	This is the end. 이것이 .... 이다.
361	He puts money under the bed. 그는 돈을 침대 밑에	374	He is a German by race. 그는 독일 .... 에 속한다.
362	He puts the gun down. 그는 총을 내려	375	The seasoning is good. .... 이 알맞다.
363	I leave today. 나는 오늘		

351) 아니 352) 방 353) 정신 354) 이른다 355) 땅 356) 이룬다 357) 아침 358) 웃는다 359) 웃음
360) 현상 361) 둔다 362) 놓는다 363) 떠난다 364) 기술 365) 전체 366) 그래 367) 네 368) 예
369) 예 370) 얻는다 371) 분 372) 아름다운 373) 끝 374) 민족 375) 간

Sentence Words(3)

	K-word	pronounce	English		K-word	pronounce	English
351	아니	a-ni	no	363	나는	na-neun	I
	나는	na-neun	I		오늘	o-neul	today
	갈 수 없다	gal su eobs-da	can't go		떠난다	tteo-nan-da	leave
352	저것이	jeo-geos-i	that	364	나는	na-neun	I
	너의	neo-ui	your		좋은	joh-eun	good
	방이니?	bang-i-ni?	is room?		기술을	gi-sul-eul	skill
353	우리는	u-ri-neun	we		가지고 있다	ga-ji-go iss-da	have
	부족	bu-jok	the tribe	365	전체	jeon-che	in total
	정신을	jeong-sin-eul	spirit		얼마에요?	eol-ma-e-yo?	how much?
	가지고 있다	ga-ji-go iss-da	have	366	그래	geu-rae	yes
354	그들은	geu-deul-eun	they		네가	ne-ga	you
	오늘	o-neul	today		맞아	maj-a	are right
	국경에	guk-gyeong-e	the border	367	너	neo	you
	이른다	i-reun-da	reach		행복하니?	haeng-bok-ha-ni?	are happy?
355	그가	geu-ga	he		네	ne	yes
	이	i	this	368	그가	geu-ga	he
	땅을	ttang-eul	land		"예"라고	ye-ra-go	"yes"
	소유하고 있다	so-yu-ha-go iss-da	own		말했다	mal-haess-da	said
356	그는	geu-neun	he	369	이것이	i-geos-i	this
	항상	hang-sang	always		좋은	joh-eun	good
	목표를	mok-pyo-reul	his goal		예	ye	example
	이룬다	i-run-da	achieve		이다	i-da	is
357	좋은	joh-eun	good	370	나는	na-neun	I
	아침입니다	a-chim-ib-ni-da	morning		운동	un-dong	exercise
	여러분	yeo-reo-bun	everybody		으로부터	eu-ro-bu-teo	from
358	그들은	geu-deul-eun	they		에너지를	e-neo-ji-reul	energy
	크게	keu-ge	loudly		얻는다	eod-neun-da	get
	웃는다	us-neun-da	laugh	371	그는	geu-neun	he
359	그녀가	geu-nyeo-ga	she		분에	bun-e	of anger
	작은	jak-eun	a little		차있다	cha-iss-da	is full
	웃음을	us-eum-eul	laugh	372	메리는	me-ri-neun	Mary
	보였다	bo-yeoss-da	showed		아름다운	a-reum-da-un	beautiful
360	태풍은	tae-pung-eun	a typhoon		여자다	yeo-ja-da	is girl
	자연	ja-yeon	natural	373	이것이	i-geos-i	this
	현상	hyeon-sang	phenomenon		끝	kkeut	the end
	이다	i-da	is		이다	i-da	is
361	그는	geu-neun	he	374	그는	geu-neun	he
	돈을	don-eul	money		독일	dok-il	German
	침대	chim-dae	the bed		민족에	min-jok-e	by race
	밑에	mit-e	under		속한다	sok-han-da	is
	둔다	dun-da	put	375	간이	gan-i	the seasoning
362	그는	geu-neun	he		알맞다	al-maj-da	is good
	총을	chong-eul	the gun				
	내려놓는다	nae-ryeo-noh-neun-da	put down				

Day4 Sentence(4)

	Write K-word in		Write K-word in ....
376	We often survey smokers. 우리는 가끔 흡연자들을	389	Have your meal. .... 먹어라
377	He seems to have gone home. 그는 집에 간	390	Enjoy your meal! .... 를 즐기세요!
378	Open your mouth! .... 을 벌리시오!	391	He wears thick coats. 그는 두꺼운 코트를 ....
379	Leave it as it is. .... 둬.	392	Rather, he did it bad. ...., 그는 그것을 잘 못했다.
380	The movie starts soon. .... 가 곧 시작된다.	393	Dreams come true. 꿈은 ....
381	There's no need to hurry. 서두를 .... 가 없다.	394	He's a stranger. 그는 .... 이다.
382	Fall in a row! .... 지어 떨어져!	395	One day is a short time. .... 는 짧은 시간이다.
383	The sky is clear. .... 이 맑다.	396	Look at this picture. 이 .... 을 보아라.
384	Science is fun. .... 은 재미있다.	397	She has no enemies. 그녀는 .... 이 없다.
385	I love nature. 나는 .... 을 사랑한다.	398	The site is nice. .... 가 좋다.
386	It was really fun. 그거 .... 재미있었다.	399	Animals also drink water. 동물들 또한 물을 ....
387	The structure of it is strong. 그것의 .... 는 강하다.	400	She hits the ball too hard. 그녀는 공을 너무 세게 ....
388	Everyone dies eventually. .... 모두는 죽는다.		

376) 조사한다 377) 듯하다 378) 입 379) 그대로 380) 영화 381) 필요 382) 줄 383) 하늘 384) 과학
385) 자연 386) 정말 387) 구조 388) 결국 389) 밥 390) 식사 391) 입는다 392) 오히려 393) 이루어진다
394) 남 395) 하루 396) 그림 397) 적 398) 터 399) 마신다 400) 친다

Sentence Words(4)

	K-word	pronounce	English		K-word	pronounce	English
376	우리는	u-ri-neun	we	390	식사를	sik-sa-reul	your meal
	가끔	ga-kkeum	often		즐기세요	jeul-gi-se-yo	enjoy
	흡연자를	heub-yeon-ja-reul	smokers	391	그는	geu-neun	he
	조사한다	jo-sa-han-da	survey		두꺼운	du-kkeo-un	thick
377	그는	geu-neun	he		코트를	ko-teu-reul	coats
	집에	jib-e	home		입는다	ib-neun-da	wear
	간듯하다	gan-deus-ha-da	seems to have gone	392	오히려	o-hi-ryeo	rather
378	입을	ib-eul	your mouth		그는	geu-neun	he
	벌리시오	beol-li-si-o	open		그것을	geu-geos-eul	it
379	그대로	geu-dae-ro	as it is		잘 못했다	jal mos-haess-da	did bad
	둬	dwo	leave it	393	꿈은	kkum-eun	dreams
380	영화가	yeong-hwa-ga	the movie		이루어진다	i-ru-eo-jin-da	come true
	곧	god	soon	394	그는	geu-neun	he
	시작된다	si-jak-doen-da	start		남	nam	a stranger
381	서두를	seo-du-reul	to hurry		이다	i-da	is
	필요가 없다	pil-yo-ga eobs-da	there's no need	395	하루는	ha-ru-neun	one day
382	줄지어	jul-ji-eo	in a row		짧은	jjalb-eun	short
	떨어져	tteol-eo-jyeo	fall		시간	si-gan	time
383	하늘이	ha-neul-i	the sky		이다	i-da	is
	맑다	malk-da	is clear	396	이	i	this
384	과학은	gwa-hak-eun	science		그림을	geu-rim-eul	picture
	재미있다	jae-mi-iss-da	is fun		보아라	bo-a-ra	look at
385	나는	na-neun	I	397	그녀는	geu-nyeo-neun	she
	자연을	ja-yeon-eul	nature		적이	jeok-i	enemies
	사랑한다	sa-rang-han-da	love		없다	eobs-da	has no
386	그거	geu-geo	it	398	터가	teo-ga	the site
	정말	jeong-mal	really		좋다	joh-da	is nice
	재미 있었다	jae-mi iss-eoss-da	was fun	399	동물들	dong-mul-deul	animals
387	그것의	geu-geos-ui	of it		또한	tto-han	also
	구조는	gu-jo-neun	the structure		물을	mul-eul	water
	강하다	gang-ha-da	is strong		마신다	ma-sin-da	drink
388	결국	gyeol-guk	eventually	400	그녀는	geu-nyeo-neun	she
	모두는	mo-du-neun	everyone		공을	gong-eul	the ball
	죽는다	juk-neun-da	die		너무	neo-mu	too
389	밥	bab	your meal		세게	se-ge	hard
	먹어라	meok-eo-ra	have		친다	chin-da	hit

Day4 Sentence Study

Final	K-word ㉔				
check	English ㉕				

K-word ⑱	English ⑲	K-word ⑳	K-word ㉑	English ㉒	K-word ㉓

1-150				
□ 1) 것	□ 31) 드린다	□ 61) 집	□ 91) 파악하고 있다	□ 121) 지닌다
□ 2) 한다	□ 32) 대한다	□ 62) 나온다	□ 92) 자신	□ 122) 가진다
□ 3) 된다	□ 33) 간다	□ 63) 따른다	□ 93) 문화	□ 123) 갖추고 있다
□ 4) 수	□ 34) 다닌다	□ 64) 그리고	□ 94) 원	□ 124) 당한다
□ 5) 수	□ 35) 년	□ 65) 및	□ 95) 생각	□ 125) 함께
□ 6) 길	□ 36) 한	□ 66) 그때	□ 96) 명	□ 126) 아이
□ 7) 쪽	□ 37) 말	□ 67) 그럼	□ 97) 통한다	□ 127) 지나간다
□ 8) 방식	□ 38) 일	□ 68) 문제	□ 98) 소리	□ 128) 많이
□ 9) 점	□ 39) 일	□ 69) 그런	□ 99) 다시	□ 129) 훨씬
□ 10) 점	□ 40) 일 한다	□ 70) 산다	□ 100) 다른	□ 130) 시간
□ 11) 나	□ 41) 작품	□ 71) 산다	□ 101) 다르다	□ 131) 너
□ 12) 내	□ 42) 작업	□ 72) 지낸다	□ 102) 여자	□ 132) 당신
□ 13) 그	□ 43) 직장	□ 73) 저	□ 103) 소녀	□ 133) 인간
□ 14) 없다	□ 44) 때문	□ 74) 생각한다	□ 104) 개	□ 134) 사실
□ 15) 않다	□ 45) 말한다	□ 75) 모른다	□ 105) 그 정도	□ 135) 과연
□ 16) 말고	□ 46) 위하여	□ 76) 속	□ 106) 뒤	□ 136) 난다
□ 17) 아니다	□ 47) 그러나	□ 77) 만든다	□ 107) 듣는다	□ 137) 자란다
□ 18) 않는다	□ 48) 온다	□ 78) 삼는다	□ 108) 다	□ 138) 어머니
□ 19) 사람	□ 49) 안다	□ 79) 시킨다	□ 109) 좀	□ 139) 엄마
□ 20) 국민	□ 50) 씨	□ 80) 두	□ 110) 조금	□ 140) 눈
□ 21) 우리	□ 51) 그렇다	□ 81) 둘	□ 111) 든다	□ 141) 눈
□ 22) 이	□ 52) 큰	□ 82) 앞	□ 112) 키운다	□ 142) 뭐
□ 23) 이	□ 53) 크다	□ 83) 경우	□ 113) 올린다	□ 143) 무엇
□ 24) 이런	□ 54) 또	□ 84) 중	□ 114) 기른다	□ 144) 무슨
□ 25) 이것	□ 55) 사회	□ 85) 중	□ 115) 싶다	□ 145) 시대
□ 26) 이거	□ 56) 안에	□ 86) 동안에	□ 116) 보인다	□ 146) 다음
□ 27) 보다	□ 57) 좋은	□ 87) 어떤	□ 117) 표정	□ 147) 이러하다
□ 28) 본다	□ 58) 더	□ 88) 잘	□ 118) 모습	□ 148) 누구
□ 29) 같다	□ 59) 받는다	□ 89) 그녀	□ 119) 가지고 있다	□ 149) 전
□ 30) 준다	□ 60) 그것	□ 90) 먹는다	□ 120) 갖고있다	□ 150) 곳

1-150				
1) thing	31) give	61) house	91) grasp	121) have
2) do	32) treat	62) come out	92) self	122) have
3) become	33) go	63) obey	93) culture	123) have
4) number	34) go	64) and	94) ₩	124) get p.p
5) way	35) year	65) and	95) thought	125) with
6) way	36) one	66) then	96) famous	126) kid
7) way	37) word	67) then	97) make sense	127) pass by
8) way	38) day	68) problem	98) sound	128) much
9) way	39) work	69) such	99) again	129) much ~er
10) store	40) work	70) buy	100) different	130) time
11) I	41) work	71) live	101) different	131) you
12) I	42) work	72) live	102) girl	132) you
13) he	43) job	73) um	103) girl	133) human
14) not have	44) because of	74) think	104) dog	134) in fact
15) not	45) speak	75) don't know	105) that much	135) indeed
16) not	46) for	76) inside	106) back	136) grow
17) not	47) but	77) make	107) hear	137) grow
18) do not	48) come	78) make	108) all	138) mother
19) people	49) know	79) make	109) a little	139) mom
20) people	50) family name	80) two	110) a little	140) eye
21) we	51) right	81) two	111) pick up	141) snow
22) tooth	52) big	82) front	112) raise	142) what
23) this	53) big	83) case	113) raise	143) what
24) this	54) once again	84) monk	114) raise	144) what
25) this	55) society	85) during	115) want	145) era
26) this	56) in	86) during	116) look	146) next
27) than	57) good	87) any	117) look	147) like this
28) see	58) more	88) well	118) appearance	148) who
29) same	59) receive	89) she	119) have	149) all
30) give	60) it	90) eat	120) have	150) place

Day1~4 List (2)

151–300				
☐ 151) 자리	☐ 181) 날	☐ 211) 인생	☐ 241) 못	☐ 271) 짓는다
☐ 152) 여러	☐ 182) 여기	☐ 212) 지금	☐ 242) 못	☐ 272) 또한
☐ 153) 많은	☐ 183) 여성	☐ 213) 뿐	☐ 243) 못한다	☐ 273) 까닭
☐ 154) 하나	☐ 184) 친구	☐ 214) 다만	☐ 244) 읽는다	☐ 274) 이유
☐ 155) 세계	☐ 185) 마음	☐ 215) 만	☐ 245) 이제	☐ 275) 또는
☐ 156) 세상	☐ 186) 관계	☐ 216) 사이에	☐ 246) 결과	☐ 276) 혹은
☐ 157) 버린다	☐ 187) 아버지	☐ 217) 방법	☐ 247) 내용	☐ 277) 필요하다
☐ 158) 위	☐ 188) 남자	☐ 218) 새롭다	☐ 248) 물론	☐ 278) 글
☐ 159) 운동	☐ 189) 남성	☐ 219) 새	☐ 249) 책	☐ 279) 생긴다
☐ 160) 학교	☐ 190) 어디	☐ 220) 우리나라	☐ 250) 일어난다	☐ 280) 남편
☐ 161) 자기	☐ 191) 몸	☐ 221) 앉는다	☐ 251) 시장	☐ 281) 밖
☐ 162) 가장	☐ 192) 얼굴	☐ 222) 처음의	☐ 252) 넣는다	☐ 282) 작은
☐ 163) 제일	☐ 193) 들어간다	☐ 223) 초기	☐ 253) 중요한	☐ 283) 탄다
☐ 164) 대부분	☐ 194) 들어온다	☐ 224) 손	☐ 254) 느낀다	☐ 284) 대학
☐ 165) 대통령	☐ 195) 왜	☐ 225) 몇	☐ 255) 어려운	☐ 285) 상황
☐ 166) 가지	☐ 196) 나타난다	☐ 226) 과정	☐ 256) 힘	☐ 286) 가운데
☐ 167) 시작한다	☐ 197) 말아라	☐ 227) 찾는다	☐ 257) 너무	☐ 287) 보낸다
☐ 168) 바로	☐ 198) 지역	☐ 228) 특히	☐ 258) 부른다	☐ 288) 즉
☐ 169) 어느	☐ 199) 물	☐ 229) 도시	☐ 259) 의미	☐ 289) 따라서
☐ 170) 그래서	☐ 200) 만난다	☐ 230) 이상	☐ 260) 뜻	☐ 290) 상태
☐ 171) 그러니까	☐ 201) 낸다	☐ 231) 이야기	☐ 261) 밝힌다	☐ 291) 이후
☐ 172) 정부	☐ 202) 쓴다	☐ 232) 얘기	☐ 262) 죽는다	☐ 292) 당시
☐ 173) 모든	☐ 203) 쓴다	☐ 233) 교육	☐ 263) 이미	☐ 293) 문학
☐ 174) 번	☐ 204) 사용한다	☐ 234) 경제	☐ 264) 정치	☐ 294) 더욱
☐ 175) 그거	☐ 205) 없이	☐ 235) 아직	☐ 265) 학생	☐ 295) 아주
☐ 176) 돈	☐ 206) 이번	☐ 236) 잡는다	☐ 266) 연구	☐ 296) 매우
☐ 177) 국가	☐ 207) 이때	☐ 237) 같이	☐ 267) 이름	☐ 297) 지방
☐ 178) 나라	☐ 208) 생활	☐ 238) 선생님	☐ 268) 내린다	☐ 298) 밤
☐ 179) 그런데	☐ 209) 삶	☐ 239) 예술	☐ 269) 사건	☐ 299) 높은
☐ 180) 근데	☐ 210) 생명	☐ 240) 일어선다	☐ 270) 쉬운	☐ 300) 최근

151-300				
151) place	181) day	211) life	241) nail	271) build
152) several	182) here	212) now	242) can't	272) also
153) many	183) female	213) only	243) can't do	273) reason
154) one	184) friend	214) only	244) read	274) reason
155) world	185) mind	215) only	245) now	275) or
156) world	186) relationship	216) between	246) result	276) or
157) dump	187) father	217) manner	247) content	277) need
158) up	188) male	218) new	248) of course	278) writing
159) exercise	189) male	219) new	249) book	279) arise
160) school	190) where	220) our country	250) happen	280) husband
161) darling	191) body	221) sit down	251) market	281) outside
162) ~est	192) face	222) initial	252) insert	282) small
163) ~est	193) go into	223) initial	253) important	283) burn
164) most	194) come in	224) hand	254) feel	284) university
165) president	195) why	225) a few	255) difficult	285) situation
166) kinds	196) emerge	226) course	256) power	286) among
167) start	197) don't	227) search	257) too	287) send
168) right away	198) area	228) especially	258) call	288) namely
169) which	199) water	229) city	259) meaning	289) thus
170) so	200) meet	230) more than	260) meaning	290) state
171) so	201) pay	231) story	261) reveal	291) since
172) government	202) write	232) story	262) die	292) at the time
173) every	203) use	233) education	263) already	293) literature
174) times	204) use	234) economy	264) politics	294) ~er
175) it	205) without	235) yet	265) student	295) very
176) money	206) this time	236) catch	266) research	296) very
177) nation	207) at this time	237) together	267) name	297) fat
178) nation	208) life	238) teacher	268) get off	298) night
179) by the way	209) life	239) art	269) incident	299) high
180) by the way	210) life	240) stand up	270) easy	300) recent

301-400				
□ 301) 만큼	□ 331) 아	□ 361) 둔다	□ 391) 입는다	
□ 302) 채	□ 332) 기다린다	□ 362) 놓는다	□ 392) 오히려	
□ 303) 대로	□ 333) 떨어진다	□ 363) 떠난다	□ 393) 이루어진다	
□ 304) 현실	□ 334) 선거	□ 364) 기술	□ 394) 남	
□ 305) 환경	□ 335) 관하여	□ 365) 전체	□ 395) 하루	
□ 306) 먼저	□ 336) 그냥	□ 366) 그래	□ 396) 그림	
□ 307) 첫	□ 337) 나눈다	□ 367) 네	□ 397) 적	
□ 308) 일단	□ 338) 이용한다	□ 368) 예	□ 398) 터	
□ 309) 얼마나	□ 339) 거의	□ 369) 예	□ 399) 마신다	
□ 310) 어쩌다	□ 340) 곧	□ 370) 얻는다	□ 400) 친다	
□ 311) 어떠하니	□ 341) 중심	□ 371) 분		
□ 312) 자체	□ 342) 중앙	□ 372) 아름다운		
□ 313) 연다	□ 343) 활동	□ 373) 끝		
□ 314) 열린다	□ 344) 오늘	□ 374) 민족		
□ 315) 머리	□ 345) 오늘날	□ 375) 간		
□ 316) 고개	□ 346) 서로	□ 376) 조사한다		
□ 317) 묻는다	□ 347) 관심	□ 377) 듯하다		
□ 318) 남는다	□ 348) 역시	□ 378) 입		
□ 319) 부분	□ 349) 광고	□ 379) 그대로		
□ 320) 일부	□ 350) 아무런	□ 380) 영화		
□ 321) 기업	□ 351) 아니	□ 381) 필요		
□ 322) 사업	□ 352) 방	□ 382) 줄		
□ 323) 거기에	□ 353) 정신	□ 383) 하늘		
□ 324) 변화	□ 354) 이른다	□ 384) 과학		
□ 325) 변한다	□ 355) 땅	□ 385) 자연		
□ 326) 바뀐다	□ 356) 이룬다	□ 386) 정말		
□ 327) 달라졌다	□ 357) 아침	□ 387) 구조		
□ 328) 바꾼다	□ 358) 웃는다	□ 388) 결국		
□ 329) 아들	□ 359) 웃음	□ 389) 밥		
□ 330) 의지	□ 360) 현상	□ 390) 식사		

301-400			
301) as~as	331) ah	361) put	391) wear
302) as	332) await	362) put	392) rather
303) as	333) fall	363) leave	393) come true
304) reality	334) election	364) skill	394) stranger
305) environment	335) about	365) total	395) one day
306) first	336) just	366) yes	396) picture
307) first	337) divide	367) yes	397) enemy
308) first	338) utilize	368) yes	398) site
309) how	339) almost	369) example	399) drink
310) how	340) soon	370) get	400) hit
311) how?	341) center	371) anger	
312) in ~self	342) center	372) beautiful	
313) open	343) activity	373) end	
314) open	344) today	374) race	
315) head	345) today	375) seasoning	
316) head	346) each other	376) survey	
317) ask	347) interest	377) seem	
318) remain	348) as well	378) mouth	
319) part	349) advertisement	379) as it is	
320) part	350) no	380) movie	
321) corporation	351) no	381) need	
322) business	352) room	382) row	
323) there	353) spirit	383) sky	
324) change	354) reach	384) science	
325) change	355) land	385) nature	
326) change	356) achieve	386) really	
327) change	357) morning	387) structure	
328) change	358) laugh	388) eventually	
329) son	359) laugh	389) meal	
330) will	360) phenomenon	390) meal	

Day1~4 List Study

Final	K-word ㉜				
check	English ㉝				

K-word ㉖	English ㉗	K-word ㉘	K-word ㉙	English ㉚	K-word ㉛

Final	K-word ㉜				
check	English ㉝				

K-word ㉖	English ㉗	K-word ㉘	K-word ㉙	English ㉚	K-word ㉛

Day1~4 List Study

Final	K-word ㉜				
check	English ㉝				

K-word ㉖	English ㉗	K-word ㉘	K-word ㉙	English ㉚	K-word ㉛

	K-word	Pronounce	English	K-word ❶	Sentence example
401	혼자	hon-ja	alone		Come alone.
402	나간다	na-gan-da	go out		I sometimes go out at night.
403	교수	gyo-su	professor		Our professor is very smart.
404	술	sul	drinking		I like drinking.
405	사랑	sa-rang	love		She's my first love.
406	사랑한다	sa-rang-han-da	love		I love you.
407	의식하는	ui-sik-ha-neun	conscious		It's not good to be self-conscious.
408	전화	jeon-hwa	telephone		The telephone rang.
409	끝난다	kkeut-nan-da	finish		The play finishes at 10.30.
410	마친다	ma-chin-da	finish		They finish works at 6.
411	돌아온다	dol-a-on-da	come back		He comes back today.
412	맞다	maj-da	be right		That's right.
413	아빠	a-ppa	dad		This is my dad.
414	걸린다	geol-lin-da	take		It takes about 2 hours to go home.
415	지킨다	ji-kin-da	protect		Tom protects her.
416	한 번	han beon	once		Once was enough.
417	커피	keo-pi	coffee		I want a cup of coffee.
418	가슴	ga-seum	chest		I have a chest pain.
419	긴	gin	long		Mary has long hair.
420	바라본다	ba-ra-bon-da	look at		She looks at the door.

Final	K-word ❽				
check	English ❾				

K-word ❷	English ❸	K-word ❹	K-word ❺	English ❻	K-word ❼

	K-word	Pronounce	English	K-word ❶	Sentence example
421	알아본다	al-a-bon-da	recognize		He doesn't recognize me.
422	회사	hoe-sa	firm		He established a firm.
423	맛	mas	taste		It has a sweet taste.
424	산업	san-eob	industry		The coal industry is dying.
425	오른다	o-reun-da	rise		Prices rise these days.
426	올라간다	ol-la-gan-da	rise		The sun rises.
427	음식	eum-sik	food		Food arrived.
428	꼭	kkok	surely		You should do homework surely.
429	요즘	yo-jeum	nowadays		I am busy nowadays.
430	계획	gye-hoek	plan		We have a training plan.
431	방안	bang-an	plan		We have a plan.
432	느낌	neu-kkim	feeling		I have a good feeling.
433	얼마	eol-ma	how much		How much is it?
434	성격	seong-gyeok	personality		She has a strong personality.
435	계속	gye-sok	over and over		He made mistakes over and over.
436	세기	se-gi	century		Viruses mark this century.
437	세운다	se-un-da	erect		They erect a church.
438	아내	a-nae	wife		His wife is French.
439	가족	ga-jok	family		This is my family.
440	여름	yeo-reum	summer		I met her in the summer.

Final	K-word ❽			
check	English ❾			

K-word ❷	English ❸	K-word ❹	K-word ❺	English ❻	K-word ❼

	K-word	Pronounce	English	K-word ❶	Sentence example
441	세	se	rent		How much rent do you pay?
442	발전	bal-jeon	advance		Recent advances are remarkable.
443	논다	non-da	play		I play with John everyday.
444	향한다	hyang-han-da	head for		He heads for America.
445	관련된	gwan-ryeon-doen	relevant		He needs relevant advice.
446	형태	hyeong-tae	form		This fruit is like an orange in form.
447	형식	hyeong-sik	form		It's just a form.
448	각	gak	angle		A square has four angles.
449	분위기	bun-wi-gi	mood		Music improves the mood.
450	기분	gi-bun	mood		His good mood brightens me.
451	그러한	geu-reo-han	such		I go for such reasons.
452	나이	na-i	age		I feel my age.
453	우선	u-seon	first of all		First of all, come here.
454	믿는다	mid-neun-da	believe		I believe you.
455	낳는다	nah-neun-da	give birth		My dog is giving birth.
456	정보	jeong-bo	information		Information is power.
457	좋아한다	joh-a-han-da	like		I like apples.
458	그린다	geu-rin-da	draw		You draw beautifully.
459	끈다	kkeun-da	turn off		He often turns off the alarm.
460	배운다	bae-un-da	learn		I learn English.

Final	K-word ❽				
check	English ❾				

K-word ❷	English ❸	K-word ❹	K-word ❺	English ❻	K-word ❼

	K-word	Pronounce	English	K-word ❶	Sentence example
461	시	si	poem		I write poems.
462	역할	yeok-hal	role		What is my role?
463	옆에	yeop-e	by		Sit by me.
464	행동	haeng-dong	behavior		His behavior is strange.
465	행위	haeng-wi	behavior		His behavior is strange.
466	국내	guk-nae	domestic		They are domestic affairs.
467	기관	gi-gwan	organ		It has a special organ.
468	입장	ib-jang	entry		Entry is free on Sundays.
469	만한	man-han	worth		Is it worth the effort?
470	가치	ga-chi	value		Its value is enormous.
471	아래	a-rae	under		There is a cat under the desk.
472	영향	yeong-hyang	influence		He's a bad influence.
473	나선다	na-seon-da	come forward		He comes forward to help them.
474	흐른다	heu-reun-da	flow		Everything flows.
475	깊은	gip-eun	deep		There is a deep well.
476	배	bae	pear		I'm eating a pear.
477	배	bae	ship		This is my ship.
478	배	bae	stomach		Your stomach came out.
479	모양	mo-yang	shape		What is the shape of the moon?
480	산	san	mountain		I was in the mountain.

Final	K-word ❽				
check	English ❾				

K-word ❷	English ❸	K-word ❹	K-word ❺	English ❻	K-word ❼

	K-word	Pronounce	English	K-word ❶	Sentence example
481	산	san	acid		Make it from acid-free paper.
482	하지만	ha-ji-man	however		However, he came home.
483	조건	jo-geon	condition		What are your conditions?
484	문	mun	door		Open the door.
485	꽃	kkocc	flower		Flowers are beautiful.
486	단계	dan-gye	step		Let's go step by step.
487	그동안	geu-dong-an	meantime		What do I do in the meantime?
488	갑자기	gab-ja-gi	suddenly		Listen!' said Tom suddenly.
489	넘는다	neom-neun-da	overstep		You often overstep your authority.
490	바람	ba-ram	wind		A strong wind was blowing.
491	마을	ma-eul	village		She lives in the village.
492	어리다	eo-ri-da	young		He is young.
493	대표	dae-pyo	representa-tive		He is our representative.
494	가능성	ga-neung-seong	chance		There's a chance of meeting her.
495	방향	bang-hyang	direction		He changed the direction.
496	대회	dae-hoe	contest		Who is the winner at the contest?
497	목소리	mok-so-ri	voice		Keep your voice down.
498	노래	no-rae	song		I know this song.
499	바다	ba-da	sea		The sea is blue.
500	힘든	him-deun	tough		He had a tough childhood.

	Final	K-word ❽				
	check	English ❾				

K-word ❷	English ❸	K-word ❹	K-word ❺	English ❻	K-word ❼

	K-word	English		K-word	English
401	혼자	Come _____ .	421	알아본다	He doesn't _____ me.
402	나간다	I sometimes _____ at night.	422	회사	He established a _____ .
403	교수	Our _____ is very smart.	423	맛	It has a sweet _____ .
404	술	I like _____ .	424	산업	The coal _____ is dying.
405	사랑	She's my first _____ .	425	오른다	Prices _____ these days.
406	사랑한다	I _____ you.	426	올라간다	The sun _____ .
407	의식하는	It's not good to be self-_____ .	427	음식	_____ arrived.
408	전화	The _____ rang.	428	꼭	You should do homework _____ .
409	끝난다	The play _____ at 10.30.	429	요즘	I am busy _____ .
410	마친다	They _____ works at 6.	430	계획	We have a training _____ .
411	돌아온다	He _____ today.	431	방안	We have a _____ .
412	맞다	That's _____ .	432	느낌	I have a good _____ .
413	아빠	This is my _____ .	433	얼마	_____ is it?
414	걸린다	It _____ about 2 hours to go home.	434	성격	She has a strong _____ .
415	지킨다	Tom _____ her.	435	계속	He made mistakes _____ .
416	한 번	_____ was enough.	436	세기	Viruses mark this _____ .
417	커피	I want a cup of _____ .	437	세운다	They _____ a church.
418	가슴	I have a _____ pain.	438	아내	His _____ is French.
419	긴	Mary has _____ hair.	439	가족	This is my _____ .
420	바라본다	She _____ the door.	440	여름	I met her in the _____ .

401) alone   402) go out   403) professor   404) drinking   405) love   406) love   407) conscious   408) telephone
409) finishes   410) finish   411) comes back   412) right   413) dad   414) takes   415) protects   416) Once
417) coffee   418) chest   419) long   420) looks at   421) recognize   422) firm   423) taste   424) industry
425) rise   426) rises   427) Food   428) surely   429) nowadays   430) plan   431) plan   432) feeling
433) How much   434) personality   435) over and over   436) century   437) erect   438) wife   439) family   440) summer

	K-word	English		K-word	English
441	세	How much .... do you pay?	461	시	I write ....
442	발전	Recent .... are remarkable.	462	역할	What is my .... ?
443	논다	I .... with John everyday.	463	옆에	Sit .... me.
444	향한다	He .... America.	464	행동	His .... is strange.
445	관련된	He needs .... advice.	465	행위	His .... is strange.
446	형태	This fruit is like an orange in	466	국내	They are .... affairs.
447	형식	It's just a	467	기관	It has a special ....
448	각	A square has four	468	입장	.... is free on Sundays.
449	분위기	Music improves the	469	만한	Is it .... the effort?
450	기분	His good .... brightens me.	470	가치	Its .... is enormous.
451	그러한	I go for .... reasons.	471	아래	There is a cat .... the desk.
452	나이	I feel my	472	영향	He's a bad ....
453	우선	..............., come here.	473	나선다	He .... to help them.
454	믿는다	I .... you.	474	흐른다	Everything ....
455	낳는다	My dog is giving	475	깊은	There is a .... well.
456	정보	.... is power.	476	배	I'm eating a ....
457	좋아한다	I .... apples.	477	배	This is my ....
458	그린다	You .... beautifully.	478	배	Your .... came out.
459	끈다	He often .... the alarm.	479	모양	What is the .... of the moon?
460	배운다	I .... English.	480	산	I was in the ....

441) rent 442) advances 443) play 444) heads for 445) relevant 446) form 447) form 448) angles
449) mood 450) mood 451) such 452) age 453) First of all 454) believe 455) birth 456) Information
457) like 458) draw 459) turns off 460) learn 461) poem 462) role 463) by 464) behavior
465) behavior 466) domestic 467) organ 468) Entry 469) worth 470) value 471) under 472) influence
473) comes forward 474) flows 475) deep 476) pear 477) ship 478) stomach 479) shape 480) mountain

	K-word	English
481	산	Make it from .... –free paper.
482	하지만	............, he came home.
483	조건	What are your ....?
484	문	Open the ....
485	꽃	.... are beautiful.
486	단계	Let's go .... by ....
487	그동안	What do I do in the ....?
488	갑자기	"Listen!" said Tom ....
489	넘는다	You often .... your authority.
490	바람	A strong .... was blowing.
491	마을	She lives in the ....
492	어리다	He is ....
493	대표	He is our ....
494	가능성	There's a .... of meeting her.
495	방향	He changed the ....
496	대회	Who is the winner at the ....?
497	목소리	Keep your .... down.
498	노래	I know this ....
499	바다	The .... is blue.
500	힘든	He had a .... childhood.

King Sejong

– The 4th king of Joseon Dynasty

King Sejong was born in 1397.
His 32 year reign marked great achievements.
Hangeul, created by King Sejong,
has been used as a common script for
the Republic of Korea and North Korea.

481) acid
482) However
483) conditions
484) door
485) Flowers
486) step, step
487) meantime
488) suddenly
489) overstep
490) wind
491) village
492) young
493) representative.
494) chance
495) direction
496) contest
497) voice
498) song
499) sea
500) tough

Final	K-word ⑯				
check	English ⑰				

K-word ⑩	English ⑪	K-word ⑫	K-word ⑬	English ⑭	K-word ⑮

	Write K-word in		Write K-word in ....
401	Come alone. .... 오세요.	414	It takes about 2 hours to go home. 집에 가는데 대략 2시간 ....
402	I sometimes go out at night. 나는 가끔 밤에	415	Tom protects her. 톰이 그녀를 ....
403	Our professor is very smart 우리 .... 님은 매우 똑똑하다.	416	Once was enough. .... 이면 충분했다.
404	I like drinking. 나는 .... 을 좋아한다.	417	I want a cup of coffee. 나는 .... 한 잔 원한다.
405	She's my first love. 그녀는 나의 첫 .... 이다.	418	I have a chest pain. 나는 .... 통증이 있다.
406	I love you. 나는 너를	419	Mary has long hair. 메리는 .... 머리를 가지고 있다.
407	It's not good to be self-conscious. 자기를 .... 것은 좋지 않다.	420	She looks at the door. 그녀가 문을 ....
408	The telephone rang. .... 가 울렸다.	421	He doesn't recognize me. 그는 나를 못 ....
409	The play finishes at 10.30. 그 연극은 10:30에	422	He established a firm. 그는 .... 를 설립했다.
410	They finish works at 6. 그들은 6시에 일을	423	It has a sweet taste. 그것은 단 .... 이 있다.
411	He comes back today. 그는 오늘	424	The coal industry is dying. 석탄 .... 은 죽어가고 있다.
412	That's right. 그것은	425	Prices rise these days. 요즘 물가가 ....
413	This is my dad. 이분은 나의 .... 이다.		

401) 혼자   402) 나간다   403) 교수   404) 술   405) 사랑   406) 사랑한다   407) 의식하는   408) 전화   409) 끝난다
410) 마친다   411) 돌아온다   412) 맞다   413) 아빠   414) 걸린다   415) 지킨다   416) 한 번   417) 커피   418) 가슴
419) 긴   420) 바라본다   421) 알아본다   422) 회사   423) 맛   424) 산업   425) 오른다

Sentence Words(1)

	K-word	pronounce	English		K-word	pronounce	English
401	혼자	hon-ja	alone	414	집에	jib-e	home
	오세요	o-se-yo	come		가는데	ga-neun-de	to go
402	나는	na-neun	I		대략	dae-ryak	about
	가끔	ga-kkeum	sometimes		2시간	du-si-gan	2 hours
	밤에	bam-e	at night		걸린다	geol-lin-da	it takes
	나간다	na-gan-da	go out	415	톰이	tom-i	Tom
403	우리	u-ri	our		그녀를	geu-nyeo-reul	her
	교수님은	gyo-su-nim-eun	professor		지킨다	ji-kin-da	protect
	매우	mae-u	very	416	한 번이면	han beon-i-myeon	once
	똑똑하다	ttok-ttok-ha-da	is smart		충분했다	chung-bun-haess-da	was enough
404	나는	na-neun	I	417	나는	na-neun	I
	술을	sul-eul	drinking		커피	keo-pi	coffee
	좋아한다	joh-a-han-da	like		한 잔	han jan	a cup of
405	그녀는	geu-nyeo-neun	she		원한다	won-han-da	want
	나의	na-ui	my	418	나는	na-neun	I
	첫	cheos	first		가슴	ga-seum	chest
	사랑	sa-rang	love		통증이	tong-jeung-i	pain
	이다	i-da	is		있다	iss-da	have
406	나는	na-neun	I	419	메리는	me-ri-neun	Mary
	너를	neo-reul	you		긴	gin	long
	사랑한다	sa-rang-han-da	love		머리를	meo-ri-reul	hair
407	자기를	ja-gi-reul	self		가지고 있다	ga-ji-go iss-da	has
	의식하는 것은	ui-sik-ha-neun geos-eun	conscious	420	그녀가	geu-nyeo-ga	she
	좋지 않다	joh-ji anh-da	it's nor good		문을	mun-eul	the door
408	전화가	jeon-hwa-ga	the telephone		바라본다	ba-ra-bon-da	look at
	울렸다	ul-lyeoss-da	rang	421	그는	geu-neun	he
409	그	geu	the		나를	na-reul	me
	연극은	yeon-geuk-eun	play		못 알아본다	mos al-a-bon-da	doesn't recognize
	10:30에	yeol-si-sam-sib-bun-e	at 10:30	422	그는	geu-neun	he
	끝난다	kkeut-nan-da	finish		회사를	hoe-sa-reul	a firm
410	그들은	geu-deul-eun	they		설립했다	seol-lib-haess-da	established
	6시에	yeo-seos-si-e	at 6	423	그것은	geu-geos-eun	it
	일을	il-eul	works		단	dan	sweet
	마친다	ma-chin-da	finish		맛이	mas-i	taste
411	그는	geu-neun	he		있다	iss-da	has
	오늘	o-neul	today	424	석탄	seok-tan	the coal
	돌아온다	dol-a-on-da	come back		산업은	san-eob-eun	industry
412	그것은	geu-geos-eun	that		죽어가고 있다	juk-eo-ga-go iss-da	is dying
	맞다	maj-da	is right	425	요즘	yo-jeum	these days
413	이 분은	i bun-eun	this		물가가	mul-ga-ga	prices
	나의	na-ui	my		오른다	o-reun-da	rise
	아빠다	a-ppa-da	is dad				

Day5 Sentence(2)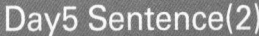

	Write K-word in		Write K-word in ....
426	The sun rises. 해가	439	This is my family. 이것이 내 .... 이다.
427	Food arrived. .... 이 도착했다.	440	I met her in the summer. 나는 .... 에 그녀를 만났다.
428	You should do homework surely. 너는 .... 숙제를 해야 한다.	441	How much rent do you pay? 너는 .... 를 얼마나 내고 있니?
429	I am busy nowadays. .... 나 바쁘다.	442	Recent advances are remarkable. 최근의 .... 은 현저하다.
430	We have a training plan. 우리는 훈련 .... 을 가지고 있다.	443	I play with John everyday. 나는 매일 존과 ....
431	We have a plan. 우리는 .... 이 있다.	444	He heads for America. 그는 미국으로 ....
432	I have a good feeling. .... 이 좋다.	445	He needs relevant advice. 그는 .... 조언이 필요하다.
433	How much is it? 이거 .... 인가요?	446	This fruit is like an orange in form. 이 과일은 .... 가 오렌지 같다.
434	She has a strong personality. 그녀는 강한 .... 을 가지고 있다.	447	It's just a form. 그것은 단지 .... 이다.
435	He made mistakes over and over. 그는 .... 실수했다.	448	A square has four angles. 정사각형은 네 .... 을 가지고 있다.
436	Viruses mark this century. 바이러스가 금 .... 를 나타낸다.	449	Music improves the mood. 음악은 .... 를 좋게 한다.
437	They erect a church. 그들이 교회를	450	His good mood brightens me. 그의 좋은 .... 이 나를 밝게 한다.
438	His wife is French. 그의 .... 는 프랑스인이다.		

426) 올라간다   427) 음식   428) 꼭   429) 요즘   430) 계획   431) 방안   432) 느낌   433) 얼마   434) 성격
435) 계속   436) 세기   437) 세운다   438) 아내   439) 가족   440) 여름   441) 세   442) 발전   443) 논다
444) 향한다   445) 관련된   446) 형태   447) 형식   448) 각   449) 분위기   450) 기분

Sentence Words(2)

	K-word	pronounce	English		K-word	pronounce	English
426	해가	hae-ga	the sun	440	나는	na-neun	I
	올라간다	ol-la-gan-da	rise		여름에	yeo-reum-e	in the summer
427	음식이	eum-sik-i	food		그녀를	geu-nyeo-reul	her
	도착했다	do-chak-haess-da	arrived		만났다	man-nass-da	met
428	너는	neo-neun	you	441	너는	neo-neun	you
	꼭	kkok	surely		세를	se-reul	rent
	숙제를	suk-je-reul	homework		얼마나	eol-ma-na	how much
	해야 한다	hae-ya han-da	should do		내고 있니?	nae-go iss-ni?	do you pay?
429	요즘	yo-jeum	nowadays	442	최근의	choe-geun-ui	recent
	나	na	I		발전은	bal-jeon-eun	advances
	바쁘다	ba-ppeu-da	am busy		현저하다	hyeon-jeo-ha-da	are remarkable
430	우리는	u-ri-neun	we	443	나는	na-neun	I
	훈련	hun-ryeon	training		매일	mae-il	everyday
	계획을	gye-hoek-eul	plan		존과	jon-gwa	with John
	가지고 있다	ga-ji-go iss-da	have		논다	non-da	play
431	우리는	u-ri-neun	we	444	그는	geu-neun	he
	방안이	bang-an-i	a plan		미국으로	mi-guk-eu-ro	for America
	있다	iss-da	have		향한다	hyang-han-da	head
432	느낌이 좋다	neu-kkim-i joh-da	I have a good feeling.	445	그는	geu-neun	he
433	이거	i-geo	it		관련된	gwan-ryeon-doen	relevant
	얼마인가요?	eol-ma-in-ga-yo?	how much is?		조언이	jo-eon-i	advice
434	그녀는	geu-nyeo-neun	she		필요하다	pil-yo-ha-da	need
	강한	gang-han	strong	446	이	i	this
	성격을	seong-gyeok-eul	personality		과일은	gwa-il-eun	fruit
	가지고 있다	ga-ji-go iss-da	has		형태가	hyeong-tae-ga	in form
435	그는	geu-neun	he		오렌지 같다	o-ren-ji gat-da	is like an orange
	계속	gye-sok	over and over	447	그것은	geu-geos-eun	it
	실수했다	sil-su-haess-da	made mistakes		단지	dan-ji	just
436	바이러스가	ba-i-reo-seu-ga	viruses		형식	hyeong-sik	a form
	금세기를	geum-se-gi-reul	this century		이다	i-da	is
	나타낸다	na-ta-naen-da	mark	448	정사각형은	jeong-sa-gak-hyeong-eun	a square
437	그들이	geu-deul-i	they		네	ne	four
	교회를	gyo-hoe-reul	a church		각을	gak-eul	angles
	세운다	se-un-da	erect		가지고 있다	ga-ji-go iss-da	has
438	그의	geu-ui	his	449	음악은	eum-ak-eun	music
	아내는	a-nae-neun	wife		분위기를	bun-wi-gi-reul	the mood
	프랑스인	peu-rang-seu-in	French		좋게 한다	joh-ge han-da	improve
	이다	i-da	is	450	그의	geu-ui	his
439	이것이	i-geos-i	this		좋은	joh-eun	good
	내	nae	my		기분이	gi-bun-i	mood
	가족	ga-jok	family		나를	na-reul	me
	이다	i-da	is		밝게 한다	balk-ge han-da	brighten

Day5 Sentence(3)

	Write K-word in		Write K-word in ....
451	I go for such reasons. 나는 .... 이유로 간다.	464	His behavior is strange. 그의 .... 이 이상하다.
452	I feel my age. 나는 나의 .... 를 느낀다.	465	His behavior is strange. 그의 .... 가 이상하다.
453	First of all, come here. ...., 이리 와.	466	They are domestic affairs. 그것들은 .... 문제다.
454	I believe you. 나는 너를	467	It has a special organ. 그것은 특별한 .... 을 가지고 있다.
455	My dog is giving birth. 내 개가 새끼를	468	Entry is free on Sundays. 일요일에는 .... 이 무료입니다.
456	Information is power. .... 는 힘이다.	469	Is it worth the effort? 그건 노력할 .... 건가요?
457	I like apples. 나는 사과를	470	Its value is enormous. 그것의 .... 는 엄청나다.
458	You draw beautifully. 너는 멋지게	471	There is a cat under the desk. 책상 .... 고양이가 있다.
459	He often turns off the alarm. 그는 종종 경보기를	472	He's a bad influence. 그는 나쁜 .... 을 끼친다.
460	I learn English. 나는 영어를	473	He comes forward to help them. 그가 그들을 돕겠다고 ....
461	I write poems. 나는 .... 를 쓴다.	474	Everything flows. 모든 것이 ....
462	What is my role? 내 .... 은 무엇인가요?	475	There is a deep well. .... 우물이 있다.
463	Sit by me. 내 .... 앉아.		

451) 그러한　　452) 나이　　453) 우선　　454) 믿는다　　455) 낳는다　　456) 정보　　457) 좋아한다　　458) 그린다　　459) 끈다
460) 배운다　　461) 시　　462) 역할　　463) 옆에　　464) 행동　　465) 행위　　466) 국내　　467) 기관　　468) 입장
469) 만한　　470) 가치　　471) 아래　　472) 영향　　473) 나선다　　474) 흐른다　　475) 깊은

Sentence Words(3)

	K-word	pronounce	English		K-word	pronounce	English
451	나는	na-neun	I	464	그의	geu-ui	hist
	그러한	geu-reo-han	such		행동이	haeng-dong-i	behavior
	이유로	i-yu-ro	for reasons		이상하다	i-sang-ha-da	is strange
	간다	gan-da	go	465	그의	geu-ui	his
452	나는	na-neun	I		행위가	haeng-wi-ga	behavior
	나의	na-ui	my		이상하다	i-sang-ha-da	is strange
	나이를	na-i-reul	age	466	그것들은	geu-geos-deul-eun	they
	느낀다	neu-kkin-da	feel		국내	guk-nae	domestic
453	우선	u-seon	first of all		문제다	mun-je-da	are affairs
	이리 와	i-ri wa	come here	467	그것은	geu-geos-eun	it
454	나는	na-neun	I		특별한	teuk-byeol-han	special
	너를	neo-reul	you		기관을	gi-gwan-eul	organ
	믿는다	mid-neun-da	believe		가지고 있다	ga-ji-go iss-da	has
455	내	nae	my	468	일요일에는	il-yo-il-e-neun	on Sundays
	개가	gae-ga	dog		입장이	ib-jang-i	entry
	새끼를 낳는다	sae-kki-reul nah-neun-da	is giving birth		무료	mu-ryo	free
456	정보는	jeong-bo-neun	information		입니다	ib-ni-da	is
	힘	him	power	469	그건	geu-geon	it
	이다	i-da	is		노력	no-ryeok	the effort
457	나는	na-neun	I		할 만한 건가요?	hal man-han geon-ga-yo?	is it worth?
	사과를	sa-gwa-reul	apples	470	그것의	geu-geos-ui	its
	좋아한다	joh-a-han-da	like		가치는	ga-chi-neun	value
458	너는	neo-neun	you		엄청나다	eom-cheong-na-da	is enormous
	멋지게	meos-ji-ge	beautifully	471	책상	chaek-sang	the desk
	그린다	geu-rin-da	draw		아래	a-rae	under
459	그는	geu-neun	he		고양이가	go-yang-i-ga	a cat
	종종	jong-jong	often		있다	iss-da	there is
	경보기를	gyeong-bo-gi-reul	the alarm	472	그는	geu-neun	he
	끈다	kkeun-da	turn off		나쁜	na-ppeun	bad
460	나는	na-neun	I		영향을 끼친다	yeong-hyang-eul kki-chin-da	is an influence
	영어를	yeong-eo-reul	English	473	그가	geu-ga	he
	배운다	bae-un-da	learn		그들을	geu-deul-eul	them
461	나는	na-neun	I		돕겠다고	dob-gess-da-go	to help
	시를	si-reul	poems		나선다	na-seon-da	come forward
	쓴다	sseun-da	write	474	모든 것이	mo-deun geos-i	everything
462	내	nae	my		흐른다	heu-reun-da	flow
	역할은	yeok-hal-eun	role	475	깊은	gip-eun	deep
	무엇인가요?	mu-eos-in-ga-yo?	what is?		우물이	u-mul-i	well
463	내	nae	me		있다	iss-da	there is
	옆에	yeop-e	by				
	앉아	anj-a	sit				

Day5 Sentence(4)

	Write K-word in _____.		Write K-word in _____.
476	I'm eating a pear. 나는 _____ 를 먹고 있다.	489	You often overstep your authority. 너는 종종 너의 권한을 _____.
477	This is my ship. 이것은 나의 _____ 이다.	490	A strong wind was blowing. 강한 _____ 이 불고 있었다.
478	Your stomach came out. 너의 _____ 가 나왔다.	491	She lives in the village. 그녀는 그 _____ 에 산다.
479	What is the shape of the moon? 달의 _____ 이 뭐야?	492	He is young. 그는 _____.
480	I was in the mountain. 나는 _____ 에 있었다.	493	He is our representative. 그는 우리들의 _____ 다.
481	Make it from acid-free paper. _____ 이 없는 종이로 그것을 만들어라.	494	There's a chance of meeting her. 그녀를 만날 _____ 이 있다.
482	However, he came home. _____, 그는 집에 왔다.	495	He changed the direction. 그는 _____ 을 바꾸었다.
483	What are your conditions? 당신의 _____ 은 무엇입니까?	496	Who is the winner at the contest? 그 _____ 에서 우승자는 누구인가요?
484	Open the door. _____ 을 열어라.	497	Keep your voice down. _____ 낮춰.
485	Flowers are beautiful. _____ 은 아름답다.	498	I know this song. 나는 이 _____ 를 안다.
486	Let's go step by step. _____ 로 가자.	499	The sea is blue. _____ 가 파랗다.
487	What do I do in the meantime? _____ 무엇을 할까요?	500	He had a tough childhood. 그에게는 _____ 어린 시절이 있었다.
488	Listen!' said Tom suddenly. 들어봐!' 톰이 _____ 말했다.		

476) 배   477) 배   478) 배   479) 모양   480) 산   481) 산   482) 하지만   483) 조건   484) 문
485) 꽃   486) 단계 단계   487) 그동안   488) 갑자기   489) 넘는다   490) 바람   491) 마을   492) 어리다   493) 대표
494) 가능성   495) 방향   496) 대회   497) 목소리   498) 노래   499) 바다   500) 힘든

174 | 2주만에 한국어 배우기

Sentence Words(4)

	K-word	pronounce	English		K-word	pronounce	English
476	나는	na-neun	I	489	너는	neo-neun	you
	배를	bae-reul	a pear		종종	jong-jong	often
	먹고 있다	meok-go iss-da	am eating		너의	neo-ui	your
477	이것은	i-geos-eun	this		권한을	gwon-han-eul	authority
	나의	na-ui	my		넘는다	neom-neun-da	overstep
	배	bae	ship	490	강한	gang-han	strong
	이다	i-da	is		바람이	ba-ram-i	wind
478	너의	neo-ui	your		불고 있었다	bul-go iss-eoss-da	was blowing
	배가	bae-ga	stomach	491	그녀는	geu-nyeo-neun	she
	나왔다	na-wass-da	came out		그 마을에	geu ma-eul-e	in the village
479	달의	dal-ui	of the moon		산다	san-da	live
	모양이	mo-yang-i	the shape	492	그는	geu-neun	he
	뭐야?	mwo-ya?	what is?		어리다	eo-ri-da	is young
480	나는	na-neun	I	493	그는	geu-neun	he
	산에	san-e	in the mountain		우리들의	u-ri-deul-ui	our
	있었다	iss-eoss-da	was		대표다	dae-pyo-da	is representative
481	산이	san-i	acid	494	그녀를	geu-nyeo-reul	her
	없는	eobs-neun	free		만날	man-nal	of meeting
	종이로	jong-i-ro	from paper		가능성이	ga-neung-seong-i	a chance
	그것을	geu-geos-eul	it		있다	iss-da	there's
	만들어라	man-deul-eo-ra	make	495	그는	geu-neun	he
482	하지만	ha-ji-man	however		방향을	bang-hyang-eul	the direction
	그는	geu-neun	he		바꾸었다	ba-kku-eoss-da	changed
	집에	jib-e	home	496	그 대회에서	geu dae-hoe-e-seo	at the contest
	왔다	wass-da	came		우승자는	u-seung-ja-neun	the winner
483	당신의	dang-sin-ui	your		누구인가요?	nu-gu-in-ga-yo?	who is?
	조건은	jo-geon-eun	condition	497	목소리	mok-so-ri	your voice
	무엇입니까?	mu-eos-ib-ni-kka?	what are?		낮춰	naj-chwo	keep down
484	문을	mun-eul	the door	498	나는	na-neun	I
	열어라	yeol-eo-ra	open		이	i	this
485	꽃은	kkocc-eun	flowers		노래를	no-rae-reul	song
	아름답다	a-reum-dab-da	are beautiful		안다	an-da	know
486	단계 단계로	dan-gye dan-gye-ro	step by step	499	바다가	ba-da-ga	the sea
	가자	ga-ja	let's go		파랗다	pa-rah-da	is blue
487	그동안	geu-dong-an	in the meantime	500	그에게는	geu-e-ge-neun	he
	무엇을	mu-eos-eul	what		힘든	him-deun	tough
	할까요?	hal-kka-yo?	do I do		어린 시절이	eo-rin si-jeol-i	childhood
488	들어봐	deul-eo-bwa	listen		있었다	iss-eoss-da	had
	톰이	tom-i	Tom				
	갑자기	gab-ja-gi	suddenly				
	말했다	mal-haess-da	said				

Day5 Sentence Study

Final	K-word ㉔				
check	English ㉕				

K-word ⑱	English ⑲	K-word ⑳	K-word ㉑	English ㉒	K-word ㉓

1-150				
☐ 1) 것	☐ 31) 드린다	☐ 61) 집	☐ 91) 파악하고 있다	☐ 121) 지닌다
☐ 2) 한다	☐ 32) 대한다	☐ 62) 나온다	☐ 92) 자신	☐ 122) 가진다
☐ 3) 된다	☐ 33) 간다	☐ 63) 따른다	☐ 93) 문화	☐ 123) 갖추고 있다
☐ 4) 수	☐ 34) 다닌다	☐ 64) 그리고	☐ 94) 원	☐ 124) 당한다
☐ 5) 수	☐ 35) 년	☐ 65) 및	☐ 95) 생각	☐ 125) 함께
☐ 6) 길	☐ 36) 한	☐ 66) 그때	☐ 96) 명	☐ 126) 아이
☐ 7) 쪽	☐ 37) 말	☐ 67) 그럼	☐ 97) 통한다	☐ 127) 지나간다
☐ 8) 방식	☐ 38) 일	☐ 68) 문제	☐ 98) 소리	☐ 128) 많이
☐ 9) 점	☐ 39) 일	☐ 69) 그런	☐ 99) 다시	☐ 129) 훨씬
☐ 10) 점	☐ 40) 일 한다	☐ 70) 산다	☐ 100) 다른	☐ 130) 시간
☐ 11) 나	☐ 41) 작품	☐ 71) 산다	☐ 101) 다르다	☐ 131) 너
☐ 12) 내	☐ 42) 작업	☐ 72) 지낸다	☐ 102) 여자	☐ 132) 당신
☐ 13) 그	☐ 43) 직장	☐ 73) 저	☐ 103) 소녀	☐ 133) 인간
☐ 14) 없다	☐ 44) 때문	☐ 74) 생각한다	☐ 104) 개	☐ 134) 사실
☐ 15) 않다	☐ 45) 말한다	☐ 75) 모른다	☐ 105) 그 정도	☐ 135) 과연
☐ 16) 말고	☐ 46) 위하여	☐ 76) 속	☐ 106) 뒤	☐ 136) 난다
☐ 17) 아니다	☐ 47) 그러나	☐ 77) 만든다	☐ 107) 듣는다	☐ 137) 자란다
☐ 18) 않는다	☐ 48) 온다	☐ 78) 삼는다	☐ 108) 다	☐ 138) 어머니
☐ 19) 사람	☐ 49) 안다	☐ 79) 시킨다	☐ 109) 좀	☐ 139) 엄마
☐ 20) 국민	☐ 50) 씨	☐ 80) 두	☐ 110) 조금	☐ 140) 눈
☐ 21) 우리	☐ 51) 그렇다	☐ 81) 둘	☐ 111) 든다	☐ 141) 눈
☐ 22) 이	☐ 52) 큰	☐ 82) 앞	☐ 112) 키운다	☐ 142) 뭐
☐ 23) 이	☐ 53) 크다	☐ 83) 경우	☐ 113) 올린다	☐ 143) 무엇
☐ 24) 이런	☐ 54) 또	☐ 84) 중	☐ 114) 기른다	☐ 144) 무슨
☐ 25) 이것	☐ 55) 사회	☐ 85) 중	☐ 115) 싶다	☐ 145) 시대
☐ 26) 이거	☐ 56) 안에	☐ 86) 동안에	☐ 116) 보인다	☐ 146) 다음
☐ 27) 보다	☐ 57) 좋은	☐ 87) 어떤	☐ 117) 표정	☐ 147) 이러하다
☐ 28) 본다	☐ 58) 더	☐ 88) 잘	☐ 118) 모습	☐ 148) 누구
☐ 29) 같다	☐ 59) 받는다	☐ 89) 그녀	☐ 119) 가지고 있다	☐ 149) 전
☐ 30) 준다	☐ 60) 그것	☐ 90) 먹는다	☐ 120) 갖고있다	☐ 150) 곳

1-150				
1) thing	31) give	61) house	91) grasp	121) have
2) do	32) treat	62) come out	92) self	122) have
3) become	33) go	63) obey	93) culture	123) have
4) number	34) go	64) and	94) ₩	124) get p.p
5) way	35) year	65) and	95) thought	125) with
6) way	36) one	66) then	96) famous	126) kid
7) way	37) word	67) then	97) make sense	127) pass by
8) way	38) day	68) problem	98) sound	128) much
9) way	39) work	69) such	99) again	129) much ~er
10) store	40) work	70) buy	100) different	130) time
11) I	41) work	71) live	101) different	131) you
12) I	42) work	72) live	102) girl	132) you
13) he	43) job	73) um	103) girl	133) human
14) not have	44) because of	74) think	104) dog	134) in fact
15) not	45) speak	75) don't know	105) that much	135) indeed
16) not	46) for	76) inside	106) back	136) grow
17) not	47) but	77) make	107) hear	137) grow
18) do not	48) come	78) make	108) all	138) mother
19) people	49) know	79) make	109) a little	139) mom
20) people	50) family name	80) two	110) a little	140) eye
21) we	51) right	81) two	111) pick up	141) snow
22) tooth	52) big	82) front	112) raise	142) what
23) this	53) big	83) case	113) raise	143) what
24) this	54) once again	84) monk	114) raise	144) what
25) this	55) society	85) during	115) want	145) era
26) this	56) in	86) during	116) look	146) next
27) than	57) good	87) any	117) look	147) like this
28) see	58) more	88) well	118) appearance	148) who
29) same	59) receive	89) she	119) have	149) all
30) give	60) it	90) eat	120) have	150) place

151–300				
☐ 151) 자리	☐ 181) 날	☐ 211) 인생	☐ 241) 못	☐ 271) 짓는다
☐ 152) 여러	☐ 182) 여기	☐ 212) 지금	☐ 242) 못	☐ 272) 또한
☐ 153) 많은	☐ 183) 여성	☐ 213) 뿐	☐ 243) 못한다	☐ 273) 까닭
☐ 154) 하나	☐ 184) 친구	☐ 214) 다만	☐ 244) 읽는다	☐ 274) 이유
☐ 155) 세계	☐ 185) 마음	☐ 215) 만	☐ 245) 이제	☐ 275) 또는
☐ 156) 세상	☐ 186) 관계	☐ 216) 사이에	☐ 246) 결과	☐ 276) 혹은
☐ 157) 버린다	☐ 187) 아버지	☐ 217) 방법	☐ 247) 내용	☐ 277) 필요하다
☐ 158) 위	☐ 188) 남자	☐ 218) 새롭다	☐ 248) 물론	☐ 278) 글
☐ 159) 운동	☐ 189) 남성	☐ 219) 새	☐ 249) 책	☐ 279) 생긴다
☐ 160) 학교	☐ 190) 어디	☐ 220) 우리나라	☐ 250) 일어난다	☐ 280) 남편
☐ 161) 자기	☐ 191) 몸	☐ 221) 앉는다	☐ 251) 시장	☐ 281) 밖
☐ 162) 가장	☐ 192) 얼굴	☐ 222) 처음의	☐ 252) 넣는다	☐ 282) 작은
☐ 163) 제일	☐ 193) 들어간다	☐ 223) 초기	☐ 253) 중요한	☐ 283) 탄다
☐ 164) 대부분	☐ 194) 들어온다	☐ 224) 손	☐ 254) 느낀다	☐ 284) 대학
☐ 165) 대통령	☐ 195) 왜	☐ 225) 몇	☐ 255) 어려운	☐ 285) 상황
☐ 166) 가지	☐ 196) 나타난다	☐ 226) 과정	☐ 256) 힘	☐ 286) 가운데
☐ 167) 시작한다	☐ 197) 말아라	☐ 227) 찾는다	☐ 257) 너무	☐ 287) 보낸다
☐ 168) 바로	☐ 198) 지역	☐ 228) 특히	☐ 258) 부른다	☐ 288) 즉
☐ 169) 어느	☐ 199) 물	☐ 229) 도시	☐ 259) 의미	☐ 289) 따라서
☐ 170) 그래서	☐ 200) 만난다	☐ 230) 이상	☐ 260) 뜻	☐ 290) 상태
☐ 171) 그러니까	☐ 201) 낸다	☐ 231) 이야기	☐ 261) 밝힌다	☐ 291) 이후
☐ 172) 정부	☐ 202) 쓴다	☐ 232) 얘기	☐ 262) 죽는다	☐ 292) 당시
☐ 173) 모든	☐ 203) 쓴다	☐ 233) 교육	☐ 263) 이미	☐ 293) 문학
☐ 174) 번	☐ 204) 사용한다	☐ 234) 경제	☐ 264) 정치	☐ 294) 더욱
☐ 175) 그거	☐ 205) 없이	☐ 235) 아직	☐ 265) 학생	☐ 295) 아주
☐ 176) 돈	☐ 206) 이번	☐ 236) 잡는다	☐ 266) 연구	☐ 296) 매우
☐ 177) 국가	☐ 207) 이때	☐ 237) 같이	☐ 267) 이름	☐ 297) 지방
☐ 178) 나라	☐ 208) 생활	☐ 238) 선생님	☐ 268) 내린다	☐ 298) 밤
☐ 179) 그런데	☐ 209) 삶	☐ 239) 예술	☐ 269) 사건	☐ 299) 높은
☐ 180) 근데	☐ 210) 생명	☐ 240) 일어선다	☐ 270) 쉬운	☐ 300) 최근

151-300				
151) place	181) day	211) life	241) nail	271) build
152) several	182) here	212) now	242) can't	272) also
153) many	183) female	213) only	243) can't do	273) reason
154) one	184) friend	214) only	244) read	274) reason
155) world	185) mind	215) only	245) now	275) or
156) world	186) relationship	216) between	246) result	276) or
157) dump	187) father	217) manner	247) content	277) need
158) up	188) male	218) new	248) of course	278) writing
159) exercise	189) male	219) new	249) book	279) arise
160) school	190) where	220) our country	250) happen	280) husband
161) darling	191) body	221) sit down	251) market	281) outside
162) ~est	192) face	222) initial	252) insert	282) small
163) ~est	193) go into	223) initial	253) important	283) burn
164) most	194) come in	224) hand	254) feel	284) university
165) president	195) why	225) a few	255) difficult	285) situation
166) kinds	196) emerge	226) course	256) power	286) among
167) start	197) don't	227) search	257) too	287) send
168) right away	198) area	228) especially	258) call	288) namely
169) which	199) water	229) city	259) meaning	289) thus
170) so	200) meet	230) more than	260) meaning	290) state
171) so	201) pay	231) story	261) reveal	291) since
172) government	202) write	232) story	262) die	292) at the time
173) every	203) use	233) education	263) already	293) literature
174) times	204) use	234) economy	264) politics	294) ~er
175) it	205) without	235) yet	265) student	295) very
176) money	206) this time	236) catch	266) research	296) very
177) nation	207) at this time	237) together	267) name	297) fat
178) nation	208) life	238) teacher	268) get off	298) night
179) by the way	209) life	239) art	269) incident	299) high
180) by the way	210) life	240) stand up	270) easy	300) recent

301-450				
☐ 301) 만큼	☐ 331) 아	☐ 361) 둔다	☐ 391) 입는다	☐ 421) 알아본다
☐ 302) 채	☐ 332) 기다린다	☐ 362) 놓는다	☐ 392) 오히려	☐ 422) 회사
☐ 303) 대로	☐ 333) 떨어진다	☐ 363) 떠난다	☐ 393) 이루어진다	☐ 423) 맛
☐ 304) 현실	☐ 334) 선거	☐ 364) 기술	☐ 394) 남	☐ 424) 산업
☐ 305) 환경	☐ 335) 관하여	☐ 365) 전체	☐ 395) 하루	☐ 425) 오른다
☐ 306) 먼저	☐ 336) 그냥	☐ 366) 그래	☐ 396) 그림	☐ 426) 올라간다
☐ 307) 첫	☐ 337) 나눈다	☐ 367) 네	☐ 397) 적	☐ 427) 음식
☐ 308) 일단	☐ 338) 이용한다	☐ 368) 예	☐ 398) 터	☐ 428) 꼭
☐ 309) 얼마나	☐ 339) 거의	☐ 369) 예	☐ 399) 마신다	☐ 429) 요즘
☐ 310) 어쩌다	☐ 340) 곧	☐ 370) 얻는다	☐ 400) 친다	☐ 430) 계획
☐ 311) 어떠하니	☐ 341) 중심	☐ 371) 분	☐ 401) 혼자	☐ 431) 방안
☐ 312) 자체	☐ 342) 중앙	☐ 372) 아름다운	☐ 402) 나간다	☐ 432) 느낌
☐ 313) 연다	☐ 343) 활동	☐ 373) 끝	☐ 403) 교수	☐ 433) 얼마
☐ 314) 열린다	☐ 344) 오늘	☐ 374) 민족	☐ 404) 술	☐ 434) 성격
☐ 315) 머리	☐ 345) 오늘날	☐ 375) 간	☐ 405) 사랑	☐ 435) 계속
☐ 316) 고개	☐ 346) 서로	☐ 376) 조사한다	☐ 406) 사랑한다	☐ 436) 세기
☐ 317) 묻는다	☐ 347) 관심	☐ 377) 듯하다	☐ 407) 의식하는	☐ 437) 세운다
☐ 318) 남는다	☐ 348) 역시	☐ 378) 입	☐ 408) 전화	☐ 438) 아내
☐ 319) 부분	☐ 349) 광고	☐ 379) 그대로	☐ 409) 끝난다	☐ 439) 가족
☐ 320) 일부	☐ 350) 아무런	☐ 380) 영화	☐ 410) 마친다	☐ 440) 여름
☐ 321) 기업	☐ 351) 아니	☐ 381) 필요	☐ 411) 돌아온다	☐ 441) 세
☐ 322) 사업	☐ 352) 방	☐ 382) 줄	☐ 412) 맞다	☐ 442) 발전
☐ 323) 거기에	☐ 353) 정신	☐ 383) 하늘	☐ 413) 아빠	☐ 443) 논다
☐ 324) 변화	☐ 354) 이른다	☐ 384) 과학	☐ 414) 걸린다	☐ 444) 향한다
☐ 325) 변한다	☐ 355) 땅	☐ 385) 자연	☐ 415) 지킨다	☐ 445) 관련된
☐ 326) 바뀐다	☐ 356) 이룬다	☐ 386) 정말	☐ 416) 한 번	☐ 446) 형태
☐ 327) 달라졌다	☐ 357) 아침	☐ 387) 구조	☐ 417) 커피	☐ 447) 형식
☐ 328) 바꾼다	☐ 358) 웃는다	☐ 388) 결국	☐ 418) 가슴	☐ 448) 각
☐ 329) 아들	☐ 359) 웃음	☐ 389) 밥	☐ 419) 긴	☐ 449) 분위기
☐ 330) 의지	☐ 360) 현상	☐ 390) 식사	☐ 420) 바라본다	☐ 450) 기분

301-450				
301) as~as	331) ah	361) put	391) wear	421) recognize
302) as	332) await	362) put	392) rather	422) firm
303) as	333) fall	363) leave	393) come true	423) taste
304) reality	334) election	364) skill	394) stranger	424) industry
305) environment	335) about	365) total	395) one day	425) rise
306) first	336) just	366) yes	396) picture	426) rise
307) first	337) divide	367) yes	397) enemy	427) food
308) first	338) utilize	368) yes	398) site	428) surely
309) how	339) almost	369) example	399) drink	429) nowadays
310) how	340) soon	370) get	400) hit	430) plan
311) how?	341) center	371) anger	401) alone	431) plan
312) in ~self	342) center	372) beautiful	402) go out	432) feeling
313) open	343) activity	373) end	403) professor	433) how much
314) open	344) today	374) race	404) drinking	434) personality
315) head	345) today	375) seasoning	405) love	435) over and over
316) head	346) each other	376) survey	406) love	436) century
317) ask	347) interest	377) seem	407) conscious	437) erect
318) remain	348) as well	378) mouth	408) telephone	438) wife
319) part	349) advertisement	379) as it is	409) finish	439) family
320) part	350) no	380) movie	410) finish	440) summer
321) corporation	351) no	381) need	411) come back	441) rent
322) business	352) room	382) row	412) be right	442) advance
323) there	353) spirit	383) sky	413) dad	443) play
324) change	354) reach	384) science	414) take	444) head for
325) change	355) land	385) nature	415) protect	445) relevant
326) change	356) achieve	386) really	416) once	446) form
327) change	357) morning	387) structure	417) coffee	447) form
328) change	358) laugh	388) eventually	418) chest	448) angle
329) son	359) laugh	389) meal	419) long	449) mood
330) will	360) phenomenon	390) meal	420) look at	450) mood

Day1~5 List (4)

451-500			
□ 451) 그러한	□ 481) 산		
□ 452) 나이	□ 482) 하지만		
□ 453) 우선	□ 483) 조건		
□ 454) 믿는다	□ 484) 문		
□ 455) 낳는다	□ 485) 꽃		
□ 456) 정보	□ 486) 단계		
□ 457) 좋아한다	□ 487) 그동안		
□ 458) 그린다	□ 488) 갑자기		
□ 459) 끈다	□ 489) 넘는다		
□ 460) 배운다	□ 490) 바람		
□ 461) 시	□ 491) 마을		
□ 462) 역할	□ 492) 어리다		
□ 463) 옆에	□ 493) 대표		
□ 464) 행동	□ 494) 가능성		
□ 465) 행위	□ 495) 방향		
□ 466) 국내	□ 496) 대회		
□ 467) 기관	□ 497) 목소리		
□ 468) 입장	□ 498) 노래		
□ 469) 만한	□ 499) 바다		
□ 470) 가치	□ 500) 힘든		
□ 471) 아래			
□ 472) 영향			
□ 473) 나선다			
□ 474) 흐른다			
□ 475) 깊은			
□ 476) 배			
□ 477) 배			
□ 478) 배			
□ 479) 모양			
□ 480) 산			

451-500				
451) such	481) acid			
452) age	482) however			
453) first of all	483) condition			
454) believe	484) door			
455) give birth	485) flower			
456) information	486) step			
457) like	487) meantime			
458) draw	488) suddenly			
459) turn off	489) overstep			
460) learn	490) wind			
461) poem	491) village			
462) role	492) young			
463) by	493) representative			
464) behavior	494) chance			
465) behavior	495) direction			
466) domestic	496) contest			
467) organ	497) voice			
468) entry	498) song			
469) worth	499) sea			
470) value	500) tough			
471) under				
472) influence				
473) come forward				
474) flow				
475) deep				
476) pear				
477) ship				
478) stomach				
479) shape				
480) mountain				

Day1~5 List Study

Final	K-word ㉜				
check	English ㉝				

K-word ㉖	English ㉗	K-word ㉘	K-word ㉙	English ㉚	K-word ㉛

Final	K-word ㉜				
check	English ㉝				

K-word ㉖	English ㉗	K-word ㉘	K-word ㉙	English ㉚	K-word ㉛

Day1~5 List Study

Final	K-word ㉜				
check	English ㉝				

K-word ㉖	English ㉗	K-word ㉘	K-word ㉙	English ㉚	K-word ㉛

Final	K-word ㉜				
check	English ㉝				

K-word ㉖	English ㉗	K-word ㉘	K-word ㉙	English ㉚	K-word ㉛

Final	K-word ㉜				
check	English ㉝				

K-word ㉖	English ㉗	K-word ㉘	K-word ㉙	English ㉚	K-word ㉛

	K-word	Pronounce	English	K-word ❶	Sentence example
501	공부	gong-bu	study		The building has a room for study.
502	공부 한다	gong-bu-han-da	study		They study very hard.
503	움직인다	um-jik-in-da	move		Lions move quietly.
504	노력	no-ryeok	effort		Make more efforts.
505	전혀	jeon-hyeo	altogether		This is altogether different.
506	언니	eon-ni	older sister		Mary is my older sister.
507	단체	dan-che	group		We're a group.
508	집단	jib-dan	group		A group of girls came.
509	알려진	al-lyeo-jin	known		The criminal is known.
510	가능하다	ga-neung-ha-da	be possible		It is possible.
511	능력	neung-ryeok	ability		Tom has a critical ability.
512	주장한다	ju-jang-han-da	insist		He insists on his innocence.
513	자식	ja-sik	child		Tom is my child.
514	어린이	eo-rin-i	child		He treats me like a child.
515	돌린다	dol-lin-da	turn		They turn wheels.
516	차례	cha-rye	turn		It's my turn.
517	불	bul	fire		Tom shouted, "Fire!"
518	주민	ju-min	resident		Local resident groups united.
519	모은다	mo-eun-da	collect		Tom collects stamps.
520	자료	ja-ryo	data		Who released the data?

Final	K-word ❽				
check	English ❾				

K-word ❷	English ❸	K-word ❹	K-word ❺	English ❻	K-word ❼

	K-word	Pronounce	English	K-word ❶	Sentence example
521	존재	jon-jae	presence		He noticed my presence.
522	학년	hak-nyeon	grade		He is in the lower grades.
523	신문	sin-mun	newspaper		This newspaper is free.
524	이해한다	i-hae-han-da	understand		I understand you.
525	제품	je-pum	product		Every product is tested.
526	분야	bun-ya	field		He is an expert in this field.
527	교사	gyo-sa	teacher		He is a teacher.
528	돌아간다	dol-a-gan-da	return		Tom returns home.
529	수준	su-jun	level		My income level is low.
530	표현	pyo-hyeon	expression		His expression is always funny.
531	대	dae	large		He wants a large company.
532	젊다	jeolm-da	young		He is young.
533	동시	dong-si	simultaneous		There were simultaneous attacks.
534	옷	os	cloths		Wear warm clothes.
535	기능	gi-neung	function		The function was canceled.
536	순간	sun-gan	moment		It was a moment's mistake.
537	전쟁	jeon-jaeng	war		The war ended.
538	꿈	kkum	dream		Sweet dreams.
539	할머니	hal-meo-ni	grandma		She is my grandma.
540	회의	hoe-ui	meeting		I have an important meeting.

Final	K-word ❽				
check	English ❾				

K-word ❷	English ❸	K-word ❹	K-word ❺	English ❻	K-word ❼

	K-word	Pronounce	English	K-word ❶	Sentence example
541	방송	bang-song	broadcast		There's a political broadcast.
542	이야기 한다	i-ya-gi han-da	talk		They talk happily.
543	얘기 한다	yae-gi han-da	talk		They talk happily.
544	나무	na-mu	tree		She plants trees.
545	잔다	jan-da	sleep		Bats sleep upside down.
546	잠	jam	sleep		Sleep gives me energy.
547	연극	yeon-geuk	play		They put on a play.
548	마찬가지로	ma-chan-ga-ji-ro	likewise		Her life was likewise happy.
549	걷는다	geod-neun-da	walk		He walks fast.
550	노동	no-dong	labor		Labor has created man.
551	과거	gwa-geo	past		We cannot change the past.
552	현대	hyeon-dae	contempo-rary		We criticize contemporary cultures.
553	살펴본다	sal-pyeo-bon-da	examine		He examines the machine.
554	장관	jang-gwan	spectacle		The carnival was a spectacle.
555	차이	cha-i	margin		He won by a narrow margin.
556	푼다	pun-da	untie		He unties the box.
557	시절	si-jeol	days		I was short in my school days.
558	물건	mul-geon	thing		She made things with her hands.
559	직접	jik-jeob	first-hand		I experienced poverty first-hand.
560	개인	gae-in	individual		Each individual is different.

Final	K-word ❽				
check	English ❾				

K-word ❷	English ❸	K-word ❹	K-word ❺	English ❻	K-word ❼

	K-word	Pronounce	English	K-word ❶	Sentence example
561	발	bal	foot		My foot hurts.
562	작가	jak-ga	writer		I'm a travel writer.
563	효과	hyo-gwa	effect		The medicine took effect.
564	불교	bul-gyo	Buddhism		Buddhism gave me enlightenment.
565	빨리	ppal-li	fast		Run fast!
566	시작된다	si-jak-doen-da	begin		School begins at 8.
567	설명한다	seol-myeong-han-da	explain		She explains in detail.
568	우주	u-ju	universe		God made the universe.
569	시기	si-gi	period		Next period will be good.
570	마치	ma-chi	as if		He acts as if he were a doctor.
571	살	sal	flesh		The flesh smells horrible.
572	생산한다	saeng-san-han-da	yield		The land yields grapes.
573	바란다	ba-ran-da	wish		I wish you luck.
574	강한	gang-han	strong		He is a strong man.
575	경험	gyeong-heom	experience		He lacks experience.
576	음악	eum-ak	music		Everybody loves music.
577	최고	choe-go	the best		It is the best choice.
578	나타낸다	na-ta-naen-da	reveal		This reveals his idea.
579	아프다	a peu-da	be ill		He is ill today.
580	적은	jeok-eun	less		I did it at a less cost.

Final K-word ❽				
check English ❾				

K-word ❷	English ❸	K-word ❹	K-word ❺	English ❻	K-word ❼

	K-word	Pronounce	English	K-word ❶	Sentence example
581	비	bi	rain		We had little rain last year.
582	고향	go-hyang	hometown		My hometown is Mapo.
583	놀란다	nol-lan-da	surprised		She is often surprised at a cat.
584	다양하다	da-yang-ha-da	so many		There are so many things.
585	운다	un-da	cry		They cry everyday.
586	농민	nong-min	farmer		Farmers left the farms.
587	은행	eun-haeng	bank		Where is the bank?
588	결혼	gyeol-hon	wedding		Their wedding is tomorrow.
589	동생	dong-saeng	younger brother		Tom is my younger brother.
590	법	beob	law		They hate laws.
591	소설	so-seol	novel		His novel sold well.
592	오후	o-hu	p.m.		It's 2:00 p.m.
593	질서	jil-seo	order		You must keep order.
594	담는다	dam-neun-da	put in		They put the cups in a box.
595	모인다	mo-in-da	gather		Everyone gathers around her.
596	시민	si-min	citizen		I am an American citizen.
597	회장	hoe-jang	chairman		He was elected chairman.
598	빠른	ppa-reun	quick		He is a quick learner.
599	스스로	seu-seu-ro	by oneself		She came by herself.
600	아기	a-gi	baby		The baby cried.

Final	K-word ❽				
check	English ❾				

K-word ❷	English ❸	K-word ❹	K-word ❺	English ❻	K-word ❼

	K-word	English		K-word	English
501	공부	The building has a room for	521	존재	He noticed my ....
502	공부한다	They .... very hard.	522	학년	He is in the lower ....
503	움직인다	Lions .... quietly.	523	신문	This .... is free.
504	노력	Make more	524	이해한다	I .... you.
505	전혀	This is .... different.	525	제품	Every .... is tested.
506	언니	Mary is my	526	분야	He is an expert in this ....
507	단체	We're a	527	교사	He is a ....
508	집단	A .... of girls came.	528	돌아간다	Tom .... home.
509	알려진	The criminal is	529	수준	My income .... is low.
510	가능하다	It is	530	표현	His .... is always funny.
511	능력	Tom has a critical	531	대	He wants a .... company.
512	주장한다	He .... on his innocence.	532	젊다	He is ....
513	자식	Tom is my	533	동시	There were .... attacks.
514	어린이	He treats me like a	534	옷	Wear warm ....
515	돌린다	They .... wheels.	535	기능	The .... was canceled.
516	차례	It's my	536	순간	It was a .... 's mistake.
517	불	Tom shouted, "........................ !"	537	전쟁	The .... ended.
518	주민	Local .... groups united.	538	꿈	Sweet ....
519	모은다	Tom .... stamps.	539	할머니	She is my ....
520	자료	Who released the .... ?	540	회의	I have an important ....

501) study 502) study 503) move 504) effort 505) altogether 506) older sister 507) group 508) group
509) known 510) possible 511) ability 512) insists 513) child 514) child 515) turn 516) turn
517) Fire 518) resident 519) collects 520) data 521) presence 522) grade 523) newspaper 524) understand
525) product 526) field 527) teacher 528) returns 529) level 530) expression 531) large 532) young
533) simultaneous 534) clothes 535) function 536) moment 537) war 538) dream 539) grandma 540) meeting

	K-word	English		K-word	English
541	방송	There's a political _____	561	발	My _____ hurts.
542	이야기한다	They _____ happily.	562	작가	I'm a travel _____.
543	얘기한다	They _____ happily.	563	효과	The medicine took _____.
544	나무	She plants _____.	564	불교	_____ gave me enlightenment.
545	잔다	Bats _____ upside down.	565	빨리	Run _____!
546	잠	_____ gives me energy.	566	시작된다	School _____ at 8.
547	연극	They put on a _____.	567	설명한다	She _____ in detail.
548	마찬가지로	Her life was _____ happy.	568	우주	God made the _____.
549	걷는다	He _____ fast.	569		Next _____ will be good.
550	노동	_____ has created man.	570		He acts _____ he were a doctor.
551	과거	We cannot change the _____.	571	살	The _____ smells horrible.
552	현대	We criticize _____ cultures.	572	생산한다	The land _____ grapes.
553	살펴본다	He _____ the machine.	573	바란다	I _____ you luck.
554	장관	The carnival was a _____.	574	강한	He is a _____ man.
555	차이	He won by a narrow _____.	575	경험	He lacks _____.
556	푼다	He _____ the box.	576	음악	Everybody loves _____.
557	시절	I was short in my school _____.	577	최고	It is the _____ choice.
558	물건	She made _____ with her hands.	578	나타낸다	This _____ his idea.
559	직접	I experienced poverty _____.	579	아프다	He is _____ today.
560	개인	Each _____ is different.	580	적은	I did it at a _____ cost.

541) broadcast 542) talk 543) talk 544) trees 545) sleep 546) Sleep 547) play 548) likewise
549) walks 550) Labor 551) past 552) contemporary 553) examines 554) spectacle 555) margin 556) unties
557) days 558) things 559) first-hand 560) individual 561) foot 562) writer 563) effect 564) Buddhism
565) fast 566) begins 567) explains 568) universe 569) period 570) as if 571) flesh 572) yields
573) wish 574) strong 575) experience 576) music 577) best 578) reveals 579) ill 580) less

	K-word	English
581	비	We had little .... last year.
582	고향	My .... is Mapo.
583	놀란다	She is often .... at a cat.
584	다양하다	There are .... things.
585	운다	They .... everyday.
586	농민	.... left the farms.
587	은행	Where is the ....?
588	결혼	Their .... is tomorrow.
589	동생	Tom is my ....
590	법	They hate ....
591	소설	His .... sold well.
592	오후	It's 2:00 ....
593	질서	You must keep ....
594	담는다	They .... the cups .... a box.
595	모인다	Everyone .... around her.
596	시민	I am an American ....
597	회장	He was elected ....
598	빠른	He is a .... learner.
599	스스로	She came ....
600	아기	The .... cried.

King Sejong

– The 4th king of Joseon Dynasty

King Sejong was born in 1397.
His 32 year reign marked great achievements.
Hangeul, created by King Sejong,
has been used as a common script for
the Republic of Korea and North Korea.

581) rain   582) hometown   583) surprised   584) so many
585) cry   586) Farmers   587) bank   588) wedding
589) younger brother   590) law   591) novel   592) p.m.
593) order   594) put, in   595) gathers   596) citizen
597) chairman   598) quick   599) by herself   600) baby

Day6 Review Study

Final	K-word ⑯				
check	English ⑰				

K-word ⑩	English ⑪	K-word ⑫	K-word ⑬	English ⑭	K-word ⑮

Day6 Sentence(1)

	Write K-word in			Write K-word in ....
501	The building has a room for study. 그 건물은 ....를 위한 방이 있다.	514	He treats me like a child. 그는 나를 ....처럼 취급한다.
502	They study very hard. 그들은 매우 열심히	515	They turn wheels. 그들은 바퀴를 ....
503	Lions move quietly. 사자들은 조용히	516	It's my turn. 내 ....이다.
504	Make more efforts. ....을 더 해라.	517	Tom shouted, "Fire!" 톰은 소리쳤다, "................이야!"
505	This is altogether different. 이것은 ....다르다.	518	Local resident groups united. 지역 ....단체들이 연합했다.
506	Mary is my older sister. 메리는 나의 ....이다.	519	Tom collects stamps. 톰은 우표를 ....
507	We're a group. 우리는 ....이다.	520	Who released the data? 누가 그 ....를 발표했나요?
508	A group of girls came. 한 ....의 여자들이 왔다.	521	He noticed my presence. 그는 내 ....를 알아차렸다.
509	The criminal is known. 범죄자는 ....다.	522	He is in the lower grades. 그는 저 ....이다.
510	It is possible. 그것은	523	This newspaper is free. 이 ....은 무료입니다.
511	Tom has a critical ability. 톰은 비판적 ....이 있다.	524	I understand you. 나는 너를 ....
512	He insists on his innocence. 그는 자신의 결백을	525	Every product is tested. 모든 ....이 테스트 된다.
513	Tom is my child. 톰은 나의 ....이다.		

501) 공부   502) 공부한다   503) 움직인다   504) 노력   505) 전혀   506) 언니   507) 단체   508) 집단   509) 알려진
510) 가능하다   511) 능력   512) 주장한다   513) 자식   514) 어린이   515) 돌린다   516) 차례   517) 불   518) 주민
519) 모은다   520) 자료   521) 존재   522) 학년   523) 신문   524) 이해한다   525) 제품

	K-word	pronounce	English		K-word	pronounce	English
501	그 건물은	geu geon-mul-eun	the building		이다	i-da	is
	공부를 위한	gong-bu-reul wi-han	for study	514	그는	geu-neun	he
	방이	bang-i	a room		나를	na-reul	me
	있다	iss-da	has		어린이	eo-rin-i	a child
502	그들은	geu-deul-eun	they		처럼	cheo-reom	like
	매우	mae-u	very		취급한다	chwi-geub-han-da	treat
	열심히	yeol-sim-hi	hard	515	그들은	geu-deul-eun	they
	공부한다	gong-bu-han-da	study		바퀴를	ba-kwi-reul	wheels
503	사자들은	sa-ja-deul-eun	lions		돌린다	dol-lin-da	turn
	조용히	jo-yong-hi	quietly	516	내	nae	my
	움직인다	um-jik-in-da	move		차례	cha-rye	turn
504	노력을	no-ryeok-eul	efforts		이다	i-da	it is
	더 해라	deo hae-ra	make more	517	톰은	tom-eun	Tom
505	이것은	i-geos-eun	this		소리쳤다	so-ri-chyeoss-da	shouted
	전혀	jeon-hyeo	altogether		불이야	bul-i-ya	fire
	다르다	da-reu-da	is different	518	지역	ji-yeok	local
506	메리는	me-ri-neun	Mary		주민	ju-min	resident
	나의	na-ui	my		단체들이	dan-che-deul-i	groups
	언니	eon-ni	older sister		연합했다	yeon-hab-haess-da	united
	이다	i-da	is	519	톰은	tom-eun	Tom
507	우리는	u-ri-neun	we		우표를	u-pyo-reul	stamps
	단체	dan-che	a group		모은다	mo-eun-da	collect
	이다	i-da	are	520	누가	nu-ga	who
508	한 집단의	han jib-dan-ui	an group of		그 자료를	geu ja-ryo-reul	the data
	여자들이	yeo-ja-deul-i	girls		발표했나요?	bal-pyo-haess-na-yo?	released
	왔다	wass-da	came	521	그는	geu-neun	he
509	범죄자는	beom-joe-ja-neun	the criminal		내	nae	my
	알려진다	al-lyeo-jin-da	is known		존재를	jon-jae-reul	presence
510	그것은	geu-geos-eun	it		알아차렸다	al-a-cha-ryeoss-da	noticed
	가능하다	ga-neung-ha-da	is possible	522	그는	geu-neun	he
511	톰은	tom-eun	Tom		저학년	jeo-hak-nyeon	in the lower grades
	비판적	bi-pan-jeok	critical		이다	i-da	is
	능력이	neung-ryeok-i	ability	523	이	i	this
	있다	iss-da	has		신문은	sin-mun-eun	newspaper
512	그는	geu-neun	he		무료입니다	mu-ryo-ib-ni-da	is free
	자신의	ja-sin-ui	his	524	나는	na-neun	I
	결백을	gyeol-baek-eul	innocence		너를	neo-reul	you
	주장한다	ju-jang-han-da	insist on		이해한다	i-hae-han-da	understand
513	톰은	tom-eun	Tom	525	모든	mo-deun	every
	나의	na-ui	my		제품이	je-pum-i	product
	자식	ja-sik	child		테스트 된다	te-seu-teu-doen-da	is tested

	Write K-word in		Write K-word in ....
526	He is an expert in this field. 그는 이 .... 에서 전문가이다.	539	She is my grandma. 그녀는 나의 .... 이다.
527	He is a teacher. 그는 .... 다.	540	I have an important meeting. 나는 중요한 .... 가 있다.
528	Tom returns home. 톰은 집으로	541	There's a political broadcast. 정책 .... 이 있다.
529	My income level is low. 나의 소득 .... 은 낮다.	542	They talk happily. 그들은 즐겁게 ....
530	His expression is always funny. 그의 .... 은 항상 웃기다.	543	They talk happily. 그들은 즐겁게 ....
531	He wants a large company. 그는 .... 기업을 원한다.	544	She plants trees. 그녀는 .... 를 심는다.
532	He is young. 그는	545	Bats sleep upside down. 박쥐는 거꾸로 ....
533	There were simultaneous attacks. .... 공격이 있었다.	546	Sleep gives me energy. .... 은 나에게 에너지를 준다.
534	Wear warm clothes. 따뜻한 .... 을 입어라.	547	They put on a play. 그들이 .... 을 상연한다.
535	The function was cancelled. 그 .... 은 취소됐다.	548	Her life was likewise happy. 그녀의 삶은 .... 행복했다.
536	It was a moment's mistake. 그것은 .... 의 실수였다.	549	He walks fast. 그는 빨리 ....
537	The war ended. .... 이 끝났다.	550	Labor has created man. .... 이 인간을 만들었다.
538	Sweet dreams. 좋은 .... 꾸어라.		

526) 분야   527) 교사   528) 돌아간다   529) 수준   530) 표현   531) 대   532) 젊다   533) 동시   534) 옷
535) 기능   536) 순간   537) 전쟁   538) 꿈   539) 할머니   540) 회의   541) 방송   542) 이야기한다   543) 얘기한다
544) 나무   545) 잔다   546) 잠   547) 연극   548) 마찬가지로   549) 걷는다   550) 노동

	K-word	pronounce	English			K-word	pronounce	English
526	그는	geu-neun	he			나의	na-ui	my
	이 분야에서	i bun-ya-e-seo	in this field			할머니	hal-meo-ni	grandma
	전문가	jeon-mun-ga	an expert			이다	i-da	is
	이다	i-da	is	540		나는	na-neun	I
527	그는	geu-neun	he			중요한	jung-yo-han	important
	교사다	gyo-sa-da	is a teacher			회의가	hoe-ui-ga	meeting
528	톰은	tom-eun	Tom			있다	iss-da	have
	집으로	jib-eu-ro	home	541		정책	jeong-chaek	political
	돌아간다	dol-a-gan-da	return			방송이	bang-song-i	broadcast
529	나의	na-ui	my			있다	iss-da	there's
	소득	so-deuk	income	542		그들은	geu-deul-eun	they
	수준은	su-jun-eun	level			즐겁게	jeul-geob-ge	happily
	낮다	naj-da	is low			이야기한다	i-ya-gi-han-da	talk
530	그의	geu-ui	his	543		그들이	geu-deul-i	they
	표현은	pyo-hyeon-eun	expression			즐겁게	jeul-geob-ge	happily
	항상	hang-sang	always			얘기한다	yae-gi-han-da	talk
	웃기다	us-gi-da	is funny	544		그녀는	geu-nyeo-neun	she
531	그는	geu-neun	he			나무를	na-mu-reul	trees
	대	dae	large			심는다	sim-neun-da	plant
	기업을	gi-eob-eul	company	545		박쥐는	bak-jwi-neun	bats
	원한다	won-han-da	want			거꾸로	geo-kku-ro	upside down
532	그는	geu-neun	he			잔다	jan-da	sleep
	젊다	jeolm-da	is young	546		잠은	jam-eun	sleep
533	동시	dong-si	simultaneous			나에게	na-e-ge	me
	공격이	gong-gyeok-i	attacks			에너지를	e-neo-ji-reul	energy
	있었다	iss-eoss-da	there were			준다	jun-da	give
534	따뜻한	tta-tteus-han	warm	547		그들이	geu-deul-i	they
	옷을	os-eul	clothes			연극을	yeon-geuk-eul	a play
	입어라	ib-eo-ra	wear			상연한다	sang-yeon-han-da	put on
535	그 기능은	geu gi-neung-eun	the function	548		그녀의	geu-nyeo-ui	her
	취소됐다	chwi-so-dwaess-da	was cancelled			삶은	salm-eun	life
536	그것은	geu-geos-eun	it			마찬가지로	ma-chan-ga-ji-ro	likewise
	순간의	sun-gan-ui	a moment's			행복했다	haeng-bok-haess-da	was happy
	실수	sil-su	mistake	549		그는	geu-neun	he
	였다	yeoss-da	was			빨리	ppal-li	fast
537	전쟁이	jeon-jaeng-i	the war			걷는다	geod-neun-da	walk
	끝났다	kkeut-nass-da	ended	550		노동이	no-dong-i	labor
538	좋은	joh-eun	sweet			인간을	in-gan-eul	man
	꿈 꾸어라	kkum kku-eo-ra	dreams			만들었다	man-deul-eoss-da	has created
539	그녀는	geu-nyeo-neun	she					

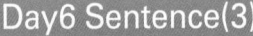

	Write K-word in ____.		Write K-word in ____.
551	We cannot change the past. 우리는 _____를 바꿀 수 없다.	564	Buddhism gave me enlightenment. _____는 나에게 깨달음을 주었다.
552	We criticize contemporary cultures. 우리는 _____ 문화를 비판한다.	565	Run fast! _____ 달려라!
553	He examines the machine. 그는 기계를 _____.	566	School begins at 8. 학교는 여덟시에 _____.
554	The carnival was a spectacle. 그 카니발은 _____이었다.	567	She explains in detail. 그녀는 자세히 _____.
555	He won by a narrow margin. 그는 작은 _____로 이겼다.	568	God made the universe. 신이 _____를 창조했다.
556	He unties the box. 그가 상자를 _____.	569	Next period will be good. 다음 _____는 좋을 것이다.
557	I was short in my school days. 나는 학창 _____에 작았다.	570	He acts as if he were a doctor. 그는 _____ 의사인 것처럼 행동한다.
558	She made things with her hands. 그녀는 손으로 _____들을 만들었다.	571	The flesh smells horrible. _____에서 지독한 냄새가 난다.
559	I experienced poverty first-hand. 나는 _____ 가난을 경험했다.	572	The land yields grapes. 그 땅은 포도를 _____.
560	Each individual is different. 각 _____이 다르다.	573	I wish you luck. 나는 당신의 행운을 _____.
561	My foot hurts. _____이 아프다.	574	He is a strong man. 그는 _____ 남자이다.
562	I'm a travel writer. 나는 여행 _____이다.	575	He lacks experience. 그는 _____이 부족하다.
563	The medicine took effect. 그 약은 _____가 있었다.		

551) 과거 552) 현대 553) 살펴본다 554) 장관 555) 차이 556) 푼다 557) 시절 558) 물건 559) 직접
560) 개인 561) 발 562) 작가 563) 효과 564) 불교 565) 빨리 566) 시작된다 567) 설명한다 568) 우주
569) 시기 570) 마치 571) 살 572) 생산한다 573) 바란다 574) 강한 575) 경험

	K-word	pronounce	English		K-word	pronounce	English
551	우리는	u-ri-neun	we	564	불교는	bul-gyo-neun	Buddhism
	과거를	gwa-geo-reul	the past		나에게	na-e-ge	me
	바꿀 수 없다	ba-kkul su eobs-da	cannot change		깨달음을	kkae-dal-eum-eul	enlightenment
552	우리는	u-ri-neun	we		주었다	ju-eoss-da	gave
	현대	hyeon-dae	comtemporary	565	빨리	ppal-li	fast
	문화를	mun-hwa-reul	cultures		달려라	dal-lyeo-ra	run
	비판한다	bi-pan-han-da	criticize	566	학교는	hak-gyo-neun	school
553	그는	geu-neun	he		여덟시에	yeo-deolb-si-e	at 8
	기계를	gi-gye-reul	the machine		시작된다	si-jak-doen-da	begin
	살펴본다	sal-pyeo-bon-da	examine	567	그녀는	geu-nyeo-neun	she
554	그 카니발은	geu ka-ni-bal-eun	the carnival		자세히	ja-se-hi	in detail
	장관	jang-gwan	a spectacle		설명한다	seol-myeong-han-da	explain
	이었다	i-eoss-da	was	568	신이	sin-i	god
555	그는	geu-neun	he		우주를	u-ju-reul	the universe
	작은	jak-eun	narrow		창조했다	chang-jo-haess-da	made
	차이로	cha-i-ro	by a margin	569	다음	da-eum	next
	이겼다	i-gyeoss-da	won		시기는	si-gi-neun	period
556	그가	geu-ga	he		좋을 것이다	joh-eul geos-i-da	will be good
	상자를	sang-ja-reul	the box	570	그는	geu-neun	he
	푼다	pun-da	untie		마치	ma-chi	as if
557	나는	na-neun	I		의사	ui-sa	a doctor
	학창시절에	hak-chang-si-jeol-e	in my school days		인 것처럼	in geos-cheo-reom	as if were
	작았다	jak-ass-da	was short		행동한다	haeng-dong-han-da	act
558	그녀는	geu-nyeo-neun	she	571	살에서	sal-e-seo	the flesh
	손으로	son-eu-ro	with her hands		지독한	ji-dok-han	horrible
	물건들을	mul-geon-deul-eul	things		냄새가 난다	naem-sae-ga nan-da	smell
	만들었다	man-deul-eoss-da	made	572	그 땅은	geu ttang-eun	the land
559	나는	na-neun	I		포도를	po-do-reul	grapes
	직접	jik-jeob	first-hand		생산한다	saeng-san-han-da	yield
	가난을	ga-nan-eul	poverty	573	나는	na-neun	I
	경험했다	gyeong-heom-haess-da	experienced		당신의	dang-sin-ui	you
560	각	gak	each		행운을	haeng-un-eul	luck
	개인이	gae-in-i	individual		바란다	ba-ran-da	wish
	다르다	da-reu-da	is different	574	그는	geu-neun	he
561	발이	bal-i	my foot		강한	gang-han	strong
	아프다	a-peu-da	hurt		남자	nam-ja	man
562	나는	na-neun	I		이다	i-da	is
	여행 작가	yeo-haeng-jak-ga	a travel writer	575	그는	geu-neun	he
	이다	i-da	am		경험이	gyeong-heom-i	experience
563	그 약은	geu yak-eun	the medicine		부족하다	bu-jok-ha-da	lack
	효과가 있었다	hyo-gwa-ga iss-eoss-da	took effect				

	Write K-word in		Write K-word in ....
576	Everybody loves music. 모든 사람들은 _____을 좋아한다.	589	Tom is my younger brother. 톰은 나의 _____이다.
757	It is the best choice. 그것이 _____ 선택이다.	590	They hate laws. 그들은 _____을 싫어한다.
578	This reveals his idea. 이것이 그의 생각을 _____.	591	His novel sold well. 그의 _____은 잘 팔렸다.
579	He is ill today. 그는 오늘 _____.	592	It's 2:00 p.m. _____ 2시다.
580	I did it at a less cost. 나는 _____ 비용으로 그것을 했다.	593	You must keep order. 너는 _____를 지켜야 한다.
581	We had little rain last year. 작년에는 _____가 거의 오지 않았다.	594	They put the cups in a box. 그들이 컵을 박스에 _____.
582	My hometown is Mapo. 나의 _____은 마포다.	595	Everyone gathers around her. 모두가 그녀 주위로 _____.
583	She is often surprised at a cat. 그녀는 종종 고양이에 _____.	596	I am an American citizen. 나는 미국 _____이다.
584	There are so many things. 물건들이 _____.	597	He was elected chairman. 그는 _____으로 뽑혔다.
585	They cry everyday. 그들은 매일 _____.	598	He is a quick learner. 그는 _____ 학습자이다.
586	Farmers left the farms. _____들이 농장을 떠났다.	599	She came by herself. 그녀는 _____ 왔다.
587	Where is the bank? _____이 어디에 있나요 ?	600	The baby cried. _____가 울었다.
588	Their wedding is tomorrow. 그들의 _____식은 내일이다.		

576) 음악   577) 최고   578) 나타낸다   579) 아프다   580) 적은   581) 비   582) 고향   583) 놀란다   584) 다양하다
585) 운다   586) 농민   587) 은행   588) 결혼   589) 동생   590) 법   591) 소설   592) 오후   593) 질서
594) 담는다   595) 모인다   596) 시민   597) 회장   598) 빠른   599) 스스로   600) 아기

Sentence Words(4)

	K-word	pronounce	English		K-word	pronounce	English
576	모든 사람들은	mo-deun sa-ram-deul-eun	everybody	589	톰은	tom-eun	Tom
	음악을	eum-ak-eul	music		나의	na-ui	my
	좋아한다	joh-a-han-da	love		동생	dong-saeng	younger brother
577	그것이	geu-geos-i	it		이다	i-da	is
	최고	choe-go	the best	590	그들은	geu-deul-eun	they
	선택	seon-taek	choice		법을	beob-eul	laws
	이다	i-da	is		싫어한다	silh-eo-han-da	hate
578	이것이	i-geos-i	this	591	그의	geu-ui	his
	그의	geu-ui	his		소설은	so-seol-eun	novel
	생각을	saeng-gak-eul	idea		잘	jal	well
	나타낸다	na-ta-naen-da	reveal		팔렸다	pal-lyeoss-da	sold
579	그는	geu-neun	he	592	오후	o-hu	p.m.
	오늘	o-neul	today		2시다	du-si-da	it's 2
	아프다	a-peu-da	is ill	593	너는	neo-neun	you
580	나는	na-neun	I		질서를	jil-seo-reul	order
	적은	jeok-eun	less		지켜야한다	ji-kyeo-ya-han-da	must keep
	비용으로	bi-yong-eu-ro	cost	594	그들이	geu-deul-i	they
	그것을	geu-geos-eul	it		컵을	keob-eul	the cups
	했다	haess-da	did		박스에	bak-seu-e	in a box
581	작년에는	jak-nyeon-e-neun	last year		담는다	dam-neun-da	put
	비가	bi-ga	rain	595	모두가	mo-du-ga	everyone
	거의 오지 않았다	geo-ui o-ji anh-ass-da	we had little		그녀	geu-nyeo	her
582	나의	na-ui	my		주위로	ju-wi-ro	around
	고향은	go-hyang-eun	hometown		모인다	mo-in-da	gather
	마포다	ma-po-da	is Mapo	596	나는	na-neun	I
583	그녀는	geu-nyeo-neun	she		미국	mi-guk	American
	종종	jong-jong	often		시민	si-min	citizen
	고양이에	go-yang-i-e	at a cat		이다	i-da	am
	놀란다	nol-lan-da	surprised	597	그는	geu-neun	he
584	물건들이	mul-geon-deul-i	things		회장으로	hoe-jang-eu-ro	chairman
	다양하다	da-yang-ha-da	there are so many		뽑혔다	ppob-hyeoss-da	was elected
585	그들은	geu-deul-eun	they	598	그는	geu-neun	he
	매일	mae-il	everyday		빠른	ppa-reun	quick
	운다	un-da	cry		학습자	hak-seub-ja	learner
586	농민들이	nong-min-deul-i	farmers		이다	i-da	is
	농장을	nong-jang-eul	the farms	599	그녀는	geu-nyeo-neun	she
	떠났다	tteo-nass-da	left		스스로	seu-seu-ro	by herself
587	은행이	eun-haeng-i	the bank		왔다	wass-da	came
	어디에 있나요?	eo-di-e iss-na-yo?	where is	600	아기가	a-gi-ga	the baby
588	그들의	geu-deul-ui	their		울었다	ul-eoss-da	crried
	결혼식은	gyeol-hon-sik-eun	wedding				
	내일이다	nae-il-i-da	is tomorrow				

Day6 Sentence Study

Final	K-word ㉔				
check	English ㉕				

K-word ⑱	English ⑲	K-word ⑳	K-word ㉑	English ㉒	K-word ㉓

1-150				
☐ 1) 것	☐ 31) 드린다	☐ 61) 집	☐ 91) 파악하고 있다	☐ 121) 지닌다
☐ 2) 한다	☐ 32) 대한다	☐ 62) 나온다	☐ 92) 자신	☐ 122) 가진다
☐ 3) 된다	☐ 33) 간다	☐ 63) 따른다	☐ 93) 문화	☐ 123) 갖추고 있다
☐ 4) 수	☐ 34) 다닌다	☐ 64) 그리고	☐ 94) 원	☐ 124) 당한다
☐ 5) 수	☐ 35) 년	☐ 65) 및	☐ 95) 생각	☐ 125) 함께
☐ 6) 길	☐ 36) 한	☐ 66) 그때	☐ 96) 명	☐ 126) 아이
☐ 7) 쪽	☐ 37) 말	☐ 67) 그럼	☐ 97) 통한다	☐ 127) 지나간다
☐ 8) 방식	☐ 38) 일	☐ 68) 문제	☐ 98) 소리	☐ 128) 많이
☐ 9) 점	☐ 39) 일	☐ 69) 그런	☐ 99) 다시	☐ 129) 훨씬
☐ 10) 점	☐ 40) 일 한다	☐ 70) 산다	☐ 100) 다른	☐ 130) 시간
☐ 11) 나	☐ 41) 작품	☐ 71) 산다	☐ 101) 다르다	☐ 131) 너
☐ 12) 내	☐ 42) 작업	☐ 72) 지낸다	☐ 102) 여자	☐ 132) 당신
☐ 13) 그	☐ 43) 직장	☐ 73) 저	☐ 103) 소녀	☐ 133) 인간
☐ 14) 없다	☐ 44) 때문	☐ 74) 생각한다	☐ 104) 개	☐ 134) 사실
☐ 15) 않다	☐ 45) 말한다	☐ 75) 모른다	☐ 105) 그 정도	☐ 135) 과연
☐ 16) 말고	☐ 46) 위하여	☐ 76) 속	☐ 106) 뒤	☐ 136) 난다
☐ 17) 아니다	☐ 47) 그러나	☐ 77) 만든다	☐ 107) 듣는다	☐ 137) 자란다
☐ 18) 않는다	☐ 48) 온다	☐ 78) 삼는다	☐ 108) 다	☐ 138) 어머니
☐ 19) 사람	☐ 49) 안다	☐ 79) 시킨다	☐ 109) 좀	☐ 139) 엄마
☐ 20) 국민	☐ 50) 씨	☐ 80) 두	☐ 110) 조금	☐ 140) 눈
☐ 21) 우리	☐ 51) 그렇다	☐ 81) 둘	☐ 111) 든다	☐ 141) 눈
☐ 22) 이	☐ 52) 큰	☐ 82) 앞	☐ 112) 키운다	☐ 142) 뭐
☐ 23) 이	☐ 53) 크다	☐ 83) 경우	☐ 113) 올린다	☐ 143) 무엇
☐ 24) 이런	☐ 54) 또	☐ 84) 중	☐ 114) 기른다	☐ 144) 무슨
☐ 25) 이것	☐ 55) 사회	☐ 85) 중	☐ 115) 싶다	☐ 145) 시대
☐ 26) 이거	☐ 56) 안에	☐ 86) 동안에	☐ 116) 보인다	☐ 146) 다음
☐ 27) 보다	☐ 57) 좋은	☐ 87) 어떤	☐ 117) 표정	☐ 147) 이러하다
☐ 28) 본다	☐ 58) 더	☐ 88) 잘	☐ 118) 모습	☐ 148) 누구
☐ 29) 같다	☐ 59) 받는다	☐ 89) 그녀	☐ 119) 가지고 있다	☐ 149) 전
☐ 30) 준다	☐ 60) 그것	☐ 90) 먹는다	☐ 120) 갖고있다	☐ 150) 곳

		1-150		
1) thing	31) give	61) house	91) grasp	121) have
2) do	32) treat	62) come out	92) self	122) have
3) become	33) go	63) obey	93) culture	123) have
4) number	34) go	64) and	94) ₩	124) get p.p
5) way	35) year	65) and	95) thought	125) with
6) way	36) one	66) then	96) famous	126) kid
7) way	37) word	67) then	97) make sense	127) pass by
8) way	38) day	68) problem	98) sound	128) much
9) way	39) work	69) such	99) again	129) much ~er
10) store	40) work	70) buy	100) different	130) time
11) I	41) work	71) live	101) different	131) you
12) I	42) work	72) live	102) girl	132) you
13) he	43) job	73) um	103) girl	133) human
14) not have	44) because of	74) think	104) dog	134) in fact
15) not	45) speak	75) don't know	105) that much	135) indeed
16) not	46) for	76) inside	106) back	136) grow
17) not	47) but	77) make	107) hear	137) grow
18) do not	48) come	78) make	108) all	138) mother
19) people	49) know	79) make	109) a little	139) mom
20) people	50) family name	80) two	110) a little	140) eye
21) we	51) right	81) two	111) pick up	141) snow
22) tooth	52) big	82) front	112) raise	142) what
23) this	53) big	83) case	113) raise	143) what
24) this	54) once again	84) monk	114) raise	144) what
25) this	55) society	85) during	115) want	145) era
26) this	56) in	86) during	116) look	146) next
27) than	57) good	87) any	117) look	147) like this
28) see	58) more	88) well	118) appearance	148) who
29) same	59) receive	89) she	119) have	149) all
30) give	60) it	90) eat	120) have	150) place

151-300				
☐ 151) 자리	☐ 181) 날	☐ 211) 인생	☐ 241) 못	☐ 271) 짓는다
☐ 152) 여러	☐ 182) 여기	☐ 212) 지금	☐ 242) 못	☐ 272) 또한
☐ 153) 많은	☐ 183) 여성	☐ 213) 뿐	☐ 243) 못한다	☐ 273) 까닭
☐ 154) 하나	☐ 184) 친구	☐ 214) 다만	☐ 244) 읽는다	☐ 274) 이유
☐ 155) 세계	☐ 185) 마음	☐ 215) 만	☐ 245) 이제	☐ 275) 또는
☐ 156) 세상	☐ 186) 관계	☐ 216) 사이에	☐ 246) 결과	☐ 276) 혹은
☐ 157) 버린다	☐ 187) 아버지	☐ 217) 방법	☐ 247) 내용	☐ 277) 필요하다
☐ 158) 위	☐ 188) 남자	☐ 218) 새롭다	☐ 248) 물론	☐ 278) 글
☐ 159) 운동	☐ 189) 남성	☐ 219) 새	☐ 249) 책	☐ 279) 생긴다
☐ 160) 학교	☐ 190) 어디	☐ 220) 우리나라	☐ 250) 일어난다	☐ 280) 남편
☐ 161) 자기	☐ 191) 몸	☐ 221) 앉는다	☐ 251) 시장	☐ 281) 밖
☐ 162) 가장	☐ 192) 얼굴	☐ 222) 처음의	☐ 252) 넣는다	☐ 282) 작은
☐ 163) 제일	☐ 193) 들어간다	☐ 223) 초기	☐ 253) 중요한	☐ 283) 탄다
☐ 164) 대부분	☐ 194) 들어온다	☐ 224) 손	☐ 254) 느낀다	☐ 284) 대학
☐ 165) 대통령	☐ 195) 왜	☐ 225) 몇	☐ 255) 어려운	☐ 285) 상황
☐ 166) 가지	☐ 196) 나타난다	☐ 226) 과정	☐ 256) 힘	☐ 286) 가운데
☐ 167) 시작한다	☐ 197) 말아라	☐ 227) 찾는다	☐ 257) 너무	☐ 287) 보낸다
☐ 168) 바로	☐ 198) 지역	☐ 228) 특히	☐ 258) 부른다	☐ 288) 즉
☐ 169) 어느	☐ 199) 물	☐ 229) 도시	☐ 259) 의미	☐ 289) 따라서
☐ 170) 그래서	☐ 200) 만난다	☐ 230) 이상	☐ 260) 뜻	☐ 290) 상태
☐ 171) 그러니까	☐ 201) 낸다	☐ 231) 이야기	☐ 261) 밝힌다	☐ 291) 이후
☐ 172) 정부	☐ 202) 쓴다	☐ 232) 얘기	☐ 262) 죽는다	☐ 292) 당시
☐ 173) 모든	☐ 203) 쓴다	☐ 233) 교육	☐ 263) 이미	☐ 293) 문학
☐ 174) 번	☐ 204) 사용한다	☐ 234) 경제	☐ 264) 정치	☐ 294) 더욱
☐ 175) 그거	☐ 205) 없이	☐ 235) 아직	☐ 265) 학생	☐ 295) 아주
☐ 176) 돈	☐ 206) 이번	☐ 236) 잡는다	☐ 266) 연구	☐ 296) 매우
☐ 177) 국가	☐ 207) 이때	☐ 237) 같이	☐ 267) 이름	☐ 297) 지방
☐ 178) 나라	☐ 208) 생활	☐ 238) 선생님	☐ 268) 내린다	☐ 298) 밤
☐ 179) 그런데	☐ 209) 삶	☐ 239) 예술	☐ 269) 사건	☐ 299) 높은
☐ 180) 근데	☐ 210) 생명	☐ 240) 일어선다	☐ 270) 쉬운	☐ 300) 최근

151-300				
151) place	181) day	211) life	241) nail	271) build
152) several	182) here	212) now	242) can't	272) also
153) many	183) female	213) only	243) can't do	273) reason
154) one	184) friend	214) only	244) read	274) reason
155) world	185) mind	215) only	245) now	275) or
156) world	186) relationship	216) between	246) result	276) or
157) dump	187) father	217) manner	247) content	277) need
158) up	188) male	218) new	248) of course	278) writing
159) exercise	189) male	219) new	249) book	279) arise
160) school	190) where	220) our country	250) happen	280) husband
161) darling	191) body	221) sit down	251) market	281) outside
162) ~est	192) face	222) initial	252) insert	282) small
163) ~est	193) go into	223) initial	253) important	283) burn
164) most	194) come in	224) hand	254) feel	284) university
165) president	195) why	225) a few	255) difficult	285) situation
166) kinds	196) emerge	226) course	256) power	286) among
167) start	197) don't	227) search	257) too	287) send
168) right away	198) area	228) especially	258) call	288) namely
169) which	199) water	229) city	259) meaning	289) thus
170) so	200) meet	230) more than	260) meaning	290) state
171) so	201) pay	231) story	261) reveal	291) since
172) government	202) write	232) story	262) die	292) at the time
173) every	203) use	233) education	263) already	293) literature
174) times	204) use	234) economy	264) politics	294) ~er
175) it	205) without	235) yet	265) student	295) very
176) money	206) this time	236) catch	266) research	296) very
177) nation	207) at this time	237) together	267) name	297) fat
178) nation	208) life	238) teacher	268) get off	298) night
179) by the way	209) life	239) art	269) incident	299) high
180) by the way	210) life	240) stand up	270) easy	300) recent

		301-450		
☐ 301) 만큼	☐ 331) 아	☐ 361) 둔다	☐ 391) 입는다	☐ 421) 알아본다
☐ 302) 채	☐ 332) 기다린다	☐ 362) 놓는다	☐ 392) 오히려	☐ 422) 회사
☐ 303) 대로	☐ 333) 떨어진다	☐ 363) 떠난다	☐ 393) 이루어진다	☐ 423) 맛
☐ 304) 현실	☐ 334) 선거	☐ 364) 기술	☐ 394) 남	☐ 424) 산업
☐ 305) 환경	☐ 335) 관하여	☐ 365) 전체	☐ 395) 하루	☐ 425) 오른다
☐ 306) 먼저	☐ 336) 그냥	☐ 366) 그래	☐ 396) 그림	☐ 426) 올라간다
☐ 307) 첫	☐ 337) 나눈다	☐ 367) 네	☐ 397) 적	☐ 427) 음식
☐ 308) 일단	☐ 338) 이용한다	☐ 368) 예	☐ 398) 터	☐ 428) 꼭
☐ 309) 얼마나	☐ 339) 거의	☐ 369) 예	☐ 399) 마신다	☐ 429) 요즘
☐ 310) 어쩌다	☐ 340) 곧	☐ 370) 얻는다	☐ 400) 친다	☐ 430) 계획
☐ 311) 어떠하니	☐ 341) 중심	☐ 371) 분	☐ 401) 혼자	☐ 431) 방안
☐ 312) 자체	☐ 342) 중앙	☐ 372) 아름다운	☐ 402) 나간다	☐ 432) 느낌
☐ 313) 연다	☐ 343) 활동	☐ 373) 끝	☐ 403) 교수	☐ 433) 얼마
☐ 314) 열린다	☐ 344) 오늘	☐ 374) 민족	☐ 404) 술	☐ 434) 성격
☐ 315) 머리	☐ 345) 오늘날	☐ 375) 간	☐ 405) 사랑	☐ 435) 계속
☐ 316) 고개	☐ 346) 서로	☐ 376) 조사한다	☐ 406) 사랑한다	☐ 436) 세기
☐ 317) 묻는다	☐ 347) 관심	☐ 377) 듯하다	☐ 407) 의식하는	☐ 437) 세운다
☐ 318) 남는다	☐ 348) 역시	☐ 378) 입	☐ 408) 전화	☐ 438) 아내
☐ 319) 부분	☐ 349) 광고	☐ 379) 그대로	☐ 409) 끝난다	☐ 439) 가족
☐ 320) 일부	☐ 350) 아무런	☐ 380) 영화	☐ 410) 마친다	☐ 440) 여름
☐ 321) 기업	☐ 351) 아니	☐ 381) 필요	☐ 411) 돌아온다	☐ 441) 세
☐ 322) 사업	☐ 352) 방	☐ 382) 줄	☐ 412) 맞다	☐ 442) 발전
☐ 323) 거기에	☐ 353) 정신	☐ 383) 하늘	☐ 413) 아빠	☐ 443) 논다
☐ 324) 변화	☐ 354) 이른다	☐ 384) 과학	☐ 414) 걸린다	☐ 444) 향한다
☐ 325) 변한다	☐ 355) 땅	☐ 385) 자연	☐ 415) 지킨다	☐ 445) 관련된
☐ 326) 바뀐다	☐ 356) 이룬다	☐ 386) 정말	☐ 416) 한 번	☐ 446) 형태
☐ 327) 달라졌다	☐ 357) 아침	☐ 387) 구조	☐ 417) 커피	☐ 447) 형식
☐ 328) 바꾼다	☐ 358) 웃는다	☐ 388) 결국	☐ 418) 가슴	☐ 448) 각
☐ 329) 아들	☐ 359) 웃음	☐ 389) 밥	☐ 419) 긴	☐ 449) 분위기
☐ 330) 의지	☐ 360) 현상	☐ 390) 식사	☐ 420) 바라본다	☐ 450) 기분

301-450				
301) as~as	331) ah	361) put	391) wear	421) recognize
302) as	332) await	362) put	392) rather	422) firm
303) as	333) fall	363) leave	393) come true	423) taste
304) reality	334) election	364) skill	394) stranger	424) industry
305) environment	335) about	365) total	395) one day	425) rise
306) first	336) just	366) yes	396) picture	426) rise
307) first	337) divide	367) yes	397) enemy	427) food
308) first	338) utilize	368) yes	398) site	428) surely
309) how	339) almost	369) example	399) drink	429) nowadays
310) how	340) soon	370) get	400) hit	430) plan
311) how?	341) center	371) anger	401) alone	431) plan
312) in ~self	342) center	372) beautiful	402) go out	432) feeling
313) open	343) activity	373) end	403) professor	433) how much
314) open	344) today	374) race	404) drinking	434) personality
315) head	345) today	375) seasoning	405) love	435) over and over
316) head	346) each other	376) survey	406) love	436) century
317) ask	347) interest	377) seem	407) conscious	437) erect
318) remain	348) as well	378) mouth	408) telephone	438) wife
319) part	349) advertisement	379) as it is	409) finish	439) family
320) part	350) no	380) movie	410) finish	440) summer
321) corporation	351) no	381) need	411) come back	441) rent
322) business	352) room	382) row	412) be right	442) advance
323) there	353) spirit	383) sky	413) dad	443) play
324) change	354) reach	384) science	414) take	444) head for
325) change	355) land	385) nature	415) protect	445) relevant
326) change	356) achieve	386) really	416) once	446) form
327) change	357) morning	387) structure	417) coffee	447) form
328) change	358) laugh	388) eventually	418) chest	448) angle
329) son	359) laugh	389) meal	419) long	449) mood
330) will	360) phenomenon	390) meal	420) look at	450) mood

451-600				
☐ 451) 그러한	☐ 481) 산	☐ 511) 능력	☐ 541) 방송	☐ 571) 살
☐ 452) 나이	☐ 482) 하지만	☐ 512) 주장한다	☐ 542) 이야기한다	☐ 572) 생산한다
☐ 453) 우선	☐ 483) 조건	☐ 513) 자식	☐ 543) 얘기한다	☐ 573) 바란다
☐ 454) 믿는다	☐ 484) 문	☐ 514) 어린이	☐ 544) 나무	☐ 574) 강한
☐ 455) 낳는다	☐ 485) 꽃	☐ 515) 돌린다	☐ 545) 잔다	☐ 575) 경험
☐ 456) 정보	☐ 486) 단계	☐ 516) 차례	☐ 546) 잠	☐ 576) 음악
☐ 457) 좋아한다	☐ 487) 그동안	☐ 517) 불	☐ 547) 연극	☐ 577) 최고
☐ 458) 그린다	☐ 488) 갑자기	☐ 518) 주민	☐ 548) 마찬가지로	☐ 578) 나타낸다
☐ 459) 끈다	☐ 489) 넘는다	☐ 519) 모은다	☐ 549) 걷는다	☐ 579) 아프다
☐ 460) 배운다	☐ 490) 바람	☐ 520) 자료	☐ 550) 노동	☐ 580) 적은
☐ 461) 시	☐ 491) 마을	☐ 521) 존재	☐ 551) 과거	☐ 581) 비
☐ 462) 역할	☐ 492) 어리다	☐ 522) 학년	☐ 552) 현대	☐ 582) 고향
☐ 463) 옆에	☐ 493) 대표	☐ 523) 신문	☐ 553) 살펴본다	☐ 583) 놀란다
☐ 464) 행동	☐ 494) 가능성	☐ 524) 이해한다	☐ 554) 장관	☐ 584) 다양하다
☐ 465) 행위	☐ 495) 방향	☐ 525) 제품	☐ 555) 차이	☐ 585) 운다
☐ 466) 국내	☐ 496) 대회	☐ 526) 분야	☐ 556) 푼다	☐ 586) 농민
☐ 467) 기관	☐ 497) 목소리	☐ 527) 교사	☐ 557) 시절	☐ 587) 은행
☐ 468) 입장	☐ 498) 노래	☐ 528) 돌아간다	☐ 558) 물건	☐ 588) 결혼
☐ 469) 만한	☐ 499) 바다	☐ 529) 수준	☐ 559) 직접	☐ 589) 동생
☐ 470) 가치	☐ 500) 힘든	☐ 530) 표현	☐ 560) 개인	☐ 590) 법
☐ 471) 아래	☐ 501) 공부	☐ 531) 대	☐ 561) 발	☐ 591) 소설
☐ 472) 영향	☐ 502) 공부한다	☐ 532) 젊다	☐ 562) 작가	☐ 592) 오후
☐ 473) 나선다	☐ 503) 움직인다	☐ 533) 동시	☐ 563) 효과	☐ 593) 질서
☐ 474) 흐른다	☐ 504) 노력	☐ 534) 옷	☐ 564) 불교	☐ 594) 담는다
☐ 475) 깊은	☐ 505) 전혀	☐ 535) 기능	☐ 565) 빨리	☐ 595) 모인다
☐ 476) 배	☐ 506) 언니	☐ 536) 순간	☐ 566) 시작된다	☐ 596) 시민
☐ 477) 배	☐ 507) 단체	☐ 537) 전쟁	☐ 567) 설명한다	☐ 597) 회장
☐ 478) 배	☐ 508) 집단	☐ 538) 꿈	☐ 568) 우주	☐ 598) 빠른
☐ 479) 모양	☐ 509) 알려진	☐ 539) 할머니	☐ 569) 시기	☐ 599) 스스로
☐ 480) 산	☐ 510) 가능하다	☐ 540) 회의	☐ 570) 마치	☐ 600) 아기

451-600				
451) such	481) acid	511) ability	541) broadcast	571) flesh
452) age	482) however	512) insist	542) talk	572) yield
453) first of all	483) condition	513) child	543) talk	573) wish
454) believe	484) door	514) child	544) tree	574) strong
455) give birth	485) flower	515) turn	545) sleep	575) experience
456) information	486) step	516) turn	546) sleep	576) music
457) like	487) meantime	517) fire	547) paly	577) the best
458) draw	488) suddenly	518) resident	548) likewise	578) reveal
459) turn off	489) overstep	519) collect	549) walk	579) be ill
460) learn	490) wind	520) data	550) labor	580) less
461) poem	491) village	521) presence	551) past	581) rain
462) role	492) young	522) grade	552) contemporary	582) hometown
463) by	493) representative	523) newspaper	553) examine	583) surprised
464) behavior	494) chance	524) understand	554) spectacle	584) so many
465) behavior	495) direction	525) product	555) margin	585) cry
466) domestic	496) contest	526) field	556) untie	586) farmer
467) organ	497) voice	527) teacher	557) days	587) bank
468) entry	498) song	528) return	558) thing	588) wedding
469) worth	499) sea	529) level	559) first-hand	589) younger brother
470) value	500) tough	530) expression	560) individual	590) law
471) under	501) study	531) large	561) foot	591) novel
472) influence	502) study	532) young	562) writer	592) p.m.
473) come forward	503) move	533) simultaneous	563) effect	593) order
474) flow	504) effort	534) cloths	564) Buddhism	594) put in
475) deep	505) altogether	535) function	565) fast	595) gather
476) pear	506) older sister	536) moment	566) begin	596) citizen
477) ship	507) group	537) war	567) explain	597) chairman
478) stomach	508) group	538) dream	568) universe	598) quick
479) shape	509) known	539) grandma	569) period	599) by oneself
480) mountain	510) be possible	540) meeting	570) as if	600) baby

Final	K-word ㉜				
check	English ㉝				

K-word ㉖	English ㉗	K-word ㉘	K-word ㉙	English ㉚	K-word ㉛

Final	K-word ㉜			
check	English ㉝			

K-word ㉖	English ㉗	K-word ㉘	K-word ㉙	English ㉚	K-word ㉛

Final	K-word ㉜				
check	English ㉝				

K-word ㉖	English ㉗	K-word ㉘	K-word ㉙	English ㉚	K-word ㉛

Day1~6 List Study

Final	K-word ㉜				
check	English ㉝				

K-word ㉖	English ㉗	K-word ㉘	K-word ㉙	English ㉚	K-word ㉛

Final	K-word ㉜				
check	English ㉝				

K-word ㉖	English ㉗	K-word ㉘	K-word ㉙	English ㉚	K-word ㉛

	K-word	Pronounce	English	K-word ❶	Sentence example
601	아저씨	a-jeo-ssi	uncle		I live with my uncle.
602	옛날	yes-nal	old days		I miss the good old days.
603	이날	i-nal	this day		Meet again this day next year.
604	제대로	je-dae-ro	properly		We did the job properly.
605	달	dal	moon		The moon is shining.
606	달	dal	month		He waited for months for it.
607	던진다	deon-jin-da	toss		You always toss things.
608	참	cham	true		Distinguish between true and false.
609	공간	gong-gan	space		He needed space.
610	이곳	i-gos	this place		I love this place.
611	딸	ttal	daughter		Your daughter is cute.
612	마지막	ma-ji-mak	final		He passed the final test.
613	병원	byeong-won	hospital		Call the hospital.
614	자세	ja-se	posture		The child's posture is good.
615	강조한다	gang-jo-han-da	emphasize		His speech emphasizes the truth.
616	경찰	gyeong-chal	police		Call the police!
617	맡는다	mat-neun-da	undertake		He undertakes the project.
618	저녁	jeo-nyeok	evening		Have a nice evening.
619	한편	han-pyeon	meanwhile		Meanwhile, you should work.
620	그러면	geu-reo-myeon	if so		If so, I won't see you.

Final	K-word ❽				
check	English ❾				

K-word ❷	English ❸	K-word ❹	K-word ❺	English ❻	K-word ❼

	K-word	Pronounce	English	K-word ❶	Sentence example
621	기자	gi-ja	reporter		He is a reporter.
622	넓은	neolb-eun	wide		The house has a wide window.
623	시험	si-heom	exam		I failed the exam.
624	주로	ju-ro	usually		I usually sleep on Sundays.
625	면	myeon	sense		In this sense, he is correct.
626	통일	tong-il	unification		Unification lies in the time.
627	들어선다	deul-eo-seon-da	enter		They enter an expressway.
628	건강	geon-gang	health		Sport means health.
629	가까이	ga-kka-i	near		My house is near.
630	건물	geon-mul	building		This building is mine.
631	시설	si-seol	facility		This is not a research facility.
632	외국	oe-guk	foreign		I like foreign languages.
633	밑	mit	beneath		He buried it beneath a rock.
634	어른	eo-reun	adult		I'm an adult.
635	주변에	ju-byeon-e	around		What is around you?
636	대신	dae-sin	instead		Work instead of chatting.
637	원인	won-in	cause		What's the cause?
638	판다	pan-da	sell		She sells vegetables.
639	군	gun	county		Tom is a county clerk.
640	열심히	yeol-sim-hi	hard		Study hard.

Final	K-word ❽				
check	English ❾				

K-word ❷	English ❸	K-word ❹	K-word ❺	English ❻	K-word ❼

	K-word	Pronounce	English	K-word ❶	Sentence example
641	재산	jae-san	property		Tom has lots of property.
642	부모	bu-mo	parent		My parents are old.
643	약간	yak-gan	some		Some juice, please.
644	언어	eon-eo	language		I like foreign languages.
645	요구한다	yo-gu-han-da	ask for		People ask for food.
646	감독	gam-dok	coach		The coach supervises the players.
647	그날	geu-nal	that day		That day snowed .
648	자주	ja-ju	often		I often meet Mary.
649	약	yak	about		It costs about $10.
650	기간	gi-gan	span		She was ill in a span of a week.
651	담배	dam-bae	tobacco		The tobacco is bad for your health.
652	일으킨다	il-eu-kin-da	cause		He often causes problems.
653	할아버지	hal-a-beo-ji	grandfather		Hello, Grandfather.
654	조직	jo-jik	tissue		Your skin tissue is thin.
655	태어난다	tae-eo-nan-da	be born		Her baby is born now.
656	공장	gong-jang	factory		That factory makes toys.
657	벌써	beol-sseo	already		Are you already here?
658	즐긴다	jeul-gin-da	enjoy		He enjoys holidays.
659	지	ji	after		It is two days after he went home.
660	환자	hwan-ja	patient		The patient looked healthy.

		K-word ❷	English ❸	K-word ❹	K-word ❺	English ❻	K-word ❼
Final	K-word ❽						
check	English ❾						

	K-word	Pronounce	English	K-word ❶	Sentence example
661	사고	sa-go	accident		Accidents happen.
662	그래도	geu-rae-do	nonetheless		I like him nonetheless.
663	아무리	a-mu-ri	however		However bad it is···
664	맞춘다	maj-chun-da	adapt		They adapt to new surroundings.
665	쌀	ssal	rice		I like rice rather than bread.
666	일반적인	il-ban-jeok-in	general		That's a general idea.
667	재미있는	jae-mi-iss-neun	interesting		That looks an interesting book.
668	가르친다	ga-reu-chin-da	teach		He teaches English.
669	대화	dae-hwa	conversation		Tom overheard our conversation.
670	막는다	mak-neun-da	prevent		The system prevents hacking.
671	올해	ol-hae	this year		We marry this year.
672	형	hyeong	older brother		He is my older brother.
673	오빠	o-ppa	older brother		Mary, is he your older brother?
674	달리	dal-li	otherwise		I can't think otherwise.
675	붙인다	but-in-da	attach		Children attach pictures on the wall.
676	인물	in-mul	figure		He is a leading figure in Korea.
677	늘	neul	always		She always criticizes me.
678	항상	hang-sang	always		Always open.
679	모두	mo-du	in total		It's $10 in total.
680	전국	jeon-guk	whole country		The whole country is hot.

		K-word ❽				
Final						
check	English ❾					

K-word ❷	English ❸	K-word ❹	K-word ❺	English ❻	K-word ❼

	K-word	Pronounce	English	K-word ❶	Sentence example
681	도움	do-um	help		I need your help.
682	가정	ga-jeong	home		I love my home.
683	건다	geon-da	hang		I hang my coat on the chair.
684	빠진다	ppa-jin-da	fall out		The water falls out of the bathtub.
685	멀다	meol-da	be far		The sea is far from the house.
686	잠시	jam-si	a while		Wait a while.
687	농업	nong-eob	agriculture		It affects agriculture.
688	댄다	daen-da	touch		He touches her forehead.
689	의견	ui-gyeon	opinion		What's your opinion?
690	무대	mu-dae	stage		It is my stage.
691	벌인다	beol-in-da	stage		They stage a strike today.
692	사진	sa-jin	photo		I like a black-and-white photo.
693	주장	ju-jang	argument		His argument was transferred.
694	표현한다	pyo-hyeon-han-da	express		He often expresses his feelings.
695	인한다	in-han-da	be caused		Accidents are caused by carelessness.
696	이상한	i-sang-han	strange		There comes a strange noise.
697	붙는다	but-neun-da	stick to		My clothes stick to my body.
698	아마	a-ma	maybe		Maybe you'll succeed.
699	잇는다	is-neun-da	connect		Bus runs connect the cities.
700	경기	gyeong-gi	economy		The economy is in recession.

Final	K-word ❽				
check	English ❾				

K-word ❷	English ❸	K-word ❹	K-word ❺	English ❻	K-word ❼

	K-word	English		K-word	English
601	아저씨	I live with my _____.	621	기자	He is a _____.
602	옛날	I miss the good _____.	622	넓은	The house has a _____ window.
603	이날	Meet again _____ next year.	623	시험	I failed the _____.
604	제대로	We did the job _____.	624	주로	I _____ sleep on Sundays.
605	달	The _____ is shining.	625	면	In this _____, he is correct.
606	달	He waited for _____ for it.	626	통일	_____ lies in the time.
607	던진다	You always _____ things.	627	들어선다	They _____ an expressway.
608	참	Distinguish between _____ and false.	628	건강	Sport means _____.
609	공간	He needed _____.	629	가까이	My house is _____.
610	이곳	I love _____.	630	건물	This _____ is mine.
611	딸	Your _____ is cute.	631	시설	This is not a research _____.
612	마지막	He passed the _____ test.	632	외국	I like _____ languages.
613	병원	Call the _____.	633	밑	He buried it _____ a rock.
614	자세	The child's _____ is good.	634	어른	I'm an _____.
615	강조한다	His speech _____ the truth.	635	주변에	What is _____ you?
616	경찰	Call the _____!	636	대신	Work _____ of chatting.
617	맡는다	He _____ the project.	637	원인	What's the _____?
618	저녁	Have a nice _____.	638	판다	She _____ vegetables.
619	한편	_____, you should work.	639	군	Tom is a _____ clerk.
620	그러면	_____, I won't see you.	640	열심히	Study _____.

601) uncle   602) old days   603) this day   604) properly   605) moon   606) months   607) toss   608) true
609) space   610) this place   611) daughter   612) final   613) hospital   614) posture   615) emphasizes   616) police
617) undertakes   618) evening   619) Meanwhile   620) If so   621) reporter   622) wide   623) exam   624) usually
625) sense   626) Unification   627) enter   628) health   629) near   630) building   631) facility   632) foreign
633) beneath   634) adult   635) around   636) instead   637) cause   638) sells   639) county   640) hard

	K-word	English		K-word	English
641	재산	Tom has lots of _____.	661	사고	_____ happen.
642	부모	My _____ are old.	662	그래도	I like him _____.
643	약간	_____ juice, please.	663	아무리	_____ bad it is…
644	언어	I like foreign _____.	664	맞춘다	They _____ to new surroundings.
645	요구한다	People _____ food.	665	쌀	I like _____ rather than bread.
646	감독	The _____ supervises the players.	666	일반적인	That's a _____ idea.
647	그날	_____ snowed .	667	재미있는	That looks an _____ book.
648	자주	I _____ meet Mary.	668	가르친다	He _____ English.
649	약	It costs _____ $10.	669	대화	Tom overheard our _____.
650	기간	She was ill in a _____ of a week.	670	막는다	The system _____ hacking.
651	담배	The _____ is bad for your health.	671	올해	We marry _____.
652	일으킨다	He often _____ problems.	672	형	He is my _____.
653	할아버지	Hello, _____.	673	오빠	Mary, is he your _____?
654	조직	Your skin _____ is thin.	674	달리	I can't think _____.
655	태어난다	Her baby is _____ now.	675	붙인다	Children _____ pictures on the wall.
656	공장	That _____ makes toys.	676	인물	He is a leading _____ in Korea.
657	벌써	Are you _____ here?	677	늘	She _____ criticizes me.
658	즐긴다	He _____ holidays.	678	항상	_____ open.
659	지	It is two days _____ he went home.	679	모두	It's $10 _____.
660	환자	The _____ looked healthy.	680	전국	The _____ is hot.

641) property   642) parents   643) Some   644) languages   645) ask for   646) coach   647) That day   648) often
649) about   650) span   651) tobacco   652) causes   653) Grandfather   654) tissue   655) born   656) factory
657) already   658) enjoys   659) after   660) patient   661) Accidents   662) nonetheless   663) However   664) adapt
665) rice   666) general   667) interesting   668) teaches   669) conversation   670) prevents   671) this year   672) older brother
673) older brother   674) otherwise   675) attach   676) figure   677) always   678) Always   679) in total   680) whole country

	K-word	English
681	도움	I need your ....
682	가정	I love my ....
683	건다	I .... my coat on the chair.
684	빠진다	The water .... out of the bathtub.
685	멀다	The sea is .... from the house.
686	잠시	Wait a ....
687	농업	It affects ....
688	댄다	He .... her forehead.
689	의견	What's your .... ?
690	무대	It is my ....
691	벌인다	They .... a strike today.
692	사진	I like a black-and-white ....
693	주장	His .... was transferred.
694	표현한다	He often .... his feelings.
695	인한다	Accidents are .... by carelessness.
696	이상한	There comes a .... noise.
697	붙는다	My clothes .... to my body.
698	아마	.... you'll succeed.
699	잇는다	Bus runs .... the cities.
700	경기	The .... is in recession.

King Sejong

– The 4th king of Joseon Dynasty

King Sejong was born in 1397.
His 32 year reign marked great achievements.
Hangeul, created by King Sejong,
has been used as a common script for
the Republic of Korea and North Korea.

681) help	682) home	683) hang	684) falls
685) far	686) while	687) agriculture	688) touches
689) opinion	690) stage	691) stage	692) photo
693) argument	694) expresses	695) caused	696) strange
697) stick to	698) Maybe	699) connect	700) economy

Day7 Review Study

Final	K-word ⑯				
check	English ⑰				

K-word ⑩	English ⑪	K-word ⑫	K-word ⑬	English ⑭	K-word ⑮

	Write K-word in			Write K-word in ....
601	I live with my uncle. 나는 나의 .... 와 살고 있다.	614		The child's posture is good. 그 아이의 .... 는 좋다.
602	I miss the good old days. 나는 좋았던 .... 을 그리워한다.	615		His speech emphasizes the truth. 그의 연설은 진실을 ....
603	Meet again this day next year. 내년 .... 에 다시 만나자.	616		Call the police! .... 을 불러라!
604	We did the job properly. 우리는 그 일을 .... 했다.	617		He undertakes the project. 그가 그 프로젝트를 ....
605	The moon is shining. .... 이 빛나고 있다.	618		Have a nice evening. 좋은 .... 보내세요.
606	He waited for months for it. 그는 그것을 위해 몇 .... 기다렸다.	619		Meanwhile, you should work. .... , 너는 일 해야 한다.
607	You always toss things. 너는 항상 물건들을	620		If so, I won't see you. .... , 나는 당신을 보지 않겠다.
608	Distinguish between true and false. .... 과 거짓을 구분해라.	621		He is a reporter. 그는 .... 다.
609	He needed space. 그는 .... 이 필요했다.	622		The house has a wide window. 그 집은 .... 창을 가지고 있다.
610	I love this place. 나는 .... 을 좋아한다.	623		I failed the exam. 나는 .... 에서 떨어졌다.
611	Your daughter is cute. 당신의 .... 은 귀엽다.	624		I usually sleep on Sundays. 나는 일요일에 .... 잔다.
612	He passed the final test. 그는 .... 시험을 통과했다.	625		In this sense, he is correct. 이런 .... 에서, 그는 옳다.
613	Call the hospital. .... 에 전화해.			

601) 아저씨　　602) 옛날　　603) 이날　　604) 제대로　　605) 달　　606) 달　　607) 던진다　　608) 참　　609) 공간
610) 이곳　　611) 딸　　612) 마지막　　613) 병원　　614) 자세　　615) 강조한다　　616) 경찰　　617) 맡는다　　618) 저녁
619) 한편　　620) 그러면　　621) 기자　　622) 넓은　　623) 시험　　624) 주로　　625) 면

	K-word	pronounce	English		K-word	pronounce	English
601	나는	na-neun	I		통과했다	tong-gwa-haess-da	passed
	나의	na-ui	my	613	병원에	byeong-won-e	the hospital
	아저씨와	a-jeo-ssi-wa	with uncle		전화해	jeon-hwa-hae	call
	살고 있다	sal-go-iss-da	live	614	그 아이의	geu a-i-ui	the child's
602	나는	na-neun	I		자세는	ja-se-neun	posture
	좋았던	joh-ass-deon	good		좋다	joh-da	is good
	옛날을	yes-nal-eul	old days	615	그의	geu-ui	his
	그리워한다	geu-ri-wo-han-da	miss		연설은	yeon-seol-eun	speech
603	내년	nae-nyeon	next year		진실을	jin-sil-eul	the truth
	이날에	i-nal-e	this day		강조한다	gang-jo-han-da	emphasize
	다시	da-si	again	616	경찰을	gyeong-chal-eul	the police
	만나자	man-na-ja	meet		불러라	bul-leo-ra	call
604	우리는	u-ri-neun	we	617	그가	geu-ga	he
	그 일을	geu il-eul	the job		그	geu	the
	제대로	je-dae-ro	properly		프로젝트를	peu-ro-jek-teu-reul	project
	했다	haess-da	did		맡는다	mat-neun-da	undertake
605	달이	dal-i	the moon	618	좋은	joh-eun	nice
	빛나고 있다	bicc-na-go iss-da	is shinning		저녁	jeo-nyeok	evening
606	그는	geu-neun	he		보내세요	bo-nae-se-yo	have
	그것을	geu-geos-eul	it	619	한편	han-pyeon	meanwhile
	위해	wi-hae	for		너는	neo-neun	you
	몇 달	myeocc dal	for months		일 해야한다	il hae-ya-han-da	should work
	기다렸다	gi-da-ryeoss-da	waited	620	그러면	geu-reo-myeon	if so
607	너는	neo-neun	you		나는	na-neun	I
	항상	hang-sang	always		당신을	dang-sin-eul	you
	물건들을	mul-geon-deul-eul	things		만나지 않겠다	man-na-ji anh-gess-da	won't see
	던진다	deon-jin-da	toss	621	그는	geu-neun	he
608	참과	cham-gwa	true and		기자다	gi-ja-da	is a reporter
	거짓을	geo-jis-eul	false	622	그 집은	geu jib-eun	the house
	구분해라	gu-bun-hae-ra	distinguish between		넓은	neolb-eun	wide
609	그는	geu-neun	he		창을	chang-eul	window
	공간이	gong-gan-i	space		가지고 있다	ga-ji-go iss-da	has
	필요했다	pil-yo-haess-da	needed	623	나는	na-neun	I
610	나는	na-neun	I		시험에	si-heom-e	the exam
	이곳을	i-gos-eul	this place		떨어졌다	tteol-eo-jyeoss-da	failed
	좋아한다	joh-a-han-da	love	624	나는	na-neun	I
611	당신의	dang-sin-ui	your		일요일에	il-yo-il-e	on Sundays
	딸은	ttal-eun	daughter		주로	ju-ro	usually
	귀엽다	gwi-yeob-da	is cute		잔다	jan-da	sleep
612	그는	geu-neun	he	625	이런 면에서	i-reon myeon-e-seo	in this sense
	마지막	ma-ji-mak	final		그는	geu-neun	he
	시험을	si-heom-eul	test		옳다	olh-da	is correct

	Write K-word in		Write K-word in ....
626	Unification lies in the time. .... 은 시간에 달려있다.	639	Tom is a county clerk. 톰은 .... 서기다.
627	They enter an expressway. 그들이 고속도로에	640	Study hard. .... 공부해라.
628	Sport means health. 스포츠는 .... 을 의미한다.	641	Tom has lots of property. 톰은 많은 .... 을 가지고 있다.
629	My house is near. 나의 집은 .... 에 있다.	642	My parents are old. 나의 .... 님은 늙었다.
630	This building is mine. 이 .... 은 나의 것이다.	643	Some juice, please. 주스 .... 주세요.
631	This is not a research facility. 이것은 연구 .... 이 아닙니다.	644	I like foreign languages. 나는 외국 .... 를 좋아한다.
632	I like foreign languages. 나는 .... 언어가 좋다.	645	People ask for food. 사람들이 음식을 ....
633	He buried it beneath a rock. 그는 그것을 바위 .... 에 묻었다.	646	The coach supervises the players. .... 이 선수들을 감독한다.
634	I'm an adult. 나는 .... 이다.	647	That day snowed . ... 눈이 왔다.
635	What is around you? 네 .... 무엇이 있니?	648	I often meet Mary. 나는 .... 메리를 만난다.
636	Work instead of chatting. 떠드는 .... 일하세요.	649	It costs about $10. 그것은 .... 10달러 비용이다.
637	What's the cause? .... 이 무엇인가요?	650	She was ill in a span of a week. 그녀는 일주일 .... 동안 아팠다.
638	She sells vegetables. 그녀는 야채를		

626) 통일　　627) 들어선다　　628) 건강　　629) 가까이　　630) 건물　　631) 시설　　632) 외국　　633) 밑　　634) 어른
635) 주변에　　636) 대신　　637) 원인　　638) 판다　　639) 군　　640) 열심히　　641) 재산　　642) 부모　　643) 약간
644) 언어　　645) 요구한다　　646) 감독　　647) 그날　　648) 자주　　649) 약　　650) 기간

Sentence Words(2)

	K-word	pronounce	English		K-word	pronounce	English
626	통일은	tong-il-eun	unification	638	그녀는	geu-nyeo-neun	she
	시간에	si-gan-e	the time		야채를	ya-chae-reul	vegetables
	달려있다	dal-lyeo-iss-da	lie in		판다	pan-da	sell
627	그들이	geu-deul-i	they	639	톰은	tom-eun	Tom
	고속도로에	go-sok-do-ro-e	an expressway		군 서기다	gun seo-gi-da	is a county clerk
	들어선다	deul-eo-seon-da	enter	640	열심히	yeol-sim-hi	hard
628	스포츠는	seu-po-cheu-neun	sport		공부해라	gong-bu-hae-ra	study
	건강을	geon-gang-eul	health	641	톰은	tom-eun	Tom
	의미한다	ui-mi-han-da	means		많은	manh-eun	lots of
629	나의	na-ui	my		재산을	jae-san-eul	property
	집은	jib-eun	house		가지고 있다	ga-ji-go iss-da	has
	가까이에	ga-kka-i-e	near	642	나의	na-ui	my
	있다	iss-da	is		부모님은	bu-mo-nim-eun	parents
630	이	i	this		늙었다	neulk-eoss-da	are old
	건물은	geon-mul-eun	building	643	주스	ju-seu	juice
	나의 것	na-ui geos	mine		약간	yak-gan	some
	이다	i-da	is		주세요	ju-se-yo	please
631	이것은	i-geos-eun	this	644	나는	na-neun	I
	연구	yeon-gu	research		외국	oe-guk	foreign
	시설이	si-seol-i	facility		언어를	eon-eo-reul	language
	아닙니다	a-nib-ni-da	is not		좋아한다	joh-a-han-da	like
632	나는	na-neun	I	645	사람들이	sa-ram-deul-i	people
	외국	oe-guk	foreign		음식을	eum-sik-eul	food
	언어가	eon-eo-ga	language		요구한다	yo-gu-han-da	ask for
	좋다	joh-da	like	646	감독이	gam-dok-i	the coach
633	그는	geu-neun	he		선수들을	seon-su-deul-eul	the players
	그것을	geu-geos-eul	it		감독한다	gam-dok-han-da	supervise
	바위	ba-wi	a rock	647	그날	geu-nal	that day
	밑에	mit-e	beneath		눈이 왔다	nun-i wass-da	snowed
	묻었다	mud-eoss-da	buried	648	나는	na-neun	I
634	나는	na-neun	I		자주	ja-ju	often
	어른	eo-reun	an adult		메리를	me-ri-reul	Mary
	이다	i-da	am		만난다	man-nan-da	meet
635	네	ne	you	649	그것은	geu-geos-eun	it
	주변에	ju-byeon-e	around		약	yak	about
	무엇이	mu-eos-i	what		10 달러	sib-dal-leo	$10
	있니?	iss-ni?	is?		비용이다	bi-yong-i-da	cost
636	떠드는	tteo-deu-neun	chatting	650	그녀는	geu-nyeo-neun	she
	대신	dae-sin	instead of		일주일	il-ju-il	a week
	일 하세요	il-ha-se-yo	work		기간 동안	gi-gan dong-an	in a span of
637	원인이	won-in-i	the cause		아팠다	a-pass-da	was ill
	무엇인가요?	mu-eos-in-ga-yo?	what's?				

Day7 Sentence(3)

	Write K-word in		Write K-word in ....
651	The tobacco is bad for your health. ....는 건강에 해롭다.	664	They adapt to new surroundings. 그들은 새로운 환경에 ....
652	He often causes problems. 그는 종종 문제를	665	I like rice rather than bread. 나는 빵보다는 ....을 좋아한다.
653	Hello, Grandfather. 안녕 하세요	666	That's a general idea. 그것은 .... 생각이다.
654	Your skin tissue is thin. 너의 피부 ....은 얇다.	667	That looks an interesting book. 저것은 .... 책 같다.
655	Her baby is born now. 그녀의 아기가 지금	668	He teaches English. 그는 영어를 ....
656	That factory makes toys. 저 ....은 장난감을 만든다.	669	Tom overheard our conversation. 톰은 우리의 ....를 엿들었다.
657	Are you already here? .... 오셨습니까?	670	The system prevents hacking. 그 시스템은 해킹을 ....
658	He enjoys holidays. 그는 휴가를	671	We marry this year. 우리는 .... 결혼한다.
659	It is two days after he went home. 그가 집에 간 .... 2일 되었다.	672	He is my older brother. 그는 나의 ....이다.
660	The patient looked healthy. 그 ....는 건강해 보였다.	673	Mary, is he your older brother? 메리야, 그가 너의 ....니?
661	Accidents happen. ....는 일어난다.	674	I can't think otherwise. 나는 .... 생각할 수 없다.
662	I like him nonetheless. .... 나는 그를 좋아한다.	675	Children attach pictures on the wall. 아이들은 그림을 벽에 ....
663	However bad it is… 그것이 .... 나빠도…		

651) 담배　652) 일으킨다　653) 할아버지　654) 조직　655) 태어난다　656) 공장　657) 벌써　658) 즐긴다　659) 지
660) 환자　661) 사고　662) 그래도　663) 아무리　664) 맞춘다　665) 쌀　666) 일반적인　667) 재미있는　668) 가르친다
669) 대화　670) 막는다　671) 올해　672) 형　673) 오빠　674) 달리　675) 붙인다

Sentence Words(3)

	K-word	pronounce	English		K-word	pronounce	English
651	담배는	dam-bae-neun	the tobacco		새로운	sae-ro-un	new
	건강에	geon-gang-e	for your health		환경에	hwan-gyeong-e	surroundings
	해롭다	hae-rob-da	is bad		맞춘다	maj-chun-da	adapt to
652	그는	geu-neun	he	665	나는	na-neun	I
	종종	jong-jong	often		빵	ppang	the bread
	문제를	mun-je-reul	problems		보다는	bo-da-neun	rather than
	일으킨다	il-eu-kin-da	cause		쌀을	ssal-eul	rice
653	안녕하세요	an-nyeong-ha-se-yo	hello		좋아한다	joh-a-han-da	like
	할아버지	hal-a-beo-ji	grandfather	666	그것은	geu-geos-eun	That
654	너의 피부	neo-ui pi-bu	your skin		일반적인	il-ban-jeok-in	general
	조직은	jo-jik-eun	tissue		생각이다	saeng-gak-i-da	is an idea
	얇다	yalb-da	is thin	667	저것은	jeo-geos-eun	that
655	그녀의	geu-nyeo-ui	her		재미있는	jae-mi-iss-neun	interesting
	아기가	a-gi-ga	baby		책	chaek	book
	지금	ji-geum	now		같다	gat-da	look
	태어난다	tae-eo-nan-da	is born	668	그는	geu-neun	he
656	저	jeo	that		영어를	yeong-eo-reul	English
	공장은	gong-jang-eun	factory		가르친다	ga-reu-chin-da	teach
	장난감을	jang-nan-gam-eul	toys	669	톰은	tom-eun	Tom
	만든다	man-deun-da	make		우리의	u-ri-ui	our
657	벌써	beol-sseo	already		대화를	dae-hwa-reul	conversation
	오셨습니까?	o-syeoss-seub-ni-kka?	are you here?		엿들었다	yeos-deul-eoss-da	overheard
658	그는	geu-neun	he	670	그 시스템은	geu si-seu-tem-eun	the system
	휴가를	hyu-ga-reul	holidays		해킹을	hae-king-eul	hacking
	즐긴다	jeul-gin-da	enjoy		막는다	mak-neun-da	prevent
659	그가	geu-ga	he	671	우리는	u-ri-neun	we
	집에	jib-e	home		올 해	ol hae	this year
	간 지	gan ji	after went		결혼한다	gyeol-hon-han-da	marry
	2일	i-il	two days	672	그는	geu-neun	he
	되었다	doe-eoss-da	it is		나의	na-ui	my
660	그 환자는	geu hwan-ja-neun	the patient		형이다	hyeong-i-da	older brother
	건강해	geon-gang-hae	health	673	메리야	me-ri-ya	Mary
	보였다	bo-yeoss-da	looked		그가	geu-ga	he
661	사고는	sa-go-neun	accidents		너의	neo-ui	your
	일어난다	il-eo-nan-da	happen		오빠니?	o-ppa-ni?	is older brother?
662	그래도	geu-rae-do	nonetheless	674	나는	na-neun	I
	나는	na-neun	I		달리	dal-li	otherwise
	그를	geu-reul	him		생각할 수 없다	saeng-gak-hal su eobs-da	can't think
	좋아한다	joh-a-han-da	like	675	아이들은	a-i-deul-eun	children
663	그것이	geu-geos-i	it		그림을	geu-rim-eul	pictures
	아무리 나빠도	a-mu-ri na-ppa-do	however bad is		벽에	byeok-e	on the wall
664	그들은	geu-deul-eun	they		붙인다	but-in-da	attach

	Write K-word in			Write K-word in ....
676	He is a leading figure in Korea. 그는 한국에서 주요한 .... 이다.	689	What's your opinion? 너의 .... 은 무엇이니?
677	She always criticizes me. 그녀는 .... 나를 비난한다.	690	It is my stage. 그것은 나의 .... 이다.
678	Always open. .... 열려있다.	691	They stage a strike today. 그들은 오늘 파업을 ....
679	It's $10 in total. .... 10달러입니다.	692	I like a black-and-white photo. 나는 흑백 .... 을 좋아한다.
680	The whole country is hot. .... 이 덥다.	693	His argument was transferred. 그의 .... 은 옳았다.
681	I need your help. 나는 너의 .... 이 필요하다.	694	He often expresses his feelings. 그는 종종 감정을 ....
682	I love my home. 나는 내 .... 을 사랑한다.	695	Accidents are caused by carelessness. 사고는 부주의로 ....
683	I hang my coat on the chair. 나는 코트를 의자에	696	There comes a strange noise. .... 소리가 난다.
684	The water falls out of the bathtub. 물이 욕조에서	697	My clothes stick to my body. 내 옷이 몸에 ....
685	The sea is far from the house. 바다는 그 집에서	698	Maybe you'll succeed. .... 너는 성공할 것이다.
686	Wait a while. .... 만 기다려주세요.	699	Bus runs connect the cities. 버스운행이 그 도시들을 ....
687	It affects agriculture. 그것은 .... 에 영향을 준다.	700	The economy is in recession. .... 가 불황에 있다.
688	He touches her forehead. 그가 그녀의 이마에 손을		

676) 인물　　677) 늘　　678) 항상　　679) 모두　　680) 전국　　681) 도움　　682) 가정　　683) 건다　　684) 빠진다
685) 멀다　　686) 잠시　　687) 농업　　688) 댄다　　689) 의견　　690) 무대　　691) 벌인다　　692) 사진　　693) 주장
694) 표현한다　　695) 인한다　　696) 이상한　　697) 붙는다　　698) 아마　　699) 잇는다　　700) 경기

	K-word	pronounce	English		K-word	pronounce	English
676	그는	geu-neun	he	689	너의	neo-ui	your
	한국에서	han-guk-e-seo	in Korea		의견은	ui-gyeon-eun	opinion
	주요한	ju-yo-han	leading		무엇이니?	mu-eos-i-ni?	what's?
	인물	in-mul	figure	690	그것은	geu-geos-eun	it
	이다	i-da	is		나의	na-ui	my
677	그녀는	geu-nyeo-neun	she		무대	mu-dae	stage
	늘	neul	always		이다	i-da	is
	나를	na-reul	me	691	그들은	geu-deul-eun	they
	비난한다	bi-nan-han-da	criticize		오늘	o-neul	today
678	항상	hang-sang	always		파업을	pa-eob-eul	a strike
	열려있다	yeol-lyeo-iss-da	open		벌인다	beol-in-da	stage
679	모두	mo-du	in total	692	나는	na-neun	I
	10달러	sib-dal-leo	$10		흑백	heuk-baek	black-and-white
	입니다	ib-ni-da	it's		사진을	sa-jin-eul	photo
680	전국이	jeon-guk-i	the whole country		좋아한다	joh-a-han-da	like
	덥다	deob-da	is hot	693	그의	geu-ui	his
681	나는	na-neun	I		주장은	ju-jang-eun	argument
	너의	neo-ui	your		옳았다	olm-ass-da	was transferred
	도움이	do-um-i	help	694	그는	geu-neun	he
	필요하다	pil-yo-ha-da	need		종종	jong-jong	often
682	나는	na-neun	I		감정을	gam-jeong-eul	his feelings
	내	nae	my		표현한다	pyo-hyeon-han-da	express
	가정을	ga-jeong-eul	home	695	사고는	sa-go-neun	accidents
	사랑한다	sa-rang-han-da	love		부주의로	bu-ju-ui-ro	by carelessness
683	나는	na-neun	I		인한다	in-han-da	are caused
	코트를	ko-teu-reul	my coat	696	이상한 소리가	i-sang-han so-ri-ga	a strange sound
	의자에	ui-ja-e	on the chair		난다	nan-da	there comes
	건다	geon-da	hang	697	내	nae	my
684	물이	mul-i	the water		옷이	os-i	clothes
	욕조에서	yok-jo-e-seo	of the bathtub		몸에	mom-e	to my body
	빠진다	ppa-jin-da	fall out		붙는다	but-neun-da	stick
685	바다는	ba-da-neun	the sea	698	아마	a-ma	maybe
	그 집에서	geu jib-e-seo	from the house		너는	neo-neun	you
	멀다	meol-da	is far		성공 할 것이다	seong-gong hal geos-i-da	will succeed
686	잠시만	jam-si-man	a while	699	버스 운행이	beo-seu un-haeng-i	bus runs
	기다려주세요	gi-da-ryeo-ju-se-yo	wait		그 도시들을	geu do-si-deul-eul	the cities
687	그것은	geu-geos-eun	it		잇는다	is-neun-da	connect
	농업에	nong-eob-e	agriculture	700	경기가	gyeong-gi-ga	the economy
	영향을 준다	yeong-hyang-eul jun-da	affect		불황에	bul-hwang-e	in recession
688	그가	geu-ga	he		있다	iss-da	is
	그녀의	geu-nyeo-ui	her				
	이마에	i-ma-e	forehead				
	손을 댄다	son-eul daen-da	touch				

Day7 Sentence Study

Final	K-word ㉔				
check	English ㉕				

K-word ⑱	English ⑲	K-word ⑳	K-word ㉑	English ㉒	K-word ㉓

1-150				
☐ 1) 것	☐ 31) 드린다	☐ 61) 집	☐ 91) 파악하고 있다	☐ 121) 지닌다
☐ 2) 한다	☐ 32) 대한다	☐ 62) 나온다	☐ 92) 자신	☐ 122) 가진다
☐ 3) 된다	☐ 33) 간다	☐ 63) 따른다	☐ 93) 문화	☐ 123) 갖추고 있다
☐ 4) 수	☐ 34) 다닌다	☐ 64) 그리고	☐ 94) 원	☐ 124) 당한다
☐ 5) 수	☐ 35) 년	☐ 65) 및	☐ 95) 생각	☐ 125) 함께
☐ 6) 길	☐ 36) 한	☐ 66) 그때	☐ 96) 명	☐ 126) 아이
☐ 7) 쪽	☐ 37) 말	☐ 67) 그럼	☐ 97) 통한다	☐ 127) 지나간다
☐ 8) 방식	☐ 38) 일	☐ 68) 문제	☐ 98) 소리	☐ 128) 많이
☐ 9) 점	☐ 39) 일	☐ 69) 그런	☐ 99) 다시	☐ 129) 훨씬
☐ 10) 점	☐ 40) 일 한다	☐ 70) 산다	☐ 100) 다른	☐ 130) 시간
☐ 11) 나	☐ 41) 작품	☐ 71) 산다	☐ 101) 다르다	☐ 131) 너
☐ 12) 내	☐ 42) 작업	☐ 72) 지낸다	☐ 102) 여자	☐ 132) 당신
☐ 13) 그	☐ 43) 직장	☐ 73) 저	☐ 103) 소녀	☐ 133) 인간
☐ 14) 없다	☐ 44) 때문	☐ 74) 생각한다	☐ 104) 개	☐ 134) 사실
☐ 15) 않다	☐ 45) 말한다	☐ 75) 모른다	☐ 105) 그 정도	☐ 135) 과연
☐ 16) 말고	☐ 46) 위하여	☐ 76) 속	☐ 106) 뒤	☐ 136) 난다
☐ 17) 아니다	☐ 47) 그러나	☐ 77) 만든다	☐ 107) 듣는다	☐ 137) 자란다
☐ 18) 않는다	☐ 48) 온다	☐ 78) 삼는다	☐ 108) 다	☐ 138) 어머니
☐ 19) 사람	☐ 49) 안다	☐ 79) 시킨다	☐ 109) 좀	☐ 139) 엄마
☐ 20) 국민	☐ 50) 씨	☐ 80) 두	☐ 110) 조금	☐ 140) 눈
☐ 21) 우리	☐ 51) 그렇다	☐ 81) 둘	☐ 111) 든다	☐ 141) 눈
☐ 22) 이	☐ 52) 큰	☐ 82) 앞	☐ 112) 키운다	☐ 142) 뭐
☐ 23) 이	☐ 53) 크다	☐ 83) 경우	☐ 113) 올린다	☐ 143) 무엇
☐ 24) 이런	☐ 54) 또	☐ 84) 중	☐ 114) 기른다	☐ 144) 무슨
☐ 25) 이것	☐ 55) 사회	☐ 85) 중	☐ 115) 싶다	☐ 145) 시대
☐ 26) 이거	☐ 56) 안에	☐ 86) 동안에	☐ 116) 보인다	☐ 146) 다음
☐ 27) 보다	☐ 57) 좋은	☐ 87) 어떤	☐ 117) 표정	☐ 147) 이러하다
☐ 28) 본다	☐ 58) 더	☐ 88) 잘	☐ 118) 모습	☐ 148) 누구
☐ 29) 같다	☐ 59) 받는다	☐ 89) 그녀	☐ 119) 가지고 있다	☐ 149) 전
☐ 30) 준다	☐ 60) 그것	☐ 90) 먹는다	☐ 120) 갖고있다	☐ 150) 곳

		1-150		
1) thing	31) give	61) house	91) grasp	121) have
2) do	32) treat	62) come out	92) self	122) have
3) become	33) go	63) obey	93) culture	123) have
4) number	34) go	64) and	94) ₩	124) get p.p
5) way	35) year	65) and	95) thought	125) with
6) way	36) one	66) then	96) famous	126) kid
7) way	37) word	67) then	97) make sense	127) pass by
8) way	38) day	68) problem	98) sound	128) much
9) way	39) work	69) such	99) again	129) much ~er
10) store	40) work	70) buy	100) different	130) time
11) I	41) work	71) live	101) different	131) you
12) I	42) work	72) live	102) girl	132) you
13) he	43) job	73) um	103) girl	133) human
14) not have	44) because of	74) think	104) dog	134) in fact
15) not	45) speak	75) don't know	105) that much	135) indeed
16) not	46) for	76) inside	106) back	136) grow
17) not	47) but	77) make	107) hear	137) grow
18) do not	48) come	78) make	108) all	138) mother
19) people	49) know	79) make	109) a little	139) mom
20) people	50) family name	80) two	110) a little	140) eye
21) we	51) right	81) two	111) pick up	141) snow
22) tooth	52) big	82) front	112) raise	142) what
23) this	53) big	83) case	113) raise	143) what
24) this	54) once again	84) monk	114) raise	144) what
25) this	55) society	85) during	115) want	145) era
26) this	56) in	86) during	116) look	146) next
27) than	57) good	87) any	117) look	147) like this
28) see	58) more	88) well	118) appearance	148) who
29) same	59) receive	89) she	119) have	149) all
30) give	60) it	90) eat	120) have	150) place

Day1~7 List (2)

151–300				
☐ 151) 자리	☐ 181) 날	☐ 211) 인생	☐ 241) 못	☐ 271) 짓는다
☐ 152) 여러	☐ 182) 여기	☐ 212) 지금	☐ 242) 못	☐ 272) 또한
☐ 153) 많은	☐ 183) 여성	☐ 213) 뿐	☐ 243) 못한다	☐ 273) 까닭
☐ 154) 하나	☐ 184) 친구	☐ 214) 다만	☐ 244) 읽는다	☐ 274) 이유
☐ 155) 세계	☐ 185) 마음	☐ 215) 만	☐ 245) 이제	☐ 275) 또는
☐ 156) 세상	☐ 186) 관계	☐ 216) 사이에	☐ 246) 결과	☐ 276) 혹은
☐ 157) 버린다	☐ 187) 아버지	☐ 217) 방법	☐ 247) 내용	☐ 277) 필요하다
☐ 158) 위	☐ 188) 남자	☐ 218) 새롭다	☐ 248) 물론	☐ 278) 글
☐ 159) 운동	☐ 189) 남성	☐ 219) 새	☐ 249) 책	☐ 279) 생긴다
☐ 160) 학교	☐ 190) 어디	☐ 220) 우리나라	☐ 250) 일어난다	☐ 280) 남편
☐ 161) 자기	☐ 191) 몸	☐ 221) 앉는다	☐ 251) 시장	☐ 281) 밖
☐ 162) 가장	☐ 192) 얼굴	☐ 222) 처음의	☐ 252) 넣는다	☐ 282) 작은
☐ 163) 제일	☐ 193) 들어간다	☐ 223) 초기	☐ 253) 중요한	☐ 283) 탄다
☐ 164) 대부분	☐ 194) 들어온다	☐ 224) 손	☐ 254) 느낀다	☐ 284) 대학
☐ 165) 대통령	☐ 195) 왜	☐ 225) 몇	☐ 255) 어려운	☐ 285) 상황
☐ 166) 가지	☐ 196) 나타난다	☐ 226) 과정	☐ 256) 힘	☐ 286) 가운데
☐ 167) 시작한다	☐ 197) 말아라	☐ 227) 찾는다	☐ 257) 너무	☐ 287) 보낸다
☐ 168) 바로	☐ 198) 지역	☐ 228) 특히	☐ 258) 부른다	☐ 288) 즉
☐ 169) 어느	☐ 199) 물	☐ 229) 도시	☐ 259) 의미	☐ 289) 따라서
☐ 170) 그래서	☐ 200) 만난다	☐ 230) 이상	☐ 260) 뜻	☐ 290) 상태
☐ 171) 그러니까	☐ 201) 낸다	☐ 231) 이야기	☐ 261) 밝힌다	☐ 291) 이후
☐ 172) 정부	☐ 202) 쓴다	☐ 232) 얘기	☐ 262) 죽는다	☐ 292) 당시
☐ 173) 모든	☐ 203) 쓴다	☐ 233) 교육	☐ 263) 이미	☐ 293) 문학
☐ 174) 번	☐ 204) 사용한다	☐ 234) 경제	☐ 264) 정치	☐ 294) 더욱
☐ 175) 그거	☐ 205) 없이	☐ 235) 아직	☐ 265) 학생	☐ 295) 아주
☐ 176) 돈	☐ 206) 이번	☐ 236) 잡는다	☐ 266) 연구	☐ 296) 매우
☐ 177) 국가	☐ 207) 이때	☐ 237) 같이	☐ 267) 이름	☐ 297) 지방
☐ 178) 나라	☐ 208) 생활	☐ 238) 선생님	☐ 268) 내린다	☐ 298) 밤
☐ 179) 그런데	☐ 209) 삶	☐ 239) 예술	☐ 269) 사건	☐ 299) 높은
☐ 180) 근데	☐ 210) 생명	☐ 240) 일어선다	☐ 270) 쉬운	☐ 300) 최근

151-300				
151) place	181) day	211) life	241) nail	271) build
152) several	182) here	212) now	242) can't	272) also
153) many	183) female	213) only	243) can't do	273) reason
154) one	184) friend	214) only	244) read	274) reason
155) world	185) mind	215) only	245) now	275) or
156) world	186) relationship	216) between	246) result	276) or
157) dump	187) father	217) manner	247) content	277) need
158) up	188) male	218) new	248) of course	278) writing
159) exercise	189) male	219) new	249) book	279) arise
160) school	190) where	220) our country	250) happen	280) husband
161) darling	191) body	221) sit down	251) market	281) outside
162) ~est	192) face	222) initial	252) insert	282) small
163) ~est	193) go into	223) initial	253) important	283) burn
164) most	194) come in	224) hand	254) feel	284) university
165) president	195) why	225) a few	255) difficult	285) situation
166) kinds	196) emerge	226) course	256) power	286) among
167) start	197) don't	227) search	257) too	287) send
168) right away	198) area	228) especially	258) call	288) namely
169) which	199) water	229) city	259) meaning	289) thus
170) so	200) meet	230) more than	260) meaning	290) state
171) so	201) pay	231) story	261) reveal	291) since
172) government	202) write	232) story	262) die	292) at the time
173) every	203) use	233) education	263) already	293) literature
174) times	204) use	234) economy	264) politics	294) ~er
175) it	205) without	235) yet	265) student	295) very
176) money	206) this time	236) catch	266) research	296) very
177) nation	207) at this time	237) together	267) name	297) fat
178) nation	208) life	238) teacher	268) get off	298) night
179) by the way	209) life	239) art	269) incident	299) high
180) by the way	210) life	240) stand up	270) easy	300) recent

301-450				
☐ 301) 만큼	☐ 331) 아	☐ 361) 둔다	☐ 391) 입는다	☐ 421) 알아본다
☐ 302) 채	☐ 332) 기다린다	☐ 362) 놓는다	☐ 392) 오히려	☐ 422) 회사
☐ 303) 대로	☐ 333) 떨어진다	☐ 363) 떠난다	☐ 393) 이루어진다	☐ 423) 맛
☐ 304) 현실	☐ 334) 선거	☐ 364) 기술	☐ 394) 남	☐ 424) 산업
☐ 305) 환경	☐ 335) 관하여	☐ 365) 전체	☐ 395) 하루	☐ 425) 오른다
☐ 306) 먼저	☐ 336) 그냥	☐ 366) 그래	☐ 396) 그림	☐ 426) 올라간다
☐ 307) 첫	☐ 337) 나눈다	☐ 367) 네	☐ 397) 적	☐ 427) 음식
☐ 308) 일단	☐ 338) 이용한다	☐ 368) 예	☐ 398) 터	☐ 428) 꼭
☐ 309) 얼마나	☐ 339) 거의	☐ 369) 예	☐ 399) 마신다	☐ 429) 요즘
☐ 310) 어쩌다	☐ 340) 곧	☐ 370) 얻는다	☐ 400) 친다	☐ 430) 계획
☐ 311) 어떠하니	☐ 341) 중심	☐ 371) 분	☐ 401) 혼자	☐ 431) 방안
☐ 312) 자체	☐ 342) 중앙	☐ 372) 아름다운	☐ 402) 나간다	☐ 432) 느낌
☐ 313) 연다	☐ 343) 활동	☐ 373) 끝	☐ 403) 교수	☐ 433) 얼마
☐ 314) 열린다	☐ 344) 오늘	☐ 374) 민족	☐ 404) 술	☐ 434) 성격
☐ 315) 머리	☐ 345) 오늘날	☐ 375) 간	☐ 405) 사랑	☐ 435) 계속
☐ 316) 고개	☐ 346) 서로	☐ 376) 조사한다	☐ 406) 사랑한다	☐ 436) 세기
☐ 317) 묻는다	☐ 347) 관심	☐ 377) 듯하다	☐ 407) 의식하는	☐ 437) 세운다
☐ 318) 남는다	☐ 348) 역시	☐ 378) 입	☐ 408) 전화	☐ 438) 아내
☐ 319) 부분	☐ 349) 광고	☐ 379) 그대로	☐ 409) 끝난다	☐ 439) 가족
☐ 320) 일부	☐ 350) 아무런	☐ 380) 영화	☐ 410) 마친다	☐ 440) 여름
☐ 321) 기업	☐ 351) 아니	☐ 381) 필요	☐ 411) 돌아온다	☐ 441) 세
☐ 322) 사업	☐ 352) 방	☐ 382) 줄	☐ 412) 맞다	☐ 442) 발전
☐ 323) 거기에	☐ 353) 정신	☐ 383) 하늘	☐ 413) 아빠	☐ 443) 논다
☐ 324) 변화	☐ 354) 이른다	☐ 384) 과학	☐ 414) 걸린다	☐ 444) 향한다
☐ 325) 변한다	☐ 355) 땅	☐ 385) 자연	☐ 415) 지킨다	☐ 445) 관련된
☐ 326) 바뀐다	☐ 356) 이룬다	☐ 386) 정말	☐ 416) 한 번	☐ 446) 형태
☐ 327) 달라졌다	☐ 357) 아침	☐ 387) 구조	☐ 417) 커피	☐ 447) 형식
☐ 328) 바꾼다	☐ 358) 웃는다	☐ 388) 결국	☐ 418) 가슴	☐ 448) 각
☐ 329) 아들	☐ 359) 웃음	☐ 389) 밥	☐ 419) 긴	☐ 449) 분위기
☐ 330) 의지	☐ 360) 현상	☐ 390) 식사	☐ 420) 바라본다	☐ 450) 기분

Day1~7 English (3)

301-450				
301) as~as	331) ah	361) put	391) wear	421) recognize
302) as	332) await	362) put	392) rather	422) firm
303) as	333) fall	363) leave	393) come true	423) taste
304) reality	334) election	364) skill	394) stranger	424) industry
305) environment	335) about	365) total	395) one day	425) rise
306) first	336) just	366) yes	396) picture	426) rise
307) first	337) divide	367) yes	397) enemy	427) food
308) first	338) utilize	368) yes	398) site	428) surely
309) how	339) almost	369) example	399) drink	429) nowadays
310) how	340) soon	370) get	400) hit	430) plan
311) how?	341) center	371) anger	401) alone	431) plan
312) in ~self	342) center	372) beautiful	402) go out	432) feeling
313) open	343) activity	373) end	403) professor	433) how much
314) open	344) today	374) race	404) drinking	434) personality
315) head	345) today	375) seasoning	405) love	435) over and over
316) head	346) each other	376) survey	406) love	436) century
317) ask	347) interest	377) seem	407) conscious	437) erect
318) remain	348) as well	378) mouth	408) telephone	438) wife
319) part	349) advertisement	379) as it is	409) finish	439) family
320) part	350) no	380) movie	410) finish	440) summer
321) corporation	351) no	381) need	411) come back	441) rent
322) business	352) room	382) row	412) be right	442) advance
323) there	353) spirit	383) sky	413) dad	443) play
324) change	354) reach	384) science	414) take	444) head for
325) change	355) land	385) nature	415) protect	445) relevant
326) change	356) achieve	386) really	416) once	446) form
327) change	357) morning	387) structure	417) coffee	447) form
328) change	358) laugh	388) eventually	418) chest	448) angle
329) son	359) laugh	389) meal	419) long	449) mood
330) will	360) phenomenon	390) meal	420) look at	450) mood

Day1~7 List (4)

451–600				
☐ 451) 그러한	☐ 481) 산	☐ 511) 능력	☐ 541) 방송	☐ 571) 살
☐ 452) 나이	☐ 482) 하지만	☐ 512) 주장한다	☐ 542) 이야기한다	☐ 572) 생산한다
☐ 453) 우선	☐ 483) 조건	☐ 513) 자식	☐ 543) 얘기한다	☐ 573) 바란다
☐ 454) 믿는다	☐ 484) 문	☐ 514) 어린이	☐ 544) 나무	☐ 574) 강한
☐ 455) 낳는다	☐ 485) 꽃	☐ 515) 돌린다	☐ 545) 잔다	☐ 575) 경험
☐ 456) 정보	☐ 486) 단계	☐ 516) 차례	☐ 546) 잠	☐ 576) 음악
☐ 457) 좋아한다	☐ 487) 그동안	☐ 517) 불	☐ 547) 연극	☐ 577) 최고
☐ 458) 그린다	☐ 488) 갑자기	☐ 518) 주민	☐ 548) 마찬가지로	☐ 578) 나타낸다
☐ 459) 끈다	☐ 489) 넘는다	☐ 519) 모은다	☐ 549) 걷는다	☐ 579) 아프다
☐ 460) 배운다	☐ 490) 바람	☐ 520) 자료	☐ 550) 노동	☐ 580) 적은
☐ 461) 시	☐ 491) 마을	☐ 521) 존재	☐ 551) 과거	☐ 581) 비
☐ 462) 역할	☐ 492) 어리다	☐ 522) 학년	☐ 552) 현대	☐ 582) 고향
☐ 463) 옆에	☐ 493) 대표	☐ 523) 신문	☐ 553) 살펴본다	☐ 583) 놀란다
☐ 464) 행동	☐ 494) 가능성	☐ 524) 이해한다	☐ 554) 장관	☐ 584) 다양하다
☐ 465) 행위	☐ 495) 방향	☐ 525) 제품	☐ 555) 차이	☐ 585) 운다
☐ 466) 국내	☐ 496) 대회	☐ 526) 분야	☐ 556) 푼다	☐ 586) 농민
☐ 467) 기관	☐ 497) 목소리	☐ 527) 교사	☐ 557) 시절	☐ 587) 은행
☐ 468) 입장	☐ 498) 노래	☐ 528) 돌아간다	☐ 558) 물건	☐ 588) 결혼
☐ 469) 만한	☐ 499) 바다	☐ 529) 수준	☐ 559) 직접	☐ 589) 동생
☐ 470) 가치	☐ 500) 힘든	☐ 530) 표현	☐ 560) 개인	☐ 590) 법
☐ 471) 아래	☐ 501) 공부	☐ 531) 대	☐ 561) 발	☐ 591) 소설
☐ 472) 영향	☐ 502) 공부한다	☐ 532) 젊다	☐ 562) 작가	☐ 592) 오후
☐ 473) 나선다	☐ 503) 움직인다	☐ 533) 동시	☐ 563) 효과	☐ 593) 질서
☐ 474) 흐른다	☐ 504) 노력	☐ 534) 옷	☐ 564) 불교	☐ 594) 담는다
☐ 475) 깊은	☐ 505) 전혀	☐ 535) 기능	☐ 565) 빨리	☐ 595) 모인다
☐ 476) 배	☐ 506) 언니	☐ 536) 순간	☐ 566) 시작된다	☐ 596) 시민
☐ 477) 배	☐ 507) 단체	☐ 537) 전쟁	☐ 567) 설명한다	☐ 597) 회장
☐ 478) 배	☐ 508) 집단	☐ 538) 꿈	☐ 568) 우주	☐ 598) 빠른
☐ 479) 모양	☐ 509) 알려진	☐ 539) 할머니	☐ 569) 시기	☐ 599) 스스로
☐ 480) 산	☐ 510) 가능하다	☐ 540) 회의	☐ 570) 마치	☐ 600) 아기

451-600				
451) such	481) acid	511) ability	541) broadcast	571) flesh
452) age	482) however	512) insist	542) talk	572) yield
453) first of all	483) condition	513) child	543) talk	573) wish
454) believe	484) door	514) child	544) tree	574) strong
455) give birth	485) flower	515) turn	545) sleep	575) experience
456) information	486) step	516) turn	546) sleep	576) music
457) like	487) meantime	517) fire	547) paly	577) the best
458) draw	488) suddenly	518) resident	548) likewise	578) reveal
459) turn off	489) overstep	519) collect	549) walk	579) be ill
460) learn	490) wind	520) data	550) labor	580) less
461) poem	491) village	521) presence	551) past	581) rain
462) role	492) young	522) grade	552) contemporary	582) hometown
463) by	493) representative	523) newspaper	553) examine	583) surprised
464) behavior	494) chance	524) understand	554) spectacle	584) so many
465) behavior	495) direction	525) product	555) margin	585) cry
466) domestic	496) contest	526) field	556) untie	586) farmer
467) organ	497) voice	527) teacher	557) days	587) bank
468) entry	498) song	528) return	558) thing	588) wedding
469) worth	499) sea	529) level	559) first-hand	589) younger brother
470) value	500) tough	530) expression	560) individual	590) law
471) under	501) study	531) large	561) foot	591) novel
472) influence	502) study	532) young	562) writer	592) p.m.
473) come forward	503) move	533) simultaneous	563) effect	593) order
474) flow	504) effort	534) cloths	564) Buddhism	594) put in
475) deep	505) altogether	535) function	565) fast	595) gather
476) pear	506) older sister	536) moment	566) begin	596) citizen
477) ship	507) group	537) war	567) explain	597) chairman
478) stomach	508) group	538) dream	568) universe	598) quick
479) shape	509) known	539) grandma	569) period	599) by oneself
480) mountain	510) be possible	540) meeting	570) as if	600) baby

601-700				
☐ 601) 아저씨	☐ 631) 시설	☐ 661) 사고	☐ 691) 벌인다	
☐ 602) 옛날	☐ 632) 외국	☐ 662) 그래도	☐ 692) 사진	
☐ 603) 이날	☐ 633) 밑	☐ 663) 아무리	☐ 693) 주장	
☐ 604) 제대로	☐ 634) 어른	☐ 664) 맞춘다	☐ 694) 표현한다	
☐ 605) 달	☐ 635) 주변에	☐ 665) 쌀	☐ 695) 인한다	
☐ 606) 달	☐ 636) 대신	☐ 666) 일반적인	☐ 696) 이상한	
☐ 607) 던진다	☐ 637) 원인	☐ 667) 재미있는	☐ 697) 붙는다	
☐ 608) 참	☐ 638) 판다	☐ 668) 가르친다	☐ 698) 아마	
☐ 609) 공간	☐ 639) 군	☐ 669) 대화	☐ 699) 잇는다	
☐ 610) 이곳	☐ 640) 열심히	☐ 670) 막는다	☐ 700) 경기	
☐ 611) 딸	☐ 641) 재산	☐ 671) 올해		
☐ 612) 마지막	☐ 642) 부모	☐ 672) 형		
☐ 613) 병원	☐ 643) 약간	☐ 673) 오빠		
☐ 614) 자세	☐ 644) 언어	☐ 674) 달리		
☐ 615) 강조한다	☐ 645) 요구한다	☐ 675) 붙인다		
☐ 616) 경찰	☐ 646) 감독	☐ 676) 인물		
☐ 617) 맡는다	☐ 647) 그날	☐ 677) 늘		
☐ 618) 저녁	☐ 648) 자주	☐ 678) 항상		
☐ 619) 한편	☐ 649) 약	☐ 679) 모두		
☐ 620) 그러면	☐ 650) 기간	☐ 680) 전국		
☐ 621) 기자	☐ 651) 담배	☐ 681) 도움		
☐ 622) 넓은	☐ 652) 일으킨다	☐ 682) 가정		
☐ 623) 시험	☐ 653) 할아버지	☐ 683) 건다		
☐ 624) 주로	☐ 654) 조직	☐ 684) 빠진다		
☐ 625) 면	☐ 655) 태어난다	☐ 685) 멀다		
☐ 626) 통일	☐ 656) 공장	☐ 686) 잠시		
☐ 627) 들어선다	☐ 657) 벌써	☐ 687) 농업		
☐ 628) 건강	☐ 658) 즐긴다	☐ 688) 댄다		
☐ 629) 가까이	☐ 659) 지	☐ 689) 의견		
☐ 630) 건물	☐ 660) 환자	☐ 690) 무대		

601-700				
601) uncle	631) facility	661) accident	691) stage	
602) old days	632) foreign	662) nonetheless	692) photo	
603) this day	633) beneath	663) however	693) argument	
604) properly	634) adult	664) adapt	694) express	
605) moon	635) around	665) rice	695) be caused	
606) month	636) instead	666) general	696) strange	
607) toss	637) cause	667) interesting	697) stick to	
608) true	638) sell	668) teach	698) maybe	
609) space	639) county	669) conversation	699) connect	
610) this place	640) hard	670) prevent	700) economy	
611) daughter	641) property	671) this year		
612) final	642) parent	672) older brother		
613) hospital	643) some	673) older brother		
614) posture	644) language	674) otherwise		
615) emphasize	645) ask for	675) attach		
616) police	646) coach	676) figure		
617) undertake	647) that day	677) always		
618) evening	648) often	678) always		
619) meanwhile	649) about	679) in total		
620) if so	650) span	680) whole country		
621) reporter	651) tobacco	681) help		
622) wide	652) cause	682) home		
623) exam	653) grandfather	683) hang		
624) usually	654) tissue	684) fall out		
625) sense	655) be born	685) be far		
626) unification	656) factory	686) a while		
627) enter	657) already	687) agriculture		
628) health	658) enjoy	688) touch		
629) near	659) after	689) opinion		
630) building	660) patient	690) stage		

Day List Study

Final	K-word ㉜				
check	English ㉝				

K-word ㉖	English ㉗	K-word ㉘	K-word ㉙	English ㉚	K-word ㉛

Day7 List Study

Final check	K-word ㉜				
	English ㉝				

K-word ㉖	English ㉗	K-word ㉘	K-word ㉙	English ㉚	K-word ㉛

Day7 List Study

Final	K-word ㉜				
check	English ㉝				

K-word ㉖	English ㉗	K-word ㉘	K-word ㉙	English ㉚	K-word ㉛

Final	K-word ㉜				
check	English ㉝				

K-word ㉖	English ㉗	K-word ㉘	K-word ㉙	English ㉚	K-word ㉛

Day7 List Study

Final	K-word ㉜				
check	English ㉝				

K-word ㉖	English ㉗	K-word ㉘	K-word ㉙	English ㉚	K-word ㉛

Day7 List Study

Final	K-word ㉜				
check	English ㉝				

K-word ㉖	English ㉗	K-word ㉘	K-word ㉙	English ㉚	K-word ㉛

Day7 List Study

Final	K-word ㉜				
check	English ㉝				

K-word ㉖	English ㉗	K-word ㉘	K-word ㉙	English ㉚	K-word ㉛

	K-word	Pronounce	English	K-word ❶	Sentence example
701	목적	mok-jeok	purpose		What is your purpose?
702	태도	tae-do	attitude		Your attitude represents yourself.
703	주위	ju-wi	surrounding		Oxford and the surrounding area
704	대책	dae-chaek	measure		Safety measures are needed.
705	그만둔다	geu-man-dun-da	quit		She quits her job.
706	발생한다	bal-saeng-han-da	happen		Accidents happen.
707	다리	da-ri	bridge		Cross the bridge.
708	재료	jae-ryo	material		I work with dangerous materials.
709	각각	gak-gak	each		Each individual is different.
710	결코	gyeol-ko	absolutely		She did absolutely no work.
711	옮긴다	olm-gin-da	transfer		They transfer to the department.
712	해	hae	sun		The sun is shining.
713	잃어버린다	ilh-eo-beo-rin-da	lose		I often lose my keys.
714	자유	ja-yu	freedom		What is freedom?
715	책임	chaek-im	charge		Who's in charge?
716	비슷한	bi-seus-han	alike		They look alike.
717	심한	sim-han	severe		He had a severe cold.
718	경쟁	gyeong-jaeng	competition		Competition is getting hotter.
719	회	hoe	gathering		I have a lot of social gatherings.
720	구체적인	gu-che-jeok-in	specific		They found no specific evidence.

Final	K-word ❽				
check	English ❾				

K-word ❷	English ❸	K-word ❹	K-word ❺	English ❻	K-word ❼

	K-word	Pronounce	English	K-word ❶	Sentence example
721	기회	gi-hoe	opportunity		Thanks for the opportunity.
722	실시한다	sil-si-han-da	enforce		They enforce regulations.
723	지구	ji-gu	earth		Love the earth.
724	번째	beon-jjae	~th		He is my 5th husband.
725	소비자	so-bi-ja	consumer		We live in a consumer culture.
726	싫다	silh-da	not like		I don't like dogs.
727	규모	gyu-mo	scale		They entertain on a large scale.
728	기준	gi-jun	criteria		You should follow the criteria.
729	반드시	ban-deu-si	certainly		Certainly, I will succeed.
730	셈	sem	count		I did a rough count.
731	받아들인다	bad-a-deul-in-da	accept		I usually accept advices.
732	현장	hyeon-jang	site		The site of the battle was terrible.
733	건설	geon-seol	construction		The construction is under way.
734	꺼낸다	kkeo-naen-da	take out		He takes out goods.
735	노동자	no-dong-ja	worker		One third of the workers are men.
736	동네	dong-ne	neighborhood		Here is a friendly neighborhood.
737	언제나	eon-je-na	at all times		She's had a good figure at all times.
738	완전히	wan-jeon-hi	completely		He is completely mad.
739	자동차	ja-dong-cha	car		I have a car.
740	차	cha	car		I have a car.

Final	K-word ❽				
check	English ❾				

K-word ❷	English ❸	K-word ❹	K-word ❺	English ❻	K-word ❼

	K-word	Pronounce	English	K-word ❶	Sentence example
741	차	cha	tea		I love to drink tea.
742	전한다	jeon-han-da	deliver		He delivers new news.
743	존재한다	jon-jae-han-da	exist		God exists.
744	개월	gae-wol	month		It took 6 months to do the work.
745	별로	byeol-lo	not very		That's not very good.
746	정한다	jeong-han-da	fix		I fix the date.
747	한마디	han-ma-di	a word		I'll say a word.
748	유지한다	yu-ji-han-da	keep		They keep quietness.
749	대중	dae-jung	public		The public gathered.
750	늘어난다	neul-eo-nan-da	stretch		The rubber band stretches.
751	닦는다	dakk-neun-da	wipe		They wipe the windows.
752	말씀	mal-sseum	words		Excuse me for my words.
753	괜찮다	gwaen-chanh-da	okay		Coffee is okay.
754	눈물	nun-mul	tear		Wipe your tears.
755	각종	gak-jong	variety		There are a variety of things.
756	빛	bicc	light		What is that bright light?
757	피한다	pi-han-da	avoid		She avoids me.
758	거친다	geo-chin-da	go through		All goods go through my inspection.
759	나아간다	na-a-gan-da	proceed		The marchers proceed slowly.
760	야	ya	hey		Hey, come here.

Final	K-word ❽				
check	English ❾				

K-word ❷	English ❸	K-word ❹	K-word ❺	English ❻	K-word ❼

	K-word	Pronounce	English	K-word ❶	Sentence example
761	지식	ji-sik	knowledge		Knowledge is power.
762	현재	hyeon-jae	present		The present is important.
763	제시한다	je-si-han-da	present		He presents its final report today.
764	여전히	yeo-jeon-hi	still		I still love you.
765	주인	ju-in	host		He's the host.
766	발견한다	bal-gyeon-han-da	discover		We discover new facts everyday.
767	선	seon	line		Draw a line on the paper.
768	인류	in-ryu	mankind		COVID-19 plagues mankind.
769	특징	teuk-jing	characteristic		Light has a dim characteristic.
770	선수	seon-su	player		Tom is a soccer player.
771	마련한다	ma-ryeon-han-da	prepare		I prepare lunch.
772	반	ban	half		Cut in half.
773	발표한다	bal-pyo-han-da	announce		They announce a new policy.
774	주제	ju-je	topic		What is the topic?
775	걸친	geol-chin	lasting		The meeting lasting 5 hours ended.
776	겪고있다	gyeokk-go-iss-da	undergo		He is undergoing a hard time.
777	관점	gwan-jeom	perspective		I'm just giving my perspective.
778	귀	gwi	ear		My ears hurt.
779	기본	gi-bon	basics		I know the basics of computers.
780	사라진다	sa-ra-jin-da	disappear		Suddenly, the ghost disappears.

Final	K-word ❽				
check	English ❾				

K-word ❷	English ❸	K-word ❹	K-word ❺	English ❻	K-word ❼

	K-word	Pronounce	English	K-word ❶	Sentence example
781	없어진다	eobs-eo-jin-da	disappear		Anxiety disappears before you.
782	감정	gam-jeong	emotion		I can't control my emotions.
783	기억	gi-eok	memory		I have a good memory.
784	놈	nom	guy		What a lucky guy!
785	인기	in-gi	popularity		His popularity has slipped recently.
786	가끔	ga-kkeum	sometimes		Sometimes I go by car.
787	구성한다	gu-seong-han-da	organize		They organize a music band today.
788	실제로	sil-je-ro	actually		It's not actually raining now.
789	짧다	jjalb-da	short		The distance is short.
790	고맙다	go-mab-da	thank you		Thank you.
791	관리	gwan-ri	managing		He is good at managing.
792	그곳	geu-gos	that place		That place was good.
793	달다	dal-da	sweet		The candy is sweet.
794	비롯된다	bi-ros-doen-da	arise		Difficulties arise from laziness.
795	들린다	deul-lin-da	sound		His voice sounds strange today.
796	달린다	dal-lin-da	run		He runs fast.
797	바쁘다	ba-ppeu-da	busy		I'm busy today.
798	이전	i-jeon	former		Tom is Mary's former husband.
799	인정한다	in-jeong-han-da	admit		I admit defeat.
800	자	ja	come on		Come on, let's go home.

K-word ❷	English ❸	K-word ❹	K-word ❺	English ❻	K-word ❼

	K-word	English		K-word	English
701	목적	What is your ____?	721	기회	Thanks for the ____.
702	태도	Your ____ represents yourself.	722	실시한다	They ____ regulations.
703	주위	Oxford and the ____ area.	723	지구	Love the ____.
704	대책	Safety ____ are needed.	724	번째	He is my 5____ husband.
705	그만둔다	She ____ her job.	725	소비자	We live in a ____ culture.
706	발생한다	Accidents ____.	726	싫다	I ____ dogs.
707	다리	Cross the ____.	727	규모	They entertain on a large ____.
708	재료	I work with dangerous ____.	728	기준	You should follow the ____.
709	각각	____ individual is different.	729	반드시	____, I will succeed.
710	결코	She did ____ no work.	730	셈	I did a rough ____.
711	옮긴다	They ____ to the department.	731	받아들인다	I usually ____ advices.
712	해	The ____ is shining.	732	현장	The ____ of the battle was terrible.
713	잃어버린다	I often ____ my keys.	733	건설	The ____ is under way.
714	자유	What is ____?	734	꺼낸다	He ____ goods.
715	책임	Who's in ____?	735	노동자	One third of the ____ are men.
716	비슷한	They look ____.	736	동네	Here is a friendly ____.
717	심한	He had a ____ cold.	737	언제나	She's had a good figure ____.
718	경쟁	____ is getting hotter.	738	완전히	He is ____ mad.
719	회	I have a lot of social ____.	739	자동차	I have a ____.
720	구체적인	They found no ____ evidence.	740	차	I have a ____.

701) purpose   702) attitude   703) surrounding   704) measures   705) quits   706) happen   707) bridge   708) material
709) Each   710) absolutely   711) transfer   712) sun   713) lose   714) freedom   715) charge   716) alike
717) severe   718) Competition   719) gatherings   720) specific   721) opportunity   722) enforce   723) earth   724) th
725) consumer   726) don't like   727) scale   728) criteria   729) Certainly   730) count   731) accept   732) site
733) construction   734) takes out   735) workers   736) neighborhood   737) at all times   738) completely   739) car   740) car

	K-word	English		K-word	English
741	차	I love to drink ⎯⎯⎯⎯⎯.	761	지식	⎯⎯⎯⎯⎯ is power.
742	전한다	He ⎯⎯⎯⎯⎯ new news.	762	현재	The ⎯⎯⎯⎯⎯ is important.
743	존재한다	God ⎯⎯⎯⎯⎯.	763	제시한다	He ⎯⎯⎯⎯⎯ its final report today.
744	개월	It took 6 ⎯⎯⎯⎯⎯ to do the work.	764	여전히	I ⎯⎯⎯⎯⎯ love you.
745	별로	That's ⎯⎯⎯⎯⎯ good.	765	주인	He's the ⎯⎯⎯⎯⎯.
746	정한다	I ⎯⎯⎯⎯⎯ the date.	766	발견한다	We ⎯⎯⎯⎯⎯ new facts everyday.
747	한마디	I'll say ⎯⎯⎯⎯⎯.	767	선	Draw a ⎯⎯⎯⎯⎯ on the paper.
748	유지한다	They ⎯⎯⎯⎯⎯ quietness.	768	인류	COVID-19 plagues ⎯⎯⎯⎯⎯.
749	대중	The ⎯⎯⎯⎯⎯ gathered.	769	특징	Light has a dim ⎯⎯⎯⎯⎯.
750	늘어난다	The rubber band ⎯⎯⎯⎯⎯.	770	선수	Tom is a soccer ⎯⎯⎯⎯⎯.
751	닦는다	They ⎯⎯⎯⎯⎯ the windows.	771	마련한다	I ⎯⎯⎯⎯⎯ lunch.
752	말씀	Excuse me for my ⎯⎯⎯⎯⎯.	772	반	Cut in ⎯⎯⎯⎯⎯.
753	괜찮다	Coffee is ⎯⎯⎯⎯⎯.	773	발표한다	They ⎯⎯⎯⎯⎯ a new policy.
754	눈물	Wipe your ⎯⎯⎯⎯⎯.	774	주제	What is the ⎯⎯⎯⎯⎯?
755	각종	There are a ⎯⎯⎯⎯⎯ of things.	775	걸친	The meeting ⎯⎯⎯⎯⎯ 5 hours ended.
756	빛	What is that bright ⎯⎯⎯⎯⎯?	776	겪고있다	He is ⎯⎯⎯⎯⎯ing a hard time.
757	피한다	She ⎯⎯⎯⎯⎯ me.	777	관점	I'm just giving my ⎯⎯⎯⎯⎯.
758	거친다	All goods ⎯⎯⎯⎯⎯ my inspection.	778	귀	My ⎯⎯⎯⎯⎯ hurt.
759	나아간다	The marchers ⎯⎯⎯⎯⎯ slowly.	779	기본	I know the ⎯⎯⎯⎯⎯ of computers.
760	야	⎯⎯⎯⎯⎯, come here.	780	사라진다	Suddenly, the ghost ⎯⎯⎯⎯⎯.

741) tea 742) delivers 743) exists 744) months 745) not very 746) fix 747) a word 748) keep
749) public 750) stretches 751) wipe 752) words 753) okay 754) tears 755) variety 756) light
757) avoids 758) go through 759) proceed 760) Hey 761) Knowledge 762) present 763) presents 764) still
765) host 766) discover 767) line 768) mankind 769) characteristic 770) player 771) prepare 772) half
773) announce 774) topic 775) lasting 776) undergo 777) perspective 778) ears 779) basics 780) disappears

	K-word	English
781	없어진다	Anxiety .... before you.
782	감정	I can't control my ....
783	기억	I have a good ....
784	놈	What a lucky ....!
785	인기	His .... has slipped recently.
786	가끔	.... I go by car.
787	구성한다	They .... a music band today.
788	실제로	It's not .... raining now.
789	짧다	The distance is ....
790	고맙다	.... you.
791	관리	He is good at ....
792	그곳	.... was good.
793	달다	The candy is ....
794	비롯된다	Difficulties .... from laziness.
795	들린다	His voice .... strange today.
796	달린다	He .... fast.
797	바쁘다	I'm .... today.
798	이전	Tom is Mary's .... husband.
799	인정한다	I .... defeat.
800	자	.... , let's go home.

King Sejong

– The 4th king of Joseon Dynasty

King Sejong was born in 1397.
His 32 year reign marked great achievements.
Hangeul, created by King Sejong,
has been used as a common script for
the Republic of Korea and North Korea.

781) disappears   782) emotions   783) memory   784) guy
785) popularity   786) Sometimes   787) organize   788) actually
789) short   790) Thank   791) managing   792) That place
793) sweet   794) arise   795) sounds   796) runs
797) busy   798) former   799) admit   800) Come on

Day8 Review Study

Final	K-word ⑯				
check	English ⑰				

K-word ⑩	English ⑪	K-word ⑫	K-word ⑬	English ⑭	K-word ⑮

	Write K-word in			Write K-word in ....
701	What is your purpose? 무엇이 당신의 .... 인가요?	714	What is freedom? .... 가 뭔가요?
702	Your attitude represents yourself. 당신의 .... 는 당신 자신을 나타낸다.	715	Who's in charge? 누가 .... 지고 있나요?
703	Oxford and the surrounding area 옥스퍼드와 그 .... 지역.	716	They look alike. 그들은 .... 모습이다.
704	Safety measures are needed. 안전 .... 이 필요하다.	717	He had a severe cold. 그는 .... 감기에 걸렸다.
705	She quits her job. 그녀는 직업을	718	Competition is getting hotter. .... 이 치열해지고 있다.
706	Accidents happen. 사고는	719	I have a lot of social gatherings. 나는 많은 친목 .... 를 가지고 있다.
707	Cross the bridge. .... 를 건너라.	720	They found no specific evidence. 그들은 .... 증거를 찾지 못했다.
708	I work with dangerous materials. 나는 위험한 .... 와 일한다.	721	Thanks for the opportunity. .... 에 대해 감사합니다.
709	Each individual is different. .... 개인은 다르다.	722	They enforce regulations. 그들이 규제를 ....
710	She did absolutely no work. 그녀는 .... 아무 일도 안 했다.	723	Love the earth. .... 를 사랑하라.
711	They transfer to the department. 그들은 그 부서로	724	He is my 5th husband. 그는 나의 다섯 .... 남편이다.
712	The sun is shining. .... 가 빛나고 있다.	725	We live in a consumer culture. 우리는 .... 문화 속에서 산다.
713	I often lose my keys. 나는 종종 내 열쇠를		

701) 목적 　　702) 태도 　　703) 주위 　　704) 대책 　　705) 그만둔다 　　706) 발생한다 　　707) 다리 　　708) 재료 　　709) 각각
710) 결코 　　711) 옮긴다 　　712) 해 　　713) 잃어버린다 　　714) 자유 　　715) 책임 　　716) 비슷한 　　717) 심한 　　718) 경쟁
719) 회 　　720) 구체적인 　　721) 기회 　　722) 실시한다 　　723) 지구 　　724) 번째 　　725) 소비자

Sentence Words(1)

	K-word	pronounce	English		K-word	pronounce	English
701	무엇이	mu-eos-i	what	714	자유가	ja-yu-ga	freedom
	당신의	dang-sin-ui	your		뭔가요?	mwon-ga-yo?	what is?
	목적	mok-jeok	purpose	715	누가	nu-ga	who
	인가요?	in-ga-yo?	is?		책임지고	chaek-im-ji-go	in charge
702	당신의	dang-sin-ui	your		있나요?	iss-na-yo?	is?
	태도는	tae-do-neun	attitude	716	그들은	geu-deul-eun	they
	당신 자신을	dang-sin ja-sin-eul	yourself		비슷한	bi-seus-han	alike
	나타낸다	na-ta-naen-da	represent		모습이다	mo-seub-i-da	look
703	옥스퍼드와	ok-seu-peo-deu-wa	Oxford and	717	그는	geu-neun	he
	그 주위	geu ju-wi	surrounding		심한	sim-han	severe
	지역	ji-yeok	area		감기에	gam-gi-e	cold
704	안전	an-jeon	safety		걸렸다	geol-lyeoss-da	had
	대책이	dae-chaek-i	measures	718	경쟁이	gyeong-jaeng-i	competition
	필요하다	pil-yo-ha-da	are needed		치열해지고	chi-yeol-hae-ji-go	hotter
705	그녀는	geu-nyeo-neun	she		있다	iss-da	is getting
	직업을	jik-eob-eul	her job	719	나는	na-neun	I
	그만둔다	geu-man-dun-da	quit		많은	manh-eun	a lot of
706	사고는	sa-go-neun	accidents		친목회를	chin-mok-hoe-reul	social gathering
	발생한다	bal-saeng-han-da	happen		가지고 있다	ga-ji-go iss-da	have
707	다리를	da-ri-reul	the bridge	720	그들은	geu-deul-eun	they
	건너라	geon-neo-ra	cross		구체적인	gu-che-jeok-in	specific
708	나는	na-neun	I		증거를	jeung-geo-reul	evidence
	위험한	wi-heom-han	dangerous		찾지 못했다	chaj-ji mos-haess-da	found no
	재료와	jae-ryo-wa	with materials	721	기회	gi-hoe	the opportunity
	일 한다	il han-da	work		에 대해	e dae-hae	for
709	각각	gak-gak	each		감사합니다	gam-sa-hab-ni-da	thanks
	개인은	gae-in-eun	individual	722	그들이	geu-deul-i	they
	다르다	da-reu-da	is different		규제를	gyu-je-reul	regulations
710	그녀는	geu-nyeo-neun	she		실시한다	sil-si-han-da	enforce
	결코	gyeol-ko	absolutely	723	지구를	ji-gu-reul	the earth
	아무 일도	a-mu il-do	work		사랑하라	sa-rang-ha-ra	love
	안 했다	an haess-da	did no	724	그는	geu-neun	he
711	그들은	geu-deul-eun	they		나의	na-ui	my
	그 부서로	geu bu-seo-ro	to the department		다섯 번째	da-seos beon-jjae	5th
	옮긴다	olm-gin-da	transfer		남편	nam-pyeon	husband
712	해가	hae-ga	the sun		이다	i-da	is
	빛나고 있다	bicc-na-go iss-da	is shining	725	우리는	u-ri-neun	we
713	나는	na-neun	I		소비자	so-bi-ja	consumer
	종종	jong-jong	often		문화	mun-hwa	culture
	내	nae	my		속에서	sok-e-seo	in
	열쇠를	yeol-soe-reul	keys		산다	san-da	live
	잃어버린다	ilh-eo-beo-rin-da	lose				

	Write K-word in		Write K-word in ....
726	I don't like dogs. 나는 개가	739	I have a car. 나는 .... 를 가지고 있다.
727	They entertain on a large scale. 그들은 큰 .... 로 접대한다.	740	I have a car. 나는 .... 를 가지고 있다.
728	You should follow the criteria. 너는 .... 을 따라야 한다.	741	I love to drink tea. 나는 .... 마시는 걸 좋아한다.
729	Certainly, I will succeed. .... , 나는 성공 할 것이다.	742	He delivers new news. 그는 새로운 소식을 ....
730	I did a rough count. 나는 대충 .... 을 해 보았다.	743	God exists. 신은 ....
731	I usually accept advices. 나는 대개 충고를	744	It took 6 months to do the work. 그 일을 하는데 육 .... 이 걸렸다.
732	The site of the battle was terrible. 전투 .... 은 끔찍했다.	745	That's not very good. 그것은 .... 좋지 않다.
733	The construction is under way. .... 이 진행되고 있다.	746	I fix the date. 내가 날짜를 ....
734	He takes out goods. 그가 상품을	747	I'll say a word. 내가 .... 할게.
735	One third of the workers are men. .... 의 3분의 1이 남자다.	748	They keep quietness. 그들은 침묵을 ....
736	Here is a friendly neighborhood. 이곳은 친절한 .... 이다.	749	The public gathered. .... 들이 모였다.
737	She's had a good figure at all times. 그녀는 .... 좋은 몸매를 가졌다.	750	The rubber band stretches. 고무줄은 ....
738	He is completely mad. 그는 .... 미쳤다.		

726) 싫다   727) 규모   728) 기준   729) 반드시   730) 셈   731) 받아들인다   732) 현장   733) 건설   734) 꺼낸다
735) 노동자   736) 동네   737) 언제나   738) 완전히   739) 자동차   740) 차   741) 차   742) 전한다   743) 존재한다
744) 개월   745) 별로   746) 정한다   747) 한마디   748) 유지한다   749) 대중   750) 늘어난다

Sentence Words(2)

	K-word	pronounce	English		K-word	pronounce	English
726	나는	na-neun	I		가졌다	ga-jyeoss-da	had
	개가	gae-ga	dogs	738	그는	geu-neun	he
	싫다	silh-da	don't like		완전히	wan-jeon-hi	completely
727	그들은	geu-deul-eun	they		미쳤다	mi-chyeoss-da	is mad
	큰	keun	large	739	나는	na-neun	I
	규모로	gyu-mo-ro	on a scale		자동차를	ja-dong-cha-reul	a car
	접대한다	jeob-dae-han-da	entertain		가지고 있다	ga-ji-go iss-da	have
728	너는	neo-neun	you	740	나는	na-neun	I
	기준을	gi-jun-eul	the criteria		차를	cha-reul	a car
	따라야 한다	tta-ra-ya han-da	should follow		가지고 있다	ga-ji-go iss-da	have
729	반드시	ban-deu-si	certainly	741	나는	na-neun	I
	나는	na-neun	I		차를	cha-reul	tea
	성공 할 것이다	seong-gong hal geos-i-da	will succeed		마시는 걸	ma-si-neun geol	to drink
730	나는	na-neun	I		좋아한다	joh-a-han-da	love
	대충	dae-chung	rough	742	그는	geu-neun	he
	셈을	sem-eul	count		새로운	sae-ro-un	new
	해 보았다	hae bo-ass-da	did		소식을	so-sik-eul	news
731	나는	na-neun	I		전한다	jeon-han-da	deliver
	대개	dae-gae	usually	743	신은	sin-eun	god
	충고를	chung-go-reul	advices		존재한다	jon-jae-han-da	exist
	받아들인다	bad-a-deul-in-da	accept	744	그 일을	geu il-eul	the work
732	전투	jeon-tu	the battle		하는데	ha-neun-de	to do
	현장은	hyeon-jang-eun	the site of		육개월이	yuk-gae-wol-i	for 6 months
	끔찍했다	kkeum-jjik-haess-da	was terrible		걸렸다	geol-lyeoss-da	it took
733	건설이	geon-seol-i	the construction	745	그것은	geu-geos-eun	that
	진행되고	jin-haeng-doe-go	under way		별로	byeol-lo	very
	있다	iss-da	is		좋지	joh-ji	good
734	그가	geu-ga	he		않다	anh-da	is not
	상품을	sang-pum-eul	goods	746	내가	nae-ga	I
	꺼낸다	kkeo-naen-da	take out		날짜를	nal-jja-reul	the date
735	노동자의	no-dong-ja-ui	the workers		정한다	jeong-han-da	fix
	3분의 1이	sam-bun-ui il-i	one third of	747	내가	nae-ga	I
	남자다	nam-ja-da	are men		한마디	han-ma-di	a word
736	이곳은	i-gos-eun	here		할게	hal-ge	will say
	친절한	chin-jeol-han	friendly	748	그들은	geu-deul-eun	they
	동네	dong-ne	neighborhood		침묵을	chim-muk-eul	quietness
	이다	i-da	is		유지한다	yu-ji-han-da	keep
737	그녀는	geu-nyeo-neun	she	749	대중들이	dae-jung-deul-i	the public
	언제나	eon-je-na	at all times		모였다	mo-yeoss-da	gathered
	좋은	joh-eun	good	750	고무줄은	go-mu-jul-eun	the rubber band
	몸매를	mom-mae-reul	figure		늘어난다	neul-eo-nan-da	stretch

	Write K-word in _____.		Write K-word in _____.
751	They wipe the windows. 그들은 창문을 _____.	764	I still love you. 나는 _____ 당신을 사랑한다.
752	Excuse me for my words. _____ 드리기 죄송합니다.	765	He's the host. 그가 _____ 이다.
753	Coffee is okay. 커피 _____.	766	We discover new facts everyday. 우리는 매일 새로운 사실을 _____.
754	Wipe your tears. _____ 을 닦아.	767	Draw a line on the paper. 종이 위에 _____ 을 그리시오.
755	There are a variety of things. _____ 물건들이 있다.	768	COVID-19 plagues mankind. 코로나 바이러스가 _____ 를 괴롭힌다.
756	What is that bright light? 저 밝은 _____ 은 무엇인가요?	769	Light has a dim characteristic. 빛은 아련한 _____ 을 갖는다.
757	She avoids me. 그녀는 나를 _____.	770	Tom is a soccer player. 톰은 축구 _____ 다.
758	All goods go through my inspection. 모든 상품이 나의 검사를 _____.	771	I prepare lunch. 내가 점심을 _____.
759	The marchers proceed slowly. 행진하는 사람들이 천천히 _____.	772	Cut in half. _____ 으로 자르시오.
760	Hey, come here. _____, 이리 와.	773	They announce a new policy. 그들은 새로운 정책을 _____.
761	Knowledge is power. _____ 은 힘 이다.	774	What is the topic? _____ 가 무엇인가요?
762	The present is important. _____ 가 중요하다.	775	The meeting lasting 5hours ended. 5시간에 _____ 회의가 끝났다.
763	He presents its final report today. 그가 오늘 최종 보고서를 _____.		

751) 닦는다　　752) 말씀　　753) 괜찮다　　754) 눈물　　755) 각종　　756) 빛　　757) 피한다　　758) 거친다　　759) 나아간다
760) 야　　761) 지식　　762) 현재　　763) 제시한다　　764) 여전히　　765) 주인　　766) 발견한다　　767) 선　　768) 인류
769) 특징　　770) 선수　　771) 마련한다　　772) 반　　773) 발표한다　　774) 주제　　775) 걸친

	K-word	pronounce	English		K-word	pronounce	English
751	그들은	geu-deul-eun	they	764	나는	na-neun	I
	창문을	chang-mun-eul	the window		여전히	yeo-jeon-hi	still
	닦는다	dakk-neun-da	wipe		당신을	dang-sin-eul	you
752	말씀드리기	mal-sseum-deu-ri-gi	for my words		사랑한다	sa-rang-han-da	love
	죄송합니다	joe-song-hab-ni-da	excuse me	765	그가	geu-ga	he
753	커피	keo-pi	coffee		주인이다	ju-in-i-da	is the host
	괜찮다	gwaen-chanh-da	is okay	766	우리는	u-ri-neun	we
754	눈물을	nun-mul-eul	your tears		매일	mae-il	everyday
	닦아	dakk-a	wipe		새로운	sae-ro-un	new
755	각종	gak-jong	a variety of		사실을	sa-sil-eul	facts
	물건들이	mul-geon-deul-i	things		발견한다	bal-gyeon-han-da	discover
	있다	iss-da	there are	767	종이	jong-i	the paper
756	저	jeo	that		위에	wi-e	on
	밝은	balk-eun	bright		선을	seon-eul	a line
	빛은	bicc-eun	light		그리시오	geu-ri-si-o	draw
	무엇인가요?	mu-eos-in-ga-yo?	what is?	768	코로나 바이러스가	ko-ro-na ba-i-reo-seu-ga	COVID-19
757	그녀는	geu-nyeo-neun	she		인류를	in-ryu-reul	mankind
	나를	na-reul	me		괴롭힌다	goe-rob-hin-da	plague
	피한다	pi-han-da	avoid	769	빛은	bicc-eun	light
758	모든	mo-deun	all		아련한	a-ryeon-han	dim
	상품이	sang-pum-i	goods		특징을	teuk-jing-eul	characteristic
	나의	na-ui	my		갖는다	gaj-neun-da	has
	검사를	geom-sa-reul	inspection	770	톰은	tom-eun	Tom
	거친다	geo-chin-da	go through		축구	chuk-gu	soccer
759	행진하는 사람들이	haeng-jin-ha-neun sa-ram-deul-i	the marchers		선수다	seon-su-da	is a player
	천천히	cheon-cheon-hi	slowly	771	내가	nae-ga	I
	나아간다	na-a-gan-da	proceed		점심을	jeom-sim-eul	lunch
760	야	ya	hey		마련한다	ma-ryeon-han-da	prepare
	이리	i-ri	here	772	반으로	ban-eu-ro	in half
	와	wa	come		자르시오	ja-reu-si-o	cut
761	지식은	ji-sik-eun	knowledge	773	그들은	geu-deul-eun	they
	힘	him	power		새로운	sae-ro-un	new
	이다	i-da	is okay		정책을	jeong-chaek-eul	policy
762	현재가	hyeon-jae-ga	the present		발표한다	bal-pyo-han-da	announce
	중요하다	jung-yo-ha-da	is important	774	주제가	ju-je-ga	the topic
763	그가	geu-ga	he		무엇인가요?	mu-eos-in-ga-yo?	what is?
	오늘	o-neul	today	775	5시간에	da-seos-si-gan-e	5 hours
	최종	choe-jong	final		걸친	geol-chin	lasting
	보고서를	bo-go-seo-reul	report		회의가	hoe-ui-ga	meeting
	제시한다	je-si-han-da	present		끝났다	kkeut-nass-da	ended

Day8 Sentence(4)

	Write K-word in		Write K-word in ....
776	He is undergoing a hard time. 그는 어려운 시기를	789	The distance is short. 거리는 ....
777	I'm just giving my perspective. 나는 그냥 내 .... 을 말하는 것이다.	790	Thank you. ....
778	My ears hurt. .... 가 아프다.	791	He is good at managing. 그는 .... 에 능숙하다.
779	I know the basics of computers. 나는 컴퓨터의 .... 은 안다.	792	That place was good. .... 은 좋았다.
780	Suddenly, the ghost disappears. 갑자기 유령이	793	The candy is sweet. 사탕이 ....
781	Anxiety disappears before you. 걱정이 너 앞에서는	794	Difficulties arise from laziness. 어려운 일들은 태만에서 ....
782	I can't control my emotions. 나는 나의 .... 을 조절할 수 없다.	795	His voice sounds strange today. 그의 목소리가 오늘 이상하게 ....
783	I have a good memory. 나는 좋은 .... 을 가지고 있다.	796	He runs fast. 그는 빨리 ....
784	What a lucky guy! 진짜 운 좋은 .... 이군!	797	I'm busy today. 나는 오늘 ....
785	His popularity has slipped recently. 그의 .... 가 최근에 떨어졌다.	798	Tom is Mary's former husband. 톰은 메리의 .... 남편이다.
786	Sometimes I go by car. .... 나는 승용차로 간다.	799	I admit defeat. 나는 패배를 ....
787	They organize a music band today. 그들은 오늘 음악밴드를	800	Come on, let's go home. .... , 집에 가자.
788	It's not actually raining now. .... 지금 비가 오지는 않는다.		

776) 겪고있다   777) 관점   778) 귀   779) 기본   780) 사라진다   781) 없어진다   782) 감정   783) 기억   784) 놈
785) 인기   786) 가끔   787) 구성한다   788) 실제로   789) 짧다   790) 고맙다   791) 관리   792) 그곳   793) 달다
794) 비롯된다   795) 들린다   796) 달린다   797) 바쁘다   798) 이전   799) 인정한다   800) 자

Sentence Words(4)

	K-word	pronounce	English		K-word	pronounce	English
776	그는	geu-neun	he		오늘	o-neul	today
	어려운	eo-ryeo-un	hard		음악	eum-ak	music
	시기를	si-gi-reul	time		밴드를	baen-deu-reul	band
	겪고 있다	gyeokk-go-iss-da	is undergoing		구성한다	gu-seong-han-da	organize
777	나는	na-neun	I	788	실제로	sil-je-ro	actually
	그냥	geu-nyang	just		지금	ji-geum	now
	내	nae	my		비가 오지는 않는다	bi-ga o-ji-neun anh-neun-da	it's not raining
	관점을	gwan-jeom-eul	perspective	789	거리는	geo-ri-neun	the distance
	말하는 것이다	mal-ha-neun geos-i-da	am giving		짧다	jjalb-da	is short
778	귀가	gwi-ga	my ears	790	고맙다	go-mab-da	thank you
	아프다	a-peu-da	hurt	791	그는	geu-neun	he
779	나는	na-neun	I		관리에	gwan-ri-e	at managing
	컴퓨터의	keom-pyu-teo-ui	of computers		능숙하다	neung-suk-ha-da	is good at
	기본은	gi-bon-eun	the basics	792	그곳은	geu-gos-eun	that place
	안다	an-da	know		좋았다	joh-ass-da	was good
780	갑자기	gab-ja-gi	suddenly	793	사탕이	sa-tang-i	the candy
	유령이	yu-ryeong-i	the ghost		달다	dal-da	is sweet
	사라진다	sa-ra-jin-da	disappear	794	어려운 일들은	eo-ryeo-un il-deul-eun	difficulties
781	걱정이	geok-jeong-i	anxiety		태만에서	tae-man-e-seo	from laziness
	너	neo	you		비롯된다	bi-ros-doen-da	arise
	앞에서는	ap-e-seo-neun	before	795	그의	geu-ui	his
	없어진다	eobs-eo-jin-da	disappear		목소리가	mok-so-ri-ga	voice
782	나는	na-neun	I		오늘	o-neul	today
	나의	na-ui	my		이상하게	i-sang-ha-ge	strange
	감정을	gam-jeong-eul	emotions		들린다	deul-lin-da	sound
	조절할 수 없다	jo-jeol-hal su eobs-da	can't control	796	그는	geu-neun	he
783	나는	na-neun	I		빨리	ppal-li	fast
	좋은	joh-eun	good		달린다	dal-lin-da	run
	기억을	gi-eok-eul	memory	797	나는	na-neun	I
	가지고 있다	ga-ji-go iss-da	have		오늘	o-neul	today
784	진짜	jin-jja	what a		바쁘다	ba-ppeu-da	am busy
	운 좋은	un joh-eun	lucky	798	톰은	tom-eun	Tom
	놈이군	nom-i-gun	guy		메리의	me-ri-ui	Mary's
785	그의	geu-ui	his		이전	i-jeon	former
	인기가	in-gi-ga	popularity		남편	nam-pyeon	husband
	최근에	choe-geun-e	recently		이다	i-da	is
	떨어졌다	tteol-eo-jyeoss-da	has slipped	799	나는	na-neun	I
786	가끔	ga-kkeum	sometimes		패배를	pae-bae-reul	dcfeat
	나는	na-neun	I		인정한다	in-jeong-han-da	admit
	승용차로	seung-yong-cha-ro	by car	800	자	ja	come on
	간다	gan-da	go		집에	jib-e	home
787	그들은	geu-deul-eun	they		가자	ga-ja	let's go

Final	K-word ㉔				
check	English ㉕				

K-word ⑱	English ⑲	K-word ⑳	K-word ㉑	English ㉒	K-word ㉓

1-150				
□ 1) 것	□ 31) 드린다	□ 61) 집	□ 91) 파악하고 있다	□ 121) 지닌다
□ 2) 한다	□ 32) 대한다	□ 62) 나온다	□ 92) 자신	□ 122) 가진다
□ 3) 된다	□ 33) 간다	□ 63) 따른다	□ 93) 문화	□ 123) 갖추고 있다
□ 4) 수	□ 34) 다닌다	□ 64) 그리고	□ 94) 원	□ 124) 당한다
□ 5) 수	□ 35) 년	□ 65) 및	□ 95) 생각	□ 125) 함께
□ 6) 길	□ 36) 한	□ 66) 그때	□ 96) 명	□ 126) 아이
□ 7) 쪽	□ 37) 말	□ 67) 그럼	□ 97) 통한다	□ 127) 지나간다
□ 8) 방식	□ 38) 일	□ 68) 문제	□ 98) 소리	□ 128) 많이
□ 9) 점	□ 39) 일	□ 69) 그런	□ 99) 다시	□ 129) 훨씬
□ 10) 점	□ 40) 일 한다	□ 70) 산다	□ 100) 다른	□ 130) 시간
□ 11) 나	□ 41) 작품	□ 71) 산다	□ 101) 다르다	□ 131) 너
□ 12) 내	□ 42) 작업	□ 72) 지낸다	□ 102) 여자	□ 132) 당신
□ 13) 그	□ 43) 직장	□ 73) 저	□ 103) 소녀	□ 133) 인간
□ 14) 없다	□ 44) 때문	□ 74) 생각한다	□ 104) 개	□ 134) 사실
□ 15) 않다	□ 45) 말한다	□ 75) 모른다	□ 105) 그 정도	□ 135) 과연
□ 16) 말고	□ 46) 위하여	□ 76) 속	□ 106) 뒤	□ 136) 난다
□ 17) 아니다	□ 47) 그러나	□ 77) 만든다	□ 107) 듣는다	□ 137) 자란다
□ 18) 않는다	□ 48) 온다	□ 78) 삼는다	□ 108) 다	□ 138) 어머니
□ 19) 사람	□ 49) 안다	□ 79) 시킨다	□ 109) 좀	□ 139) 엄마
□ 20) 국민	□ 50) 씨	□ 80) 두	□ 110) 조금	□ 140) 눈
□ 21) 우리	□ 51) 그렇다	□ 81) 둘	□ 111) 든다	□ 141) 눈
□ 22) 이	□ 52) 큰	□ 82) 앞	□ 112) 키운다	□ 142) 뭐
□ 23) 이	□ 53) 크다	□ 83) 경우	□ 113) 올린다	□ 143) 무엇
□ 24) 이런	□ 54) 또	□ 84) 중	□ 114) 기른다	□ 144) 무슨
□ 25) 이것	□ 55) 사회	□ 85) 중	□ 115) 싶다	□ 145) 시대
□ 26) 이거	□ 56) 안에	□ 86) 동안에	□ 116) 보인다	□ 146) 다음
□ 27) 보다	□ 57) 좋은	□ 87) 어떤	□ 117) 표정	□ 147) 이러하다
□ 28) 본다	□ 58) 더	□ 88) 잘	□ 118) 모습	□ 148) 누구
□ 29) 같다	□ 59) 받는다	□ 89) 그녀	□ 119) 가지고 있다	□ 149) 전
□ 30) 준다	□ 60) 그것	□ 90) 먹는다	□ 120) 갖고있다	□ 150) 곳

1-150				
1) thing	31) give	61) house	91) grasp	121) have
2) do	32) treat	62) come out	92) self	122) have
3) become	33) go	63) obey	93) culture	123) have
4) number	34) go	64) and	94) ₩	124) get p.p
5) way	35) year	65) and	95) thought	125) with
6) way	36) one	66) then	96) famous	126) kid
7) way	37) word	67) then	97) make sense	127) pass by
8) way	38) day	68) problem	98) sound	128) much
9) way	39) work	69) such	99) again	129) much ~er
10) store	40) work	70) buy	100) different	130) time
11) I	41) work	71) live	101) different	131) you
12) I	42) work	72) live	102) girl	132) you
13) he	43) job	73) um	103) girl	133) human
14) not have	44) because of	74) think	104) dog	134) in fact
15) not	45) speak	75) don't know	105) that much	135) indeed
16) not	46) for	76) inside	106) back	136) grow
17) not	47) but	77) make	107) hear	137) grow
18) do not	48) come	78) make	108) all	138) mother
19) people	49) know	79) make	109) a little	139) mom
20) people	50) family name	80) two	110) a little	140) eye
21) we	51) right	81) two	111) pick up	141) snow
22) tooth	52) big	82) front	112) raise	142) what
23) this	53) big	83) case	113) raise	143) what
24) this	54) once again	84) monk	114) raise	144) what
25) this	55) society	85) during	115) want	145) era
26) this	56) in	86) during	116) look	146) next
27) than	57) good	87) any	117) look	147) like this
28) see	58) more	88) well	118) appearance	148) who
29) same	59) receive	89) she	119) have	149) all
30) give	60) it	90) eat	120) have	150) place

151-300				
☐ 151) 자리	☐ 181) 날	☐ 211) 인생	☐ 241) 못	☐ 271) 짓는다
☐ 152) 여러	☐ 182) 여기	☐ 212) 지금	☐ 242) 못	☐ 272) 또한
☐ 153) 많은	☐ 183) 여성	☐ 213) 뿐	☐ 243) 못한다	☐ 273) 까닭
☐ 154) 하나	☐ 184) 친구	☐ 214) 다만	☐ 244) 읽는다	☐ 274) 이유
☐ 155) 세계	☐ 185) 마음	☐ 215) 만	☐ 245) 이제	☐ 275) 또는
☐ 156) 세상	☐ 186) 관계	☐ 216) 사이에	☐ 246) 결과	☐ 276) 혹은
☐ 157) 버린다	☐ 187) 아버지	☐ 217) 방법	☐ 247) 내용	☐ 277) 필요하다
☐ 158) 위	☐ 188) 남자	☐ 218) 새롭다	☐ 248) 물론	☐ 278) 글
☐ 159) 운동	☐ 189) 남성	☐ 219) 새	☐ 249) 책	☐ 279) 생긴다
☐ 160) 학교	☐ 190) 어디	☐ 220) 우리나라	☐ 250) 일어난다	☐ 280) 남편
☐ 161) 자기	☐ 191) 몸	☐ 221) 앉는다	☐ 251) 시장	☐ 281) 밖
☐ 162) 가장	☐ 192) 얼굴	☐ 222) 처음의	☐ 252) 넣는다	☐ 282) 작은
☐ 163) 제일	☐ 193) 들어간다	☐ 223) 초기	☐ 253) 중요한	☐ 283) 탄다
☐ 164) 대부분	☐ 194) 들어온다	☐ 224) 손	☐ 254) 느낀다	☐ 284) 대학
☐ 165) 대통령	☐ 195) 왜	☐ 225) 몇	☐ 255) 어려운	☐ 285) 상황
☐ 166) 가지	☐ 196) 나타난다	☐ 226) 과정	☐ 256) 힘	☐ 286) 가운데
☐ 167) 시작한다	☐ 197) 말아라	☐ 227) 찾는다	☐ 257) 너무	☐ 287) 보낸다
☐ 168) 바로	☐ 198) 지역	☐ 228) 특히	☐ 258) 부른다	☐ 288) 즉
☐ 169) 어느	☐ 199) 물	☐ 229) 도시	☐ 259) 의미	☐ 289) 따라서
☐ 170) 그래서	☐ 200) 만난다	☐ 230) 이상	☐ 260) 뜻	☐ 290) 상태
☐ 171) 그러니까	☐ 201) 낸다	☐ 231) 이야기	☐ 261) 밝힌다	☐ 291) 이후
☐ 172) 정부	☐ 202) 쓴다	☐ 232) 얘기	☐ 262) 죽는다	☐ 292) 당시
☐ 173) 모든	☐ 203) 쓴다	☐ 233) 교육	☐ 263) 이미	☐ 293) 문학
☐ 174) 번	☐ 204) 사용한다	☐ 234) 경제	☐ 264) 정치	☐ 294) 더욱
☐ 175) 그거	☐ 205) 없이	☐ 235) 아직	☐ 265) 학생	☐ 295) 아주
☐ 176) 돈	☐ 206) 이번	☐ 236) 잡는다	☐ 266) 연구	☐ 296) 매우
☐ 177) 국가	☐ 207) 이때	☐ 237) 같이	☐ 267) 이름	☐ 297) 지방
☐ 178) 나라	☐ 208) 생활	☐ 238) 선생님	☐ 268) 내린다	☐ 298) 밤
☐ 179) 그런데	☐ 209) 삶	☐ 239) 예술	☐ 269) 사건	☐ 299) 높은
☐ 180) 근데	☐ 210) 생명	☐ 240) 일어선다	☐ 270) 쉬운	☐ 300) 최근

151-300				
151) place	181) day	211) life	241) nail	271) build
152) several	182) here	212) now	242) can't	272) also
153) many	183) female	213) only	243) can't do	273) reason
154) one	184) friend	214) only	244) read	274) reason
155) world	185) mind	215) only	245) now	275) or
156) world	186) relationship	216) between	246) result	276) or
157) dump	187) father	217) manner	247) content	277) need
158) up	188) male	218) new	248) of course	278) writing
159) exercise	189) male	219) new	249) book	279) arise
160) school	190) where	220) our country	250) happen	280) husband
161) darling	191) body	221) sit down	251) market	281) outside
162) ~est	192) face	222) initial	252) insert	282) small
163) ~est	193) go into	223) initial	253) important	283) burn
164) most	194) come in	224) hand	254) feel	284) university
165) president	195) why	225) a few	255) difficult	285) situation
166) kinds	196) emerge	226) course	256) power	286) among
167) start	197) don't	227) search	257) too	287) send
168) right away	198) area	228) especially	258) call	288) namely
169) which	199) water	229) city	259) meaning	289) thus
170) so	200) meet	230) more than	260) meaning	290) state
171) so	201) pay	231) story	261) reveal	291) since
172) government	202) write	232) story	262) die	292) at the time
173) every	203) use	233) education	263) already	293) literature
174) times	204) use	234) economy	264) politics	294) ~er
175) it	205) without	235) yet	265) student	295) very
176) money	206) this time	236) catch	266) research	296) very
177) nation	207) at this time	237) together	267) name	297) fat
178) nation	208) life	238) teacher	268) get off	298) night
179) by the way	209) life	239) art	269) incident	299) high
180) by the way	210) life	240) stand up	270) easy	300) recent

301-450				
☐ 301) 만큼	☐ 331) 아	☐ 361) 둔다	☐ 391) 입는다	☐ 421) 알아본다
☐ 302) 채	☐ 332) 기다린다	☐ 362) 놓는다	☐ 392) 오히려	☐ 422) 회사
☐ 303) 대로	☐ 333) 떨어진다	☐ 363) 떠난다	☐ 393) 이루어진다	☐ 423) 맛
☐ 304) 현실	☐ 334) 선거	☐ 364) 기술	☐ 394) 남	☐ 424) 산업
☐ 305) 환경	☐ 335) 관하여	☐ 365) 전체	☐ 395) 하루	☐ 425) 오른다
☐ 306) 먼저	☐ 336) 그냥	☐ 366) 그래	☐ 396) 그림	☐ 426) 올라간다
☐ 307) 첫	☐ 337) 나눈다	☐ 367) 네	☐ 397) 적	☐ 427) 음식
☐ 308) 일단	☐ 338) 이용한다	☐ 368) 예	☐ 398) 터	☐ 428) 꼭
☐ 309) 얼마나	☐ 339) 거의	☐ 369) 예	☐ 399) 마신다	☐ 429) 요즘
☐ 310) 어쩌다	☐ 340) 곧	☐ 370) 얻는다	☐ 400) 친다	☐ 430) 계획
☐ 311) 어떠하니	☐ 341) 중심	☐ 371) 분	☐ 401) 혼자	☐ 431) 방안
☐ 312) 자체	☐ 342) 중앙	☐ 372) 아름다운	☐ 402) 나간다	☐ 432) 느낌
☐ 313) 연다	☐ 343) 활동	☐ 373) 끝	☐ 403) 교수	☐ 433) 얼마
☐ 314) 열린다	☐ 344) 오늘	☐ 374) 민족	☐ 404) 술	☐ 434) 성격
☐ 315) 머리	☐ 345) 오늘날	☐ 375) 간	☐ 405) 사랑	☐ 435) 계속
☐ 316) 고개	☐ 346) 서로	☐ 376) 조사한다	☐ 406) 사랑한다	☐ 436) 세기
☐ 317) 묻는다	☐ 347) 관심	☐ 377) 듯하다	☐ 407) 의식하는	☐ 437) 세운다
☐ 318) 남는다	☐ 348) 역시	☐ 378) 입	☐ 408) 전화	☐ 438) 아내
☐ 319) 부분	☐ 349) 광고	☐ 379) 그대로	☐ 409) 끝난다	☐ 439) 가족
☐ 320) 일부	☐ 350) 아무런	☐ 380) 영화	☐ 410) 마친다	☐ 440) 여름
☐ 321) 기업	☐ 351) 아니	☐ 381) 필요	☐ 411) 돌아온다	☐ 441) 세
☐ 322) 사업	☐ 352) 방	☐ 382) 줄	☐ 412) 맞다	☐ 442) 발전
☐ 323) 거기에	☐ 353) 정신	☐ 383) 하늘	☐ 413) 아빠	☐ 443) 논다
☐ 324) 변화	☐ 354) 이른다	☐ 384) 과학	☐ 414) 걸린다	☐ 444) 향한다
☐ 325) 변한다	☐ 355) 땅	☐ 385) 자연	☐ 415) 지킨다	☐ 445) 관련된
☐ 326) 바뀐다	☐ 356) 이룬다	☐ 386) 정말	☐ 416) 한 번	☐ 446) 형태
☐ 327) 달라졌다	☐ 357) 아침	☐ 387) 구조	☐ 417) 커피	☐ 447) 형식
☐ 328) 바꾼다	☐ 358) 웃는다	☐ 388) 결국	☐ 418) 가슴	☐ 448) 각
☐ 329) 아들	☐ 359) 웃음	☐ 389) 밥	☐ 419) 긴	☐ 449) 분위기
☐ 330) 의지	☐ 360) 현상	☐ 390) 식사	☐ 420) 바라본다	☐ 450) 기분

301-450				
301) as~as	331) ah	361) put	391) wear	421) recognize
302) as	332) await	362) put	392) rather	422) firm
303) as	333) fall	363) leave	393) come true	423) taste
304) reality	334) election	364) skill	394) stranger	424) industry
305) environment	335) about	365) total	395) one day	425) rise
306) first	336) just	366) yes	396) picture	426) rise
307) first	337) divide	367) yes	397) enemy	427) food
308) first	338) utilize	368) yes	398) site	428) surely
309) how	339) almost	369) example	399) drink	429) nowadays
310) how	340) soon	370) get	400) hit	430) plan
311) how?	341) center	371) anger	401) alone	431) plan
312) in ~self	342) center	372) beautiful	402) go out	432) feeling
313) open	343) activity	373) end	403) professor	433) how much
314) open	344) today	374) race	404) drinking	434) personality
315) head	345) today	375) seasoning	405) love	435) over and over
316) head	346) each other	376) survey	406) love	436) century
317) ask	347) interest	377) seem	407) conscious	437) erect
318) remain	348) as well	378) mouth	408) telephone	438) wife
319) part	349) advertisement	379) as it is	409) finish	439) family
320) part	350) no	380) movie	410) finish	440) summer
321) corporation	351) no	381) need	411) come back	441) rent
322) business	352) room	382) row	412) be right	442) advance
323) there	353) spirit	383) sky	413) dad	443) play
324) change	354) reach	384) science	414) take	444) head for
325) change	355) land	385) nature	415) protect	445) relevant
326) change	356) achieve	386) really	416) once	446) form
327) change	357) morning	387) structure	417) coffee	447) form
328) change	358) laugh	388) eventually	418) chest	448) angle
329) son	359) laugh	389) meal	419) long	449) mood
330) will	360) phenomenon	390) meal	420) look at	450) mood

451-600				
☐ 451) 그러한	☐ 481) 산	☐ 511) 능력	☐ 541) 방송	☐ 571) 살
☐ 452) 나이	☐ 482) 하지만	☐ 512) 주장한다	☐ 542) 이야기한다	☐ 572) 생산한다
☐ 453) 우선	☐ 483) 조건	☐ 513) 자식	☐ 543) 얘기한다	☐ 573) 바란다
☐ 454) 믿는다	☐ 484) 문	☐ 514) 어린이	☐ 544) 나무	☐ 574) 강한
☐ 455) 낳는다	☐ 485) 꽃	☐ 515) 돌린다	☐ 545) 잔다	☐ 575) 경험
☐ 456) 정보	☐ 486) 단계	☐ 516) 차례	☐ 546) 잠	☐ 576) 음악
☐ 457) 좋아한다	☐ 487) 그동안	☐ 517) 불	☐ 547) 연극	☐ 577) 최고
☐ 458) 그린다	☐ 488) 갑자기	☐ 518) 주민	☐ 548) 마찬가지로	☐ 578) 나타낸다
☐ 459) 끈다	☐ 489) 넘는다	☐ 519) 모은다	☐ 549) 걷는다	☐ 579) 아프다
☐ 460) 배운다	☐ 490) 바람	☐ 520) 자료	☐ 550) 노동	☐ 580) 적은
☐ 461) 시	☐ 491) 마을	☐ 521) 존재	☐ 551) 과거	☐ 581) 비
☐ 462) 역할	☐ 492) 어리다	☐ 522) 학년	☐ 552) 현대	☐ 582) 고향
☐ 463) 옆에	☐ 493) 대표	☐ 523) 신문	☐ 553) 살펴본다	☐ 583) 놀란다
☐ 464) 행동	☐ 494) 가능성	☐ 524) 이해한다	☐ 554) 장관	☐ 584) 다양하다
☐ 465) 행위	☐ 495) 방향	☐ 525) 제품	☐ 555) 차이	☐ 585) 운다
☐ 466) 국내	☐ 496) 대회	☐ 526) 분야	☐ 556) 푼다	☐ 586) 농민
☐ 467) 기관	☐ 497) 목소리	☐ 527) 교사	☐ 557) 시절	☐ 587) 은행
☐ 468) 입장	☐ 498) 노래	☐ 528) 돌아간다	☐ 558) 물건	☐ 588) 결혼
☐ 469) 만한	☐ 499) 바다	☐ 529) 수준	☐ 559) 직접	☐ 589) 동생
☐ 470) 가치	☐ 500) 힘든	☐ 530) 표현	☐ 560) 개인	☐ 590) 법
☐ 471) 아래	☐ 501) 공부	☐ 531) 대	☐ 561) 발	☐ 591) 소설
☐ 472) 영향	☐ 502) 공부한다	☐ 532) 젊다	☐ 562) 작가	☐ 592) 오후
☐ 473) 나선다	☐ 503) 움직인다	☐ 533) 동시	☐ 563) 효과	☐ 593) 질서
☐ 474) 흐른다	☐ 504) 노력	☐ 534) 옷	☐ 564) 불교	☐ 594) 담는다
☐ 475) 깊은	☐ 505) 전혀	☐ 535) 기능	☐ 565) 빨리	☐ 595) 모인다
☐ 476) 배	☐ 506) 언니	☐ 536) 순간	☐ 566) 시작된다	☐ 596) 시민
☐ 477) 배	☐ 507) 단체	☐ 537) 전쟁	☐ 567) 설명한다	☐ 597) 회장
☐ 478) 배	☐ 508) 집단	☐ 538) 꿈	☐ 568) 우주	☐ 598) 빠른
☐ 479) 모양	☐ 509) 알려진	☐ 539) 할머니	☐ 569) 시기	☐ 599) 스스로
☐ 480) 산	☐ 510) 가능하다	☐ 540) 회의	☐ 570) 마치	☐ 600) 아기

451-600				
451) such	481) acid	511) ability	541) broadcast	571) flesh
452) age	482) however	512) insist	542) talk	572) yield
453) first of all	483) condition	513) child	543) talk	573) wish
454) believe	484) door	514) child	544) tree	574) strong
455) give birth	485) flower	515) turn	545) sleep	575) experience
456) information	486) step	516) turn	546) sleep	576) music
457) like	487) meantime	517) fire	547) play	577) the best
458) draw	488) suddenly	518) resident	548) likewise	578) reveal
459) turn off	489) overstep	519) collect	549) walk	579) be ill
460) learn	490) wind	520) data	550) labor	580) less
461) poem	491) village	521) presence	551) past	581) rain
462) role	492) young	522) grade	552) contemporary	582) hometown
463) by	493) representative	523) newspaper	553) examine	583) surprised
464) behavior	494) chance	524) understand	554) spectacle	584) so many
465) behavior	495) direction	525) product	555) margin	585) cry
466) domestic	496) contest	526) field	556) untie	586) farmer
467) organ	497) voice	527) teacher	557) days	587) bank
468) entry	498) song	528) return	558) thing	588) wedding
469) worth	499) sea	529) level	559) first-hand	589) younger brother
470) value	500) tough	530) expression	560) individual	590) law
471) under	501) study	531) large	561) foot	591) novel
472) influence	502) study	532) young	562) writer	592) p.m.
473) come forward	503) move	533) simultaneous	563) effect	593) order
474) flow	504) effort	534) cloths	564) Buddhism	594) put in
475) deep	505) altogether	535) function	565) fast	595) gather
476) pear	506) older sister	536) moment	566) begin	596) citizen
477) ship	507) group	537) war	567) explain	597) chairman
478) stomach	508) group	538) dream	568) universe	598) quick
479) shape	509) known	539) grandma	569) period	599) by oneself
480) mountain	510) be possible	540) meeting	570) as if	600) baby

601-750				
☐ 601) 아저씨	☐ 631) 시설	☐ 661) 사고	☐ 691) 벌인다	☐ 721) 기회
☐ 602) 옛날	☐ 632) 외국	☐ 662) 그래도	☐ 692) 사진	☐ 722) 실시한다
☐ 603) 이날	☐ 633) 밑	☐ 663) 아무리	☐ 693) 주장	☐ 723) 지구
☐ 604) 제대로	☐ 634) 어른	☐ 664) 맞춘다	☐ 694) 표현한다	☐ 724) 번째
☐ 605) 달	☐ 635) 주변에	☐ 665) 쌀	☐ 695) 인한다	☐ 725) 소비자
☐ 606) 달	☐ 636) 대신	☐ 666) 일반적인	☐ 696) 이상한	☐ 726) 싫다
☐ 607) 던진다	☐ 637) 원인	☐ 667) 재미있는	☐ 697) 붙는다	☐ 727) 규모
☐ 608) 참	☐ 638) 판다	☐ 668) 가르친다	☐ 698) 아마	☐ 728) 기준
☐ 609) 공간	☐ 639) 군	☐ 669) 대화	☐ 699) 잇는다	☐ 729) 반드시
☐ 610) 이곳	☐ 640) 열심히	☐ 670) 막는다	☐ 700) 경기	☐ 730) 셈
☐ 611) 딸	☐ 641) 재산	☐ 671) 올해	☐ 701) 목적	☐ 731) 받아들인다
☐ 612) 마지막	☐ 642) 부모	☐ 672) 형	☐ 702) 태도	☐ 732) 현장
☐ 613) 병원	☐ 643) 약간	☐ 673) 오빠	☐ 703) 주위	☐ 733) 건설
☐ 614) 자세	☐ 644) 언어	☐ 674) 달리	☐ 704) 대책	☐ 734) 꺼낸다
☐ 615) 강조한다	☐ 645) 요구한다	☐ 675) 붙인다	☐ 705) 그만둔다	☐ 735) 노동자
☐ 616) 경찰	☐ 646) 감독	☐ 676) 인물	☐ 706) 발생한다	☐ 736) 동네
☐ 617) 맡는다	☐ 647) 그날	☐ 677) 늘	☐ 707) 다리	☐ 737) 언제나
☐ 618) 저녁	☐ 648) 자주	☐ 678) 항상	☐ 708) 재료	☐ 738) 완전히
☐ 619) 한편	☐ 649) 약	☐ 679) 모두	☐ 709) 각각	☐ 739) 자동차
☐ 620) 그러면	☐ 650) 기간	☐ 680) 전국	☐ 710) 결코	☐ 740) 차
☐ 621) 기자	☐ 651) 담배	☐ 681) 도움	☐ 711) 옮긴다	☐ 741) 차
☐ 622) 넓은	☐ 652) 일으킨다	☐ 682) 가정	☐ 712) 해	☐ 742) 전한다
☐ 623) 시험	☐ 653) 할아버지	☐ 683) 건다	☐ 713) 잃어버린다	☐ 743) 존재한다
☐ 624) 주로	☐ 654) 조직	☐ 684) 빠진다	☐ 714) 자유	☐ 744) 개월
☐ 625) 면	☐ 655) 태어난다	☐ 685) 멀다	☐ 715) 책임	☐ 745) 별로
☐ 626) 통일	☐ 656) 공장	☐ 686) 잠시	☐ 716) 비슷한	☐ 746) 정한다
☐ 627) 들어선다	☐ 657) 벌써	☐ 687) 농업	☐ 717) 심한	☐ 747) 한마디
☐ 628) 건강	☐ 658) 즐긴다	☐ 688) 댄다	☐ 718) 경쟁	☐ 748) 유지한다
☐ 629) 가까이	☐ 659) 지	☐ 689) 의견	☐ 719) 회	☐ 749) 대중
☐ 630) 건물	☐ 660) 환자	☐ 690) 무대	☐ 720) 구체적인	☐ 750) 늘어난다

601-750				
601) uncle	631) facility	661) accident	691) stage	721) opportunity
602) old days	632) foreign	662) nonetheless	692) photo	722) enforce
603) this day	633) beneath	663) however	693) argument	723) earth
604) properly	634) adult	664) adapt	694) express	724) ~th
605) moon	635) around	665) rice	695) be caused	725) consumer
606) month	636) instead	666) general	696) strange	726) not like
607) toss	637) cause	667) interesting	697) stick to	727) scale
608) true	638) sell	668) teach	698) maybe	728) criteria
609) space	639) county	669) conversation	699) connect	729) certainly
610) this place	640) hard	670) prevent	700) economy	730) count
611) daughter	641) property	671) this year	701) purpose	731) accept
612) final	642) parent	672) older brother	702) attitude	732) site
613) hospital	643) some	673) older brother	703) surrounding	733) construction
614) posture	644) language	674) otherwise	704) measure	734) takeout
615) emphasize	645) ask for	675) attach	705) quit	735) workforce
616) police	646) coach	676) figure	706) happen	736) neighborhood
617) undertake	647) that day	677) always	707) bridge	737) at all times
618) evening	648) often	678) always	708) material	738) completely
619) meanwhile	649) about	679) in total	709) each	739) car
620) if so	650) span	680) whole country	710) absolutely	740) car
621) reporter	651) tobacco	681) help	711) transfer	741) tea
622) wide	652) cause	682) home	712) sun	742) deliver
623) exam	653) grandfather	683) hang	713) lose	743) exist
624) usually	654) tissue	684) fall out	714) freedom	744) month
625) sense	655) be born	685) be far	715) charge	745) not very
626) unification	656) factory	686) a while	716) alike	746) fix
627) enter	657) already	687) agriculture	717) severe	747) a word
628) health	658) enjoy	688) touch	718) competition	748) keep
629) near	659) after	689) opinion	719) gathering	749) public
630) building	660) patient	690) stage	720) specific	750) stretch

Day1~8 List (6)

751-800				
☐ 751) 닦는다	☐ 781) 없어진다			
☐ 752) 말씀	☐ 782) 감정			
☐ 753) 괜찮다	☐ 783) 기억			
☐ 754) 눈물	☐ 784) 놈			
☐ 755) 각종	☐ 785) 인기			
☐ 756) 빛	☐ 786) 가끔			
☐ 757) 피한다	☐ 787) 구성한다			
☐ 758) 거친다	☐ 788) 실제로			
☐ 759) 나아간다	☐ 789) 짧다			
☐ 760) 야	☐ 790) 고맙다			
☐ 761) 지식	☐ 791) 관리			
☐ 762) 현재	☐ 792) 그곳			
☐ 763) 제시한다	☐ 793) 달다			
☐ 764) 여전히	☐ 794) 비롯된다			
☐ 765) 주인	☐ 795) 들린다			
☐ 766) 발견한다	☐ 796) 달린다			
☐ 767) 선	☐ 797) 바쁘다			
☐ 768) 인류	☐ 798) 이전			
☐ 769) 특징	☐ 799) 인정한다			
☐ 770) 선수	☐ 800) 자			
☐ 771) 마련한다				
☐ 772) 반				
☐ 773) 발표한다				
☐ 774) 주제				
☐ 775) 걸친				
☐ 776) 겪고있다				
☐ 777) 관점				
☐ 778) 귀				
☐ 779) 기본				
☐ 780) 사라진다				

751-800				
751) wipe	781) disappear			
752) words	782) emotion			
753) okay	783) memory			
754) tear	784) guy			
755) variety	785) popularity			
756) light	786) sometimes			
757) avoid	787) organize			
758) go through	788) actually			
759) proceed	789) short			
760) hey	790) thank you			
761) knowledge	791) managing			
762) present	792) that place			
763) present	793) sweet			
764) still	794) arise			
765) host	795) sound			
766) discover	796) run			
767) line	797) busy			
768) mankind	798) former			
769) characteristic	799) admit			
770) player	800) come on			
771) prepare				
772) half				
773) announce				
774) topic				
775) lasting				
776) undergo				
777) perspective				
778) ear				
779) basics				
780) disappear				

Day1~8 List Study

Final	K-word ㉜			
check	English ㉝			

K-word ㉖	English ㉗	K-word ㉘	K-word ㉙	English ㉚	K-word ㉛

Final	K-word ㉜				
check	English ㉝				

K-word ㉖	English ㉗	K-word ㉘	K-word ㉙	English ㉚	K-word ㉛

Final	K-word ㉜				
check	English ㉝				

K-word ㉖	English ㉗	K-word ㉘	K-word ㉙	English ㉚	K-word ㉛

Final	K-word ㉜				
check	English ㉝				

K-word ㉖	English ㉗	K-word ㉘	K-word ㉙	English ㉚	K-word ㉛

| Final | K-word ㉜ | | | | |
| check | English ㉝ | | | | |

K-word ㉖	English ㉗	K-word ㉘	K-word ㉙	English ㉚	K-word ㉛

	K-word	Pronounce	English	K-word ❶	Sentence example
801	나쁘다	na-ppeu-da	bad		Their service is bad.
802	불구하고	bul-gu-ha-go	despite		I go despite the rain.
803	국제적인	guk-je-jeok-in	international		English is international.
804	그룹	geu-rup	band		I love this band.
805	전통	jeon-tong	tradition		This is our tradition.
806	잔	jan	cup		I had two cups of coffee.
807	있다	iss-da	be		He is in the house.
808	시인	si-in	poet		He is a poet.
809	언제	eon-je	when		When's dinner?
810	외에는	oe-e-neun	except		I know nobody except her.
811	평가	pyeong-ga	evaluation		He received a favorable evaluation.
812	내려온다	nae-ryeo-on-da	descend		The plane descends.
813	위치	wi-chi	position		We have the best position.
814	줄인다	jul-in-da	reduce		They reduce the cost.
815	가격	ga-gyeok	price		Prices have jumped.
816	비어있다	bi-eo-iss-da	empty		The room is empty.
817	삼국	sam-guk	three nations		The three nations met in Seoul.
818	손님	son-nim	guest		We have guests.
819	원한다	won-han-da	want		I want money.
820	통신	tong-sin	communi-cation		Communication develops.

		K-word ❷	English ❸	K-word ❹	K-word ❺	English ❻	K-word ❼
Final	K-word ❽						
check	English ❾						

	K-word	Pronounce	English	K-word ❶	Sentence example
821	확인한다	hwak-in-han-da	check		The police check the dead body.
822	모임	mo-im	meeting		Yesterday was our first meeting.
823	아무	a-mu	any		Give me anything.
824	기계	gi-gye	machine		Who invented this machine?
825	물질	mul-jil	substance		Do not use this substance.
826	뉴스	nyu-seu	news		What's the latest news?
827	편다	pyeon-da	unfold		He unfolds a map.
828	수업	su-eob	lesson		She gives piano lessons.
829	종교	jong-gyo	religion		What is your religion?
830	층	cheung	floor		It is on the second floor.
831	자연스럽다	ja-yeon-seu-reob-da	natural		His behavior is natural.
832	장	jang	paste		I like soybean paste.
833	돈다	don-da	orbit		Planets orbit the sun.
834	잊는다	ij-neun-da	forget		Everyone forgets.
835	실천한다	sil-cheon-han-da	practice		He practices his words.
836	보호	bo-ho	custody		Tom is in a custody of Mother.
837	씻는다	ssis-neun-da	wash		He washes hands fast.
838	늦는다	neuj-neun-da	late		He is late.
839	이웃	i-us	neighbor		Love your neighbors.
840	편지	pyeon-ji	letter		Bill wrote a letter.

Final	K-word ❽				
check	English ❾				

K-word ❷	English ❸	K-word ❹	K-word ❺	English ❻	K-word ❼

	K-word	Pronounce	English	K-word ❶	Sentence example
841	공동	gong-dong	joint		We have a joint account.
842	팔	pal	arm		My arm hurts.
843	분명하다	bun-myeong-ha-da	clear		The result is clear.
844	분석	bun-seok	analysis		Your analysis is accurate.
845	상품	sang-pum	goods		Prices are marked on the goods.
846	설명	seol-myeong	explanation		Your explanation is simple.
847	이어진다	i-eo-jin-da	continue		The story continues until July.
848	종류	jong-ryu	types		You have three types of goods.
849	어깨	eo-kkae	shoulder		He pushed my shoulder.
850	지적한다	ji-jeok-han-da	point out		He often points out my mistakes.
851	부부	bu-bu	man and wife		The man and wife was happy.
852	오랫동안	o-raes-dong-an	for a long time		I've loved him for a long time.
853	눕는다	nub-neun-da	lie		He lies on the bed.
854	발달한다	bal-dal-han-da	develop		Children develop slowly.
855	발전한다	bal-jeon-han-da	make progress		We are making progress.
856	여행	yeo-haeng	journey		Have a safe journey.
857	죽음	juk-eum	death		I fear death.
858	고통	go-tong	pain		No pain, no gain.
859	등장한다	deung-jang-han-da	appear		Actors appear on the stage.
860	공	gong	ball		I hit the ball.

Final	K-word ❽				
check	English ❾				

K-word ❷	English ❸	K-word ❹	K-word ❺	English ❻	K-word ❼

	K-word	Pronounce	English	K-word ❶	Sentence example
861	어울린다	eo-ul-lin-da	look good		The clothes look good on you.
862	쉰다	swin-da	rest		The tiger rests on the rock.
863	알린다	al-lin-da	inform		He informs deaths.
864	찬다	chan-da	kick		He usually kicks stones.
865	멀리	meol-li	far		Tom went too far.
866	뺀다	ppaen-da	pull out	`	He pulls the key out of the car.
867	예정	ye-jeong	schedule		The trip was not scheduled.
868	즐겁다	jeul-geob-da	happy		I am happy.
869	한계	han-gye	limit		There are limits.
870	흔히	heun-hi	commonly		It is commonly known as Ecstasy.
871	바탕	ba-tang	background		The background is nice.
872	싸운다	ssa-un-da	contend		They contend each other.
873	예쁘다	ye-ppeu-da	pretty		She is pretty.
874	갈등	gal-deung	conflict		Conflict is good actually.
875	전문	jeon-mun	specialty		Her specialty is law.
876	정확하다	jeong-hwak-ha-da	accurate		His memory is accurate.
877	나중에	na-jung-e	later		See you later.
878	등	deung	back		My back hurts.
879	맛있다	mas-iss-da	delicious		This food is delicious.
880	며칠	myeo-chil	a few days		See you a few days later.

Final	K-word ❽				
check	English ❾				

K-word ❷	English ❸	K-word ❹	K-word ❺	English ❻	K-word ❼

	K-word	Pronounce	English	K-word ❶	Sentence example
881	신경	sin-gyeong	nerves		Everyone's nerves were on edge.
882	미	mi	beauty		Beauty is not the standard.
883	시선	si-seon	gaze		His gaze is burdensome.
884	언론	eon-ron	media		They avoided the media.
885	투자	tu-ja	investment		Be careful about the investment.
886	지원	ji-won	support		His support is cut off.
887	결정한다	gyeol-jeong-han-da	decide		You decide.
888	경영	gyeong-yeong	management		Your management is loose.
889	목표	mok-pyo	goal		I reached my goal.
890	성장	seong-jang	growth		Future depends on economic growth.
891	숲	sup	forest		He lives alone in the forest.
892	작년	jak-nyeon	last year		I met her last year.
893	지난 해	ji-nan hae	last year		He came here last year.
894	내려간다	naer-yeo-gan-da	go down		The price of oil goes down.
895	미친다	mi-chin-da	crazy		I'm crazy about soccer.
896	새벽	sae-byeok	dawn		Dawn is coming.
897	쓰레기	sseu-re-gi	trash		Throw away the trash.
898	임금	im-geum	wage		What's the minimum wage?
899	피해	pi-hae	damage		The typhoon damage is great.
900	무섭다	mu-seob-da	scared		I'm scared of her.

Final	K-word ❽				
check	English ❾				

K-word ❷	English ❸	K-word ❹	K-word ❺	English ❻	K-word ❼

	K-word	English		K-word	English
801	나쁘다	Their service is	821	확인한다	The police .... the dead body.
802	불구하고	I go .... the rain.	822	모임	Yesterday was our first ....
803	국제적인	English is	823	아무	Give me .... thing.
804	그룹	I love this	824	기계	Who invented this .... ?
805	전통	This is our	825	물질	Do not use this ....
806	잔	I had two .... of coffee.	826	뉴스	What's the latest .... ?
807	있다	He .... in the house.	827	편다	He .... a map.
808	시인	He is a	828	수업	She gives piano ....
809	언제	.... 's dinner?	829	종교	What is your .... ?
810	외에는	I know nobody .... her.	830	층	It is on the second ....
811	평가	He received a favorable	831	자연스럽다	His behavior is ....
812	내려온다	The plane	832	장	I like soybean ....
813	위치	We have the best	833	돈다	Planets .... the sun.
814	줄인다	They .... the cost.	834	잊는다	Everyone ....
815	가격	.... s have jumped.	835	실천한다	He .... his words.
816	비어있다	The room is	836	보호	Tom is in a .... of Mother.
817	삼국	The .... met in Seoul.	837	씻는다	He .... hands fast.
818	손님	We have	838	늦는다	He is ....
819	원한다	I .... money.	839	이웃	Love your ....
820	통신	.... develops.	840	편지	Bill wrote a ....

801) bad 802) despite 803) international 804) band
805) tradition 806) cups 807) is 808) poet
809) When 810) except 811) evaluation 812) descends
813) position 814) reduce 815) Price 816) empty
817) three nations 818) guests 819) want 820) Communication
821) check 822) meeting 823) any 824) machine
825) substance 826) news 827) unfolds 828) lessons
829) religion 830) floor 831) natural 832) paste
833) orbit 834) forgets 835) practices 836) custody
837) washes 838) late 839) neighbor 840) letter

	K-word	English		K-word	English
841	공동	We have a .... account.	861	어울린다	The clothes .... on you.
842	팔	My .... hurts.	862	쉰다	The tiger .... on the rock.
843	분명하다	The result is	863	알린다	He .... deaths.
844	분석	Your .... is accurate.	864	찬다	He usually .... stones.
845	상품	Prices are marked on the	865	멀리	Tom went too ....
846	설명	Your .... is simple.	866	뺀다	He .... the key .... of the car.
847	이어진다	The story .... until July.	867	예정	The trip was not .... ed.
848	종류	You have three .... of goods.	868	즐겁다	I am ....
849	어깨	He pushed my	869	한계	There are ....
850	지적한다	He often .... my mistakes.	870	흔히	It is .... known as Ecstasy.
851	부부	The .... was happy.	871	바탕	The .... is nice.
852	오랫동안	I've loved him	872	싸운다	They .... each other.
853	눕는다	He .... on the bed.	873	예쁘다	She is ....
854	발달한다	Children .... slowly.	874	갈등	.... is good actually.
855	발전한다	We are making	875	전문	Her .... is law.
856	여행	Have a safe	876	정확하다	His memory is ....
857	죽음	I fear	877	나중에	See you ....
858	고통	No .... , no gain.	878	등	My .... hurts.
859	등장한다	Actors .... on the stage.	879	맛있다	This food is ....
860	공	I hit the	880	며칠	See you .... later.

841) joint 842) arm 843) clear 844) analysis 845) goods 846) explanation 847) continues 848) types
849) shoulder 850) points out 851) man and wife 852) for a long time 853) lies 854) develop 855) progress 856) journey
857) death 858) pain 859) appear 860) ball 861) look good 862) rests 863) informs 864) kicks
865) far 866) pulls, out 867) schedule 868) happy 869) limits 870) commonly 871) background 872) contend
873) pretty 874) Conflict 875) specialty 876) accurate 877) later 878) back 879) delicious 880) a few days

	K-word	English
881	신경	Everyone's _____ were on edge.
882	미	_____ is not the standard.
883	시선	His _____ is burdensome.
884	언론	They avoided the _____.
885	투자	Be careful about the _____.
886	지원	His _____ is cut off.
887	결정한다	You _____.
888	경영	Your _____ is loose.
889	목표	I reached my _____.
890	성장	Future depends on economic _____.
891	숲	He lives alone in the _____.
892	작년	I met her _____.
893	지난 해	He came here _____.
894	내려간다	The price of oil _____.
895	미친다	I'm _____ about soccer.
896	새벽	_____ is coming.
897	쓰레기	Throw away the _____.
898	임금	What's the minimum _____?
899	피해	The typhoon _____ is great.
900	무섭다	I'm _____ of her.

King Sejong

– The 4th king of Joseon Dynasty

King Sejong was born in 1397.
His 32 year reign marked great achievements.
Hangeul, created by King Sejong,
has been used as a common script for
the Republic of Korea and North Korea.

881) nerves　　882) Beauty　　883) gaze　　884) media
885) Investment　886) support　887) decide　888) management
889) goal　　890) growth　891) forest　892) last year
893) last year　894) goes down　895) crazy　896) Dawn
897) trash　　898) wage　899) damage　900) scared

Day9 Review Study

Final	K-word ⑯			
check	English ⑰			

K-word ⑩	English ⑪	K-word ⑫	K-word ⑬	English ⑭	K-word ⑮

	Write K-word in		Write K-word in ....
801	Their service is bad. 그들의 서비스는	814	They reduce the cost. 그들은 비용을 ....
802	I go despite the rain. 비에도 .... 나는 간다.	815	Prices have jumped. .... 이 올랐다.
803	English is international. 영어는 .... 것이다.	816	The room is empty. 그 방은 ....
804	I love this band. 나는 이 .... 을 좋아한다.	817	The three nations met in Seoul. .... 이 서울에서 만났다.
805	This is our tradition. 이것이 우리 .... 입니다 .	818	We have guests. 우리는 .... 들이 있다.
806	I had two cups of coffee. 나는 커피 2 .... 마셨다.	819	I want money. 나는 돈을 ....
807	He is in the house. 그는 집에	820	Communication develops. .... 은 발전한다.
808	He is a poet. 그는 .... 이다.	821	The police check the dead body. 경찰이 죽은 몸을 ....
809	When's dinner? 저녁은 .... 인가요?	822	Yesterday was our first meeting. 어제가 우리의 첫 .... 이었다.
810	I know nobody except her. 나는 그녀 .... 아무도 모른다.	823	Give me anything. .... 것이나 주세요.
811	He received a favorable evaluation. 그는 좋은 .... 를 받았다.	824	Who invented this machine? 누가 이 .... 를 발명했나요?
812	The plane descends. 비행기가	825	Do not use this substance. 이 .... 을 사용하지 마시오.
813	We have the best position. 우리는 최고의 .... 를 가진다.		

801) 나쁘다   802) 불구하고   803) 국제적인   804) 그룹   805) 전통   806) 잔   807) 있다   808) 시인   809) 언제
810) 외에는   811) 평가   812) 내려온다   813) 위치   814) 줄인다   815) 가격   816) 비어있다   817) 삼국   818) 손님
819) 원한다   820) 통신   821) 확인한다   822) 모임   823) 아무   824) 기계   825) 물질

Sentence Words(1)

	K-word	pronounce	English		K-word	pronounce	English
801	그들의	geu-deul-ui	their		최고의	choe-go-ui	the best
	서비스는	seo-bi-seu-neun	service		위치를	wi-chi-reul	position
	나쁘다	na-ppeu-da	is bad		가진다	ga-jin-da	have
802	비에도	bi-e-do	the rain	814	그들은	geu-deul-eun	they
	불구하고	bul-gu-ha-go	despite		비용을	bi-yong-eul	the cost
	나는	na-neun	I		줄인다	jul-in-da	reduce
	간다	gan-da	go	815	가격이	ga-gyeok-i	prices
803	영어는	yeong-eo-neun	English		올랐다	ol-lass-da	have jumped
	국제적인	guk-je-jeok-in	international	816	그 방은	geu bang-eun	the room
	것이다	geos-i-da	is		비어있다	bi-eo-iss-da	is empty
804	나는	na-neun	I	817	삼국이	sam-guk-i	the three nations
	이	i	this		서울에서	seo-ul-e-seo	in Seoul
	그룹을	geu-rub-eul	band		만났다	man-nass-da	met
	좋아한다	joh-a-han-da	love	818	우리는	u-ri-neun	we
805	이것이	i-geos-i	this		손님들이	son-nim-deul-i	guests
	우리	u-ri	our		있다	iss-da	have
	전통	jeon-tong	tradition	819	나는	na-neun	I
	입니다	ib-ni-da	is		돈을	don-eul	money
806	나는	na-neun	I		원한다	won-han-da	want
	커피	keo-pi	coffee	820	통신은	tong-sin-eun	communication
	2잔	du-jan	two cups of		발전한다	bal-jeon-han-da	develop
	마셨다	ma-syeoss-da	had	821	경찰이	gyeong-chal-i	the police
807	그는	geu-neun	he		죽은	juk-eun	dead
	집에	jib-e	in the house		몸을	mom-eul	the body
	있다	iss-da	is		확인한다	hwak-in-han-da	check
808	그는	geu-neun	he	822	어제가	eo-je-ga	yesterday
	시인	si-in	a poet		우리의	u-ri-ui	our
	이다	i-da	is		첫	cheos	first
809	저녁은	jeo-nyeok-eun	dinner		모임	mo-im	meeting
	언제인가요?	eon-je-in-ga-yo?	when's?		이었다	i-eoss-da	was
810	나는	na-neun	I	823	아무것이나	a-mu-geos-i-na	anything
	그녀	geu-nyeo	her		주세요	ju-se-yo	give me
	외에는	oe-e-neun	except	824	누가	nu-ga	who
	아무도 모른다	a-mu-do mo-reun-da	know nobody		이	i	this
811	그는	geu-neun	he		기계를	gi-gye-reul	machine
	좋은	joh-eun	favorable		발명했나요?	bal-myeong-haess-na-yo?	invented
	평가를	pyeong-ga-reul	evaluation	825	이	i	this
	받았다	bad-ass-da	received		물질을	mul-jil-eul	substance
812	비행기가	bi-haeng-gi-ga	the plane		사용하지	sa-yong-ha-ji	use
	내려온다	nae-ryeo-on-da	descend		마시오	ma-si-o	do not
813	우리는	u-ri-neun	we				

Day9 Sentence(2)

	Write K-word in		Write K-word in ....
826	What's the latest news? 최신 ....는 뭐니?	839	Love your neighbors. 당신의 ....을 사랑하라.
827	He unfolds a map. 그가 지도를	840	Bill wrote a letter. 빌은 ....를 썼다.
828	She gives piano lessons. 그녀는 피아노 ....을 한다.	841	We have a joint account. 우리는 ....계좌를 가지고 있다.
829	What is your religion? 당신의 ....가 뭐야?	842	My arm hurts. 내 ....이 아프다.
830	It is on the second floor. 그것은 2 ....에 있다.	843	The result is clear. 결과는 ....
831	His behavior is natural. 그의 행동은	844	Your analysis is accurate. 너의 ....은 정확하다.
832	I like soybean paste. 나는 된 ....을 좋아한다.	845	Prices are marked on the goods. 가격은 ....에 표시되어 있다.
833	Planets orbit the sun. 행성은 태양의 주위를	846	Your explanation is simple. 너의 ....은 간단하다.
834	Everyone forgets. 모두가	847	The story continues until July. 그 이야기는 7월까지 ....
835	He practices his words. 그는 자신의 말을	848	You have three types of goods. 너는 세 ....의 상품을 갖는다.
836	Tom is in the custody of Mother. 톰은 엄마의 ....속에 있다.	849	He pushed my shoulder. 그는 나의 ....를 밀쳤다.
837	He washes hands fast. 그는 빨리 손을	850	He often points out my mistakes. 그는 종종 나의 실수를 ....
838	He is late. 그가		

826) 뉴스   827) 편다   828) 수업   829) 종교   830) 층   831) 자연스럽다   832) 장   833) 돈다   834) 잊는다
835) 실천한다   836) 보호   837) 씻는다   838) 늦는다   839) 이웃   840) 편지   841) 공동   842) 팔   843) 분명하다
844) 분석   845) 상품   846) 설명   847) 이어진다   848) 종류   849) 어깨   850) 지적한다

Sentence Words(2)

	K-word	pronounce	English		K-word	pronounce	English
826	최신	choe-sin	the latest		이웃을	i-us-eul	neighbors
	뉴스는	nyu-seu-neun	news		사랑하라	sa-rang-ha-ra	love
	뭐니?	mwo-ni?	what's?	840	빌은	bil-eun	Bill
827	그가	geu-ga	he		편지를	pyeon-ji-reul	a litter
	지도를	ji-do-reul	a map		썼다	sseoss-da	wrote
	편다	pyeon-da	unfold	841	우리는	u-ri-neun	we
828	그녀는	geu-nyeo-neun	she		공동	gong-dong	joint
	피아노	pi-a-no	piano		계좌를	gye-jwa-reul	account
	수업을	su-eob-eul	lessons		가지고 있다	ga-ji-go iss-da	have
	한다	han-da	give	842	내	nae	my
829	당신의	dang-sin-ui	your		팔이	pal-i	arm
	종교가	jong-gyo-ga	religion		아프다	a-peu-da	hurt
	뭐야?	mwo-ya?	what is?	843	결과는	gyeol-gwa-neun	the result
830	그것은	geu-geos-eun	it		분명하다	bun-myeong-ha-da	is clear
	2층에	i-cheung-e	on the second floor	844	너의	neo-ui	your
	있다	iss-da	is		분석은	bun-seok-eun	analysis
831	그의	geu-ui	his		정확하다	jeong-hwak-ha-da	is accurate
	행동은	haeng-dong-eun	behavior	845	가격은	ga-gyeok-eun	prices
	자연스럽다	ja-yeon-seu-reob-da	is natural		상품에	sang-pum-e	on the goods
832	나는	na-neun	I		표시되어 있다	pyo-si-doe-eo iss-da	are marked
	된장을	doen-jang-eul	soybean paste	846	너의	neo-ui	your
	좋아한다	joh-a-han-da	like		설명은	seol-myeong-eun	explanation
833	행성은	haeng-seong-eun	planets		간단하다	gan-dan-ha-da	is simple
	태양의	tae-yang-ui	the sun	847	그 이야기는	geu i-ya-gi-neun	the story
	주위를 돈다	ju-wi-reul don-da	orbit		7월	chil-wol	July
834	모두가	mo-du-ga	everyone		까지	kka-ji	until
	잊는다	ij-neun-da	forget		이어진다	i-eo-jin-da	continue
835	그는	geu-neun	he	848	너는	neo-neun	you
	자신의 말을	ja-sin-ui mal-eul	his words		세 종류의	se jong-ryu-ui	three types of
	실천한다	sil-cheon-han-da	practice		상품을	sang-pum-eul	goods
836	톰은	tom-eun	Tom		가진다	ga-jin-da	have
	엄마의	eom-ma-ui	of Mother	849	그는	geu-neun	he
	보호속에	bo-ho-sok-e	in the custody		나의	na-ui	my
	있다	iss-da	is		어깨를	eo-kkae-reul	shoulder
837	그는	geu-neun	he		밀쳤다	mil-chyeoss-da	pushed
	빨리	ppal-li	fast	850	그는	geu-neun	he
	손을	son-eul	hands		종종	jong-jong	often
	씻는다	ssis-neun-da	wash		나의	na-ui	my
838	그가	geu-ga	he		실수를	sil-su-reul	mistakes
	늦는다	neuj-neun-da	is late		지적한다	ji-jeok-han-da	point out
839	당신의	dang-sin-ui	your				

	Write K-word in			Write K-word in ....
851	The man and wife was happy. 그 .... 는 행복했다.	864	He usually kicks stones. 그는 대개 돌을 ....
852	I've loved him for a long time. 나는 .... 그를 사랑했다.	865	Tom went too far. 톰은 너무 .... 갔다.
853	He lies on the bed. 그가 침대에	866	He pulls the key out of the car. 그가 차에서 키를 ....
854	Children develop slowly. 아이들은 서서히	867	The trip was not scheduled. 그 여행은 .... 에 없었다.
855	We are making progress. 우리는	868	I am happy. 나는 ....
856	Have a safe journey. 안전한 .... 되세요.	869	There are limits. .... 가 있다.
857	I fear death. 나는 .... 이 두렵다.	870	It is commonly known as Ecstasy. 그것은 .... 엑스터시로 알려져 있다.
858	No pain, no gain. .... 이 없으면 얻는 건 없다.	871	The background is nice. .... 이 멋지다.
859	Actors appear on the stage. 배우들이 무대에	872	They contend each other. 그들은 서로 ....
860	I hit the ball. 나는 .... 을 쳤다.	873	She is pretty. 그녀는 ....
861	The clothes look good on you. 옷이 너한테	874	Conflict is good actually. .... 은 실제로 좋다.
862	The tiger rests on the rock. 호랑이가 바위에서	875	Her specialty is law. 그녀의 .... 은 법이다.
863	He informs deaths. 그는 죽음을		

851) 부부   852) 오랫동안   853) 눕는다   854) 발달한다   855) 발전한다   856) 여행   857) 죽음   858) 고통   859) 등장한다
860) 공   861) 어울린다   862) 쉰다   863) 알린다   864) 찬다   865) 멀리   866) 뺀다   867) 예정   868) 즐겁다
869) 한계   870) 흔히   871) 바탕   872) 싸운다   873) 예쁘다   874) 갈등   875) 전문

	K-word	pronounce	English		K-word	pronounce	English
851	그	geu	the	864	그는	geu-neun	he
	부부는	bu-bu-neun	man and wife		대개	dae-gae	usually
	행복했다	haeng-bok-haess-da	was happy		돌을	dol-eul	stones
852	나는	na-neun	I		찬다	chan-da	kick
	오랫동안	o-raes-dong-an	for a long time	865	톰은	tom-eun	Tom
	그를	geu-reul	he		너무	neo-mu	too
	사랑했다	sa-rang-haess-da	have loved		멀리	meol-li	far
853	그가	geu-ga	he		갔다	gass-da	went
	침대에	chim-dae-e	on the bed	866	그가	geu-ga	he
	눕는다	nub-neun-da	lie		차에서	cha-e-seo	of the car
854	아이들은	a-i-deul-eun	children		키를	ki-reul	the key
	서서히	seo-seo-hi	slowly		뺀다	ppaen-da	pull out
	발달한다	bal-dal-han-da	develop	867	그 여행은	geu yeo-haeng-eun	the trip
855	우리는	u-ri-neun	we		예정에 없었다	ye-jeong-e eobs-eoss-da	was not scheduled
	발전한다	bal-jeon-han-da	are making progress	868	나는	na-neun	I
856	안전한	an-jeon-han	safety		즐겁다	jeul-geob-da	am happy
	여행	yeo-haeng	a journey	869	한계가	han-gye-ga	limits
	되세요	doe-se-yo	have		있다	iss-da	there are
857	나는	na-neun	I	870	그것은	geu-geos-eun	it
	죽음이	juk-eum-i	death		흔히	heun-hi	commonly
	두렵다	du-ryeob-da	fear		엑스터시로	ek-seu-teo-si-ro	as Ectasy
858	고통이 없으면	go-tong-i eobs-eu-myeon	no pain		알려져 있다	al-lyeo-jyeo iss-da	is known
	얻는 건 없다	eot-neun geon eobs-da	no gain	871	바탕이	ba-tang-i	the background
859	배우들이	bae-u-deul-i	actors		멋지다	meos-ji-da	is nice
	무대에	mu-dae-e	on the stage	872	그들은	geu-deul-eun	they
	등장한다	deung-jang-han-da	appear		서로	seo-ro	each other
860	나는	na-neun	I		싸운다	ssa-un-da	contend
	공을	gong-eul	the ball	873	그녀는	geu-nyeo-neun	she
	쳤다	chyeoss-da	hit		예쁘다	ye-ppeu-da	is pretty
861	옷이	os-i	the clothes	874	갈등은	gal-deung-eun	conflict
	너한테	neo-han-te	on you		실제로	sil-je-ro	actually
	어울린다	eo-ul-lin-da	look good		좋다	joh-da	is good
862	호랑이가	ho-rang-i-ga	the tiger	875	그녀의	geu-nyeo-ui	her
	바위에서	ba-wi-e-seo	on the rock		전문은	jeon-mun-eun	specialty
	쉰다	swin-da	rest		법	beob	law
863	그는	geu-neun	he		이다	i-da	is
	죽음을	juk-eum-eul	deaths				
	알린다	al-lin-da	inform				

	Write K-word in			Write K-word in ....
876	His memory is accurate. 그의 기억은	889	I reached my goal. 나는 나의 .... 에 도달했다.
877	See you later. .... 보자.	890	Future depends on economic growth. 미래는 경제 .... 에 달려있다.
878	My back hurts. .... 이 아프다.	891	He lives alone in the forest. 그는 .... 에서 혼자 산다.
879	This food is delicious. 이 음식은	892	I met her last year. 나는 .... 에 그녀를 만났다.
880	See you a few days later. .... 후에 보자.	893	He came here last year. 그는 .... 여기에 왔다.
881	Everyone's nerves were on edge. 모두의 .... 이 날카로워 있었다.	894	The price of oil goes down. 유가가 ....
882	Beauty is not the standard. .... 가 기준이 아니다.	895	I'm crazy about soccer. 나는 축구에 ....
883	His gaze is burdensome. 그의 .... 이 부담 된다.	896	Dawn is coming. .... 이 오고 있다.
884	They avoided the media. 그들은 .... 을 피했다.	897	Throw away the trash. .... 를 버려라.
885	Be careful about the investment. .... 에 조심해라.	898	What's the minimum wage? 최저 .... 이 얼마입니까?
886	His support is cut off. 그의 .... 이 끊어졌다.	899	The typhoon damage is great. 태풍 .... 가 크다.
887	You decide. 당신이	900	I'm scared of her. 나는 그녀가 ....
888	Your management is loose. 너의 .... 은 느슨하다.		

876) 정확하다 877) 나중에 878) 등 879) 맛있다 880) 며칠 881) 신경 882) 미 883) 시선 884) 언론
885) 투자 886) 지원 887) 결정한다 888) 경영 889) 목표 890) 성장 891) 숲 892) 작년 893) 지난 해
894) 내려간다 895) 미친다 896) 새벽 897) 쓰레기 898) 임금 899) 피해 900) 무섭다

	K-word	pronounce	English		K-word	pronounce	English
876	그의	geu-ui	his	890	미래는	mi-rae-neun	future
	기억은	gi-eok-eun	memory		경제	gyeong-je	economic
	정확하다	jeong-hwak-ha-da	is accurate		성장에	seong-jang-e	growth
877	나중에	na-jung-e	later		달려있다	dal-lyeo-iss-da	depend on
	보자	bo-ja	see you	891	그는	geu-neun	he
878	등이	deung-i	my back		숲에서	sup-e-seo	in the forest
	아프다	a-peu-da	hurt		혼자	hon-ja	alone
879	이	i	this		산다	san-da	live
	음식은	eum-sik-eun	food	892	나는	na-neun	I
	맛있다	mas-iss-da	is delicious		작년에	jak-nyeon-e	last year
880	며칠	myeo-chil	a few days		그녀를	geu-nyeo-reul	her
	후에	hu-e	later		만났다	man-nass-da	met
	보자	bo-ja	see you	893	그는	geu-neun	he
881	모두의	mo-du-ui	everyone's		지난 해	ji-nan hae	last year
	신경이	sin-gyeong-i	nerves		여기에	yeo-gi-e	here
	날카로워	nal-ka-ro-wo	on edge		왔다	wass-da	came
	있었다	iss-eoss-da	were	894	유가가	yu-ga-ga	the price of oil
882	미가	mi-ga	beauty		내려간다	nae-ryeo-gan-da	goes down
	기준이	gi-jun-i	the standard	895	나는	na-neun	I
	아니다	a-ni-da	is not		축구에	chuk-gu-e	about soccer
883	그의	geu-ui	his		미친다	mi-chin-da	am crazy
	시선이	si-seon-i	gaze	896	새벽이	sae-byeok-i	dawn
	부담 된다	bu-dam-doen-da	is burdensome		오고 있다	o-go iss-da	is coming
884	그들은	geu-deul-eun	they	897	쓰레기를	sseu-re-gi-reul	the trash
	언론을	eon-ron-eul	the media		버려라	beo-ryeo-ra	throw away
	피했다	pi-haess-da	avoided	898	최저	choe-jeo	minimum
885	투자에	tu-ja-e	about the investment		임금이	im-geum-i	wage
	조심해라	jo-sim-hae-ra	be careful		얼마입니까?	eol-ma-ib-ni-kka?	what's?
886	그의	geu-ui	his	899	태풍	tae-pung	the typhoon
	지원이	ji-won-i	support		피해가	pi-hae-ga	damage
	끊어졌다	kkeunh-eo-jyeoss-da	is cut off		크다	keu-da	is great
887	당신이	dang-sin-i	you	900	나는	na-neun	I
	결정한다	gyeol-jeong-han-da	decide		그녀가	geu-nyeo-ga	her
888	너의	neo-ui	your		무섭다	mu-seob-da	am scared of
	경영은	gyeong-yeong-eun	management				
	느슨하다	neu-seun-ha-da	is loose				
889	나는	na-neun	I				
	나의	na-ui	my				
	목표에	mok-pyo-e	goal				
	도달했다	do-dal-haess-da	reached				

Final	K-word ㉔				
check	English ㉕				

K-word ⑱	English ⑲	K-word ⑳	K-word ㉑	English ㉒	K-word ㉓

1-150				
☐ 1) 것	☐ 31) 드린다	☐ 61) 집	☐ 91) 파악하고 있다	☐ 121) 지닌다
☐ 2) 한다	☐ 32) 대한다	☐ 62) 나온다	☐ 92) 자신	☐ 122) 가진다
☐ 3) 된다	☐ 33) 간다	☐ 63) 따른다	☐ 93) 문화	☐ 123) 갖추고 있다
☐ 4) 수	☐ 34) 다닌다	☐ 64) 그리고	☐ 94) 원	☐ 124) 당한다
☐ 5) 수	☐ 35) 년	☐ 65) 및	☐ 95) 생각	☐ 125) 함께
☐ 6) 길	☐ 36) 한	☐ 66) 그때	☐ 96) 명	☐ 126) 아이
☐ 7) 쪽	☐ 37) 말	☐ 67) 그럼	☐ 97) 통한다	☐ 127) 지나간다
☐ 8) 방식	☐ 38) 일	☐ 68) 문제	☐ 98) 소리	☐ 128) 많이
☐ 9) 점	☐ 39) 일	☐ 69) 그런	☐ 99) 다시	☐ 129) 훨씬
☐ 10) 점	☐ 40) 일 한다	☐ 70) 산다	☐ 100) 다른	☐ 130) 시간
☐ 11) 나	☐ 41) 작품	☐ 71) 산다	☐ 101) 다르다	☐ 131) 너
☐ 12) 내	☐ 42) 작업	☐ 72) 지낸다	☐ 102) 여자	☐ 132) 당신
☐ 13) 그	☐ 43) 직장	☐ 73) 저	☐ 103) 소녀	☐ 133) 인간
☐ 14) 없다	☐ 44) 때문	☐ 74) 생각한다	☐ 104) 개	☐ 134) 사실
☐ 15) 않다	☐ 45) 말한다	☐ 75) 모른다	☐ 105) 그 정도	☐ 135) 과연
☐ 16) 말고	☐ 46) 위하여	☐ 76) 속	☐ 106) 뒤	☐ 136) 난다
☐ 17) 아니다	☐ 47) 그러나	☐ 77) 만든다	☐ 107) 듣는다	☐ 137) 자란다
☐ 18) 않는다	☐ 48) 온다	☐ 78) 삼는다	☐ 108) 다	☐ 138) 어머니
☐ 19) 사람	☐ 49) 안다	☐ 79) 시킨다	☐ 109) 좀	☐ 139) 엄마
☐ 20) 국민	☐ 50) 씨	☐ 80) 두	☐ 110) 조금	☐ 140) 눈
☐ 21) 우리	☐ 51) 그렇다	☐ 81) 둘	☐ 111) 든다	☐ 141) 눈
☐ 22) 이	☐ 52) 큰	☐ 82) 앞	☐ 112) 키운다	☐ 142) 뭐
☐ 23) 이	☐ 53) 크다	☐ 83) 경우	☐ 113) 올린다	☐ 143) 무엇
☐ 24) 이런	☐ 54) 또	☐ 84) 중	☐ 114) 기른다	☐ 144) 무슨
☐ 25) 이것	☐ 55) 사회	☐ 85) 중	☐ 115) 싶다	☐ 145) 시대
☐ 26) 이거	☐ 56) 안에	☐ 86) 동안에	☐ 116) 보인다	☐ 146) 다음
☐ 27) 보다	☐ 57) 좋은	☐ 87) 어떤	☐ 117) 표정	☐ 147) 이러하다
☐ 28) 본다	☐ 58) 더	☐ 88) 잘	☐ 118) 모습	☐ 148) 누구
☐ 29) 같다	☐ 59) 받는다	☐ 89) 그녀	☐ 119) 가지고 있다	☐ 149) 전
☐ 30) 준다	☐ 60) 그것	☐ 90) 먹는다	☐ 120) 갖고있다	☐ 150) 곳

1-150				
1) thing	31) give	61) house	91) grasp	121) have
2) do	32) treat	62) come out	92) self	122) have
3) become	33) go	63) obey	93) culture	123) have
4) number	34) go	64) and	94) ₩	124) get p.p
5) way	35) year	65) and	95) thought	125) with
6) way	36) one	66) then	96) famous	126) kid
7) way	37) word	67) then	97) make sense	127) pass by
8) way	38) day	68) problem	98) sound	128) much
9) way	39) work	69) such	99) again	129) much ~er
10) store	40) work	70) buy	100) different	130) time
11) I	41) work	71) live	101) different	131) you
12) I	42) work	72) live	102) girl	132) you
13) he	43) job	73) um	103) girl	133) human
14) not have	44) because of	74) think	104) dog	134) in fact
15) not	45) speak	75) don't know	105) that much	135) indeed
16) not	46) for	76) inside	106) back	136) grow
17) not	47) but	77) make	107) hear	137) grow
18) do not	48) come	78) make	108) all	138) mother
19) people	49) know	79) make	109) a little	139) mom
20) people	50) family name	80) two	110) a little	140) eye
21) we	51) right	81) two	111) pick up	141) snow
22) tooth	52) big	82) front	112) raise	142) what
23) this	53) big	83) case	113) raise	143) what
24) this	54) once again	84) monk	114) raise	144) what
25) this	55) society	85) during	115) want	145) era
26) this	56) in	86) during	116) look	146) next
27) than	57) good	87) any	117) look	147) like this
28) see	58) more	88) well	118) appearance	148) who
29) same	59) receive	89) she	119) have	149) all
30) give	60) it	90) eat	120) have	150) place

151-300				
☐ 151) 자리	☐ 181) 날	☐ 211) 인생	☐ 241) 못	☐ 271) 짓는다
☐ 152) 여러	☐ 182) 여기	☐ 212) 지금	☐ 242) 못	☐ 272) 또한
☐ 153) 많은	☐ 183) 여성	☐ 213) 뿐	☐ 243) 못한다	☐ 273) 까닭
☐ 154) 하나	☐ 184) 친구	☐ 214) 다만	☐ 244) 읽는다	☐ 274) 이유
☐ 155) 세계	☐ 185) 마음	☐ 215) 만	☐ 245) 이제	☐ 275) 또는
☐ 156) 세상	☐ 186) 관계	☐ 216) 사이에	☐ 246) 결과	☐ 276) 혹은
☐ 157) 버린다	☐ 187) 아버지	☐ 217) 방법	☐ 247) 내용	☐ 277) 필요하다
☐ 158) 위	☐ 188) 남자	☐ 218) 새롭다	☐ 248) 물론	☐ 278) 글
☐ 159) 운동	☐ 189) 남성	☐ 219) 새	☐ 249) 책	☐ 279) 생긴다
☐ 160) 학교	☐ 190) 어디	☐ 220) 우리나라	☐ 250) 일어난다	☐ 280) 남편
☐ 161) 자기	☐ 191) 몸	☐ 221) 앉는다	☐ 251) 시장	☐ 281) 밖
☐ 162) 가장	☐ 192) 얼굴	☐ 222) 처음의	☐ 252) 넣는다	☐ 282) 작은
☐ 163) 제일	☐ 193) 들어간다	☐ 223) 초기	☐ 253) 중요한	☐ 283) 탄다
☐ 164) 대부분	☐ 194) 들어온다	☐ 224) 손	☐ 254) 느낀다	☐ 284) 대학
☐ 165) 대통령	☐ 195) 왜	☐ 225) 몇	☐ 255) 어려운	☐ 285) 상황
☐ 166) 가지	☐ 196) 나타난다	☐ 226) 과정	☐ 256) 힘	☐ 286) 가운데
☐ 167) 시작한다	☐ 197) 말아라	☐ 227) 찾는다	☐ 257) 너무	☐ 287) 보낸다
☐ 168) 바로	☐ 198) 지역	☐ 228) 특히	☐ 258) 부른다	☐ 288) 즉
☐ 169) 어느	☐ 199) 물	☐ 229) 도시	☐ 259) 의미	☐ 289) 따라서
☐ 170) 그래서	☐ 200) 만난다	☐ 230) 이상	☐ 260) 뜻	☐ 290) 상태
☐ 171) 그러니까	☐ 201) 낸다	☐ 231) 이야기	☐ 261) 밝힌다	☐ 291) 이후
☐ 172) 정부	☐ 202) 쓴다	☐ 232) 얘기	☐ 262) 죽는다	☐ 292) 당시
☐ 173) 모든	☐ 203) 쓴다	☐ 233) 교육	☐ 263) 이미	☐ 293) 문학
☐ 174) 번	☐ 204) 사용한다	☐ 234) 경제	☐ 264) 정치	☐ 294) 더욱
☐ 175) 그거	☐ 205) 없이	☐ 235) 아직	☐ 265) 학생	☐ 295) 아주
☐ 176) 돈	☐ 206) 이번	☐ 236) 잡는다	☐ 266) 연구	☐ 296) 매우
☐ 177) 국가	☐ 207) 이때	☐ 237) 같이	☐ 267) 이름	☐ 297) 지방
☐ 178) 나라	☐ 208) 생활	☐ 238) 선생님	☐ 268) 내린다	☐ 298) 밤
☐ 179) 그런데	☐ 209) 삶	☐ 239) 예술	☐ 269) 사건	☐ 299) 높은
☐ 180) 근데	☐ 210) 생명	☐ 240) 일어선다	☐ 270) 쉬운	☐ 300) 최근

151-300				
151) place	181) day	211) life	241) nail	271) build
152) several	182) here	212) now	242) can't	272) also
153) many	183) female	213) only	243) can't do	273) reason
154) one	184) friend	214) only	244) read	274) reason
155) world	185) mind	215) only	245) now	275) or
156) world	186) relationship	216) between	246) result	276) or
157) dump	187) father	217) manner	247) content	277) need
158) up	188) male	218) new	248) of course	278) writing
159) exercise	189) male	219) new	249) book	279) arise
160) school	190) where	220) our country	250) happen	280) husband
161) darling	191) body	221) sit down	251) market	281) outside
162) ~est	192) face	222) initial	252) insert	282) small
163) ~est	193) go into	223) initial	253) important	283) burn
164) most	194) come in	224) hand	254) feel	284) university
165) president	195) why	225) a few	255) difficult	285) situation
166) kinds	196) emerge	226) course	256) power	286) among
167) start	197) don't	227) search	257) too	287) send
168) right away	198) area	228) especially	258) call	288) namely
169) which	199) water	229) city	259) meaning	289) thus
170) so	200) meet	230) more than	260) meaning	290) state
171) so	201) pay	231) story	261) reveal	291) since
172) government	202) write	232) story	262) die	292) at the time
173) every	203) use	233) education	263) already	293) literature
174) times	204) use	234) economy	264) politics	294) ~er
175) it	205) without	235) yet	265) student	295) very
176) money	206) this time	236) catch	266) research	296) very
177) nation	207) at this time	237) together	267) name	297) fat
178) nation	208) life	238) teacher	268) get off	298) night
179) by the way	209) life	239) art	269) incident	299) high
180) by the way	210) life	240) stand up	270) easy	300) recent

301-450				
☐ 301) 만큼	☐ 331) 아	☐ 361) 둔다	☐ 391) 입는다	☐ 421) 알아본다
☐ 302) 채	☐ 332) 기다린다	☐ 362) 놓는다	☐ 392) 오히려	☐ 422) 회사
☐ 303) 대로	☐ 333) 떨어진다	☐ 363) 떠난다	☐ 393) 이루어진다	☐ 423) 맛
☐ 304) 현실	☐ 334) 선거	☐ 364) 기술	☐ 394) 남	☐ 424) 산업
☐ 305) 환경	☐ 335) 관하여	☐ 365) 전체	☐ 395) 하루	☐ 425) 오른다
☐ 306) 먼저	☐ 336) 그냥	☐ 366) 그래	☐ 396) 그림	☐ 426) 올라간다
☐ 307) 첫	☐ 337) 나눈다	☐ 367) 네	☐ 397) 적	☐ 427) 음식
☐ 308) 일단	☐ 338) 이용한다	☐ 368) 예	☐ 398) 터	☐ 428) 꼭
☐ 309) 얼마나	☐ 339) 거의	☐ 369) 예	☐ 399) 마신다	☐ 429) 요즘
☐ 310) 어쩌다	☐ 340) 곧	☐ 370) 얻는다	☐ 400) 친다	☐ 430) 계획
☐ 311) 어떠하니	☐ 341) 중심	☐ 371) 분	☐ 401) 혼자	☐ 431) 방안
☐ 312) 자체	☐ 342) 중앙	☐ 372) 아름다운	☐ 402) 나간다	☐ 432) 느낌
☐ 313) 연다	☐ 343) 활동	☐ 373) 끝	☐ 403) 교수	☐ 433) 얼마
☐ 314) 열린다	☐ 344) 오늘	☐ 374) 민족	☐ 404) 술	☐ 434) 성격
☐ 315) 머리	☐ 345) 오늘날	☐ 375) 간	☐ 405) 사랑	☐ 435) 계속
☐ 316) 고개	☐ 346) 서로	☐ 376) 조사한다	☐ 406) 사랑한다	☐ 436) 세기
☐ 317) 묻는다	☐ 347) 관심	☐ 377) 듯하다	☐ 407) 의식하는	☐ 437) 세운다
☐ 318) 남는다	☐ 348) 역시	☐ 378) 입	☐ 408) 전화	☐ 438) 아내
☐ 319) 부분	☐ 349) 광고	☐ 379) 그대로	☐ 409) 끝난다	☐ 439) 가족
☐ 320) 일부	☐ 350) 아무런	☐ 380) 영화	☐ 410) 마친다	☐ 440) 여름
☐ 321) 기업	☐ 351) 아니	☐ 381) 필요	☐ 411) 돌아온다	☐ 441) 세
☐ 322) 사업	☐ 352) 방	☐ 382) 줄	☐ 412) 맞다	☐ 442) 발전
☐ 323) 거기에	☐ 353) 정신	☐ 383) 하늘	☐ 413) 아빠	☐ 443) 논다
☐ 324) 변화	☐ 354) 이른다	☐ 384) 과학	☐ 414) 걸린다	☐ 444) 향한다
☐ 325) 변한다	☐ 355) 땅	☐ 385) 자연	☐ 415) 지킨다	☐ 445) 관련된
☐ 326) 바뀐다	☐ 356) 이룬다	☐ 386) 정말	☐ 416) 한 번	☐ 446) 형태
☐ 327) 달라졌다	☐ 357) 아침	☐ 387) 구조	☐ 417) 커피	☐ 447) 형식
☐ 328) 바꾼다	☐ 358) 웃는다	☐ 388) 결국	☐ 418) 가슴	☐ 448) 각
☐ 329) 아들	☐ 359) 웃음	☐ 389) 밥	☐ 419) 긴	☐ 449) 분위기
☐ 330) 의지	☐ 360) 현상	☐ 390) 식사	☐ 420) 바라본다	☐ 450) 기분

301-450				
301) as~as	331) ah	361) put	391) wear	421) recognize
302) as	332) await	362) put	392) rather	422) firm
303) as	333) fall	363) leave	393) come true	423) taste
304) reality	334) election	364) skill	394) stranger	424) industry
305) environment	335) about	365) total	395) one day	425) rise
306) first	336) just	366) yes	396) picture	426) rise
307) first	337) divide	367) yes	397) enemy	427) food
308) first	338) utilize	368) yes	398) site	428) surely
309) how	339) almost	369) example	399) drink	429) nowadays
310) how	340) soon	370) get	400) hit	430) plan
311) how?	341) center	371) anger	401) alone	431) plan
312) in ~self	342) center	372) beautiful	402) go out	432) feeling
313) open	343) activity	373) end	403) professor	433) how much
314) open	344) today	374) race	404) drinking	434) personality
315) head	345) today	375) seasoning	405) love	435) over and over
316) head	346) each other	376) survey	406) love	436) century
317) ask	347) interest	377) seem	407) conscious	437) erect
318) remain	348) as well	378) mouth	408) telephone	438) wife
319) part	349) advertisement	379) as it is	409) finish	439) family
320) part	350) no	380) movie	410) finish	440) summer
321) corporation	351) no	381) need	411) come back	441) rent
322) business	352) room	382) row	412) be right	442) advance
323) there	353) spirit	383) sky	413) dad	443) play
324) change	354) reach	384) science	414) take	444) head for
325) change	355) land	385) nature	415) protect	445) relevant
326) change	356) achieve	386) really	416) once	446) form
327) change	357) morning	387) structure	417) coffee	447) form
328) change	358) laugh	388) eventually	418) chest	448) angle
329) son	359) laugh	389) meal	419) long	449) mood
330) will	360) phenomenon	390) meal	420) look at	450) mood

451-600				
☐ 451) 그러한	☐ 481) 산	☐ 511) 능력	☐ 541) 방송	☐ 571) 살
☐ 452) 나이	☐ 482) 하지만	☐ 512) 주장한다	☐ 542) 이야기한다	☐ 572) 생산한다
☐ 453) 우선	☐ 483) 조건	☐ 513) 자식	☐ 543) 얘기한다	☐ 573) 바란다
☐ 454) 믿는다	☐ 484) 문	☐ 514) 어린이	☐ 544) 나무	☐ 574) 강한
☐ 455) 낳는다	☐ 485) 꽃	☐ 515) 돌린다	☐ 545) 잔다	☐ 575) 경험
☐ 456) 정보	☐ 486) 단계	☐ 516) 차례	☐ 546) 잠	☐ 576) 음악
☐ 457) 좋아한다	☐ 487) 그동안	☐ 517) 불	☐ 547) 연극	☐ 577) 최고
☐ 458) 그린다	☐ 488) 갑자기	☐ 518) 주민	☐ 548) 마찬가지로	☐ 578) 나타낸다
☐ 459) 끈다	☐ 489) 넘는다	☐ 519) 모은다	☐ 549) 걷는다	☐ 579) 아프다
☐ 460) 배운다	☐ 490) 바람	☐ 520) 자료	☐ 550) 노동	☐ 580) 적은
☐ 461) 시	☐ 491) 마을	☐ 521) 존재	☐ 551) 과거	☐ 581) 비
☐ 462) 역할	☐ 492) 어리다	☐ 522) 학년	☐ 552) 현대	☐ 582) 고향
☐ 463) 옆에	☐ 493) 대표	☐ 523) 신문	☐ 553) 살펴본다	☐ 583) 놀란다
☐ 464) 행동	☐ 494) 가능성	☐ 524) 이해한다	☐ 554) 장관	☐ 584) 다양하다
☐ 465) 행위	☐ 495) 방향	☐ 525) 제품	☐ 555) 차이	☐ 585) 운다
☐ 466) 국내	☐ 496) 대회	☐ 526) 분야	☐ 556) 푼다	☐ 586) 농민
☐ 467) 기관	☐ 497) 목소리	☐ 527) 교사	☐ 557) 시절	☐ 587) 은행
☐ 468) 입장	☐ 498) 노래	☐ 528) 돌아간다	☐ 558) 물건	☐ 588) 결혼
☐ 469) 만한	☐ 499) 바다	☐ 529) 수준	☐ 559) 직접	☐ 589) 동생
☐ 470) 가치	☐ 500) 힘든	☐ 530) 표현	☐ 560) 개인	☐ 590) 법
☐ 471) 아래	☐ 501) 공부	☐ 531) 대	☐ 561) 발	☐ 591) 소설
☐ 472) 영향	☐ 502) 공부한다	☐ 532) 젊다	☐ 562) 작가	☐ 592) 오후
☐ 473) 나선다	☐ 503) 움직인다	☐ 533) 동시	☐ 563) 효과	☐ 593) 질서
☐ 474) 흐른다	☐ 504) 노력	☐ 534) 옷	☐ 564) 불교	☐ 594) 담는다
☐ 475) 깊은	☐ 505) 전혀	☐ 535) 기능	☐ 565) 빨리	☐ 595) 모인다
☐ 476) 배	☐ 506) 언니	☐ 536) 순간	☐ 566) 시작된다	☐ 596) 시민
☐ 477) 배	☐ 507) 단체	☐ 537) 전쟁	☐ 567) 설명한다	☐ 597) 회장
☐ 478) 배	☐ 508) 집단	☐ 538) 꿈	☐ 568) 우주	☐ 598) 빠른
☐ 479) 모양	☐ 509) 알려진	☐ 539) 할머니	☐ 569) 시기	☐ 599) 스스로
☐ 480) 산	☐ 510) 가능하다	☐ 540) 회의	☐ 570) 마치	☐ 600) 아기

451-600				
451) such	481) acid	511) ability	541) broadcast	571) flesh
452) age	482) however	512) insist	542) talk	572) yield
453) first of all	483) condition	513) child	543) talk	573) wish
454) believe	484) door	514) child	544) tree	574) strong
455) give birth	485) flower	515) turn	545) sleep	575) experience
456) information	486) step	516) turn	546) sleep	576) music
457) like	487) meantime	517) fire	547) paly	577) the best
458) draw	488) suddenly	518) resident	548) likewise	578) reveal
459) turn off	489) overstep	519) collect	549) walk	579) be ill
460) learn	490) wind	520) data	550) labor	580) less
461) poem	491) village	521) presence	551) past	581) rain
462) role	492) young	522) grade	552) contemporary	582) hometown
463) by	493) representative	523) newspaper	553) examine	583) surprised
464) behavior	494) chance	524) understand	554) spectacle	584) so many
465) behavior	495) direction	525) product	555) margin	585) cry
466) domestic	496) contest	526) field	556) untie	586) farmer
467) organ	497) voice	527) teacher	557) days	587) bank
468) entry	498) song	528) return	558) thing	588) wedding
469) worth	499) sea	529) level	559) first-hand	589) younger brother
470) value	500) tough	530) expression	560) individual	590) law
471) under	501) study	531) large	561) foot	591) novel
472) influence	502) study	532) young	562) writer	592) p.m.
473) come forward	503) move	533) simultaneous	563) effect	593) order
474) flow	504) effort	534) cloths	564) Buddhism	594) put in
475) deep	505) altogether	535) function	565) fast	595) gather
476) pear	506) older sister	536) moment	566) begin	596) citizen
477) ship	507) group	537) war	567) explain	597) chairman
478) stomach	508) group	538) dream	568) universe	598) quick
479) shape	509) known	539) grandma	569) period	599) by oneself
480) mountain	510) be possible	540) meeting	570) as if	600) baby

601-750				
□ 601) 아저씨	□ 631) 시설	□ 661) 사고	□ 691) 벌인다	□ 721) 기회
□ 602) 옛날	□ 632) 외국	□ 662) 그래도	□ 692) 사진	□ 722) 실시한다
□ 603) 이날	□ 633) 밑	□ 663) 아무리	□ 693) 주장	□ 723) 지구
□ 604) 제대로	□ 634) 어른	□ 664) 맞춘다	□ 694) 표현한다	□ 724) 번째
□ 605) 달	□ 635) 주변에	□ 665) 쌀	□ 695) 인한다	□ 725) 소비자
□ 606) 달	□ 636) 대신	□ 666) 일반적인	□ 696) 이상한	□ 726) 싫다
□ 607) 던진다	□ 637) 원인	□ 667) 재미있는	□ 697) 붙는다	□ 727) 규모
□ 608) 참	□ 638) 판다	□ 668) 가르친다	□ 698) 아마	□ 728) 기준
□ 609) 공간	□ 639) 군	□ 669) 대화	□ 699) 잇는다	□ 729) 반드시
□ 610) 이곳	□ 640) 열심히	□ 670) 막는다	□ 700) 경기	□ 730) 셈
□ 611) 딸	□ 641) 재산	□ 671) 올해	□ 701) 목적	□ 731) 받아들인다
□ 612) 마지막	□ 642) 부모	□ 672) 형	□ 702) 태도	□ 732) 현장
□ 613) 병원	□ 643) 약간	□ 673) 오빠	□ 703) 주위	□ 733) 건설
□ 614) 자세	□ 644) 언어	□ 674) 달리	□ 704) 대책	□ 734) 꺼낸다
□ 615) 강조한다	□ 645) 요구한다	□ 675) 붙인다	□ 705) 그만둔다	□ 735) 노동자
□ 616) 경찰	□ 646) 감독	□ 676) 인물	□ 706) 발생한다	□ 736) 동네
□ 617) 맡는다	□ 647) 그날	□ 677) 늘	□ 707) 다리	□ 737) 언제나
□ 618) 저녁	□ 648) 자주	□ 678) 항상	□ 708) 재료	□ 738) 완전히
□ 619) 한편	□ 649) 약	□ 679) 모두	□ 709) 각각	□ 739) 자동차
□ 620) 그러면	□ 650) 기간	□ 680) 전국	□ 710) 결코	□ 740) 차
□ 621) 기자	□ 651) 담배	□ 681) 도움	□ 711) 옮긴다	□ 741) 차
□ 622) 넓은	□ 652) 일으킨다	□ 682) 가정	□ 712) 해	□ 742) 전한다
□ 623) 시험	□ 653) 할아버지	□ 683) 건다	□ 713) 잃어버린다	□ 743) 존재한다
□ 624) 주로	□ 654) 조직	□ 684) 빠진다	□ 714) 자유	□ 744) 개월
□ 625) 면	□ 655) 태어난다	□ 685) 멀다	□ 715) 책임	□ 745) 별로
□ 626) 통일	□ 656) 공장	□ 686) 잠시	□ 716) 비슷한	□ 746) 정한다
□ 627) 들어선다	□ 657) 벌써	□ 687) 농업	□ 717) 심한	□ 747) 한마디
□ 628) 건강	□ 658) 즐긴다	□ 688) 댄다	□ 718) 경쟁	□ 748) 유지한다
□ 629) 가까이	□ 659) 지	□ 689) 의견	□ 719) 회	□ 749) 대중
□ 630) 건물	□ 660) 환자	□ 690) 무대	□ 720) 구체적인	□ 750) 늘어난다

		601-750		
601) uncle	631) facility	661) accident	691) stage	721) opportunity
602) old days	632) foreign	662) nonetheless	692) photo	722) enforce
603) this day	633) beneath	663) however	693) argument	723) earth
604) properly	634) adult	664) adapt	694) express	724) ~th
605) moon	635) around	665) rice	695) be caused	725) consumer
606) month	636) instead	666) general	696) strange	726) not like
607) toss	637) cause	667) interesting	697) stick to	727) scale
608) true	638) sell	668) teach	698) maybe	728) criteria
609) space	639) county	669) conversation	699) connect	729) certainly
610) this place	640) hard	670) prevent	700) economy	730) count
611) daughter	641) property	671) this year	701) purpose	731) accept
612) final	642) parent	672) older brother	702) attitude	732) site
613) hospital	643) some	673) older brother	703) surrounding	733) construction
614) posture	644) language	674) otherwise	704) measure	734) takeout
615) emphasize	645) ask for	675) attach	705) quit	735) workforce
616) police	646) coach	676) figure	706) happen	736) neighborhood
617) undertake	647) that day	677) always	707) bridge	737) at all times
618) evening	648) often	678) always	708) material	738) completely
619) meanwhile	649) about	679) in total	709) each	739) car
620) if so	650) span	680) whole country	710) absolutely	740) car
621) reporter	651) tobacco	681) help	711) transfer	741) tea
622) wide	652) cause	682) home	712) sun	742) deliver
623) exam	653) grandfather	683) hang	713) lose	743) exist
624) usually	654) tissue	684) fall out	714) freedom	744) month
625) sense	655) be born	685) be far	715) charge	745) not very
626) unification	656) factory	686) a while	716) alike	746) fix
627) enter	657) already	687) agriculture	717) severe	747) a word
628) health	658) enjoy	688) touch	718) competition	748) keep
629) near	659) after	689) opinion	719) gathering	749) public
630) building	660) patient	690) stage	720) specific	750) stretch

751-900				
☐ 751) 닦는다	☐ 781) 없어진다	☐ 811) 평가	☐ 841) 공동	☐ 871) 바탕
☐ 752) 말씀	☐ 782) 감정	☐ 812) 내려온다	☐ 842) 팔	☐ 872) 싸운다
☐ 753) 괜찮다	☐ 783) 기억	☐ 813) 위치	☐ 843) 분명하다	☐ 873) 예쁘다
☐ 754) 눈물	☐ 784) 놈	☐ 814) 줄인다	☐ 844) 분석	☐ 874) 갈등
☐ 755) 각종	☐ 785) 인기	☐ 815) 가격	☐ 845) 상품	☐ 875) 전문
☐ 756) 빛	☐ 786) 가끔	☐ 816) 비어있다	☐ 846) 설명	☐ 876) 정확하다
☐ 757) 피한다	☐ 787) 구성한다	☐ 817) 삼국	☐ 847) 이어진다	☐ 877) 나중에
☐ 758) 거친다	☐ 788) 실제로	☐ 818) 손님	☐ 848) 종류	☐ 878) 등
☐ 759) 나아간다	☐ 789) 짧다	☐ 819) 원한다	☐ 849) 어깨	☐ 879) 맛있다
☐ 760) 야	☐ 790) 고맙다	☐ 820) 통신	☐ 850) 지적한다	☐ 880) 며칠
☐ 761) 지식	☐ 791) 관리	☐ 821) 확인한다	☐ 851) 부부	☐ 881) 신경
☐ 762) 현재	☐ 792) 그곳	☐ 822) 모임	☐ 852) 오랫동안	☐ 882) 미
☐ 763) 제시한다	☐ 793) 달다	☐ 823) 아무	☐ 853) 눕는다	☐ 883) 시선
☐ 764) 여전히	☐ 794) 비롯된다	☐ 824) 기계	☐ 854) 발달한다	☐ 884) 언론
☐ 765) 주인	☐ 795) 들린다	☐ 825) 물질	☐ 855) 발전한다	☐ 885) 투자
☐ 766) 발견한다	☐ 796) 달린다	☐ 826) 뉴스	☐ 856) 여행	☐ 886) 지원
☐ 767) 선	☐ 797) 바쁘다	☐ 827) 편다	☐ 857) 죽음	☐ 887) 결정한다
☐ 768) 인류	☐ 798) 이전	☐ 828) 수업	☐ 858) 고통	☐ 888) 경영
☐ 769) 특징	☐ 799) 인정한다	☐ 829) 종교	☐ 859) 등장한다	☐ 889) 목표
☐ 770) 선수	☐ 800) 자	☐ 830) 층	☐ 860) 공	☐ 890) 성장
☐ 771) 마련한다	☐ 801) 나쁘다	☐ 831) 자연스럽다	☐ 861) 어울린다	☐ 891) 숲
☐ 772) 반	☐ 802) 불구하고	☐ 832) 장	☐ 862) 쉰다	☐ 892) 작년
☐ 773) 발표한다	☐ 803) 국제적인	☐ 833) 돈다	☐ 863) 알린다	☐ 893) 지난 해
☐ 774) 주제	☐ 804) 그룹	☐ 834) 잊는다	☐ 864) 찬다	☐ 894) 내려간다
☐ 775) 걸친	☐ 805) 전통	☐ 835) 실천한다	☐ 865) 멀리	☐ 895) 미친다
☐ 776) 겪고있다	☐ 806) 잔	☐ 836) 보호	☐ 866) 뺀다	☐ 896) 새벽
☐ 777) 관점	☐ 807) 있다	☐ 837) 씻는다	☐ 867) 예정	☐ 897) 쓰레기
☐ 778) 귀	☐ 808) 시인	☐ 838) 늦는다	☐ 868) 즐겁다	☐ 898) 임금
☐ 779) 기본	☐ 809) 언제	☐ 839) 이웃	☐ 869) 한계	☐ 899) 피해
☐ 780) 사라진다	☐ 810) 외에는	☐ 840) 편지	☐ 870) 흔히	☐ 900) 무섭다

751-900				
751) wipe	781) disappear	811) evaluation	841) joint	871) background
752) words	782) emotion	812) descend	842) arm	872) contend
753) okay	783) memory	813) position	843) clear	873) pretty
754) tear	784) guy	814) reduce	844) analysis	874) conflict
755) variety	785) popularity	815) price	845) goods	875) specialty
756) light	786) sometimes	816) empty	846) explanation	876) accurate
757) avoid	787) organize	817) three nations	847) continue	877) later
758) go through	788) actually	818) guest	848) types	878) back
759) proceed	789) short	819) want	849) shoulder	879) delicious
760) hey	790) thank you	820) communication	850) point out	880) a few days
761) knowledge	791) managing	821) check	851) man and wife	881) nerves
762) present	792) that place	822) meeting	852) for a long time	882) beauty
763) present	793) sweet	823) any	853) lie	883) gaze
764) still	794) arise	824) machine	854) develop	884) media
765) host	795) sound	825) substance	855) progress	885) investment
766) discover	796) run	826) news	856) journey	886) support
767) line	797) busy	827) unfold	857) death	887) decide
768) mankind	798) former	828) lesson	858) pain	888) management
769) characteristic	799) admit	829) religion	859) appear	889) goal
770) player	800) come on	830) floor	860) ball	890) growth
771) prepare	801) bad	831) natural	861) look good	891) forest
772) half	802) despite	832) paste	862) rest	892) last year
773) announce	803) international	833) orbit	863) inform	893) last year
774) topic	804) band	834) forget	864) kick	894) go down
775) lasting	805) tradition	835) practice	865) far	895) crazy
776) undergo	806) cup	836) custody	866) pull out	896) dawn
777) perspective	807) be	837) wash	867) schedule	897) trash
778) ear	808) poet	838) late	868) happy	898) wage
779) basics	809) when	839) neighbor	869) limit	899) damage
780) disappear	810) except	840) letter	870) commonly	900) scared

Day1~9 List Study

Final	K-word ㉜				
check	English ㉝				

K-word ㉖	English ㉗	K-word ㉘	K-word ㉙	English ㉚	K-word ㉛

Final	K-word ㉜				
check	English ㉝				

K-word ㉖	English ㉗	K-word ㉘	K-word ㉙	English ㉚	K-word ㉛

Day1~9 List Study

Final	K-word ㉜				
check	English ㉝				

K-word ㉖	English ㉗	K-word ㉘	K-word ㉙	English ㉚	K-word ㉛

Day1~9 List Study

Final	K-word ㉜				
check	English ㉝				

K-word ㉖	English ㉗	K-word ㉘	K-word ㉙	English ㉚	K-word ㉛

Day1~9 List Study

Final	K-word ㉜				
check	English ㉝				

K-word ㉖	English ㉗	K-word ㉘	K-word ㉙	English ㉚	K-word ㉛

Final	K-word ㉜				
check	English ㉝				

K-word ㉖	English ㉗	K-word ㉘	K-word ㉙	English ㉚	K-word ㉛

Final	K-word ㉜				
check	English ㉝				

K-word ㉖	English ㉗	K-word ㉘	K-word ㉙	English ㉚	K-word ㉛

Final	K-word ㉜				
check	English ㉝				

K-word ㉖	English ㉗	K-word ㉘	K-word ㉙	English ㉚	K-word ㉛

Day1~9 List Study

Final	K-word ㉜				
check	English ㉝				

K-word ㉖	English ㉗	K-word ㉘	K-word ㉙	English ㉚	K-word ㉛

	K-word	English		K-word	English
1	것 geos		21	우리 u-ri	
2	한다 han-da		22	이 i	
3	된다 doen-da		23	이 i	
4	수 su		24	이런 i-reon	
5	수 su		25	이것 i-geos	
6	길 gil		26	이거 i-geo	
7	쪽 jjok		27	보다 bo-da	
8	방식 bang-sik		28	본다 bon-da	
9	점 jeom		29	같다 gat-da	
10	점 jeom		30	준다 jun-da	
11	나 na		31	드린다 deu-rin-da	
12	내 nae		32	대한다 dae-han-da	
13	그 geu		33	간다 gan-da	
14	없다 eobs-da		34	다닌다 da-nin-da	
15	않다 anh-da		35	년 nyeon	
16	말고 mal-go		36	한 han	
17	아니다 a-ni-da		37	말 mal	
18	않는다 anh-neun-da		38	일 il	
19	사람 sa-ram		39	일 il	
20	국민 guk-min		40	일 한다 il han-da	

1) thing　　2) do　　3) becom e　　4) number　　5) way　　6) way　　7) way　　8) way
9) way　　10) store　　11) I　　12) I　　13) he　　14) not have　　15) not　　16) not
17) not　　18) do not　　19) people　　20) people　　21) we　　22) tooth　　23) this　　24) this
25) this　　26) this　　27) than　　28) see　　29) same　　30) give　　31) give　　32) treat
33) go　　34) go　　35) year　　36) one　　37) word　　38) day　　39) work　　40) work

	K-word	English		K-word	English
41	작품 jak-pum		61	집 jib	
42	작업 jak-eob		62	나온다 na-on-da	
43	직장 jik-jang		63	따른다 tta-reun-da	
44	때문 ttae-mun		64	그리고 geu-ri-go	
45	말한다 mal-han-da		65	및 micc	
46	위하여 wi-ha-yeo		66	그때 geu-ttae	
47	그러나 geu-reo-na		67	그럼 geu-reom	
48	온다 on-da		68	문제 mun-je	
49	안다 an-da		69	그런 geu-reon	
50	씨 ssi		70	산다 san-da	
51	그렇다 geu-reoh-da		71	산다 san-da	
52	큰 keun		72	지낸다 ji-naen-da	
53	크다 keu-da		73	저 jeo	
54	또 tto		74	생각한다 saeng-gak-han-da	
55	사회 sa-hoe		75	모른다 mo-reun-da	
56	안에 an-e		76	속 sok	
57	좋은 joh-eun		77	만든다 man-deun-da	
58	더 deo		78	삼는다 sam-neun-da	
59	받는다 bad-neun-da		79	시킨다 si-kin-da	
60	그것 geu-geos		80	두 du	

41) work   42) work   43) job   44) because of   45) speak   46) for   47) but   48) come
49) know   50) family name   51) right   52) big   53) big   54) once again   55) society   56) in
57) good   58) more   59) receive   60) it   61) house   62) come out   63) obey   64) and
65) and   66) then   67) then   68) problem   69) such   70) buy   71) live   72) live
73) um   74) thinks   75) don't know   76) inside   77) make   78) make   79) make   80) two

	K-word	English		K-word	English
81	둘 dul		101	다르다 da-reu-da	
82	앞 ap		102	여자 yeo-ja	
83	경우 gyeong-u		103	소녀 so-nyeo	
84	중 jung		104	개 gae	
85	중 jung		105	그정도 geu-jeong-do	
86	동안에 dong-an-e		106	뒤 dwi	
87	어떤 eo-tteon		107	듣는다 deud-neun-da	
88	잘 jal		108	다 da	
89	그녀 geu-nyeo		109	좀 jom	
90	먹는다 meok-neun-da		110	조금 jo-geum	
91	파악하고 있다 pa-ak-ha-go issda		111	든다 deun-da	
92	자신 ja-sin		112	키운다 ki-un-da	
93	문화 mun-hwa		113	올린다 ol-lin-da	
94	원 won		114	기른다 gi-reun-da	
95	생각 saeng-gak		115	싶다 sip-da	
96	명 myeong		116	보인다 bo-in-da	
97	통한다 tong-han-da		117	표정 pyo-jeong	
98	소리 sori		118	모습 mo-seub	
99	다시 da-si		119	가지고 있다 ga-ji-go iss-da	
100	다른 da-reun		120	갖고 있다 gaj-go iss-da	

81) two　　82) front　　83) case　　84) monk　　85) during　　86) during　　87) any　　88) well
89) she　　90) eat　　91) grasp　　92) self　　93) culture　　94) ₩　　95) thought　　96) famous
97) make sense　　98) sound　　99) again　　100) different　　101) different　　102) girl　　103) girl　　104) dog
105) that much　　106) back　　107) hear　　108) all　　109) al ittle　　110) a little　　111) pick up　　112) raise
113) raise　　114) raise　　115) want　　116) look　　117) look　　118) appearance　　119) have　　120) have

	K-word	English		K-word	English
121	지닌다 ji-nin-da		141	눈 nun	
122	가진다 ga-jin-da		142	뭐 mwo	
123	갖추고 있다 gaj-chu-go iss-da		143	무엇 mu-eos	
124	당한다 dang-han-da		144	무슨 mu-seun	
125	함께 ham-kke		145	시대 si-dae	
126	아이 a-i		146	다음 da-eum	
127	지나간다 ji-na-gan-da		147	이러하다 i-reo-ha-da	
128	많이 manh-i		148	누구 nu-gu	
129	훨씬 hwol-ssin		149	전 jeon	
130	시간 si-gan		150	곳 gos	
131	너 neo		151	자리 ja-ri	
132	당신 dang-sin		152	여러 yeo-reo	
133	인간 in-gan		153	많은 manh-eun	
134	사실 sa-sil		154	하나 ha-na	
135	과연 gwa-yeon		155	세계 se-gye	
136	난다 nan-da		156	세상 se-sang	
137	자란다 ja-ran-da		157	버린다 beo-rin-da	
138	어머니 eo-meo-ni		158	위 wi	
139	엄마 eom-ma		159	운동 un-dong	
140	눈 nun		160	학교 hak-gyo	

121) have 122) have 123) have 124) get p.p 125) with 126) kid 127) pass by 128) much
129) much ~er 130) time 131) you 132) you 133) human 134) in fact 135) indeed 136) grow
137) grow 138) mother 139) mom 140) eye 141) snow 142) what 143) what 144) what
145) era 146) next 147) like this 148) who 149) all 150) place 151) place 152) several
153) many 154) one 155) world 156) world 157) dump 158) up 159) exercise 160) school

	K-word	English		K-word	English
161	자기 ja-gi		181	날 nal	
162	가장 ga-jang		182	여기 yeo-gi	
163	제일 je-il		183	여성 yeo-seong	
164	대부분 dae-bu-bun		184	친구 chin-gu	
165	대통령 dae-tong-ryeong		185	마음 ma-eum	
166	가지 ga-ji		186	관계 gwan-gye	
167	시작한다 si-jak-han-da		187	아버지 a-beo-ji	
168	바로 ba-ro		188	남자 nam-ja	
169	어느 eo-neu		189	남성 nam-seong	
170	그래서 geu-rae-seo		190	어디 eo-di	
171	그러니까 geu-reo-ni-kka		191	몸 mom	
172	정부 jeong-bu		192	얼굴 eol-gul	
173	모든 mo-deun		193	들어간다 deul-eo-gan-da	
174	번 beon		194	들어온다 deul-eo-on-da	
175	그거 geu-geo		195	왜 wae	
176	돈 don		196	나타난다 na-ta-nan-da	
177	국가 guk-ga		197	말아라 mal-a-ra	
178	나라 na-ra		198	지역 ji-yeok	
179	그런데 geu-reon-de		199	물 mul	
180	근데 geun-de		200	만난다 man-nan-da	

161) darling   162) ~est   163) ~est   164) most   165) president   166) kinds   167) start   168) right away
169) which   170) so   171) so   172) government   173) every   174) times   175) it   176) money
177) nation   178) nation   179) by the way   180) by the way   181) day   182) here   183) female   184) friend
185) mind   186) relationship   187) father   188) male   189) male   190) where   191) body   192) face
193) go into   194) come in   195) why   196) emerge   197) don't   198) area   199) water   200) meet

	K-word	English		K-word	English
201	낸다 naen-da		221	앉는다 anj-neun-da	
202	쓴다 sseun-da		222	처음의 cheo-eum-ui	
203	쓴다 sseun-da		223	초기 cho-gi	
204	사용한다 sa-yong-han-da		224	손 son	
205	없이 eobs-i		225	몇 myeocc	
206	이번 i-beon		226	과정 gwa-jeong	
207	이때 i-ttae		227	찾는다 chaj-neun-da	
208	생활 saeng-hwal		228	특히 teuk-hi	
209	삶 salm		229	도시 do-si	
210	생명 saeng-myeong		230	이상 i-sang	
211	인생 in-saeng		231	이야기 i-ya-gi	
212	지금 ji-geum		232	얘기 yae-gi	
213	뿐 ppun		233	교육 gyo-yuk	
214	다만 da-man		234	경제 gyeong-je	
215	만 man		235	아직 a-jik	
216	사이에 sa-i-e		236	잡는다 jab-neun-da	
217	방법 bang-beob		237	같이 gat-i	
218	새롭다 sae-rob-da		238	선생님 seon-saeng-nim	
219	새 sae		239	예술 ye-sul	
220	우리나라 u-ri-na-ra		240	일어선다 il-eo-seon-da	

201) pay   202) write   203) use   204) use   205) without   206) this time   207) at this time   208) life
209) life   210) life   211) life   212) now   213) only   214) only   215) only   216) between
217) manner   218) new   219) new   220) our country   221) sit down   222) initial   223) initial   224) hand
225) a few   226) course   227) search   228) especially   229) city   230) more than   231) story   232) story
233) education   234) economy   235) yet   236) catch   237) together   238) teacher   239) art   240) stand up

	K-word	English		K-word	English
241	못 mos		261	밝힌다 balk-hin-da	
242	못 mos		262	죽는다 juk-neun-da	
243	못한다 mos-han-da		263	이미 i-mi	
244	읽는다 ilk-neun-da		264	정치 jeong-chi	
245	이제 i-je		265	학생 hak-saeng	
246	결과 gyeol-gwa		266	연구 yeon-gu	
247	내용 nae-yong		267	이름 i-reum	
248	물론 mul-lon		268	내린다 nae-rin-da	
249	책 chaek		269	사건 sa-geon	
250	일어난다 il-eo-nan-da		270	쉬운 swi-un	
251	시장 si-jang		271	짓는다 jis-neun-da	
252	넣는다 neoh-neun-da		272	또한 tto-han	
253	중요한 jung-yo-han		273	까닭 kka-dalk	
254	느낀다 neu-kkin-da		274	이유 i-yu	
255	어려운 eo-ryeo-un		275	또는 tto-neun	
256	힘 him		276	혹은 hok-eun	
257	너무 neo-mu		277	필요하다 pil-yo-ha-da	
258	부른다 bu-reun-da		278	글 geul	
259	의미 ui-mi		279	생긴다 saeng-gin-da	
260	뜻 tteus		280	남편 nam-pyeon	

241) nail   242) can't   243) can't do   244) read   245) now   246) result   247) content   248) of course
249) book   250) happen   251) market   252) insert   253) important 254) feel   255) difficult   256) power
257) too   258) call   259) meaning   260) meaning   261) reveal   262) die   263) already   264) politics
265) student   266) research   267) name   268) get off   269) incident   270) easy   271) build   272) also
273) reason   274) reason   275) or   276) or   277) need   278) writing   279) arise   280) husband

	K-word	English		K-word	English
281	밖 bakk		301	만큼 man-keum	
282	작은 jak-eun		302	채 chae	
283	탄다 tan-da		303	대로 dae-ro	
284	대학 dae-hak		304	현실 hyeon-sil	
285	상황 sang-hwang		305	환경 hwan-gyeong	
286	가운데 ga-un-de		306	먼저 meon-jeo	
287	보낸다 bo-naen-da		307	첫 cheos	
288	즉 jeuk		308	일단 il-dan	
289	따라서 tta-ra-seo		309	얼마나 eol-ma-na	
290	상태 sang-tae		310	어쩌다 eo-jjeo-da	
291	이후 i-hu		311	어떠하니? eo-tteo-ha-ni	
292	당시 dang-si		312	자체 ja-che	
293	문학 mun-hak		313	연다 yeon-da	
294	더욱 deo-uk		314	열린다 yeol-lin-da	
295	아주 a-ju		315	머리 meo-ri	
296	매우 mae-u		316	고개 go-gae	
297	지방 ji-bang		317	묻는다 mud-neun-da	
298	밤 bam		318	남는다 nam-neun-da	
299	높은 nop-eun		319	부분 bu-bun	
300	최근 choe-geun		320	일부 il-bu	

281) outside   282) small   283) burn   284) university   285) situation   286) among   287) send   288) namely
289) thus   290) state   291) since   292) at the time   293) literature   294) ~er   295) very   296) very
297) fat   298) night   299) high   300) recent   301) as~as   302) as   303) as   304) reality
305) environment   306) first   307) first   308) first   309) how   310) how   311) how?   312) ~self
313) open   314) open   315) head   316) head   317) ask   318) remain   319) part   320) part

	K-word	English		K-word	English
321	기업 gi-eob		341	중심 jung-sim	
322	사업 sa-eob		342	중앙 jung-ang	
323	거기에 geo-gi-e		343	활동 hwal-dong	
324	변화 byeon-hwa		344	오늘 o-neul	
325	변한다 byeon-han-da		345	오늘날 o-neul-nal	
326	바뀐다 ba-kkwin-da		346	서로 seo-ro	
327	달라졌다 dal-la-jyeoss-da		347	관심 gwan-sim	
328	바꾼다 ba-kkun-da		348	역시 yeok-si	
329	아들 a-deul		349	광고 gwang-go	
330	의지 ui-ji		350	아무런 a-mu-reon	
331	아 a		351	아니 a-ni	
332	기다린다 gi-da-rin-da		352	방 bang	
333	떨어진다 tteol-eo-jin-da		353	정신 jeong-sin	
334	선거 seon-geo		354	이른다 i-reun-da	
335	관하여 gwan-ha-yeo		355	땅 ttang	
336	그냥 geu-nyang		356	이룬다 i-run-da	
337	나눈다 na-nun-da		357	아침 a-chim	
338	이용한다 i-yong-han-da		358	웃는다 us-neun-da	
339	거의 geo-ui		359	웃음 us-eum	
340	곧 god		360	현상 hyeon-sang	

321) corporation 322) business 323) there 324) change 325) change 326) change 327) change 328) change
329) son 330) will 331) ah 332) await 333) fall 334) election 335) about 336) just
337) divide 338) utilize 339) almost 340) soon 341) center 342) center 343) activity 344) today
345) today 346) each other 347) interest 348) as well 349) advertisement 350) no 351) no 352) room
353) spirit 354) reach 355) land 356) achieve 357) morning 358) laugh 359) laugh 360) phenomenon

	K-word	English		K-word	English
361	둔다 dun-da		381	필요 pil-yo	
362	놓는다 noh-neun-da		382	줄 jul	
363	떠난다 tteo-nan-da		383	하늘 ha-neul	
364	기술 gi-sul		384	과학 gwa-hak	
365	전체 jeon-che		385	자연 ja-yeon	
366	그래 geu-rae		386	정말 jeong-mal	
367	네 ne		387	구조 gu-jo	
368	예 ye		388	결국 gyeol-guk	
369	예 ye		389	밥 bab	
370	얻는다 eod-neun-da		390	식사 sik-sa	
371	분 bun		391	입는다 ib-neun-da	
372	아름다운 a-reum-da-un		392	오히려 o-hi-ryeo	
373	끝 kkeut		393	이루어진다 i-ru-eo-jin-da	
374	민족 min-jok		394	남 nam	
375	간 gan		395	하루 ha-ru	
376	조사한다 jo-sa-han-da		396	그림 geu-rim	
377	듯하다 deus-ha-da		397	적 jeok	
378	입 ib		398	터 teo	
379	그대로 geu-dae-ro		399	마신다 ma-sin-da	
380	영화 yeong-hwa		400	친다 chin-da	

361) put 362) put 363) leave 364) skill 365) total 366) yes 367) yes 368) yes
369) example 370) get 371) anger 372) beautiful 373) end 374) race 375) seasoning 376) survey
377) seem 378) mouth 379) as it is 380) movie 381) need 382) row 383) sky 384) science
385) nature 386) really 387) structure 388) eventually 389) meal 390) meal 391) wear 392) rather
393) come true 394) stranger 395) one day 396) picture 397) enemy 398) site 399) drink 400) hit

	K-word	English		K-word	English
401	혼자 hon-ja		421	알아본다 al-a-bon-da	
402	나간다 na-gan-da		422	회사 hoe-sa	
403	교수 gyo-su		423	맛 mas	
404	술 sul		424	산업 san-eob	
405	사랑 sa-rang		425	오른다 o-reun-da	
406	사랑한다 sa-rang-han-da		426	올라간다 ol-la-gan-da	
407	의식하는 ui-sik-ha-neun		427	음식 eum-sik	
408	전화 jeon-hwa		428	꼭 kkok	
409	끝난다 kkeut-nan-da		429	요즘 yo-jeum	
410	마친다 ma-chin-da		430	계획 gye-hoek	
411	돌아온다 dol-a-on-da		431	방안 bang-an	
412	맞다 maj-da		432	느낌 neu-kkim	
413	아빠 a-ppa		433	얼마 eol-ma	
414	걸린다 geol-lin-da		434	성격 seong-gyeok	
415	지킨다 ji-kin-da		435	계속 gye-sok	
416	한 번 han beon		436	세기 se-gi	
417	커피 keo-pi		437	세운다 se-un-da	
418	가슴 ga-seum		438	아내 a-nae	
419	긴 gin		439	가족 ga-jok	
420	바라본다 ba-ra-bon-da		440	여름 yeo-reum	

401) alone 402) go out 403) professor 404) drinking 405) love 406) love 407) conscious 408) telephone
409) finish 410) finish 411) come back 412) right 413) dad 414) take 415) protect 416) once
417) coffee 418) chest 419) long 420) look at 421) recognize 422) firm 423) taste 424) industry
425) rise 426) rise 427) food 428) surely 429) nowadays 430) plan 431) plan 432) feeling
433) how much 434) personality 435) over and over 436) century 437) erect 438) wife 439) family 440) summer

	K-word	English		K-word	English
441	세 se		461	시 si	
442	발전 bal-jeon		462	역할 yeok-hal	
443	논다 non-da		463	옆에 yeop-e	
444	향한다 hyang-han-da		464	행동 haeng-dong	
445	관련된 gwan-ryeon-doen		465	행위 haeng-wi	
446	형태 hyeong-tae		466	국내 guk-nae	
447	형식 hyeong-sik		467	기관 gi-gwan	
448	각 gak		468	입장 ib-jang	
449	분위기 bun-wi-gi		469	만한 man-han	
450	기분 gi-bun		470	가치 ga-chi	
451	그러한 geu-reo-han		471	아래 a-rae	
452	나이 na-i		472	영향 yeong-hyang	
453	우선 u-seon		473	나선다 na-seon-da	
454	믿는다 mid-neun-da		474	흐른다 heu-reun-da	
455	낳는다 nah-neun-da		475	깊은 gip-eun	
456	정보 jeong-bo		476	배 bae	
457	좋아한다 joh-a-han-da		477	배 bae	
458	그린다 geu-rin-da		478	배 bae	
459	끈다 kkeun-da		479	모양 mo-yang	
460	배운다 bae-un-da		480	산 san	

441) rent 442) advance 443) play 444) head for 445) relevant 446) form 447) form 448) angle
449) mood 450) mood 451) such 452) age 453) first of all 454) believe 455) give birth 456) information
457) like 458) draw 459) turn off 460) learn 461) poem 462) role 463) by 464) behavior
465) behavior 466) domestic 467) organ 468) entry 469) worth 470) value 471) under 472) influence
473) come forward 474) flow 475) deep 476) pear 477) ship 478) stomach 479) shape 480) mountain

#	K-word	English	#	K-word	English
481	산 san		501	공부 gong-bu	
482	하지만 ha-ji-man		502	공부한다 gong-bu-han-da	
483	조건 jo-geon		503	움직인다 um-jik-in-da	
484	문 mun		504	노력 no-ryeok	
485	꽃 kkocc		505	전혀 jeon-hyeo	
486	단계 dan-gye		506	언니 eon-ni	
487	그동안 geu-dong-an		507	단체 dan-che	
488	갑자기 gab-ja-gi		508	집단 jib-dan	
489	넘는다 neom-neun-da		509	알려진 al-lyeo-jin	
490	바람 ba-ram		510	가능하다 ga-neung-ha-da	
491	마을 ma-eul		511	능력 neung-ryeok	
492	어리다 eo-ri-da		512	주장한다 ju-jang-han-da	
493	대표 dae-pyo		513	자식 ja-sik	
494	가능성 ga-neung-seong		514	어린이 eo-rin-i	
495	방향 bang-hyang		515	돌린다 dol-lin-da	
496	대회 dae-hoe		516	차례 cha-rye	
497	목소리 mok-so-ri		517	불 bul	
498	노래 no-rae		518	주민 ju-min	
499	바다 ba-da		519	모은다 mo-eun-da	
500	힘든 him-deun		520	자료 ja-ryo	

481) acid 482)however 483) condition 484) door 485) flower 486) step 487) meantime 488) suddenly
489) overstep 490) wind 491) village 492) young 493) representative. 494) chance 495) direction 496) contest
497) voice 498) song 499) sea 500) tough 501) study 502) study 503) move 504) effort
505) altogether 506) older sister 507) group 508) group 509) known 510) possible 511) ability 512) insist
513) child 514) child 515) turn 516) turn 517) fire 518) resident 519) collect 520) data

	K-word	English		K-word	English
521	존재 jon-jae		541	방송 bang-song	
522	학년 hak-nyeon		542	이야기 한다 i-ya-gi han-da	
523	신문 sin-mun		543	얘기 한다 yae-gi han-da	
524	이해한다 i-hae-han-da		544	나무 na-mu	
525	제품 je-pum		545	잔다 jan-da	
526	분야 bun-ya		546	잠 jam	
527	교사 gyo-sa		547	연극 yeon-geuk	
528	돌아간다 dol-a-gan-da		548	마찬가지로 ma-chan-ga-ji-ro	
529	수준 su-jun		549	걷는다 geod-neun-da	
530	표현 pyo-hyeon		550	노동 no-dong	
531	대 dae		551	과거 gwa-geo	
532	젊다 jeolm-da		552	현대 hyeon-dae	
533	동시 dong-si		553	살펴본다 sal-pyeo-bon-da	
534	옷 os		554	장관 jang-gwan	
535	기능 gi-neung		555	차이 cha-i	
536	순간 sun-gan		556	푼다 pun-da	
537	전쟁 jeon-jaeng		557	시절 si-jeol	
538	꿈 kkum		558	물건 mul-geon	
539	할머니 hal-meo-ni		559	직접 jik-jeob	
540	회의 hoe-ui		560	개인 gae-in	

521) presence   522) grade   523) newspaper   524) understand   525) product   526) field   527) teacher   528) return
529) level   530) expression   531) large   532) young   533) simultaneous   534) cloths   535) function   536) moment
537) war   538) dream   539) grandma   540) meeting   541) broadcast   542) talk   543) talk   544) tree
545) sleep   546) sleep   547) play   548) likewise   549) walk   550) labor   551) past   552) contemporary
553) examine   554) spectacle   555) margin   556) untie   557) days   558) thing   559) first-hand   560) individual

	K-word	English		K-word	English
561	발 bal		581	비 bi	
562	작가 jak-ga		582	고향 go-hyang	
563	효과 hyo-gwa		583	놀란다 nol-lan-da	
564	불교 bul-gyo		584	다양하다 da-yang-ha-da	
565	빨리 ppal-li		585	운다 un-da	
566	시작된다 si-jak-doen-da		586	농민 nong-min	
567	설명한다 seol-myeong-han-da		587	은행 eun-haeng	
568	우주 u-ju		588	결혼 gyeol-hon	
569	시기 si-gi		589	동생 dong-saeng	
570	마치 ma-chi		590	법 beob	
571	살 sal		591	소설 so-seol	
572	생산한다 saeng-san-han-da		592	오후 o-hu	
573	바란다 ba-ran-da		593	질서 jil-seo	
574	강한 gang-han		594	담는다 dam-neun-da	
575	경험 gyeong-heom		595	모인다 mo-in-da	
576	음악 eum-ak		596	시민 si-min	
577	최고 choe-go		597	회장 hoe-jang	
578	나타낸다 na-ta-naen-da		598	빠른 ppa-reun	
579	아프다 a-peu-da		599	스스로 seu-seu-ro	
580	적은 jeok-eun		600	아기 a-gi	

561) foot   562) writer   563) effect   564) Buddhism   565) fast   566) begin   567) explain   568) universe
569) period   570) as if   571) flesh   572) yield   573) wish   574) strong   575) experience   576) music
577) the best   578) reveal   579) ill   580) less   581) rain   582) hometown   583) surprised   584) so many
585) cry   586) farmer   587) bank   588) wedding   589) younger brother   590) law   591) novel   592) p.m.
593) order   594) put in   595) gather   596) citizen   597) chairman   598) quick   599) by oneself   600) baby

	K-word	English		K-word	English
601	아저씨 a-jeo-ssi		621	기자 gi-ja	
602	옛날 yes-nal		622	넓은 neolb-eun	
603	이날 i-nal		623	시험 si-heom	
604	제대로 je-dae-ro		624	주로 ju-ro	
605	달 dal		625	면 myeon	
606	달 dal		626	통일 tong-il	
607	던진다 deon-jin-da		627	들어선다 deul-eo-seon-da	
608	참 cham		628	건강 geon-gang	
609	공간 gong-gan		629	가까이 ga-kka-i	
610	이곳 i-gos		630	건물 geon-mul	
611	딸 ttal		631	시설 si-seol	
612	마지막 ma-ji-mak		632	외국 oe-guk	
613	병원 byeong-won		633	밑 mit	
614	자세 ja-se		634	어른 eo-reun	
615	강조한다 gang-jo-han-da		635	주변에 ju-byeon-e	
616	경찰 gyeong-chal		636	대신 dae-sin	
617	맡는다 mat-neun-da		637	원인 won-in	
618	저녁 jeo-nyeok		638	판다 pan-da	
619	한편 han-pyeon		639	군 gun	
620	그러면 geu-reo-myeon		640	열심히 yeol-sim-hi	

601) uncle   602) old days   603) this day   604) properly   605) moon   606) month   607) toss   608) true
609) space   610) this place   611) daughter   612) final   613) hospital   614) posture   615) emphasize   616) police
617) undertake   618) evening   619) meanwhile   620) if so   621) reporter   622) wide   623) exam   624) usually
625) sense   626) unification   627) enter   628) health   629) near   630) building   631) facility   632) foreign
633) beneath   634) adult   635) around   636) instead   637) cause   638) sell   639) county   640) hard

	K-word	English		K-word	English
641	재산 jae-san		661	사고 sa-go	
642	부모 bu-mo		662	그래도 geu-rae-do	
643	약간 yak-gan		663	아무리 a-mu-ri	
644	언어 eon-eo		664	맞춘다 maj-chun-da	
645	요구한다 yo-gu-han-da		665	쌀 ssal	
646	감독 gam-dok		666	일반적인 il-ban-jeok-in	
647	그날 geu-nal		667	재미있는 jae-mi-iss-neun	
648	자주 ja-ju		668	가르친다 ga-reu-chin-da	
649	약 yak		669	대화 dae-hwa	
650	기간 gi-gan		670	막는다 mak-neun-da	
651	담배 dam-bae		671	올해 ol-hae	
652	일으킨다 il-eu-kin-da		672	형 hyeong	
653	할아버지 hal-a-beo-ji		673	오빠 o-ppa	
654	조직 jo-jik		674	달리 dal-li	
655	태어난다 tae-eo-nan-da		675	붙인다 but-in-da	
656	공장 gong-jang		676	인물 in-mul	
657	벌써 beol-sseo		677	늘 neul	
658	즐긴다 jeul-gin-da		678	항상 hang-sang	
659	지 ji		679	모두 mo-du	
660	환자 hwan-ja		680	전국 jeon-guk	

641) property   642) parent   643) some   644) language   645) ask for   646) coach   647) that day   648) often
649) about   650) span   651) tobacco   652) cause   653) grandfather   654) tissue   655) be born   656) factory
657) already   658) enjoy   659) after   660) patient   661) accident   662) nonetheless   663) however   664) adapt
665) rice   666) general   667) interesting   668) teach   669) conversation   670) prevent   671) this year   672) older brother
673) older brother   674) otherwise   675) attach   676) figure   677) always   678) always   679) altogether   680) whole country

	K-word	English		K-word	English
681	도움 do-um		701	목적 mok-jeok	
682	가정 ga-jeong		702	태도 tae-do	
683	걷다 geon-da		703	주위 ju-wi	
684	빠진다 ppa-jin-da		704	대책 dae-chaek	
685	멀다 meol-da		705	그만둔다 geu-man-dun-da	
686	잠시 jam-si		706	발생한다 bal-saeng-han-da	
687	농업 nong-eob		707	다리 da-ri	
688	댄다 daen-da		708	재료 jae-ryo	
689	의견 ui-gyeon		709	각각 gak-gak	
690	무대 mu-dae		710	결코 gyeol-ko	
691	벌인다 beol-in-da		711	옮긴다 olm-gin-da	
692	사진 sa-jin		712	해 hae	
693	주장 ju-jang		713	잃어버린다 ilh-eo-beo-rin-da	
694	표현한다 pyo-hyeon-han-da		714	자유 ja-yu	
695	인한다 in-han-da		715	책임 chaek-im	
696	이상한 i-sang-han		716	비슷한 bi-seus-han	
697	붙는다 but-neun-da		717	심한 sim-han	
698	아마 a-ma		718	경쟁 gyeong-jaeng	
699	잇는다 is-neun-da		719	회 hoe	
700	경기 gyeong-gi		720	구체적인 gu-che-jeok-in	

681) help 682) home 683) hang 684) fall out 685) be far 686) while 687) agriculture 688) touch
689) opinion 690) stage 691) stage 692) photo 693) argument 694) express 695) caused 696) strange
697) stick to 698) maybe 699) connect 700) economy 701) purpose 702) attitude 703) surrounding 704) measure
705) quit 706) happen 707) bridge 708) material 709) each 710) absolutely 711) transfer 712) sun
713) lose 714) freedom 715) charge 716) alike 717) severe 718) competition 719) gathering 720) specific

	K-word	English		K-word	English
721	기회 gi-hoe		741	차 cha	
722	실시한다 sil-si-han-da		742	전한다 jeon-han-da	
723	지구 ji-gu		743	존재한다 jon-jae-han-da	
724	번째 beon-jjae		744	개월 gae-wol	
725	소비자 so-bi-ja		745	별로 byeol-lo	
726	싫다 silh-da		746	정한다 jeong-han-da	
727	규모 gyu-mo		747	한마디 han-ma-di	
728	기준 gi-jun		748	유지한다 yu-ji-han-da	
729	반드시 ban-deu-si		749	대중 dae-jung	
730	셈 sem		750	늘어난다 neul-eo-nan-da	
731	받아들인다 bad-a-deul-in-da		751	닦는다 dakk-neun-da	
732	현장 hyeon-jang		752	말씀 mal-sseum	
733	건설 geon-seol		753	괜찮다 gwaen-chanh-da	
734	꺼낸다 kkeo-naen-da		754	눈물 nun-mul	
735	노동자 no-dong-ja		755	각종 gak-jong	
736	동네 dong-ne		756	빛 bicc	
737	언제나 eon-je-na		757	피한다 pi-han-da	
738	완전히 wan-jeon-hi		758	거친다 geo-chin-da	
739	자동차 ja-dong-cha		759	나아간다 na-a-gan-da	
740	차 cha		760	야 ya	

721) opportunity   722) enforce   723) earth   724) th   725) consumer   726) not like   727) scale   728) criteria
729) certainly   730) count   731) accept   732) site   733) construction   734) take out   735) worker   736) neighborhood
737) at all times   738) completely   739) car   740) car   741) tea   742) deliver   743) exist   744) month
745) not very   746) fix   747) a word   748) keep   749) public   750) stretch   751) wipe   752) words
753) okay   754) tear   755) variety   756) light   757) avoid   758) go through   759) proceed   760) hey

	K-word	English		K-word	English
761	지식 ji-sik		781	없어진다 eobs-eo-jinda	
762	현재 hyeon-jae		782	감정 gam-jeong	
763	제시한다 je-si-han-da		783	기억 gi-eok	
764	여전히 yeo-jeon-hi		784	놈 nom	
765	주인 ju-in		785	인기 in-gi	
766	발견한다 bal-gyeon-han-da		786	가끔 ga-kkeum	
767	선 seon		787	구성한다 gu-seong-han-da	
768	인류 in-ryu		788	실제로 sil-je-ro	
769	특징 teuk-jing		789	짧다 jjalb-da	
770	선수 seon-su		790	고맙다 go-mab-da	
771	마련한다 ma-ryeon-han-da		791	관리 gwan-ri	
772	반 ban		792	그곳 geu-gos	
773	발표한다 bal-pyo-han-da		793	달다 dal-da	
774	주제 ju-je		794	비롯된다 bi-ros-doen-da	
775	걸친 geol-chin		795	들린다 deul-lin-da	
776	겪고 있다 gyeokk-go-iss-da		796	달린다 dal-lin-da	
777	관점 gwan-jeom		797	바쁘다 ba-ppeu-da	
778	귀 gwi		798	이전 i-jeon	
779	기본 gi-bon		799	인정한다 in-jeong-han-da	
780	사라진다 sa-ra-jin-da		800	자 ja	

761) knowledge   762) present   763) present   764) still   765) host   766) discover   767) line   768) mankind
769) characteristic 770) player   771) prepare   772) half   773) announce   774) topic   775) lasting   776) undergo
777) perspective   778) ear   779) basics   780) disappear   781) disappear   782) emotion   783) memory   784) guy
785) popularity   786) sometimes   787) organize   788) actually   789) short   790) thank you   791) managing   792) that place
793) sweet   794) arise   795) sound   796) run   797) busy   798) former   799) admit   800) come on

	K-word	English		K-word	English
801	나쁘다 na-ppeu-da		821	확인한다 hwak-in-han-da	
802	불구하고 bul-gu-ha-go		822	모임 mo-im	
803	국제적인 guk-je-jeok-in		823	아무 a-mu	
804	그룹 geu-rub		824	기계 gi-gye	
805	전통 jeon-tong		825	물질 mul-jil	
806	잔 jan		826	뉴스 nyu-seu	
807	있다 iss-da		827	편다 pyeon-da	
808	시인 si-in		828	수업 su-eob	
809	언제 eon-je		829	종교 jong-gyo	
810	외에는 oe-e-neun		830	층 cheung	
811	평가 pyeong-ga		831	자연스럽다 ja-yeon-seu-reob-da	
812	내려온다 nae-ryeo-on-da		832	장 jang	
813	위치 wi-chi		833	돈다 don-da	
814	줄인다 jul-in-da		834	잊는다 ij-neun-da	
815	가격 ga-gyeok		835	실천한다 sil-cheon-han-da	
816	비어있다 bi-eo-iss-da		836	보호 bo-ho	
817	삼국 sam-guk		837	씻는다 ssis-neun-da	
818	손님 son-nim		838	늦는다 neuj-neun-da	
819	원한다 won-han-da		839	이웃 i-us	
820	통신 tong-sin		840	편지 pyeon-ji	

801) bad 802) despite 803) international 804) band 805) tradition 806) cup 807) be 808) poet
809) when 810) except 811) evaluation 812) descend 813) position 814) reduce 815) price 816) empty
817) three nations 818) guest 819) want 820) communication 821) check 822) meeting 823) any 824) machine
825) substance 826) news 827) unfold 828) lesson 829) religion 830) floor 831) natural 832) paste
833) orbit 834) forget 835) practice 836) custody 837) wash 838) late 839) neighbor 840) letter

	K-word	English		K-word	English
841	공동 gong-dong		861	어울린다 eo-ul-lin-da	
842	팔 pal		862	쉰다 swin-da	
843	분명하다 bun-myeong-ha-da		863	알린다 al-lin-da	
844	분석 bun-seok		864	찬다 chan-da	
845	상품 sang-pum		865	멀리 meol-li	
846	설명 seol-myeong		866	뺀다 ppaen-da	
847	이어진다 i-eo-jin-da		867	예정 ye-jeong	
848	종류 jong-ryu		868	즐겁다 jeul-geob-da	
849	어깨 eo-kkae		869	한계 han-gye	
850	지적한다 ji-jeok-han-da		870	흔히 heun-hi	
851	부부 bu-bu		871	바탕 ba-tang	
852	오랫동안 o-raes-dong-an		872	싸운다 ssa-un-da	
853	눕는다 nub-neun-da		873	예쁘다 ye-ppeu-da	
854	발달한다 bal-dal-han-da		874	갈등 gal-deung	
855	발전한다 bal-jeon-han-da		875	전문 jeon-mun	
856	여행 yeo-haeng		876	정확하다 jeong-hwak-ha-da	
857	죽음 juk-eum		877	나중에 na-jung-e	
858	고통 go-tong		878	등 deung	
859	등장한다 deung-jang-han-da		879	맛있다 mas-iss-da	
860	공 gong		880	며칠 myeo-chil	

841) joint 842) arm 843) clear 844) analysis 845) goods 846) explanation 847) continue 848) types
849) shoulder 850) point out 851) man and wife 852) for a long time 853) lie 854) develop 855) progress 856) journey
857) death 858) pain 859) appear 860) ball 861) look good 862) rest 863) inform 864) kick
865) far 866) pull out 867) schedule 868) happy 869) limit 870) commonly 871) background 872) contend
873) pretty 874) conflict 875) specialty 876) accurate 877) later 878) back 879) delicious 880) a few days

	K-word	English
881	신경 sin-gyeong	
882	미 mi	
883	시선 si-seon	
884	언론 eon-ron	
885	투자 tu-ja	
886	지원 ji-won	
887	결정한다 gyeol-jeong-han-da	
888	경영 gyeong-yeong	
889	목표 mok-pyo	
890	성장 seong-jang	
891	숲 sup	
892	작년 jak-nyeon	
893	지난 해 ji-nan hae	
894	내려간다 nae-ryeo-gan-da	
895	미친다 mi-chin-da	
896	새벽 sae-byeok	
897	쓰레기 sseu-re-gi	
898	임금 im-geum	
899	피해 pi-hae	
900	무섭다 mu-seob-da	

King Sejong

– The 4th king of Joseon Dynasty

King Sejong was born in 1397.
His 32 year reign marked great achievements.
Hangeul, created by King Sejong,
has been used as a common script for
the Republic of Korea and North Korea.

881) nerves   882) beauty   883) gaze   884) media
885) investment 886) support   887) decide 888) management
889) goal   890) growth   891) forest   892) last year
893) last year 894) go down   895) crazy   896) dawn
897) trash   898) wage   899) damage   900) scared

900 Total Review Study

Final	K-word ⑳				
check	English ㊶				

K-word ㉞	English ㉟	K-word ㊱	K-word ㊲	English ㊳	K-word ㊴

Final	K-word ⑩				
check	English ㊶				

K-word ㉞	English ㉟	K-word ㊱	K-word ㊲	English ㊳	K-word ㊴

Final	K-word ㊵				
check	English ㊶				

K-word ㉞	English ㉟	K-word ㊱	K-word ㊲	English ㊳	K-word ㊴

Final	K-word ㊵				
check	English ㊶				

K-word ㉞	English ㉟	K-word ㊱	K-word ㊲	English ㊳	K-word ㊴

Final	K-word ㊽				
check	English ㊶				

K-word ㉞	English ㉟	K-word ㊱	K-word ㊲	English ㊳	K-word ㊴

Final	K-word ④⓪				
check	English ④①				

K-word ㉞	English ㉟	K-word ㊱	K-word ㊲	English ㊳	K-word ㊴

Final	K-word ⑩				
check	English ㊶				

K-word ㉞	English ㉟	K-word ㊱	K-word ㊲	English ㊳	K-word ㊴

Final	K-word ㊵				
check	English ㊶				

K-word ㉞	English ㉟	K-word ㊱	K-word ㊲	English ㊳	K-word ㊴

Final	K-word ㊵				
check	English ㊶				

K-word ㉞	English ㉟	K-word ㊱	K-word ㊲	English ㊳	K-word ㊴

	Final	K-word ㊵				
	check	English ㊶				

K-word ㉞	English ㉟	K-word ㊱	K-word ㊲	English ㊳	K-word ㊳

1-150				
☐ 1) 것	☐ 31) 드린다	☐ 61) 집	☐ 91) 파악하고 있다	☐ 121) 지닌다
☐ 2) 한다	☐ 32) 대한다	☐ 62) 나온다	☐ 92) 자신	☐ 122) 가진다
☐ 3) 된다	☐ 33) 간다	☐ 63) 따른다	☐ 93) 문화	☐ 123) 갖추고 있다
☐ 4) 수	☐ 34) 다닌다	☐ 64) 그리고	☐ 94) 원	☐ 124) 당한다
☐ 5) 수	☐ 35) 년	☐ 65) 및	☐ 95) 생각	☐ 125) 함께
☐ 6) 길	☐ 36) 한	☐ 66) 그때	☐ 96) 명	☐ 126) 아이
☐ 7) 쪽	☐ 37) 말	☐ 67) 그럼	☐ 97) 통한다	☐ 127) 지나간다
☐ 8) 방식	☐ 38) 일	☐ 68) 문제	☐ 98) 소리	☐ 128) 많이
☐ 9) 점	☐ 39) 일	☐ 69) 그런	☐ 99) 다시	☐ 129) 훨씬
☐ 10) 점	☐ 40) 일 한다	☐ 70) 산다	☐ 100) 다른	☐ 130) 시간
☐ 11) 나	☐ 41) 작품	☐ 71) 산다	☐ 101) 다르다	☐ 131) 너
☐ 12) 내	☐ 42) 작업	☐ 72) 지낸다	☐ 102) 여자	☐ 132) 당신
☐ 13) 그	☐ 43) 직장	☐ 73) 저	☐ 103) 소녀	☐ 133) 인간
☐ 14) 없다	☐ 44) 때문	☐ 74) 생각한다	☐ 104) 개	☐ 134) 사실
☐ 15) 않다	☐ 45) 말한다	☐ 75) 모른다	☐ 105) 그 정도	☐ 135) 과연
☐ 16) 말고	☐ 46) 위하여	☐ 76) 속	☐ 106) 뒤	☐ 136) 난다
☐ 17) 아니다	☐ 47) 그러나	☐ 77) 만든다	☐ 107) 듣는다	☐ 137) 자란다
☐ 18) 않는다	☐ 48) 온다	☐ 78) 삼는다	☐ 108) 다	☐ 138) 어머니
☐ 19) 사람	☐ 49) 안다	☐ 79) 시킨다	☐ 109) 좀	☐ 139) 엄마
☐ 20) 국민	☐ 50) 씨	☐ 80) 두	☐ 110) 조금	☐ 140) 눈
☐ 21) 우리	☐ 51) 그렇다	☐ 81) 둘	☐ 111) 든다	☐ 141) 눈
☐ 22) 이	☐ 52) 큰	☐ 82) 앞	☐ 112) 키운다	☐ 142) 뭐
☐ 23) 이	☐ 53) 크다	☐ 83) 경우	☐ 113) 올린다	☐ 143) 무엇
☐ 24) 이런	☐ 54) 또	☐ 84) 중	☐ 114) 기른다	☐ 144) 무슨
☐ 25) 이것	☐ 55) 사회	☐ 85) 중	☐ 115) 싶다	☐ 145) 시대
☐ 26) 이거	☐ 56) 안에	☐ 86) 동안에	☐ 116) 보인다	☐ 146) 다음
☐ 27) 보다	☐ 57) 좋은	☐ 87) 어떤	☐ 117) 표정	☐ 147) 이러하다
☐ 28) 본다	☐ 58) 더	☐ 88) 잘	☐ 118) 모습	☐ 148) 누구
☐ 29) 같다	☐ 59) 받는다	☐ 89) 그녀	☐ 119) 가지고 있다	☐ 149) 전
☐ 30) 준다	☐ 60) 그것	☐ 90) 먹는다	☐ 120) 갖고있다	☐ 150) 곳

1-150				
1) thing	31) give	61) house	91) grasp	121) have
2) do	32) treat	62) come out	92) self	122) have
3) become	33) go	63) obey	93) culture	123) have
4) number	34) go	64) and	94) ₩	124) get p.p
5) way	35) year	65) and	95) thought	125) with
6) way	36) one	66) then	96) famous	126) kid
7) way	37) word	67) then	97) make sense	127) pass by
8) way	38) day	68) problem	98) sound	128) much
9) way	39) work	69) such	99) again	129) much ~er
10) store	40) work	70) buy	100) different	130) time
11) I	41) work	71) live	101) different	131) you
12) I	42) work	72) live	102) girl	132) you
13) he	43) job	73) um	103) girl	133) human
14) not have	44) because of	74) think	104) dog	134) in fact
15) not	45) speak	75) don't know	105) that much	135) indeed
16) not	46) for	76) inside	106) back	136) grow
17) not	47) but	77) make	107) hear	137) grow
18) do not	48) come	78) make	108) all	138) mother
19) people	49) know	79) make	109) a little	139) mom
20) people	50) family name	80) two	110) a little	140) eye
21) we	51) right	81) two	111) pick up	141) snow
22) tooth	52) big	82) front	112) raise	142) what
23) this	53) big	83) case	113) raise	143) what
24) this	54) once again	84) monk	114) raise	144) what
25) this	55) society	85) during	115) want	145) era
26) this	56) in	86) during	116) look	146) next
27) than	57) good	87) any	117) look	147) like this
28) see	58) more	88) well	118) appearance	148) who
29) same	59) receive	89) she	119) have	149) all
30) give	60) it	90) eat	120) have	150) place

151-300				
☐ 151) 자리	☐ 181) 날	☐ 211) 인생	☐ 241) 못	☐ 271) 짓는다
☐ 152) 여러	☐ 182) 여기	☐ 212) 지금	☐ 242) 못	☐ 272) 또한
☐ 153) 많은	☐ 183) 여성	☐ 213) 뿐	☐ 243) 못한다	☐ 273) 까닭
☐ 154) 하나	☐ 184) 친구	☐ 214) 다만	☐ 244) 읽는다	☐ 274) 이유
☐ 155) 세계	☐ 185) 마음	☐ 215) 만	☐ 245) 이제	☐ 275) 또는
☐ 156) 세상	☐ 186) 관계	☐ 216) 사이에	☐ 246) 결과	☐ 276) 혹은
☐ 157) 버린다	☐ 187) 아버지	☐ 217) 방법	☐ 247) 내용	☐ 277) 필요하다
☐ 158) 위	☐ 188) 남자	☐ 218) 새롭다	☐ 248) 물론	☐ 278) 글
☐ 159) 운동	☐ 189) 남성	☐ 219) 새	☐ 249) 책	☐ 279) 생긴다
☐ 160) 학교	☐ 190) 어디	☐ 220) 우리나라	☐ 250) 일어난다	☐ 280) 남편
☐ 161) 자기	☐ 191) 몸	☐ 221) 앉는다	☐ 251) 시장	☐ 281) 밖
☐ 162) 가장	☐ 192) 얼굴	☐ 222) 처음의	☐ 252) 넣는다	☐ 282) 작은
☐ 163) 제일	☐ 193) 들어간다	☐ 223) 초기	☐ 253) 중요한	☐ 283) 탄다
☐ 164) 대부분	☐ 194) 들어온다	☐ 224) 손	☐ 254) 느낀다	☐ 284) 대학
☐ 165) 대통령	☐ 195) 왜	☐ 225) 몇	☐ 255) 어려운	☐ 285) 상황
☐ 166) 가지	☐ 196) 나타난다	☐ 226) 과정	☐ 256) 힘	☐ 286) 가운데
☐ 167) 시작한다	☐ 197) 말아라	☐ 227) 찾는다	☐ 257) 너무	☐ 287) 보낸다
☐ 168) 바로	☐ 198) 지역	☐ 228) 특히	☐ 258) 부른다	☐ 288) 즉
☐ 169) 어느	☐ 199) 물	☐ 229) 도시	☐ 259) 의미	☐ 289) 따라서
☐ 170) 그래서	☐ 200) 만난다	☐ 230) 이상	☐ 260) 뜻	☐ 290) 상태
☐ 171) 그러니까	☐ 201) 낸다	☐ 231) 이야기	☐ 261) 밝힌다	☐ 291) 이후
☐ 172) 정부	☐ 202) 쓴다	☐ 232) 얘기	☐ 262) 죽는다	☐ 292) 당시
☐ 173) 모든	☐ 203) 쓴다	☐ 233) 교육	☐ 263) 이미	☐ 293) 문학
☐ 174) 번	☐ 204) 사용한다	☐ 234) 경제	☐ 264) 정치	☐ 294) 더욱
☐ 175) 그거	☐ 205) 없이	☐ 235) 아직	☐ 265) 학생	☐ 295) 아주
☐ 176) 돈	☐ 206) 이번	☐ 236) 잡는다	☐ 266) 연구	☐ 296) 매우
☐ 177) 국가	☐ 207) 이때	☐ 237) 같이	☐ 267) 이름	☐ 297) 지방
☐ 178) 나라	☐ 208) 생활	☐ 238) 선생님	☐ 268) 내린다	☐ 298) 밤
☐ 179) 그런데	☐ 209) 삶	☐ 239) 예술	☐ 269) 사건	☐ 299) 높은
☐ 180) 근데	☐ 210) 생명	☐ 240) 일어선다	☐ 270) 쉬운	☐ 300) 최근

151-300				
151) place	181) day	211) life	241) nail	271) build
152) several	182) here	212) now	242) can't	272) also
153) many	183) female	213) only	243) can't do	273) reason
154) one	184) friend	214) only	244) read	274) reason
155) world	185) mind	215) only	245) now	275) or
156) world	186) relationship	216) between	246) result	276) or
157) dump	187) father	217) manner	247) content	277) need
158) up	188) male	218) new	248) of course	278) writing
159) exercise	189) male	219) new	249) book	279) arise
160) school	190) where	220) our country	250) happen	280) husband
161) darling	191) body	221) sit down	251) market	281) outside
162) ~est	192) face	222) initial	252) insert	282) small
163) ~est	193) go into	223) initial	253) important	283) burn
164) most	194) come in	224) hand	254) feel	284) university
165) president	195) why	225) a few	255) difficult	285) situation
166) kinds	196) emerge	226) course	256) power	286) among
167) start	197) don't	227) search	257) too	287) send
168) right away	198) area	228) especially	258) call	288) namely
169) which	199) water	229) city	259) meaning	289) thus
170) so	200) meet	230) more than	260) meaning	290) state
171) so	201) pay	231) story	261) reveal	291) since
172) government	202) write	232) story	262) die	292) at the time
173) every	203) use	233) education	263) already	293) literature
174) times	204) use	234) economy	264) politics	294) ~er
175) it	205) without	235) yet	265) student	295) very
176) money	206) this time	236) catch	266) research	296) very
177) nation	207) at this time	237) together	267) name	297) fat
178) nation	208) life	238) teacher	268) get off	298) night
179) by the way	209) life	239) art	269) incident	299) high
180) by the way	210) life	240) stand up	270) easy	300) recent

Day1~9 List (3)

301-450				
☐ 301) 만큼	☐ 331) 아	☐ 361) 둔다	☐ 391) 입는다	☐ 421) 알아본다
☐ 302) 채	☐ 332) 기다린다	☐ 362) 놓는다	☐ 392) 오히려	☐ 422) 회사
☐ 303) 대로	☐ 333) 떨어진다	☐ 363) 떠난다	☐ 393) 이루어진다	☐ 423) 맛
☐ 304) 현실	☐ 334) 선거	☐ 364) 기술	☐ 394) 남	☐ 424) 산업
☐ 305) 환경	☐ 335) 관하여	☐ 365) 전체	☐ 395) 하루	☐ 425) 오른다
☐ 306) 먼저	☐ 336) 그냥	☐ 366) 그래	☐ 396) 그림	☐ 426) 올라간다
☐ 307) 첫	☐ 337) 나눈다	☐ 367) 네	☐ 397) 적	☐ 427) 음식
☐ 308) 일단	☐ 338) 이용한다	☐ 368) 예	☐ 398) 터	☐ 428) 꼭
☐ 309) 얼마나	☐ 339) 거의	☐ 369) 예	☐ 399) 마신다	☐ 429) 요즘
☐ 310) 어쩌다	☐ 340) 곧	☐ 370) 얻는다	☐ 400) 친다	☐ 430) 계획
☐ 311) 어떠하니	☐ 341) 중심	☐ 371) 분	☐ 401) 혼자	☐ 431) 방안
☐ 312) 자체	☐ 342) 중앙	☐ 372) 아름다운	☐ 402) 나간다	☐ 432) 느낌
☐ 313) 연다	☐ 343) 활동	☐ 373) 끝	☐ 403) 교수	☐ 433) 얼마
☐ 314) 열린다	☐ 344) 오늘	☐ 374) 민족	☐ 404) 술	☐ 434) 성격
☐ 315) 머리	☐ 345) 오늘날	☐ 375) 간	☐ 405) 사랑	☐ 435) 계속
☐ 316) 고개	☐ 346) 서로	☐ 376) 조사한다	☐ 406) 사랑한다	☐ 436) 세기
☐ 317) 묻는다	☐ 347) 관심	☐ 377) 듯하다	☐ 407) 의식하는	☐ 437) 세운다
☐ 318) 남는다	☐ 348) 역시	☐ 378) 입	☐ 408) 전화	☐ 438) 아내
☐ 319) 부분	☐ 349) 광고	☐ 379) 그대로	☐ 409) 끝난다	☐ 439) 가족
☐ 320) 일부	☐ 350) 아무런	☐ 380) 영화	☐ 410) 마친다	☐ 440) 여름
☐ 321) 기업	☐ 351) 아니	☐ 381) 필요	☐ 411) 돌아온다	☐ 441) 세
☐ 322) 사업	☐ 352) 방	☐ 382) 줄	☐ 412) 맞다	☐ 442) 발전
☐ 323) 거기에	☐ 353) 정신	☐ 383) 하늘	☐ 413) 아빠	☐ 443) 논다
☐ 324) 변화	☐ 354) 이른다	☐ 384) 과학	☐ 414) 걸린다	☐ 444) 향한다
☐ 325) 변한다	☐ 355) 땅	☐ 385) 자연	☐ 415) 지킨다	☐ 445) 관련된
☐ 326) 바뀐다	☐ 356) 이룬다	☐ 386) 정말	☐ 416) 한 번	☐ 446) 형태
☐ 327) 달라졌다	☐ 357) 아침	☐ 387) 구조	☐ 417) 커피	☐ 447) 형식
☐ 328) 바꾼다	☐ 358) 웃는다	☐ 388) 결국	☐ 418) 가슴	☐ 448) 각
☐ 329) 아들	☐ 359) 웃음	☐ 389) 밥	☐ 419) 긴	☐ 449) 분위기
☐ 330) 의지	☐ 360) 현상	☐ 390) 식사	☐ 420) 바라본다	☐ 450) 기분

301-450				
301) as~as	331) ah	361) put	391) wear	421) recognize
302) as	332) await	362) put	392) rather	422) firm
303) as	333) fall	363) leave	393) come true	423) taste
304) reality	334) election	364) skill	394) stranger	424) industry
305) environment	335) about	365) total	395) one day	425) rise
306) first	336) just	366) yes	396) picture	426) rise
307) first	337) divide	367) yes	397) enemy	427) food
308) first	338) utilize	368) yes	398) site	428) surely
309) how	339) almost	369) example	399) drink	429) nowadays
310) how	340) soon	370) get	400) hit	430) plan
311) how?	341) center	371) anger	401) alone	431) plan
312) in ~self	342) center	372) beautiful	402) go out	432) feeling
313) open	343) activity	373) end	403) professor	433) how much
314) open	344) today	374) race	404) drinking	434) personality
315) head	345) today	375) seasoning	405) love	435) over and over
316) head	346) each other	376) survey	406) love	436) century
317) ask	347) interest	377) seem	407) conscious	437) erect
318) remain	348) as well	378) mouth	408) telephone	438) wife
319) part	349) advertisement	379) as it is	409) finish	439) family
320) part	350) no	380) movie	410) finish	440) summer
321) corporation	351) no	381) need	411) come back	441) rent
322) business	352) room	382) row	412) be right	442) advance
323) there	353) spirit	383) sky	413) dad	443) play
324) change	354) reach	384) science	414) take	444) head for
325) change	355) land	385) nature	415) protect	445) relevant
326) change	356) achieve	386) really	416) once	446) form
327) change	357) morning	387) structure	417) coffee	447) form
328) change	358) laugh	388) eventually	418) chest	448) angle
329) son	359) laugh	389) meal	419) long	449) mood
330) will	360) phenomenon	390) meal	420) look at	450) mood

451-600				
☐ 451) 그러한	☐ 481) 산	☐ 511) 능력	☐ 541) 방송	☐ 571) 살
☐ 452) 나이	☐ 482) 하지만	☐ 512) 주장한다	☐ 542) 이야기한다	☐ 572) 생산한다
☐ 453) 우선	☐ 483) 조건	☐ 513) 자식	☐ 543) 얘기한다	☐ 573) 바란다
☐ 454) 믿는다	☐ 484) 문	☐ 514) 어린이	☐ 544) 나무	☐ 574) 강한
☐ 455) 낳는다	☐ 485) 꽃	☐ 515) 돌린다	☐ 545) 잔다	☐ 575) 경험
☐ 456) 정보	☐ 486) 단계	☐ 516) 차례	☐ 546) 잠	☐ 576) 음악
☐ 457) 좋아한다	☐ 487) 그동안	☐ 517) 불	☐ 547) 연극	☐ 577) 최고
☐ 458) 그린다	☐ 488) 갑자기	☐ 518) 주민	☐ 548) 마찬가지로	☐ 578) 나타낸다
☐ 459) 끈다	☐ 489) 넘는다	☐ 519) 모은다	☐ 549) 걷는다	☐ 579) 아프다
☐ 460) 배운다	☐ 490) 바람	☐ 520) 자료	☐ 550) 노동	☐ 580) 적은
☐ 461) 시	☐ 491) 마을	☐ 521) 존재	☐ 551) 과거	☐ 581) 비
☐ 462) 역할	☐ 492) 어리다	☐ 522) 학년	☐ 552) 현대	☐ 582) 고향
☐ 463) 옆에	☐ 493) 대표	☐ 523) 신문	☐ 553) 살펴본다	☐ 583) 놀란다
☐ 464) 행동	☐ 494) 가능성	☐ 524) 이해한다	☐ 554) 장관	☐ 584) 다양하다
☐ 465) 행위	☐ 495) 방향	☐ 525) 제품	☐ 555) 차이	☐ 585) 운다
☐ 466) 국내	☐ 496) 대회	☐ 526) 분야	☐ 556) 푼다	☐ 586) 농민
☐ 467) 기관	☐ 497) 목소리	☐ 527) 교사	☐ 557) 시절	☐ 587) 은행
☐ 468) 입장	☐ 498) 노래	☐ 528) 돌아간다	☐ 558) 물건	☐ 588) 결혼
☐ 469) 만한	☐ 499) 바다	☐ 529) 수준	☐ 559) 직접	☐ 589) 동생
☐ 470) 가치	☐ 500) 힘든	☐ 530) 표현	☐ 560) 개인	☐ 590) 법
☐ 471) 아래	☐ 501) 공부	☐ 531) 대	☐ 561) 발	☐ 591) 소설
☐ 472) 영향	☐ 502) 공부한다	☐ 532) 젊다	☐ 562) 작가	☐ 592) 오후
☐ 473) 나선다	☐ 503) 움직인다	☐ 533) 동시	☐ 563) 효과	☐ 593) 질서
☐ 474) 흐른다	☐ 504) 노력	☐ 534) 옷	☐ 564) 불교	☐ 594) 담는다
☐ 475) 깊은	☐ 505) 전혀	☐ 535) 기능	☐ 565) 빨리	☐ 595) 모인다
☐ 476) 배	☐ 506) 언니	☐ 536) 순간	☐ 566) 시작된다	☐ 596) 시민
☐ 477) 배	☐ 507) 단체	☐ 537) 전쟁	☐ 567) 설명한다	☐ 597) 회장
☐ 478) 배	☐ 508) 집단	☐ 538) 꿈	☐ 568) 우주	☐ 598) 빠른
☐ 479) 모양	☐ 509) 알려진	☐ 539) 할머니	☐ 569) 시기	☐ 599) 스스로
☐ 480) 산	☐ 510) 가능하다	☐ 540) 회의	☐ 570) 마치	☐ 600) 아기

451-600				
451) such	481) acid	511) ability	541) broadcast	571) flesh
452) age	482) however	512) insist	542) talk	572) yield
453) first of all	483) condition	513) child	543) talk	573) wish
454) believe	484) door	514) child	544) tree	574) strong
455) give birth	485) flower	515) turn	545) sleep	575) experience
456) information	486) step	516) turn	546) sleep	576) music
457) like	487) meantime	517) fire	547) paly	577) the best
458) draw	488) suddenly	518) resident	548) likewise	578) reveal
459) turn off	489) overstep	519) collect	549) walk	579) be ill
460) learn	490) wind	520) data	550) labor	580) less
461) poem	491) village	521) presence	551) past	581) rain
462) role	492) young	522) grade	552) contemporary	582) hometown
463) by	493) representative	523) newspaper	553) examine	583) surprised
464) behavior	494) chance	524) understand	554) spectacle	584) so many
465) behavior	495) direction	525) product	555) margin	585) cry
466) domestic	496) contest	526) field	556) untie	586) farmer
467) organ	497) voice	527) teacher	557) days	587) bank
468) entry	498) song	528) return	558) thing	588) wedding
469) worth	499) sea	529) level	559) first-hand	589) younger brother
470) value	500) tough	530) expression	560) individual	590) law
471) under	501) study	531) large	561) foot	591) novel
472) influence	502) study	532) young	562) writer	592) p.m.
473) come forward	503) move	533) simultaneous	563) effect	593) order
474) flow	504) effort	534) cloths	564) Buddhism	594) put in
475) deep	505) altogether	535) function	565) fast	595) gather
476) pear	506) older sister	536) moment	566) begin	596) citizen
477) ship	507) group	537) war	567) explain	597) chairman
478) stomach	508) group	538) dream	568) universe	598) quick
479) shape	509) known	539) grandma	569) period	599) by oneself
480) mountain	510) be possible	540) meeting	570) as if	600) baby

601-750				
□ 601) 아저씨	□ 631) 시설	□ 661) 사고	□ 691) 벌인다	□ 721) 기회
□ 602) 옛날	□ 632) 외국	□ 662) 그래도	□ 692) 사진	□ 722) 실시한다
□ 603) 이날	□ 633) 밑	□ 663) 아무리	□ 693) 주장	□ 723) 지구
□ 604) 제대로	□ 634) 어른	□ 664) 맞춘다	□ 694) 표현한다	□ 724) 번째
□ 605) 달	□ 635) 주변에	□ 665) 쌀	□ 695) 인한다	□ 725) 소비자
□ 606) 달	□ 636) 대신	□ 666) 일반적인	□ 696) 이상한	□ 726) 싫다
□ 607) 던진다	□ 637) 원인	□ 667) 재미있는	□ 697) 붙는다	□ 727) 규모
□ 608) 참	□ 638) 판다	□ 668) 가르친다	□ 698) 아마	□ 728) 기준
□ 609) 공간	□ 639) 군	□ 669) 대화	□ 699) 잇는다	□ 729) 반드시
□ 610) 이곳	□ 640) 열심히	□ 670) 막는다	□ 700) 경기	□ 730) 셈
□ 611) 딸	□ 641) 재산	□ 671) 올해	□ 701) 목적	□ 731) 받아들인다
□ 612) 마지막	□ 642) 부모	□ 672) 형	□ 702) 태도	□ 732) 현장
□ 613) 병원	□ 643) 약간	□ 673) 오빠	□ 703) 주위	□ 733) 건설
□ 614) 자세	□ 644) 언어	□ 674) 달리	□ 704) 대책	□ 734) 꺼낸다
□ 615) 강조한다	□ 645) 요구한다	□ 675) 붙인다	□ 705) 그만둔다	□ 735) 노동자
□ 616) 경찰	□ 646) 감독	□ 676) 인물	□ 706) 발생한다	□ 736) 동네
□ 617) 맡는다	□ 647) 그날	□ 677) 늘	□ 707) 다리	□ 737) 언제나
□ 618) 저녁	□ 648) 자주	□ 678) 항상	□ 708) 재료	□ 738) 완전히
□ 619) 한편	□ 649) 약	□ 679) 모두	□ 709) 각각	□ 739) 자동차
□ 620) 그러면	□ 650) 기간	□ 680) 전국	□ 710) 결코	□ 740) 차
□ 621) 기자	□ 651) 담배	□ 681) 도움	□ 711) 옮긴다	□ 741) 차
□ 622) 넓은	□ 652) 일으킨다	□ 682) 가정	□ 712) 해	□ 742) 전한다
□ 623) 시험	□ 653) 할아버지	□ 683) 건다	□ 713) 잃어버린다	□ 743) 존재한다
□ 624) 주로	□ 654) 조직	□ 684) 빠진다	□ 714) 자유	□ 744) 개월
□ 625) 면	□ 655) 태어난다	□ 685) 멀다	□ 715) 책임	□ 745) 별로
□ 626) 통일	□ 656) 공장	□ 686) 잠시	□ 716) 비슷한	□ 746) 정한다
□ 627) 들어선다	□ 657) 벌써	□ 687) 농업	□ 717) 심한	□ 747) 한마디
□ 628) 건강	□ 658) 즐긴다	□ 688) 댄다	□ 718) 경쟁	□ 748) 유지한다
□ 629) 가까이	□ 659) 지	□ 689) 의견	□ 719) 회	□ 749) 대중
□ 630) 건물	□ 660) 환자	□ 690) 무대	□ 720) 구체적인	□ 750) 늘어난다

601-750				
601) uncle	631) facility	661) accident	691) stage	721) opportunity
602) old days	632) foreign	662) nonetheless	692) photo	722) enforce
603) this day	633) beneath	663) however	693) argument	723) earth
604) properly	634) adult	664) adapt	694) express	724) ~th
605) moon	635) around	665) rice	695) be caused	725) consumer
606) month	636) instead	666) general	696) strange	726) not like
607) toss	637) cause	667) interesting	697) stick to	727) scale
608) true	638) sell	668) teach	698) maybe	728) criteria
609) space	639) county	669) conversation	699) connect	729) certainly
610) this place	640) hard	670) prevent	700) economy	730) count
611) daughter	641) property	671) this year	701) purpose	731) accept
612) final	642) parent	672) older brother	702) attitude	732) site
613) hospital	643) some	673) older brother	703) surrounding	733) construction
614) posture	644) language	674) otherwise	704) measure	734) takeout
615) emphasize	645) ask for	675) attach	705) quit	735) worker
616) police	646) coach	676) figure	706) happen	736) neighborhood
617) undertake	647) that day	677) always	707) bridge	737) at all times
618) evening	648) often	678) always	708) material	738) completely
619) meanwhile	649) about	679) in total	709) each	739) car
620) if so	650) span	680) whole country	710) absolutely	740) car
621) reporter	651) tobacco	681) help	711) transfer	741) tea
622) wide	652) cause	682) home	712) sun	742) deliver
623) exam	653) grandfather	683) hang	713) lose	743) exist
624) usually	654) tissue	684) fall out	714) freedom	744) month
625) sense	655) be born	685) be far	715) charge	745) not very
626) unification	656) factory	686) a while	716) alike	746) fix
627) enter	657) already	687) agriculture	717) severe	747) a word
628) health	658) enjoy	688) touch	718) competition	748) keep
629) near	659) after	689) opinion	719) gathering	749) public
630) building	660) patient	690) stage	720) specific	750) stretch

751-900				
☐ 751) 닦는다	☐ 781) 없어진다	☐ 811) 평가	☐ 841) 공동	☐ 871) 바탕
☐ 752) 말씀	☐ 782) 감정	☐ 812) 내려온다	☐ 842) 팔	☐ 872) 싸운다
☐ 753) 괜찮다	☐ 783) 기억	☐ 813) 위치	☐ 843) 분명하다	☐ 873) 예쁘다
☐ 754) 눈물	☐ 784) 놈	☐ 814) 줄인다	☐ 844) 분석	☐ 874) 갈등
☐ 755) 각종	☐ 785) 인기	☐ 815) 가격	☐ 845) 상품	☐ 875) 전문
☐ 756) 빛	☐ 786) 가끔	☐ 816) 비어있다	☐ 846) 설명	☐ 876) 정확하다
☐ 757) 피한다	☐ 787) 구성한다	☐ 817) 삼국	☐ 847) 이어진다	☐ 877) 나중에
☐ 758) 거친다	☐ 788) 실제로	☐ 818) 손님	☐ 848) 종류	☐ 878) 등
☐ 759) 나아간다	☐ 789) 짧다	☐ 819) 원한다	☐ 849) 어깨	☐ 879) 맛있다
☐ 760) 야	☐ 790) 고맙다	☐ 820) 통신	☐ 850) 지적한다	☐ 880) 며칠
☐ 761) 지식	☐ 791) 관리	☐ 821) 확인한다	☐ 851) 부부	☐ 881) 신경
☐ 762) 현재	☐ 792) 그곳	☐ 822) 모임	☐ 852) 오랫동안	☐ 882) 미
☐ 763) 제시한다	☐ 793) 달다	☐ 823) 아무	☐ 853) 눕는다	☐ 883) 시선
☐ 764) 여전히	☐ 794) 비롯된다	☐ 824) 기계	☐ 854) 발달한다	☐ 884) 언론
☐ 765) 주인	☐ 795) 들린다	☐ 825) 물질	☐ 855) 발전한다	☐ 885) 투자
☐ 766) 발견한다	☐ 796) 달린다	☐ 826) 뉴스	☐ 856) 여행	☐ 886) 지원
☐ 767) 선	☐ 797) 바쁘다	☐ 827) 편다	☐ 857) 죽음	☐ 887) 결정한다
☐ 768) 인류	☐ 798) 이전	☐ 828) 수업	☐ 858) 고통	☐ 888) 경영
☐ 769) 특징	☐ 799) 인정한다	☐ 829) 종교	☐ 859) 등장한다	☐ 889) 목표
☐ 770) 선수	☐ 800) 자	☐ 830) 층	☐ 860) 공	☐ 890) 성장
☐ 771) 마련한다	☐ 801) 나쁘다	☐ 831) 자연스럽다	☐ 861) 어울린다	☐ 891) 숲
☐ 772) 반	☐ 802) 불구하고	☐ 832) 장	☐ 862) 쉰다	☐ 892) 작년
☐ 773) 발표한다	☐ 803) 국제적인	☐ 833) 돈다	☐ 863) 알린다	☐ 893) 지난 해
☐ 774) 주제	☐ 804) 그룹	☐ 834) 잊는다	☐ 864) 찬다	☐ 894) 내려간다
☐ 775) 걸친	☐ 805) 전통	☐ 835) 실천한다	☐ 865) 멀리	☐ 895) 미친다
☐ 776) 겪고있다	☐ 806) 잔	☐ 836) 보호	☐ 866) 뺀다	☐ 896) 새벽
☐ 777) 관점	☐ 807) 있다	☐ 837) 씻는다	☐ 867) 예정	☐ 897) 쓰레기
☐ 778) 귀	☐ 808) 시인	☐ 838) 늦는다	☐ 868) 즐겁다	☐ 898) 임금
☐ 779) 기본	☐ 809) 언제	☐ 839) 이웃	☐ 869) 한계	☐ 899) 피해
☐ 780) 사라진다	☐ 810) 외에는	☐ 840) 편지	☐ 870) 흔히	☐ 900) 무섭다

751-900				
751) wipe	781) disappear	811) evaluation	841) joint	871) background
752) words	782) emotion	812) descend	842) arm	872) contend
753) okay	783) memory	813) position	843) clear	873) pretty
754) tear	784) guy	814) reduce	844) analysis	874) conflict
755) variety	785) popularity	815) price	845) goods	875) specialty
756) light	786) sometimes	816) empty	846) explanation	876) accurate
757) avoid	787) organize	817) three nations	847) continue	877) later
758) go through	788) actually	818) guest	848) types	878) back
759) proceed	789) short	819) want	849) shoulder	879) delicious
760) hey	790) thank you	820) communication	850) point out	880) a few days
761) knowledge	791) managing	821) check	851) man and wife	881) nerves
762) present	792) that place	822) meeting	852) for a long time	882) beauty
763) present	793) sweet	823) any	853) lie	883) gaze
764) still	794) arise	824) machine	854) develop	884) media
765) host	795) sound	825) substance	855) progress	885) investment
766) discover	796) run	826) news	856) journey	886) support
767) line	797) busy	827) unfold	857) death	887) decide
768) mankind	798) former	828) lesson	858) pain	888) management
769) characteristic	799) admit	829) religion	859) appear	889) goal
770) player	800) come on	830) floor	860) ball	890) growth
771) prepare	801) bad	831) natural	861) look good	891) forest
772) half	802) despite	832) paste	862) rest	892) last year
773) announce	803) international	833) orbit	863) inform	893) last year
774) topic	804) band	834) forget	864) kick	894) go down
775) lasting	805) tradition	835) practice	865) far	895) crazy
776) undergo	806) cup	836) custody	866) pull out	896) dawn
777) perspective	807) be	837) wash	867) schedule	897) trash
778) ear	808) poet	838) late	868) happy	898) wage
779) basics	809) when	839) neighbor	869) limit	899) damage
780) disappear	810) except	840) letter	870) commonly	900) scared

Final	K-word ㊽						
check	English ㊾						

K-word ㊷	English ㊸	K-word ㊹	K-word ㊺	English ㊻	K-word ㊼

		K-word ㊽				
Final					
check	English ㊾				

K-word ㊷	English ㊸	K-word ㊹	K-word ㊺	English ㊻	K-word ㊼

Final	K-word ㊽				
check	English ㊾				

K-word ㊷	English ㊸	K-word ㊹	K-word ㊺	English ㊻	K-word ㊼

Final	K-word ㊽				
check	English ㊾				

K-word ㊷	English ㊸	K-word ㊹	K-word ㊺	English ㊻	K-word ㊼

- Korean's Most Used Sentence Practice

- Everyday Korean Words

- Korean Writing Practice

- Korean Sentence Writing Practice

- Korean Communication Culture

- Most used Korean words 4440

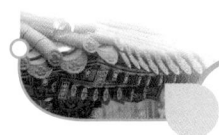

오랜만이에요.	오랜 친구예요.	He's an old friend.
o-raen-man-i-e-yo.	o-raen chin-gu-ye-yo.	
Long time, no see.	오랜 가뭄이에요.	It's a long drought.
	o-raen ga-mum-i-eyo	
오랜만이에요	2년 만이에요.	It's been two years.
	i-nyeon man-i-e-yo.	
	하루 만이에요.	It's just one day.
	ha-ru man-i-e-yo.	

몸 관리 잘하세요.	몸 관리 맡기세요.	Let me take care of your body.
mom gwan-ri jal-ha-se-yo.	mom gwan-ri mat-gi-se-yo.	
Take care of your body.	몸 관리 시작하세요.	Start taking care of your body.
	mom gwan-ri si-jak-ha-se-yo.	
몸 관리 잘하세요	돈 관리 잘하세요.	Take good care of your money.
	don gwan-ri jal-ha-se-yo.	
	머리 관리 잘하세요.	Take good care of your hair.
	meo-ri gwan-ri jal-ha-se-yo.	

생일축하해요.	생일 기억해요.	Remember your birthday.
saeng-il-chuk-ha-hae-yo.	saeng-il gi-eok-hae-yo.	
Happy birthday.	생일 잊으세요.	Forget your birthday.
	saeng-il ij-eu-se-yo.	
생일축하해요	합격 축하해요.	Congratulations on passing.
	hab-gyeok chuk-ha-hae-yo.	
	당선 축하해요	Congratulations on winning.
	dang-seon chuk-ha-hae-yo	

축하드려요.	축하 받았어요.	I got congratulations.
chuk-ha-deu-ryeo-yo.	chuk-ha bad-ass-eo-yo.	
Congratulations.	축하 합니다.	Congratulations.
	chuk-ha hab-ni-da	
축하드려요	감사 드려요.	Thank you.
	gam-sa deu-ryeo-yo.	
	부탁 드려요.	Please.
	bu-tak deu-ryeo-yo.	

감기에 걸렸어요.	감기에 효과 있어요.	It works for a cold.
gam-gi-e geol-lyeoss-eo-yo.	gam-gi-e hyo-gwa iss-eo-yo.	
I caught a cold.	감기에 대비하세요.	Be prepared for a cold.
감기에 걸렸어요	gam-gi-e dae-bi-ha-se-yo.	
	간암에 걸렸어요.	I have liver cancer.
	gan-am-e geol-lyeoss-eo-yo.	
	교통신호에 걸렸어요.	I got a traffic signal.
	gyo-tong-sin-ho-e geol-lyeoss-eo-yo.	

머리가 좀 아파요.	머리가 좀 멍해요.	My head is a bit fuzzy.
meo-ri-ga jom a-pa-yo.	meo-ri-ga jom meong-hae-yo.	
I have a little headache.	머리가 좀 이상해요.	My head is a bit weird.
머리가 좀 아파요	meo-ri-ga jom i-sang-hae-yo.	
	다리가 좀 아파요.	My legs hurt a little.
	da-ri-ga jom a-pa-yo.	
	배가 좀 아파요.	I have a stomachache.
	bae-ga jom a-pa-yo.	

많이 좋아졌어요.	많이 나빠졌어요.	It's got a lot worse.
manh-i joh-a-jyeoss-eo-yo.	manh-i na-ppa-jyeoss-eo-yo.	
It's gotten a lot better.	많이 길어졌어요.	It got a lot longer.
많이 좋아졌어요	manh-i gil-eo-jyeoss-eo-yo.	
	조금 좋아졌어요.	It got a little better.
	jo-geum joh-a-jyeoss-eo-yo.	
	매우 좋아졌어요.	It got a lot better.
	mae-u joh-a-jyeoss-eo-yo	

걱정하지 마세요.	염려하지 마세요.	Don't worry.
geok-jeong-ha-ji ma-se-yo.	yeom-ryeo-ha-ji ma-se-yo.	
Don't worry.	놀라지 마세요.	Don't be surprised.
걱정하지 마세요	nol-la-ji ma-se-yo	
	두려워하지 마세요.	Don't be afraid.
	du-ryeo-wo-ha-ji ma-se-yo.	
	부끄러워하지 마세요.	Don't be shy.
	bu-kkeu-reo-wo-ha-ji ma-se-yo.	

	객실카드를 찾았어요.	I found the room card.
객실카드를 잃어버렸어요.	gaek-sil-ka-deu-reul chaj-ass-eo-yo.	
gaek-sil-ka-deu-reul ilh-eo-beo-ryeoss-eo-yo.	객실카드를 주세요.	Give me your room card.
I lost my room card.	gaek-sil-ka-deu-reul ju-se-yo.	
객실카드를 잃어버렸어요	핸드폰을 잃어버렸어요.	I lost my phone.
	haen-deu-pon-eul ilh-eo-beo-ryeoss-eo-yo.	
	열쇠를 잃어버렸어요.	I lost my key.
	yeol-soe-reul ilh-eo-beo-ryeoss-eo-yo.	

	부탁 전해주세요.	Please tell him.
부탁드려요.	bu-tak jeon-hae-ju-se-yo.	
bu-tak-deu-ryeo-yo.	부탁 잊지 마세요.	Please don't forget to ask.
Please.	bu-tak ij-ji ma-se-yo.	
부탁드려요	감사 드려요.	Thank you.
	gam-sa-deu-ryeo-yo	
	인사 드려요.	Greetings.
	in-sa-deu-ryeo-yo	

	먼저 가세요.	Go first.
먼저 하세요.	meon-jeo ga-se-yo.	
meon-jeo ha-se-yo.	먼저 드세요.	Eat first.
Please, you first.	meon-jeo deu-se-yo.	
먼저 하세요	나중에 하세요.	Do it later.
	na-jung-e ha-se-yo.	
	오후에 하세요.	Do it in the afternoon.
	o-hu-e ha-se-yo.	

	정말 반가워요.	Nice to meet you.
정말 아쉬워요.	jeong-mal ban-ga-wo-yo.	
jeong-mal a-swi-wo-yo.	정말 감사해요.	Thank you so much.
I'm very sad.	jeong-mal gam-sa-hae-yo.	
정말 아쉬워요	조금 아쉬워요.	It's a bit disappointing.
	jo-geum a-swi-wo-yo.	
	많이 아쉬워요.	It's very unfortunate.
	manh-i a-swi-wo-yo.	

조심하세요.	조심히 걸으세요.	Please walk carefully.
jo-sim-ha-se-yo.	jo-sim-hi geol-eu-se-yo.	
Be careful.	조심히 가세요.	Take care.
	jo-sim-hi ga-se-yo.	
조심하세요	식사하세요.	Have a meal.
	sik-sa-ha-se-yo.	
	운동하세요.	Work out.
	un-dong-ha-se-yo.	

앉으세요.	일어나세요.	Stand up.
anj-eu-se-yo.	il-eo-na-se-yo.	
Please take a seat.	엎드리세요.	Lie down.
	eop-deu-ri-se-yo.	
앉으세요	멈추세요.	Please stop.
	meom-chu-se-yo	
	공부하세요.	Please study.
	gong-bu-ha-se-yo.	

제가 계산할게요.	제가 옮길게요.	I'll move it.
je-ga gye-san-hal-ge-yo.	je-ga olm-gil-ge-yo.	
I'll pay.	제가 할게요.	I'll do it.
	je-ga hal-ge-yo.	
제가 계산할게요	그가 계산할게요.	He'll pay for it.
	geu-ga gye-san-hal-ge-yo.	
	그녀가 계산할게요.	She'll pay for it.
	geu-nyeo-ga gye-san-hal-ge-yo.	

드셔보세요.	일어나보세요.	Try getting up.
deu-syeo-bo-se-yo.	il-eo-na-bo-se-yo	
Taste it.	뱉어보세요.	Spit it out.
	baet-eo-bo-se-yo	
드셔보세요	마셔보세요.	Drink it.
	ma-syeo-bo-se-yo.	
	앉아보세요.	Please sit down.
	anj-a-bo-se-yo	

너무 맛있어요.	너무 매워요.	This is too spicy.
neo-mu mas-iss-eo-yo.	neo-mu mae-wo-yo.	
It's so delicious.	너무 멋져요.	It's really fantastic.
너무 맛있어요	neo-mu meos-jyeo-yo.	
	매우 맛있어요.	It's very delicious.
	mae-u mas-iss-eo-yo.	
	조금 맛있어요.	It's kind of delicious.
	jo-geum mas-iss-eo-yo.	

많이 드세요.	많이 가지세요.	Have a lot.
manh-i deu-se-yo.	manh-i ga-ji-se-yo.	
Please, help yourself.	많이 넣으세요.	Put in a lot.
많이 드세요	manh-i neoh-eu-se-yo.	
	전부 드세요	Eat it all.
	jeon-bu deu-se-yo	
	조금 드세요.	Eat a little bit.
	jo-geum deu-se-yo.	

조금 매워요.	조금 싱거워요.	It's a little bland.
jo-geum mae-wo-yo.	jo-geum sing-geo-wo-yo.	
It's a bit spicy.	조금 짜요.	It's a little salty.
조금 매워요	jo-geum jja-yo.	
	매우 매워요.	It's very spicy.
	mae-u mae-wo-yo.	
	약간 매워요.	It's a bit spicy.
	yak-gan mae-wo-yo.	

작은 걸로 주세요.	작은 걸로 가지세요.	Take the small one.
jak-eun geol-lo ju-se-yo.	jak-eun geol-lo ga-ji-se-yo.	
Please give me a small one.	작은 걸로 넣으세요.	Put the small one in.
작은 걸로 주세요	jak-eun geol-lo neoh-eu-se-yo.	
	적당한 걸로 주세요.	Please give me the right one.
	jeok-dang-han geol-lo ju-se-yo.	
	보통 걸로 주세요.	Give me a normal one.
	bo-tong geol-lo ju-se-yo.	

큰 걸로 주세요.	큰 걸로 가지세요.	Take the big one.
keun geol-lo ju-se-yo.	keun geol-lo ga-ji-se-yo.	
Give me a big one.	큰 걸로 넣으세요.	Put the big one in.
큰 걸로 주세요	keun geol-lo neoh-eu-se-yo.	
	짠 걸로 주세요.	Please give me something salty.
	jjan geol-lo ju-se-yo.	
	매운 걸로 주세요.	Please give me something spicy.
	mae-un geol-lo ju-se-yo.	

조금 더 주세요.	조금 더 드세요.	Eat some more.
jo-geum deo ju-se-yo.	jo-geum deo deu-se-yo.	
Give me a little more.	조금 더 하세요.	Do a little more.
조금 더 주세요	jo-geum deo ha-se-yo.	
	많이 더 주세요.	Give me a lot more.
	manh-i deo ju-se-yo.	
	만 원어치 주세요.	Give me 10,000 won worth.
	man won eo-chi ju-se-yo.	

아무것도 아니에요.	아무것도 없어요.	I don't have any.
a-mu-geos-do a-ni-ye-yo.	a-mu-geos-do eobs-eo-yo.	
Nothing is wrong.	아무것도 맛없어요.	Nothing tastes good.
아무것도 아니에요	a-mu-geos-do mas-eobs-eo-yo.	
	사소한 것 아니에요.	It's not a small thing.
	sa-so-han geos a-ni-ye-yo.	
	중요한 것 아니에요.	It's not an important thing.
	jung-yo-han geos a-ni-ye-yo.	

너무 예뻐요.	너무 길어요.	It's too long.
neo-mu ye-ppeo-yo.	neo-mu gil-eo-yo.	
It's so pretty.	너무 짧아요.	It's too short.
너무 예뻐요	neo-mu jjalb-a-yo.	
	조금 예뻐요.	It's a little pretty.
	jo geum ye-ppeo-yo.	
	매우 예뻐요.	It's very pretty.
	mae-u ye-ppeo-yo.	

다른 걸로 바꾸고 싶어요.	다른 걸로 주세요.	Please give me something else.
da-reun geol-lo ba-kku-go sip-eo-yo.	da-reun geol-lo ju-se-yo.	
I want to change it to something else.	다른 걸로 가지세요.	Take something else.
다른 걸로 바꾸고 싶어요	da-reun geol-lo ga-ji-se-yo.	
	작은 걸로 바꾸고 싶어요.	I want to change it to a small one.
	jag-eun geol-lo ba-kku-go sip-eo-yo.	
	이것을 바꾸고 싶어요.	I want to change this.
	i-geos-eul ba-kku-go sip-eo-yo.	

저것 좀 보여주세요.	저것 좀 주세요.	Please give me that.
jeo-geos jom bo-yeo-ju-se-yo.	jeo-geos jom ju-se-yo.	
Please show me that one.	저것 좀 바꾸세요.	Please change that.
저것 좀 보여주세요	jeo-geos jom ba-kku-se-yo.	
	당신 것 좀 보여주세요.	Please show us yours.
	dang-sin geos jom bo-yeo-ju-se-yo.	
	얇은 것 좀 보여주세요.	Please show us something thin.
	yalb-eun geos jom bo-yeo-ju-se-yo.	

휴지 좀 가져다주시겠어요?	휴지 좀 버리겠어요?	Can you throw away some tissues?
hyu-ji jom ga-jyeo-da-ju-si-gess-eo-yo?	hyu-ji jom beo-ri-gess-eo-yo?	
Can you bring me some tissue?	휴지 좀 넣으시겠어요?	Can you put in some tissues?
휴지 좀 가져다 주시겠어요	hyu-ji jom neoh-eu-si-gess-eo-yo?	
	수저 좀 가져다주시겠어요?	Can you bring me a spoon?
	su-jeo jom ga-jyeo-da-ju-si-gess-eo-yo?	
	물 좀 가져다주시겠어요?	Can you bring me some water?
	mul jom ga-jyeo-da-ju-si-gess-eo-yo?	

테이블 좀 치워주시겠어요?	테이블 좀 펴주시겠어요?	Can you open the table?
te-i-beul jom chi-wo-ju-si-gess-eo-yo?	te-i-beul jom pyeo-ju-si-gess-eo-yo?	
Can you move the table?	테이블 좀 접으시겠어요?	Can you fold the table?
테이블 좀 치워주시겠어요	te-i-beul jom jeob-eu-si-gess-eo-yo?	
	손 좀 치워주시겠어요?	Can you move your hands?
	son jom chi-wo-ju-si-gess-eo-yo?	
	책 좀 치워주시겠어요?	Can you move the books?
	chaek jom chi-wo-ju-si-gess-eo-yo?	

나눠서 담아주세요.	나눠서 드세요.	Divide it and eat it.
na-nwo-seo dam-a-ju-se-yo.	na-nwo-seo deu-se-yo.	
Please divide it and put it in.	나눠서 가지세요.	Divide it and take it.
	na-nwo-seo ga-ji-se-yo.	
나눠서 담아주세요	합쳐서 담아주세요.	Please put them together.
	hab-chyeo-seo dam-a-ju-se-yo.	
	모두 담아주세요.	Please put everything in.
	mo-du dam-a-ju-se-yo.	

영수증 좀 주세요.	영수증 좀 버리세요.	Please throw away the receipt.
yeong-su-jeung jom ju-se-yo.	yeong-su-jeung jom beo-ri-se-yo.	
Please give me the receipt.	영수증 좀 넣으세요.	Put the receipt in.
	yeong-su-jeung jom neoh-eu-se-yo.	
영수증 좀 주세요	표 좀 주세요.	Please give me the ticket.
	pyo jom ju-se-yo.	
	돈 좀 주세요.	Please give me some money.
	don jom ju-se-yo.	

핸드폰 충전 좀 할 수 있을까요?	핸드폰 충전 좀 부탁할까요?	Can you charge my phone?
haen-deu-pon chung-jeon jom hal-su-iss-eul-kka-yo?	haen-deu-pon chung-jeon jom bu-tak-hal-kka-yo?	
Can I charge my phone?	핸드폰 충전 좀 멈출까요?	Could you stop charging my phone?
	haen-deu-pon chung-jeon jom meom-chul-kka-yo?	
핸드폰 충전 좀 할 수 있을까요	식사 좀 할 수 있을까요?	Can I have a meal?
	sik-sa jom hal su iss-eul-kka-yo?	
	세차 좀 할 수 있을까요?	Can I wash my car?
	se-cha jom hal su iss-eul-kka-yo?	

Everyday Korean Words

생활 saeng-hwal (LIfe)					
간식	gan-sik	snack	바늘	ba-neul	needle
거울	geo-ul	mirror	바닥	ba-dak	floor
걸레	geol-le	duster	바지	ba-ji	pants
게임	ge-im	game	밤	bam	night
게임기	ge-im-gi	game console	방망이	bang-mang-i	bat
경첩	gyeong-cheob	hinges	배터리	bae-teo-ri	battery
고무줄	go-mu-jul	rubber band	베개	be-gae	pillow
고스톱	go-seu-tob	go-stop	벽	byeok	wall
공유기	gong-yu-gi	internet modem	변기	byeon-gi	toilet
과자	gwa-ja	snacks	보면대	bo-myeon-dae	music stand
국가	guk-ga	nation	보온병	bo-on-byeong	thermos
국기	guk-gi	national flag	부엌	bu-eok	kitchen
귀이개	gwi-i-gae	earpick	빗	bis	comb
그릇	geu-reus	bowl	빨랫줄	ppal-laes-jul	laundry line
기타	gi-ta	guitar	서랍	seo-rab	drawer
냉장고	naeng-jang-go	refrigerator	선풍기	seon-pung-gi	fan
노트북	no-teu-buk	laptop	셔츠	syeo-cheu	shirts
달력	dal-lyeok	calendar	소독제	so-dok-je	disinfectant
담배	dam-bae	cigarette	소주잔	so-ju-jan	soju cup
담요	dam-yo	blanket	소파	so-pa	sofa
도끼	do-kki	axe	손 소독제	son so-dok-je	hand sanitizer
도시락	do-si-rak	lunch box	송곳	song-gos	awl
드라이버	deu-ra-i-beo	screwdriver	수저	su-jeo	spoon
마스크	ma-seu-keu	mask	숟가락	sud-ga-rak	spoon
마우스	ma-u-seu	mouse	숙제	suk-je	homework
망치	mang-chi	hammer	스피커	seu-pi-keo	speaker
맥주잔	maek-ju-jan	beer glass	슬리퍼	seul-li-peo	slippers
못	mos	nail	시계	si-gye	clock
물	mul	water	식칼	sik-kal	kitchen knife
물병	mul-byeong	water bottle	식탁	sik-tak	table

신발	sin-bal	shoes	조명	jo-myeong	lighting
쓰레기통	sseu-re-gi-tong	trash can	주전자	ju-jeon-ja	kettle
아침	a-chim	morning	지갑	ji-gab	wallet
아침	a-chim	breakfast	지팡이	ji-pang-i	cane
안경	an-gyeong	glasses	집게	jib-ge	tongs
액자	aek-ja	frame	치약	chi-yak	toothpaste
약	yak	medicine	침대	chim-dae	bed
양말	yang-mal	socks	칫솔	chis-sol	toothbrush
에어컨	e-eo-keon	air conditioner	커피	keo-pi	coffee
열쇠	yeol-soe	key	컴퓨터	keom-pyu-teo	computer
영상	yeong-sang	video	컵	keob	cup
영양제	yeong-yang-je	nutritional supplements	톱	tob	saw
온도계	on-do-gye	thermometer	항아리	hang-a-ri	jar
와인잔	wa-in-jan	wine glass	핸드크림	haen-deu-keu-rim	hand cream
욕조	yok-jo	bathtub	행주	haeng-ju	dishcloth
우산	u-san	umbrella	헤어밴드	he-eo-baen-deu	hairband
의자	ui-ja	chair	화분	hwa-bun	flowerpot
이불	i-bul	bedclothes	화장대	hwa-jang-dae	dressing table
이쑤시개	i-ssu-si-gae	toothpick	휴지	hyu-ji	waste paper
이어폰	i-eo-pon	earphones			

학용품 hak-yong-pum (Stationery)

자물쇠	ja-mul-soe	lock
장갑	jang-gab	gloves
장롱	jang-rong	wardrobe
쟁반	jaeng-ban	tray
저녁	jeo-nyeok	dinner
전등	jeon-deung	light
점심	jeom-sim	lunch
접시	jeob-si	plate
젓가락	jeos-ga-rak	chopsticks
정수기	jeong-su-gi	water purifier

가방	ga-bang	bag
가위	ga-wi	scissors
게시판	ge-si-pan	bulletin board
공책	gong-chaek	notebook
교과서	gyo-gwa-seo	textbook
노트	no-teu	notebook
독서대	dok-seo-dae	reading table
마커펜	ma-keo-pen	marker pen
먹	meok	ink stick

			스포츠 seu-po-cheu (Sports)		
문제집	mun-je-jib	workbook	격투기	gyeok-tu-gi	martial arts
복사기	bok-sa-gi	copy machine	골프	gol-peu	golf
볼펜	bol-pen	ballpoint pen	공	gong	ball
분필	bun-pil	chalk	권투	gwon-tu	boxing
붓	bus	brush	농구	nong-gu	basketball
사인펜	sa-in-pen	magic marker	달리기	dal-li-gi	running
색연필	saek-yeon-pil	colored pencil	럭비	reok-bi	rugby
샤프심	sya-peu-sim	sharp lead	레슬링	re-seul-ling	wrestling
알림장	al-lim-jang	homework diary	마라톤	ma-ra-ton	marathon
압정	ab-jeong	tack	미식축구	mi-sik-chuk-gu	American football
연필	yeon-pil	pencil	배구	bae-gu	volleyball
연필깎이	yeon-pil-kkagi-i	pencil sharpener	배드민턴	bae-deu-min-teon	badminton
일기장	il-gi-jang	diary	배드민턴채	bae-deu-min-teon-chae	badminton racket
자	ja	ruler	볼링	bol-ling	bowling
종이	jong-i	paper	사격	sa-gyeok	shooting
지우개	ji-u-gae	eraser	수구	su-gu	water polo
책	chaek	book	수영	su-yeong	swimming
책가방	chaek-ga-bang	backpack	스케이트	seu-ke-i-teu	skating
책갈피	chaek-gal-pi	bookmark	스키	seu-ki	ski
책상	chaek-sang	desk	썰매	sseol-mae	sled
칠판	chil-pan	blackboard	야구	ya-gu	baseball
칼	kal	knife	양궁	yang-gung	archery
크레파스	keu-re-pa-seu	crayon	역도	yeok-do	weightlifting
테이프	te-i-peu	tape	유도	yu-do	judo
풀	pul	glue	육상	yuk-sang	athletics
필통	pil-tong	pencil case	인라인 스케이트	in-ra-in seu-ke-it-eu	inline skate
한지	han-ji	Korean paper	조정	jo-jeong	rowing
형광펜	hyeong-gwang-pen	highlighter	족구	jok-gu	foot volleyball
화이트펜	hwa-i-teu-pen	white pen	체조	che-jo	gymnastics
			축구	chuk-gu	soccer

탁구	tak-gu	table tennis	발가락	bal-ga-rak	toe
태권도	tae-gwon-do	taekwondo	발목	bal-mok	ankle
테니스	te-ni-seu	tennis	발바닥	bal-ba-dak	sole
펜싱	pen-sing	fencing	발톱	bal-tob	claw
하키	ha-ki	hockey	방광	bang-gwang	bladder
핸드볼	haen-deu-bol	handball	배	bae	abdomen
			배꼽	bae-kkob	navel

신체 sin-che (Body)

가슴	ga-seum	chest	볼	bol	cheek
간	gan	liver	뺨	ppyam	cheek
갈비뼈	gal-bi-ppyeo	rib	뼈	ppyeo	bone
갑상선	gab-sang-seon	thyroid	성기	seong-gi	genitals
귀	gwi	ear	소뇌	so-noe	cerebellum
기관지	gi-gwan-ji	bronchial tube	소장	so-jang	small intestine
뇌	noe	brain	손	son	hand
눈	nun	eye	손가락	son-ga-rak	finger
눈썹	nun-sseob	eyebrow	손목	son-mok	wrist
다리	da-ri	leg	손톱	son-tob	fingernail
담낭	dam-nang	gall bladder	식도	sik-do	esophagus
대뇌	dae-noe	cerebrum	십이지장	sib-i-ji-jang	duodenum
대장	dae-jang	large intestine	어깨	eo-kkae	shoulder
동맥	dong-maek	artery	위	wi	stomach
뒤꿈치	dwi-kkum-chi	heel	이마	i-ma	forehead
등	deung	back	이빨	i-ppal	tooth
맹장	maeng-jang	appendix	입	ib	mouth
머리	meo-ri	head	정맥	jeong-maek	vein
머리카락	meo-ri-ka-rak	hair	지문	ji-mun	fingerprint
목	mok	neck	척추	cheok-chu	spine
무릎	mu-reup	knee	침	chim	saliva
발	bal	feet	코	ko	nose
			콩팥	kong-pat	kidney

병 byeong (Disease)		
간암	gan-am	liver cancer
감기	gam-gi	cold
갑상선암	gab-sang-seon-am	thyroid cancer
거북목	geo-buk-mok	turtle neck
뇌암	noe-am	brain cancer
눈병	nun-byeong	eye disease
당뇨	dang-nyo	diabetes
독감	dok-gam	flu
두통	du-tong	headache
바이러스	ba-i-reo-seu	virus
배탈	bae-tal	stomachache
변비	byeon-bi	constipation
복통	bok-tong	abdominal pain
설사	seol-sa	diarrhea
설암	seol-am	tongue cancer
수전증	su-jeon-jeung	hand tremor
식도염	sik-do-yeom	esophagitis
심장마비	sim-jang-ma-bi	heart attack
아토피	a-to-pi	atopy
암	am	cancer
염증	yeom-jeung	inflammation
장염	jang-yeom	enteritis
장티푸스	jang-ti-pu-seu	typhoid
전신마비	jeon-sin-ma-bi	general paralysis
췌장암	chwe-jang-am	pancreatic cancer
치매	chi-mae	dementia
치질	chi-jil	hemorrhoids
치통	chi-tong	toothache
코로나	ko-ro-na	COVID-19

탈모	tal-mo	hair loss
폐렴	pye-ryeom	pneumonia
폐암	pye-am	lung cancer
피부암	pi-bu-am	skin cancer
하반신마비	ha-ban-sin-ma-bi	paraparesis
후두암	hu-du-am	laryngeal cancer
흑사병	heuk-sa-byeong	The Black Death

주변 ju-byeon (Surroundings)		
가게	ga-ge	store
고깃집	go-gis-jib	meat restaurant
고등학교	go-deung-hak-gyo	high school
공원	gong-won	park
교차로	gyo-cha-ro	intersection
교회	gyo-hoe	church
노래방	no-rae-bang	karaoke room
놀이터	nol-i-teo	playground
다리	da-ri	bridge
도로	do-ro	road
만화방	man-hwa-bang	comic book store
버스정거장	beo-seu-jeong-geo-jang	bus stop
병원	byeong-won	hospital
부동산	bu-dong-san	real estate
빌라	bil-la	villa
성당	seong-dang	catholic church
시장	si-jang	market
식당	sik-dang	restaurant
신호등	sin-ho-deung	traffic light
아파트	a-pa-teu	apartment
약국	yak-guk	pharmacy
엘리베이터	el-li-be-i-teo	elevator

			꽃 kkocc (Flower)		
오토바이	o-to-ba-i	motorcycle	강아지풀	gang-a-ji-pul	foxtail
유치원	yu-chi-won	kindergarten	개나리	gae-na-ri	forsythia
자동차	ja-dong-cha	car	거베라	geo-be-ra	gerbera
절	jeol	Buddhist temple	국화	guk-hwa	chrysanthemum
정비소	jeong-bi-so	repair shop	나팔꽃	na-pal-kkocc	morning glory
정육점	jeong-yuk-jeom	butcher shop	난초	nan-cho	orchid
주유소	ju-yu-so	gas station	다알리아	da-al-lia	dahlia
주차장	ju-cha-jang	parking lot	달리아	dal-li-a	dahila
주택	ju-taek	housing	데이지	de-i-ji	daisy
중학교	jung-hak-gyo	middle school	동백꽃	dong-baek-kkocc	camellia
지하철역	ji-ha-cheol-yeok	subway station	들장미	deul-jang-mi	briar
집	jib	home	라벤더	ra-ben-deo	lavender
철도	cheol-do	railroad	라일락	ra-il-lak	lilac
체육관	che-yuk-gwan	gym	로즈마리	ro-jeu-ma-ri	rosemary
초등학교	cho-deung-hak-gyo	elementary school	메리골드	me-ri-gol-deu	marigold
카페	ka-pe	cafe	모란	mo-ran	peony
편의점	pyeon-ui-jeom	convenience store	목련	mok-ryeon	magnolia
피시방	pi-si-bang	internet cafe	무궁화	mu-gung-hwa	rose of Sharon
학원	hag-won	academy	민들레	min-deul-le	dandelion
			백일홍	baek-il-hong	zinnia
			백합	baek-hab	lily
			벚꽃	beoj-kkocc	cherry blossom
			붓꽃	bus-kkocc	iris
			선인장꽃	seon-in-jang-kkocc	cactus flower
			수국	su-guk	hydrangea
			수선화	su-seon-hwa	daffodil
			안개꽃	an-gae-kkocc	gypsophila
			양귀비꽃	yang-gwi-bi-kkocc	poppy
			억새풀	eok-sae-pul	silver grass
			연꽃	yeon-kkocc	lotus

자스민	ja-seu-min	jasmine	매실나무	mae-sil-na-mu	Japanese apricot tree
잔디	jan-di	grass	메타세콰이	me-ta-se-kwa-i	metasequoia
잡초	jab-cho	weeds	박달나무	bak-dal-na-mu	kind of birch
장미	jang-mi	rose	밤나무	bam-na-mu	chestnut tree
제비꽃	je-bi-kkocc	violet	배나무	bae-na-mu	pear tree
진달래	jin-dal-lae	azalea	백송	baek-song	Pinus bungeana
카네이션	ka-ne-i-syeon	carnation	버드나무	beo-deu-na-mu	willow
캐모마일	kae-mo-ma-il	chamomile	벚꽃나무	beocc-kkocc-na-mu	cherry blossoms
코스모스	ko-seu-mo-seu	cosmos	보리수나무	bo-ri-su-na-mu	oleaster
클로버	keul-lo-beo	clover	사과나무	sa-gwa-na-mu	apple tree
튤립	tyul-lib	tulip	석류나무	seok-ryu-na-mu	pomegranate tree
팬지	paen-ji	pansy	소나무	so-na-mu	pine tree
풀	pul	grass	소철	so-cheol	cycad
프리지아	peu-ri-ji-a	freesia	야자나무	ya-ja-na-mu	palm tree
해바라기	hae-ba-ra-gi	sunflower	올리브나무	ol-li-beu-na-mu	olive tree
히비스커스	hi-bi-seu-keo-seu	hibiscus	유자나무	yu-ja-na-mu	citron tree
			은행나무	eun-haeng-na-mu	ginkgo

나무 na-mu (Tree)

			자작나무	ja-jak-na-mu	birch tree
가로수나무	ga-ro-su-na-mu	American elm	전나무	jeon-na-mu	fir tree
가시나무	ga-si-na-mu	thorny plant	참나무	cham-na-mu	oak
감나무	gam-na-mu	persimmon tree	편백나무	pyeon-baek-na-mu	cypress essential
고무나무	go-mu-na-mu	rubber tree			
금식나무	geum-sik-na-mu	spotted laurel			

방향 bang-hyang (Direction)

느티나무	neu-ti-na-mu	zelkova	동	dong	east
대나무	dae-na-mu	bamboo	서	seo	west
대추나무	dae-chu-na-mu	jujube tree	남	nam	south
도토리나무	do-to-ri-na-mu	oak tree	북	buk	north
돌참나무	dol-cham-na-mu	Lithocarpus edulis			
떡갈나무	tteok-gal-na-mu	old oak			
마루나무	ma-ru-na-mu	poplar			

꽃 kkocc (Flower) 2		
개화기	gae-hwa-gi	flowering season
거름	geo-reum	manure
꽃	kkocc	flower
꽃가루	kkocc-ga-ru	pollen
꽃말	kkocc-mal	flower language
꽃봉오리	kkocc-bong-o-ri	bud
꽃잎	kkocc-ip	petal
낙엽	nag-yeob	fallen leaf
단풍	dan-pung	maple
뿌리	ppu-ri	root
새싹	sae-ssak	sprout
수술	su-sul	stamen
씨앗	ssi-as	seed
암술	am-sul	pistil
잎	ip	leaf
줄기	jul-gi	stem
화분	hwa-bun	flowerpot
흙	heulk	soil

동물 dong-mul (Animal)		
가마우지	ga-ma-u-ji	cormorant
갈매기	gal-mae-gi	gull
강아지	gang-a-ji	puppy
개	gae	dog
개구리	gae-gu-ri	frog
개미	gae-mi	ant
거머리	geo-meo-ri	leech
거미	geo-mi	spider
거북	geo-buk	turtle
거위	geo-wi	goose

고래	go-rae	whale
고릴라	go-ril-la	gorilla
고슴도치	go-seum-do-chi	hedgehog
곰	gom	bear
까마귀	kka-ma-gwi	crow
까치	kka-chi	magpie
꿩	kkwong	pheasant
나무늘보	na-mu-neul-bo	sloth
나비	na-bi	butterfly
너구리	neo-gu-ri	raccoon
늑대	neuk-dae	wolf
다람쥐	da-ram-jwi	squirrel
닭	dalk	chicken
도요새	do-yo-sae	snipe
독수리	dok-su-ri	eagle
돌고래	dol-go-rae	dolphin
돼지	dwae-ji	pig
두꺼비	du-kkeo-bi	toad
두더지	du-deo-ji	mole
두루미	du-ru-mi	crane
뜸부기	tteum-bu-gi	crake
말	mal	horse
매	mae	hawk
매미	mae-mi	cicada
메뚜기	me-ttu-gi	grasshopper
모기	mo-gi	mosquito
물개	mul-gae	seal
백조	baek-jo	swan
뱀	baem	snake
벌	beol	bee

부엉이	bu-eong-i	owl
비둘기	bi-dul-gi	pigeon
비버	bi-beo	beaver
뻐꾸기	ppeo-kku-gi	cuckoo
사슴	sa-seum	deer
사자	sa-ja	lion
소	so	cow
수달	su-dal	otter
악어	ak-eo	crocodile
앵무새	aeng-mu-sae	parrot
양	yang	sheep
어치	eo-chi	jay
얼룩말	eol-luk-mal	zebra
여우	yeo-u	fox
염소	yeom-so	goat
영양	yeong-yang	antelope
오리	o-ri	duck
오소리	o-so-ri	badger
원숭이	won-sung-i	monkey
재규어	jae-gyu-eo	jaguar
전갈	jeon-gal	scorpion
쥐	jwi	mouse
지렁이	ji-reong-i	earthworm
찌르레기	jji-reu-re-gi	starling
치타	chi-ta	cheetah
캥거루	kaeng-geo-ru	kangaroo
코끼리	ko-kki-ri	elephant
코뿔소	ko-ppul-so	rhinoceros
타조	ta-jo	turkey
토끼	to-kki	rabbit

판다	pan-da	panda
펠리컨	pel-li-keon	pelican
펭귄	peng-gwin	penguin
표범	pyo-beom	leopard
풍뎅이	pung-deng-i	goldbug
하마	ha-ma	hippo
하이에나	ha-i-e-na	hyena
할미새	hal-mi-sae	wagtail
해마	hae-ma	seahorse
호랑이	ho-rang-i	tiger
홍학	hong-hak	flamingo
황새	hwang-sae	stork
황소	hwang-so	bull

물고기 mul-go-gi (Fish)

갑오징어	gab-o-jing-eo	cuttlefish
가자미	ga-ja-mi	plaice
가재	ga-jae	crayfish
갈치	gal-chi	cutlass fish
감성돔	gam-seong-dom	sea bream
게	ge	crab
고등어	go-deung-eo	mackerel
광어	gwang-eo	flatfish
굴	gul	oyster
굴비	gul-bi	dried yellow croaker
김	gim	laver
꼬막	kko-mak	cockle
꽁치	kkong-chi	mackerel pike
꽃게	kkocc-ge	blue crab
날치	nal-chi	flying fish

넙치	neob-chi	halibut	삼치	sam-chi	Spanish mackerel
농어	nong-eo	sea bass	상어	sang-eo	shark
다금바리	da-geum-ba-ri	long tooth grouper	새우	sae-u	shrimp
다시마	da-si-ma	tang	서대	seo-dae	sole
달팽이	dal-paeng-i	snail	성게	seong-ge	sea urchin
대구	dae-gu	cod	소라	so-ra	conch
대합	dae-hab	clam	송어	song-eo	trout
도다리	do-da-ri	flounder	숭어	sung-eo	mullet
도루묵	do-ru-muk	sandfish	쏘가리	sso-ga-ri	mandarin fish
돌돔	dol-dom	rock bream	아귀	a-gwi	monkfish
동태	dong-tae	frozen pollack	연어	yeon-eo	salmon
망둥이	mang-dung-i	goby	오징어	o-jing-eo	squid
멍게	meong-ge	sea squirt	옥돔	ok-dom	tile fish
메기	me-gi	catfish	왕게	wang-ge	king crab
멸치	myeol-chi	anchovy	우럭	u-reok	rockfish
명태	myeong-tae	pollock	우렁이	u-reng-i	mud snail
문어	mun-eo	octopus	잉어	ing-eo	carp
미꾸라지	mi-kku-ra-ji	mudfish	전갱이	jeon-gaeng-i	horse mackerel
미역	mi-yeok	seaweed	전복	jeon-bok	sea ear
민어	min-eo	croaker	점성어	jeom-seong-eo	red drum
바닷가재	ba-das-ga-jae	lobster	정어리	jeong-eo-ri	sardine
방어	bang-eo	yellowtail	조개류	jo-gae-ryu	shellfish
백조기	baek-jo-gi	white croaker	쥐노래미	jwi-no-rae-mi	Atka mackerel
뱀장어	baem-jang-eo	eel	참돔	cham-dom	red snapper
병어	byeong-eo	butterfish	참조기	cham-jo-gi	yellow croaker
복어	bok-eo	blowfish	참치	cham-chi	tuna
북어(황태)	buk-eo(hwang-tae)	dried pollack	청어	cheong-eo	herring
불가사리	bul-ga-sa-ri	starfish	파래	pa-rae	sea lettuce
붕어	bung-eo	crucian carp	패주	pae ju	scallop
빙어	bing-eo	pond smelt	해마	hae-ma	seahorse

해삼	hae-sam	sea cucumber
해파리	hae-pa-ri	jellyfish
홍어	hong-eo	thornback
홍합	hong-hab	mussel

류 ryu (Class)

포유류	po-yu-ryu	mammal
파충류	pa-chung-ryu	reptile
조류	jo-ryu	birds
영장류	yeong-jang-ryu	primates
양서류	yang-seo-ryu	amphibian
갑각류	gab-gak-ryu	crustacean
설치류	seol-chi-ryu	rodent
해조류	hae-jo-ryu	algae
어패류	eo-pae-ryu	fish and shells
곤충류	gon-chung-ryu	insecta

달 dal (month)

일월	il-wol	January
이월	i-wol	February
삼월	sam-wol	March
사월	sa-wol	April
오월	o-wol	May
유월	yu-wol	June
칠월	chil-wol	July
팔월	pal-wol	August
구월	gu-wol	September
시월	si-wol	October
십일월	sib-il-wol	November
십이월	sib-i-wol	December

요일 yo-il (Day)

월요일	wol-yo-il	Monday
화요일	hwa-yo-il	Tuesday
수요일	su-yo-il	Wednesday
목요일	mok-yo-il	Thursday
금요일	geum-yo-il	Friday
토요일	to-yo-il	Saturday
일요일	il-yo-il	Sunday

날짜 nal-jja (Date)

이천이십일년	i-cheon-i-sib-il-nyeon	2021
천구백구십구년	cheon-gu-baek-gu-sib-gu-nyeon	1999
이천이십일년 구월 이십칠일	i-cheon-i-sib-il-nyeon gu-wol i-sib-chil-il	Sep 27th, 2021
천구백육십년대	cheon-gu-baeg-yug-sib-nyeon-dae	1960's

색깔 saek-kkal (Color)

빨간색	ppal-gan-saek	red
핑크색	ping-keu-saek	pink
노란색	no-ran-saek	yellow
금색	geum-saek	gold
오렌지색	o-ren-ji-saek	orange
자주색	ja-ju-saek	purple
보라색	bo-ra-saek	violet
까만색	kka-man-saek	black
녹색	nok-saek	green
흰색	huin-saek	white
파란색	pa-ran-saek	blue
은색	eun-saek	silver
갈색	gal-saek	brown
회색	hoe-saek	grey

기수1 gi-su (Cardinal Number1)			기수2 gi-su (Cardinal Number2)		
일	il	1	하나	ha-na	1
이	i	2	둘	dul	2
삼	sam	3	셋	ses	3
사	sa	4	넷	nes	4
오	o	5	다섯	da-seos	5
육	yuk	6	여섯	yeo-seos	6
칠	chil	7	일곱	il-gob	7
팔	pal	8	여덟	yeo-teolb	8
구	gu	9	아홉	a-hob	9
십	sib	10	열	yeol	10
십일	sib-il	11	열하나	yeol-ha-na	11
십이	sib-i	12	열둘	yeol-dul	12
십삼	sib-sam	13	열셋	yeol-ses	13
십사	sib-sa	14	열넷	yeol-nes	14
십오	sib-o	15	열다섯	yeol-da-seos	15
십육	sib-yuk	16	열여섯	yeol-yeo-seos	16
십칠	sib-chil	17	열일곱	yeol-il-gob	17
십팔	sib-pal	18	열여덟	yeol-yeo-deolb	18
십구	sib-gu	19	열아홉	yeol-a-hob	19
이십	i-sib	20	스물	seu-mul	20
이십일	i-sib-il	21	스물하나	seu-mul-ha-na	21
이십이	i-sib-i	22	스물둘	seu-mul-dul	22
삼십	sam-sib	30	서른	seo-reun	30
사십	sa-sib	40	마흔	ma-heun	40
오십	o-sib	50	쉰	swin	50
육십	yuk-sib	60	예순	ye-sun	60
칠십	chil-sib	70	일흔	il-heun	70
팔십	pal-sib	80	여든	yeo-deun	80
구십	gu-sib	90	아흔	a-heun	90
백	baek	100	백	baek	100

백일	baek-il	101	백하나	baek-ha-na	101
백이	baek-i	102	백둘	baek-dul	102
백삼	baek-sam	103	백셋	baek-ses	103
백십	baek-sib	110	백열	baek-yeol	110
백십일	baek-sib-il	111	백열하나	baek-yeol-ha-na	111
백십이	baek-sib-i	112	백열둘	baek-yeol-dul	112
백십삼	baek-sib-sam	113	백열셋	baek-yeol-ses	113
백이십	baek-i-sib	120	백스물	baek-seu-mul	120
천	cheon	1,000	천	cheon	1,000
천일	cheon-il	1,001	천하나	cheon-ha-na	1,001
천이	cheon-i	1,002	천둘	cheon-dul	1,002
천백	cheon-baek	1,100	천백	cheon-baek	1,100
천백일	cheon-baek-il	1,101	천백하나	cheon-baek-ha-na	1,101
천백이	cheon-baek-i	1,102	천백둘	cheon-baek-dul	1,102
천백십	cheon-baek-sib	1,110	천백십	cheon-baek-sib	1,110
천백이십	cheon-baek-i-sib	1,120	천백이십	cheon-baek-i-sib	1,120
천이백	cheon-i-baek	1,200	천이백	cheon-i-baek	1,200
이천	i-cheon	2,000	이천	i-cheon	2,000
이천일	i-cheon-il	2,001	이천하나	i-cheon-ha-na	2,001
만	man	10,000	만	man	10,000
만일	man-il	10,001	만하나	man-ha-na	10,001
이만	i-man	20,000	이만	i-man	20,000
이만일	i-man-il	20,001	이만하나	i-man ha-na	20,001
십만	sib-man	100,000	십만	sib-man	100,000
이십만	i-sib-man	200,000	이십만	i-sib-man	200,000
백만	baek-man	1,000,000	백만	baek-man	1,000,000
백만일	baek-man-il	1,000,001	백만 하나	baek-man-ha-na	1,000,001
천만	cheon-man	10,000,000	천만	cheon-man	10,000,000
억	eok	100,000,000	억	eok	100,000,000
일억일	il-eok-il	100,000,001	일억 하나	il-eok-ha-na	100,000,001
십억	sib-eok	1,000,000,000	십억	sib-eok	1,000,000,000

과일 gwa-il (Fruit)

감	gam	persimmon
귤	gyul	tangerine
도토리	do-to-ri	acorns
딸기	ttal-gi	strawberry
망고	mang-go	mango
바나나	ba-na-na	banana
밤	bam	chestnut
배	bae	pear
복숭아	bok-sung-a	peach
사과	sa-gwa	apple
살구	sal-gu	apricot
수박	su-bak	watermelon
오렌지	o-ren-ji	orange
은행	eun-haeng	ginko
자두	ja-du	plum
체리	che-ri	cherry
포도	po-do	grape

기념일 gi-nyeom-il (Anniversary)

구정(설날)	gu-jeong(seol-nal)	Lunar New Year
신정	sin-jeong	New Year's Day
추석	chu-seok	August 15th in the lunar calendar
제사	je-sa	ancestral rites
정월 대보름	jeong-wol dae-bo-reum	January 15th in the lunar calendar
단오	dan-o	May 5th in the lunar calendar
칠석	chil-seok	July 7th in the lunar calendar
복날	bok-nal	3days from June to July in the lunar calendar
3.1절	sam-il-jeol	March 1st
광복절	gwang-bok-jeol	August15th
개천절	gae-cheon-jeol	October 3rd

한글날	han-geul-nal	October 9th
부처님오신 날	bu-cheo-nim o-sin-nal	April 8th in the lunar calendar
어린이날	eo-rin-i-nal	May 5th
현충일	hyeon-chung-il	June 6th
크리스마스	keu-ri-seu-ma-seu	December 25th
식목일	sik-mok-il	April 5th
제헌절	je-heon-jeol	July 17th
국군의 날	guk-gun-ui-nal	October 1st
유엔의 날	yu-en-ui-nal	October 24th

도시 do-si (City)

서울	seo-ul	강원도	gang-won-do
경기도	gyeong-gi-do	충청북도	chung-cheong-buk-do
인천	in-cheon	울릉도	ul-reung-do
충청남도	chung-cheong-nam-do	독도	dok-do
세종시	se-jong-si	경상북도	gyeong-sang-buk-do
대전	dae-jeon	대구	dae-gu
전라북도	jeon-ra-buk-do	울산	ul-san
광주	gwang-ju	부산	bu-san
전라남도	jeon-ra-nam-do	경상남도	gyeong-sang-nam-do
제주도	je-ju-do		

악기 ak-gi (Musical Instrument)

거문고	geo-mun-go	geomungo
기타	gita	guitar
나팔	na-pal	trumpet
드럼	deu-reom	drum
바이올린	ba-i-ol-lin	violin
북	buk	drum
색소폰	saek-so-pon	saxophone
심벌즈	sim-beol-jeu	cymbals
아코디언	a-ko-di-eon	accordion
오르간	o-reu-gan	organ
오카리나	o-ka-ri-na	ocarina
우쿨렐레	u-kul-lel-le	ukulele
트럼펫	teu-reom-pes	trumpet
피리	pi-ri	flute
피아노	pi-a-no	piano
하모니카	ha-mo-ni-ka	harmonica

가족 ga-jok (Family)

증조부	jeung-jo-bu	great-grandfather
증조모	jeung-jo-mo	great grandmother
할아버지	hal-a-beo-ji	grandfather
할머니	hal-meo-ni	grandmother
아버지	a-beo-ji	father
아빠	a-ppa	dad
어머니	eo-meo-ni	mother
엄마	eom-ma	mom
시아버지	si-a-beo-ji	husband's father
시어머니	si-eo-meo-ni	husband's mother
장인	jang-in	wife's father
장모	jang-mo	wife's mother
큰아버지	keun-a-beo-ji	elder brother of father
큰어머니	keun-eo-meo-ni	wife of the elder brother of father
삼촌	sam-chon	father's brother
외삼촌	oe-sam-chon	mother's brother
외숙모	oe-suk-mo	wife of mother's brother
고모	go-mo	father's sister
고모부	go-mo-bu	husband of father's sister
이모	i-mo	mother's sister
이모부	i-mo-bu	husband of mother's sister
시아주버니	si-a-ju-beo-ni	elder brother of husband
숙모	suk-mo	wife of father's brother
남편	nam-pyeon	husband
아내	a-nae	wife
자식	ja-sik	sons and daughters
손자	son-ja	grandson
손녀	son-nyeo	granddaughter
며느리	myeo-neu-ri	son's wife
사위	sa-wi	daughter's husband
증손자	jeung-son-ja	great grandson
증손녀	jeung-son-nyeo	great granddaughter
사촌	sa-chon	cousin
조카	jo-ka	nephew
자매	ja-mae	sisters
형제	hyeong-je	brothers
아들	a-deul	son
딸	ttal	daughter
오빠	o-ppa	girl's older brother
언니	eon-ni	girl's older sister
누나	nu-na	boy's older sister
남동생	nam-dong-saeng	younger brother
여동생	yeo-dong-saeng	younger sister

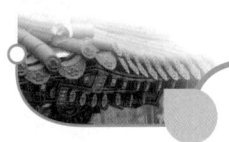

Korean Writing Practice *Write according to the letter.

ㄱ	ㄴ	ㄷ	ㄹ	ㅁ	ㅂ	ㅅ	ㅇ	ㅈ	ㅊ	ㅋ	ㅌ	ㅍ	ㅎ
g/k	n	d/t	r/l	m	b/p	s	ng	j	ch	k	t	p	h
ㄱ	ㄴ	ㄷ	ㄹ	ㅁ	ㅂ	ㅅ	ㅇ	ㅈ	ㅊ	ㅋ	ㅌ	ㅍ	ㅎ
ㄱ	ㄴ	ㄷ	ㄹ	ㅁ	ㅂ	ㅅ	ㅇ	ㅈ	ㅊ	ㅋ	ㅌ	ㅍ	ㅎ
ㄱ	ㄴ	ㄷ	ㄹ	ㅁ	ㅂ	ㅅ	ㅇ	ㅈ	ㅊ	ㅋ	ㅌ	ㅍ	ㅎ
ㄱ	ㄴ	ㄷ	ㄹ	ㅁ	ㅂ	ㅅ	ㅇ	ㅈ	ㅊ	ㅋ	ㅌ	ㅍ	ㅎ
ㄱ	ㄴ	ㄷ	ㄹ	ㅁ	ㅂ	ㅅ	ㅇ	ㅈ	ㅊ	ㅋ	ㅌ	ㅍ	ㅎ

ㄲ		ㄸ		ㅃ		ㅆ		ㅉ	
kk		tt		pp		ss		jj	
ㄲ		ㄸ		ㅃ		ㅆ		ㅉ	

ㄲ	ㄲ	ㄸ	ㄸ	ㅃ	ㅃ	ㅆ	ㅆ	ㅉ	ㅉ
ㄲ	ㄲ	ㄸ	ㄸ	ㅃ	ㅃ	ㅆ	ㅆ	ㅉ	ㅉ

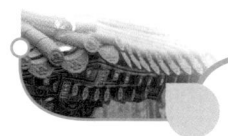

Korean Writing Practice

ㅏ	ㅑ	ㅓ	ㅕ	ㅗ	ㅛ	ㅜ	ㅠ	ㅡ	ㅣ
a	ya	eo	yeo	o	yo	u	yu	eu	i
ㅏ	ㅑ	ㅓ	ㅕ	ㅗ	ㅛ	ㅜ	ㅠ	ㅡ	ㅣ
ㅏ	ㅑ	ㅓ	ㅕ	ㅗ	ㅛ	ㅜ	ㅠ	ㅡ	ㅣ
ㅏ	ㅑ	ㅓ	ㅕ	ㅗ	ㅛ	ㅜ	ㅠ	ㅡ	ㅣ
ㅏ	ㅑ	ㅓ	ㅕ	ㅗ	ㅛ	ㅜ	ㅠ	ㅡ	ㅣ
ㅐ	ㅒ	ㅔ	ㅖ	ㅚ	ㅟ	ㅢ	ㅘ	ㅝ	ㅙ
ae	yae	e	ye	oe	wi	ui	wa	wo	wae
ㅐ	ㅒ	ㅔ	ㅖ	ㅚ	ㅟ	ㅢ	ㅘ	ㅝ	ㅙ
ㅐ	ㅒ	ㅔ	ㅖ	ㅚ	ㅟ	ㅢ	ㅘ	ㅝ	ㅙ
ㅐ	ㅒ	ㅔ	ㅖ	ㅚ	ㅟ	ㅢ	ㅘ	ㅝ	ㅙ
ㅐ	ㅒ	ㅔ	ㅖ	ㅚ	ㅟ	ㅢ	ㅘ	ㅝ	ㅙ
ㅞ we		ㅞ		ㅞ		ㅞ		ㅞ	

Korean Writing Practice

가	갸	거	겨	고	교	구	규	그	기
ga	gya	geo	gyeo	go	gyo	gu	gyu	geu	gi
가	갸	거	겨	고	교	구	규	그	기
가	갸	거	겨	고	교	구	규	그	기

나	냐	너	녀	노	뇨	누	뉴	느	니
na	nya	neo	nyeo	no	nyo	nu	nyu	neu	ni
나	냐	너	녀	노	뇨	누	뉴	느	니
나	냐	너	녀	노	뇨	누	뉴	느	니

다	댜	더	뎌	도	됴	두	듀	드	디
da	dya	deo	dyeo	do	dyo	du	dyu	deu	di
다	댜	더	뎌	도	됴	두	듀	드	디
다	댜	더	뎌	도	됴	두	듀	드	디

라 ra	랴 rya	러 reo	려 ryeo	로 ro	료 ryo	루 ru	류 ryu	르 reu	리 ri
라	랴	러	려	로	료	루	류	르	리
라	랴	러	려	로	료	루	류	르	리

마 ma	먀 mya	머 meo	며 myeo	모 mo	묘 myo	무 mu	뮤 myu	므 meu	미 mi
마	먀	머	며	모	묘	무	뮤	므	미
마	먀	머	며	모	묘	무	뮤	므	미

바 ba	뱌 bya	버 beo	벼 byeo	보 bo	뵤 byo	부 bu	뷰 byu	브 beu	비 bi
바	뱌	버	벼	보	뵤	부	뷰	브	비
바	뱌	버	벼	보	뵤	부	뷰	브	비

사 sa	샤 sya	서 seo	셔 syeo	소 so	쇼 syo	수 su	슈 syu	스 seu	시 si
사	샤	서	셔	소	쇼	수	슈	스	시
사	샤	서	셔	소	쇼	수	슈	스	시

아	야	어	여	오	요	우	유	으	이
a	ya	eo	yeo	o	yo	u	yu	eu	i
아	야	어	여	오	요	우	유	으	이
아	야	어	여	오	요	우	유	으	이

자	쟈	저	져	조	죠	주	쥬	즈	지
ja	jya	jeo	jyeo	jo	jyo	ju	jyu	jeu	ji
자	쟈	저	져	조	죠	주	쥬	즈	지
자	쟈	저	져	조	죠	주	쥬	즈	지

차	챠	쳐	쳐	쵸	쵸	추	츄	츠	치
cha	chya	cheo	chyeo	cho	chyo	chu	chyu	cheu	chi
차	챠	쳐	쳐	쵸	쵸	추	츄	츠	치
차	챠	쳐	쳐	쵸	쵸	추	츄	츠	치

카	캬	커	켜	코	쿄	쿠	큐	크	키
ka	kya	keo	kyeo	ko	kyo	ku	kyu	keu	ki
카	캬	커	켜	코	쿄	쿠	큐	크	키
카	캬	커	켜	코	쿄	쿠	큐	크	키

타	탸	터	텨	토	툐	투	튜	트	티
ta	tya	teo	tyeo	to	tyo	tu	tyu	teu	ti
타	탸	터	텨	토	툐	투	튜	트	티
타	탸	터	텨	토	툐	투	튜	트	티

파	퍄	퍼	펴	포	표	푸	퓨	프	피
pa	pya	peo	pyeo	po	pyo	pu	pyu	peu	pi
파	퍄	퍼	펴	포	표	푸	퓨	프	피
파	퍄	퍼	펴	포	표	푸	퓨	프	피

하	햐	허	혀	호	효	후	휴	흐	히
ha	hya	heo	hyeo	ho	hyo	hu	hyu	heu	hi
하	햐	허	혀	호	효	후	휴	흐	히
하	햐	허	혀	호	효	후	휴	흐	히

까	꺄	꺼	껴	꼬	꾜	꾸	뀨	끄	끼
kka	kkya	kkeo	kkyeo	kko	kkyo	kku	kkyu	kkeu	kki
까	꺄	꺼	껴	꼬	꾜	꾸	뀨	끄	끼

따	땨	떠	뗘	또	뚀	뚜	뜌	뜨	띠
tta	ttya	tteo	ttyeo	tto	ttyo	ttu	ttyu	tteu	tti
따	땨	떠	뗘	또	뚀	뚜	뜌	뜨	띠

빠	뺘	뻐	뼈	뽀	뾰	뿌	쀼	쁘	삐
ppa	ppya	ppeo	ppyeo	ppo	ppyo	ppu	ppyu	ppeu	ppi
빠	뺘	뻐	뼈	뽀	뾰	뿌	쀼	쁘	삐

싸	쌰	써	쎠	쏘	쑈	쑤	쓔	쓰	씨
ssa	ssya	sseo	ssyeo	sso	ssyo	ssu	ssyu	sseu	ssi
싸	쌰	써	쎠	쏘	쑈	쑤	쓔	쓰	씨

짜	쨔	쩌	쪄	쪼	쬬	쭈	쮸	쯔	찌
jja	jjya	jjeo	jjyeo	jjo	jjyo	jju	jjyu	jjeu	jji
짜	쨔	쩌	쪄	쪼	쬬	쭈	쮸	쯔	찌

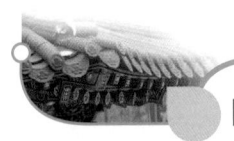

Korean Writing Practice

각	간	갈	감	갑	갓	강	개	객	거
gak(g)	gan	gal	gam	gap(b)	gat(s)	gang	gae	gaek	geo
각	간	갈	감	갑	갓	강	개	객	거

건	걸	검	겁	게	겨	격	견	결	겸
geon	geol	geom	geop(b)	ge	gyeo	gyeok(g)	gyeon	gyeol	gyeom
따	걸	검	겁	게	겨	격	견	결	겸

겹	경	계	고	곡	곤	골	곳	공	곶
gyeop(b)	gyeong	gye	go	gok	gon	gol	got(s)	gong	got(j)
겹	경	계	고	곡	곤	골	곳	공	곶

과	곽	관	괄	광	괘	괴	굉	교	구
gwa	gwak	gwan	gwal	gwang	gwae	goe	goeng	gyo	gu
과	곽	관	괄	광	괘	괴	굉	교	구

국	군	굴	굿	궁	권	궐	귀	규	균
guk(g)	gun	gul	gut(s)	gung	gwon	gwol	gwi	gyu	gyun
국	군	굴	굿	궁	권	궐	귀	규	균

귤	그	극	근	글	금	급	긍	기	긴
gyul	geu	geuk(g)	geun	geul	geum	geup(b)	geung	gi	gin
귤	그	극	근	글	금	급	긍	기	긴

길	김	까	깨	꼬	꼭	꽃	꾀	꾸	꿈
gil	gim	kka	kkae	kko	kkok(g)	kkot(cc)	kkoe	kku	kkum
길	김	까	깨	꼬	꼭	꽃	꾀	꾸	꿈

끝	끼								
kkeut	kki								
끝	끼								

낙	난	날	남	납	낭	내	냉	너	널
nak(g)	nan	nal	nam	nap(b)	nang	nae	naeng	neo	neol
낙	난	날	남	납	낭	내	냉	너	널

네	녀	녁	년	념	녕	노	녹	논	놀
ne	nyeo	nyeok(g)	nyeon	nyeom	nyeong	no	nok(g)	non	nol
네	녀	녁	년	념	녕	노	녹	논	놀

농	뇌	누	눈	눌	느	늑	늠	능	뇌
nong	noe	nu	nun	nul	neu	neuk(g)	neum	neung	nui
농	뇌	누	눈	눌	느	늑	늠	능	뇌

니	닉	닌	닐	님
ni	nik(g)	nin	nil	nim
니	닉	닌	닐	님

단	달	담	답	당	대	댁	더	덕	도
dan	dal	dam	dap(b)	dang	dae	daek(g)	deo	deok	do
단	달	담	답	당	대	댁	더	덕	도

독	돈	돌	동	돼	되	된	두	둑	둔
dok(g)	don	dol	dong	dwae	doe	doen	du	duk(g)	dun
독	돈	돌	동	돼	되	된	두	둑	둔

뒤	드	득	들	등	디	따	땅	때	또
dwi	deu	deuk(g)	deul	deung	di	tta	ttang	ttae	tto
뒤	드	득	들	등	디	따	땅	때	또

뚜	뚝	뜨	띠						
ttu	ttuk(g)	tteu	tti						
뚜	뚝	뜨	띠						

락	란	람	랑	래	랭	량	렁	레	려
rak(g)	ran	ram	rang	rae	raeng	ryang	reong	re	ryeo
락	란	람	랑	래	랭	량	렁	레	려

력	련	렬	렴	렵	령	례	로	록	론
ryeok(g)	ryeon	ryeol	ryeom	ryeop(b)	ryeong	rye	ro	rok(g)	ron
력	련	렬	렴	렵	령	례	로	록	론

롱	뢰	료	룡	루	류	륙	륜	률	룽
rong	roe	ryo	ryong	ru	ryu	ryuk(g)	ryun	ryul	ryung
롱	뢰	료	룡	루	류	륙	륜	률	룽

르	륵	른	름	릉	리	린	림	립	
reu	reuk(g)	reun	reum	reung	ri	rin	rim	rip(b)	
르	륵	른	름	릉	리	린	림	립	

막	만	말	망	매	맥	맨	맹	머	먹
mak(g)	man	mal	mang	mae	maek(g)	maen	maeng	meo	meok(g)
막	만	말	망	매	맥	맨	맹	머	먹

메	며	멱	면	멸	명	모	목	몰	못
me	myeo	myeok(g)	myeon	myeol	myeong	mo	mok(g)	mol	mot(s)
메	며	멱	면	멸	명	모	목	몰	못

몽	뫼	묘	무	묵	밀	문	물	므	미
mong	moe	myo	mu	muk(g)	mil	mun	mul	meu	mi
몽	뫼	묘	무	묵	밀	문	물	므	미

민									
min									
민									

박	반	발	밥	방	배	백	뱀	버	번
bak(g)	ban	bal	bap(b)	bang	bae	baek(g)	baem	beo	beon
박	반	발	밥	방	배	백	뱀	버	번

벌	범	법	벼	벽	변	별	병	보	복
beol	beom	beop(b)	byeo	byeok(g)	byeon	byeol	byeong	bo	bok(g)
벌	범	법	벼	벽	변	별	병	보	복

본	봉	부	북	분	불	붕	비	빈	빌
bon	bong	bu	buk(g)	bun	bul	bung	bi	bin	bil
본	봉	부	북	분	불	붕	비	빈	빌

빔	빙	빠	빼	뻐	뽀	뿌	쁘	삐	
bim	bing	ppa	ppae	ppeo	ppo	ppu	ppeu	ppi	
빔	빙	빠	빼	뻐	뽀	뿌	쁘	삐	

삭	산	살	삼	삽	상	샅	새	색	생
sak(g)	san	sal	sam	sap(b)	sang	sat	sae	saek(g)	saeng
삭	산	살	삼	삽	상	샅	새	색	생

서	석	선	설	섬	섭	성	세	셔	소
seo	seok(g)	seon	seol	seom	seop(b)	seong	se	syeo	so
서	석	선	설	섬	섭	성	세	셔	소

속	손	솔	솟	송	쇄	쇠	수	숙	순
sok(g)	son	sol	sot(s)	song	swae	soe	su	suk(g)	sun
속	손	솔	솟	송	쇄	쇠	수	숙	순

술	숨	숭	쉬	스	슬	슴	습	승	시
sul	sum	sung	swi	seu	seul	seum	seup(b)	seung	si
술	숨	숭	쉬	스	슬	슴	습	승	시

식	신	실	심	십	싱	싸	쌍	쌔	쏘
sik(g)	sin	sil	sim	sip(b)	sing	ssa	ssang	ssae	sso
식	신	실	심	십	싱	싸	쌍	쌔	쏘

쑥	씨								
ssuk(g)	ssi								
쑥	씨								

악	안	알	암	압	앙	앞	애	액	앵
ak(g)	an	al	am	ap(b)	ang	ap	ae	aek(g)	aeng
악	안	알	암	압	앙	앞	애	액	앵

야	약	얀	양	어	억	언	얼	엄	업
ya	yak(g)	yan	yang	eo	eok(g)	eon	eol	eom	eop(b)
야	약	얀	양	어	억	언	얼	엄	업

에	여	역	연	열	염	엽	영	예	오
e	yeo	yeok(g)	yeon	yeol	yeom	yeop(b)	yeong	ye	o
에	여	역	연	열	염	엽	영	예	오

옥	온	올	옴	옹	와	완	왈	왕	왜
ok(g)	on	ol	om	ong	wa	wan	wal	wang	wae
옥	온	올	옴	옹	와	완	왈	왕	왜

외	원	요	욕	용	우	욱	운	울	움
oe	oen	yo	yok(g)	yong	u	uk(g)	un	ul	um
외	원	요	욕	용	우	욱	운	울	움

웅	워	원	월	위	유	육	윤	율	융
ung	wo	won	wol	wi	yu	yuk(g)	yun	yul	yung
웅	워	원	월	위	유	육	윤	율	융

윷	으	은	을	음	읍	응	의	이	익
yut(yucc)	eu	eun	eul	eum	eup(b)	eung	ui	i	ik(g)
윷	으	은	을	음	읍	응	의	이	익

인	일	임	입	잉
in	il	im	ip(b)	ing
인	일	임	입	잉

작	잔	잠	잡	장	재	쟁	저	적	전
jak(g)	jan	jam	jap(b)	jang	jae	jaeng	jeo	jeok(g)	jeon
작	잔	잠	잡	장	재	쟁	저	적	전

절	점	접	정	제	조	족	존	졸	종
jeol	jeom	jeop(b)	jeong	je	jo	jok(g)	jon	jol	jong
절	점	접	정	제	조	족	존	졸	종

좌	죄	주	죽	준	줄	중	쥐	즈	즉
jwa	joe	ju	juk(g)	jun	jul	jung	jwi	jeu	jeuk(g)
좌	죄	주	죽	준	줄	중	쥐	즈	즉

즐	즘	즙	증	지	직	진	질	짐	집
jeul	jeum	jeup(b)	jeung	ji	jik(g)	jin	jil	jim	jip(b)
즐	즘	즙	증	지	직	진	질	짐	집

징	짜	째	쪼	찌					
jing	jja	jjae	jjo	jji					
징	짜	째	쪼	찌					

착	찬	찰	참	창	채	책	처	척	천
chak(g)	chan	chal	cham	chang	chae	chaek	cheo	cheok(g)	cheon
착	찬	찰	참	창	채	책	처	척	천

철	첨	첩	청	제	초	촉	춘	총	최
cheol	cheom	cheop(b)	cheong	che	cho	chok(g)	chon	chong	choe
철	첨	첩	청	제	초	촉	춘	총	최

추	축	춘	출	춤	충	측	층	치	칙
chu	chuk(g)	chun	chul	chum	chung	cheuk(g)	cheung	chi	chik(g)
추	축	춘	출	춤	충	측	층	치	칙

친	칠	침	칩	칭					
chin	chil	chim	chip(b)	ching					
친	칠	침	칩	칭					

코	쾌	크	큰	키					
ko	kwae	keu	keun	ki					
코	쾌	크	큰	키					

탁	탄	탈	탐	탑	탕	태	택	탱	터
tak(g)	tan	tal	tam	tap(b)	tang	tae	taek(g)	taeng	teo
탁	탄	탈	탐	탑	탕	태	택	탱	터

테	토	톤	톨	통	퇴	투	퉁	튀	트
te	to	ton	tol	tong	toe	tu	tung	twi	teu
테	토	톤	톨	통	퇴	투	퉁	튀	트

특	틈	티							
teuk(g)	teum	ti							
특	틈	티							

판	팔	패	팽	퍼	페	펴	편	폄	평
pan	pal	pae	paeng	peo	pe	pyeo	pyeon	pyeom	pyeong
판	팔	패	팽	퍼	페	펴	편	폄	평

폐	포	폭	표	푸	품	풍	프	피	픽
pye	po	pok(g)	pyo	pu	pum	pung	peu	pi	pik(g)
폐	포	폭	표	푸	품	풍	프	피	픽

필 pil	핍 pip(b)								
필	핍								

학 hak(g)	한 han	할 hal	함 ham	합 hap(b)	항 hang	해 hae	핵 haek(g)	행 haeng	향 hyang
학	한	할	함	합	항	해	핵	행	향

허 heo	헌 heon	험 heom	헤 he	혀 hyeo	혁 hyeok(g)	현 hyeon	혈 hyeol	혐 hyeom	협 hyeop(b)
허	헌	험	헤	혀	혁	현	혈	혐	협

형	혜	호	혹	혼	홀	홉	홍	화	확
hyeong	hye	ho	hok(g)	hon	hol	hop(b)	hong	hwa	hwak(g)
형	혜	호	혹	혼	홀	홉	홍	화	확

환	활	황	홰	횃	회	획	횡	효	후
hwan	hwal	hwang	hwae	hwaet(s)	hoe	hoek(g)	hoeng	hyo	hu
환	활	황	홰	횃	회	획	횡	효	후

훈	훤	훼	휘	유	율	융	흐	흑	흔
hun	hwon	hwe	hwi	hyu	hyul	hyung	heu	heuk(g)	heun
훈	훤	훼	휘	유	율	융	흐	흑	흔

흘	흠	흡	흥	희	흰	히	힘		
heul	heum	heup(b)	heung	hui	huin	hi	him		
흘	흠	흡	흥	희	흰	히	힘		

Korean Sentence Writing Practice

(p401)

오랜 친구에요	o-raen chin-gu-e-yo	He's an old friend.
오랜 가뭄이에요	o-raen ga-mum-i-eyo	It's a long drought.
2년 만이에요	i-nyeon man-i-e-yo	It's been two years.
하루 만이에요	ha-ru man-i-e-yo	It's just one day.
몸 관리 맡기세요	mom gwan-ri mat-gi-se-yo	Let me take care of your body.
몸 관리 시작하세요	mom gwan-ri si-jak-ha-se-yo	Start taking care of your body.
돈 관리 잘하세요	don gwan-ri jal-ha-se-yo	Take good care of your money.
머리 관리 잘하세요	meo-ri gwan-ri jal-ha-se-yo	Take good care of your hair.
생일 기억해요	saeng-il gi-eok-hae-yo	Remember your birthday.
생일 잊으세요	saeng-il ij-eu-se-yo	Forget about your birthday.
합격 축하해요	hab-gyeok chuk-ha-hae-yo	Congratulations on passing.
당선 축하해요	dang-seon chuk-ha-hae-yo	Congratulations on winning.
축하 받았어요	chuk-ha bad-ass-eo-yo	I got congratulations.
축하 합니다	chuk-ha hab-ni-da	Congratulations!.
감사 드려요	gam-sa deu-ryeo-yo	Thank you.
부탁 드려요	bu-tak deu-ryeo-yo	I beg you.

(p402)

감기에 효과 있어요	gam-gi-e hyo-gwa iss-eo-yo	It's effective for colds.
감기에 대비하세요	gam-gi-e dae-bi-ha-se-yo	Be prepared for a cold.
간암에 걸렸어요	gan-am-e geol-lyeoss-eo-yo	I have liver cancer.
교통신호에 걸렸어요	gyo-tong-sin-ho-e geol-lyeoss-eo-yo	I got a traffic signal.
머리가 좀 멍해요	meo-ri-ga jom meong-hae-yo	My head is a bit fuzzy.
머리가 좀 이상해요	meo-ri-ga jom i-sang-hae-yo	My head is a bit weird.
다리가 좀 아파요	da-ri-ga jom a-pa-yo	My legs hurt a little.
배가 좀 아파요	bae-ga jom a-pa-yo	I have a stomachache.
많이 나빠졌어요	manh-i na-ppa-jyeoss-eo-yo	It got a lot worse.
많이 길어졌어요	manh-i gil-eo-jyeoss-eo-yo	It got a lot longer.
조금 좋아졌어요	jo-geum joh-a-jyeoss-eo-yo	It got a little better.
매우 좋아졌어요	mae-u joh-a-jyeoss-eo-yo	It got a lot better.
염려하지 마세요	yeom-ryeo-ha-ji ma-se-yo	Don't worry.
놀라지 마세요	nol-la-ji ma-se-yo	Don't be surprised.
두려워하지 마세요	du-ryeo-wo-ha-ji ma-se-yo	Don't be afraid.
부끄러워하지 마세요	bu-kkeu-reo-wo-ha-ji ma-se-yo	Don't be embarrassed.

객실카드를 찾았어요	gaek-sil-ka-deu-reul chaj-ass-eo-yo I found a room card.
객실카드를 주세요	gaek-sil-ka-deu-reul ju-se-yo Give me your room card.
핸드폰을 잃어버렸어요	haen-deu-pon-eul ilh-eo-beo-ryeoss-eo-yo. I lost my phone.
열쇠를 잃어버렸어요	yeol-soe-reul ilh-eo-beo-ryeoss-eo-yo I lost my key.
부탁 전해주세요	bu-tak jeon-hae-ju-se-yo Please tell him.
부탁 잊지 마세요	bu-tak ij-ji ma-se-yo Don't forget to ask.
먼저 가세요	meon-jeo ga-se-yo After you.
먼저 드세요	meon-jeo deu-se-yo Eat first.
나중에 하세요	na-jung-e ha-se-yo You can do that later.
오후에 하세요	o-hu-e ha-se-yo Do it in the afternoon.
정말 반가워요	jeong-mal ban-ga-wo-yo It is so nice to meet you.
정말 감사해요	jeong-mal gam-sa-hae-yo Thank you so much.
조금 아쉬워요	jo-geum a-swi-wo-yo It's a bit disappointing.
많이 아쉬워요	manh-i a-swi-wo-yo It's very unfortunate.

(p404)

조심히 걸으세요　jo-sim-hi geol-eu-se-yo　Please walk carefully.

조심히 가세요　jo-sim-hi ga-se-yo　Take care.

식사하세요　sik-sa-ha-se-yo　Have a meal.

운동하세요　un-dong-ha-se-yo　Work out.

일어나세요　il-eo-na-se-yo　Stand up.

엎드리세요　eop-deu-ri-se-yo　Lie down.

멈추세요　meom-chu-se-yo　Please stop.

공부하세요　gong-bu-ha-se-yo　Study.

제가 옮길게요　je-ga olm-gil-ge-yo　I'll move it.

제가 할게요　je-ga hal-ge-yo　I'll do it.

그가 계산할게요　geu-ga gye-san-hal-ge-yo　He'll pay for it.

그녀가 계산할게요　geu-nyeo-ga gye-san-hal-ge-yo　She'll pay for it.

일어나보세요　il-eo-na-bo-se-yo　Try getting up.

뱉어보세요　baet-eo-bo-se-yo　Spit it out.

마셔보세요　ma-syeo-bo-se-yo　Drink it.

앉아보세요　anj-a-bo-se-yo　Please sit down.

(p405)

너무 매워요	neo-mu mae-wo-yo	This is too spicy.
너무 멋져요	neo-mu meos-jyeo-yo	It's really fantastic.
매우 맛있어요	mae-u mas-iss-eo-yo	It's very delicious.
조금 맛있어요	jo-geum mas-iss-eo-yo	It's kind of delicious.
많이 가지세요	manh-i ga-ji-se-yo	Have a lot.
많이 넣으세요	manh-i neoh-eu-se-yo	Put in a lot.
전부 드세요	jeon-bu deu-se-yo	Eat everything.
조금 드세요	jo-geum deu-se-yo	Eat a little bit.
조금 싱거워요	jo-geum sing-geo-wo-yo	It's a little bland.
조금 짜요	jo-geum jja-yo	It's a little salty.
매우 매워요	mae-u mae-wo-yo	It's very spicy.
약간 매워요	yak-gan mae-wo-yo	It's a bit spicy.
작은 걸로 가지세요	jak-eun geol-lo ga-ji-se-yo	Take the small one.
작은 걸로 넣으세요	jak-eun geol-lo neoh-eu-se-yo	Put the small one in.
적당한 걸로 주세요	jeok-dang-han geol-lo ju-se-yo	Please give me the right one.
보통 걸로 주세요	bo-tong geol-lo ju-se-yo	Give me a normal one.

(p406)

큰 걸로 가지세요	keun geol-lo ga-ji-se-yo	Take the big one.
큰 걸로 넣으세요	gkeun geol-lo neoh-eu-se-yo	Put the big one in.
짠 걸로 주세요	jjan geol-lo ju-se-yo	Please give me something salty.
매운 걸로 주세요	mae-un geol-lo ju-se-yo	I'd like something spicy, please.
조금 더 드세요	jo-geum deo deu-se-yo	Eat some more.
조금 더 하세요	jo-geum deo ha-se-yo	Do a little more.
많이 더 주세요	manh-i deo ju-se-yo	Please give me more.
만 원 어치 주세요	man won eo-chi ju-se-yo	Give me 10,000 won worth.
아무것도 없어요	a-mu-geos-do eobs-eo-yo	I don't have any.
아무것도 맛없어요	a-mu-geos-do mas-eobs-eo-yo	Nothing tastes good.
사소한 것 아니에요	sa-so-han geos a-ni-ye-yo	It's not a small thing.
중요한 것 아니에요	jung-yo-han geos a-ni-ye-yo	It's not an important thing.
너무 길어요	neo-mu gil-eo-yo	It's too long.
너무 짧아요	neo-mu jjalb-a-yo	It's so short.
조금 예뻐요	jo-geum ye-ppeo-yo	It's a little pretty.
매우 예뻐요	mae-u ye-ppeo-yo	It's very pretty.

| 다른 걸로 주세요 | da-reun geol-lo ju-se-yo | Please give me something else. |

| 다른 걸로 가지세요 | da-reun geol-lo ga-ji-se-yo | Take something else. |

| 작은 걸로 바꾸고 싶어요 | jak-eun geol-lo ba-kku-go sip-eo-yo
I want to change it to a small one. |

| 이것을 바꾸고 싶어요 | i-geos-eul ba-kku-go sip-eo-yo
I want to change this. |

| 저것 좀 주세요 | jeo-geos jom ju-se-yo | Please give me that. |

| 저것 좀 바꾸세요 | jeo-geos jom ba-kku-se-yo | Please change that. |

| 당신 것 좀 보여주세요 | dang-sin geos jom bo-yeo-ju-se-yo
Please show us yours. |

| 얇은 것 좀 보여주세요 | yalb-eun geos jom bo-yeo-ju-se-yo
Please show us something thin. |

| 휴지 좀 버리겠어요? | hyu-ji jom beo-ri-gess-eo-yo
Can you throw away some tissues? |

| 휴지 좀 넣으시겠어요? | hyu-ji jom neoh-eu-si-gess-eo-yo
Can you put in some tissues? |

| 수저 좀 가져다주시겠어요? | su-jeo jom ga-jyeo-da-ju-si-gess-eo-yo
Can you bring me a spoon? |

| 물 좀 가져다주시겠어요? | mul jom ga-jyeo-da-ju-si-gess-eo-yo
Can you bring me some water? |

| 테이블 좀 펴주시겠어요? | te-i-beul jom pyeo-ju-si-gess-eo-yo
Can you open the table? |

| 테이블 좀 접으시겠어요? | te-i-beul jom jeob-eu-si-gess-eo-yo
Can you fold the table? |

| 손 좀 치워주시겠어요? | son jom chi-wo-ju-si-gess-eo-yo
Can you move your hands? |

| 책 좀 치워주시겠어요? | chaek jom chi-wo-ju-si-gess-eo-yo
Can you move the books? |

(p408)

나눠서 드세요   na-nwo-seo deu-se-yo   Share it and eat it.

나눠서 가지세요   na-nwo-seo ga-ji-se-yo   Divide it and take it.

합쳐서 담아주세요   hab-chyeo-seo dam-a-ju-se-yo
Please put them together.

모두 담아주세요   mo-du dam-a-ju-se-yo   Please put everything in.

영수증 좀 버리세요   yeong-su-jeung jom beo-ri-se-yo
Please throw away the receipt.

영수증 좀 넣으세요   yeong-su-jeung jom neoh-eu-se-yo
Put the receipt in.

표 좀 주세요   pyo jom ju-se-yo   Please give me the ticket.

돈 좀 주세요   don jom ju-se-yo   Please give me some money.

핸드폰 충전 좀 부탁할까요?   haen-deu-pon chung-jeon jom bu-tak-hal-kka-yo
Can you charge my phone?

핸 드폰 충전 좀 멈출까요?   haen-deu-pon chung-jeon jom meom-chul-kka-yo
Could you stop charging my phone?

식사 좀 할 수 있을까요?   sik-sa jom hal su iss-eul-kka-yo
Can I have a meal?

세차 좀 할 수 있을까요?   se-cha jom hal su iss-eul-kka-yo
Can I wash my car?

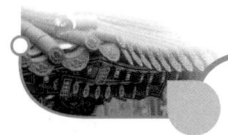

Korean Communication Culture

1. Korean composition.

1) Korean is in the order of subject + object + verb.

나는   그를 보았다. na-neun geu-reul bo-ass-da / I   saw him.
(subject) (object) (verb)   (subject) (verb) (object)

나는   어제 공원에서 그를 보았다. na-neun eo-je gong-won-e-seo geu-reul bo-ass-da
(subject) (adverb) (adverb) (object) (verb)

I   saw him in the park yesterday.
(subject) (verb) (object)   (adverb)   (adverb)

2) Changing the word order does not significantly change the meaning of the sentence.

나는 어제 공원에서 그를 보았다. / 어제 공원에서 나는 그를 보았다.

na-neun eo-je gong-won-e-seo geu-reul bo-ass-da

나는 그를 보았다 어제 공원에서. / 공원에서 나는 보았다 그를 어제.

3) In most cases, modifiers come in front of the modificand.

마음에 행복한 천사를 가진 아이 ma-eum-e haeng-bok-han cheon-sa-reul ga-jin a-i
                      modificand

a child with a happy angel in his heart
modificand

2. Korean has no fricative that can indicate [f], [v], [θ], [ʒ].

3. It is natural to ask the age of the person you meet for the first time.

- Usually, it's to choose honorific and plain language.
- Knowing each other's ages, older person is called "형", "누나", "오빠", "언니" and younger person is called "너". neo   hyeong nu-na   o-ppa   eon-ni

4. The address and reference forms are delicately developed.

English	Korean
aunt	이모 (mother's sister) i-mo, 숙모 (wife of father's brother) suk-mo, 외숙모 (wife of mother's brother) oe-suk-mo, 고모 (father's sister) go-mo, 큰어머니 (elder brother 's wife of father) keun-eo-meo-ni, 작은어머니 (younger brother 's wife of father) jak-eun-eo-meo-ni
uncle	삼촌 (father's brother) sam-chon, 숙부 (younger brother of father) suk-bu, 외숙부 (brother of mother) oe-suk-bu, 큰아버지 (elder brother of father) keun-a-beo-ji, 작은아버지 (younger brother of father) jak-eun-a-beo-ji.
brother	형 (older brother of man) hyeong, 오빠 (older brother of woman) o-ppa, 작은형 (a man's second older brother) jak-eun-hyeong, 큰형 (a man's eldest brother) keun-hyeong
sister	누나 (older sister of man) nu-na, 언니 (older sister of woman) eon-ni, 작은누나 (a man's second older sister) jak-eun-nu-na, 큰누나 (a man's eldest sister) keun-nu-na

5. Koreans don't use the word "당신" except for very close relationships.
dang-sin

- They use "선생님", "사모님", "여사님", "사장님", "이모님", "저기요", "여기요".
  "seon-saeng-nim", "sa-mo-nim", "yeo-sa-nim", "sa-jang-nim", "i-mo-nim", "jeo-gi-yo", "yeo-gi-yo"

6. They don't just call people in higher positions by their names.

– They only call a relationship or position or add a last name in front of the position:
"삼촌", "할아버지", "사장님", "김 사장님", "박 부장님", "길동 오빠".....
"sam-chon", "hal-a-beo-ji", "sa-jang-nim", "Kim sa-jang-nim", "Bak bu-jang-nim", "gil-dong o-ppa"

7. Koreans use plain and honorific language depending on the upper and lower relationships of age or class and whether they are close or not.

		plain	honorific
formal	declarative	산다 san-da	삽니다 sab-ni-da
	interrogative	사니? sa-ni?	삽니까? sab-ni-kka?
	imperative	사라 sa-ra	사십시오 sa-sib-si-yo
	propositive	사자 sa-ja	삽시다 sab-si-da
informal	declarative	사 sa	사요 sa-yo
	interrogative	사? sa?	사요? sa-yo?
	imperative	사 sa	사세요 sa-se-yo
	propositive	사 sa	사요 sa-yo

＊You should be careful because plain language can cause discomfort.

8. The actual form of use is divided into four categories: plain, one-sided talk-down, polite, and one-sided honorific, depending on whether they are close or not.

close (plain)	plain	해라체, 해체 hae-ra-che, hae-che
	one-sided talk down	하게체, 해라체, 해체 ha-ge-che, hae-ra-che, hae-che
not close (honorific)	polite	해요체, 하오체 hae-yo-che, ha-o-che
	one-sided honorific	하십시오체 ha-sib-si-o-che

9. The basic form of Korean consists of two types: honorific and plain, but practically there are four formal types(하십시오체, 하오체, 하게체, 해라체) and two informal ones(해요체, 해체).

ha-sib-si-o-che ha-o-che ha-ge-che hae-ra-che

hae-yo-che hae-che

	type final ending	declarative	interrogative	imperative	propositive	exclamatory
formal	하십시오체 ha-sib-si-o-che (very honorific) -ㅂ니다, -ㅂ니까, -십시오, -ㅂ시오, -십시다, -시지요, -소서	물이 mul-i 보입니다. bo-ib-ni-da	언제 eon-je 식사 sik-sa- 하셨습니까? ha-syeoss- seub-ni-kka	앉으 anj-eu 십시오. -sib-si-o	책을 chaek-eul 읽으십시오. ilk-eu-sib-si-o	정말 jeong-mal 반갑습니다. ban-gab-seub-ni-da.
	하오체 ha-o-che (honorific) -오, -소, -구려	물이 mul-i 보이오. bo-i-o	언제 eon-je 식사했소? sik-sa-haess-so	앉으 오. anj-eu-o	책을 읽읍시다. chaek-eul ilk-eub-si-da	정말 jeong-mal 반갑구려. ban-gab-gu-ryeo
	하게체 ha-ge-che (talk-down) -게, -네, -일세, -나, -세, -는가	물이 mul-i 보이네. bo-i-ne	언제 eon-je 식사했는가? sik-sa-hass-neun-ga	앉 anj- 게. ge	책을 chaek-eul 읽게. ilk-ge	정말 jeong-mal 반갑구만. ban-gab-gu-man
	해라체 hae-ra-che (very talk-down) -어, -아라, -ㄴ다, -느냐, -니, -자, -해라	물이 mul-i 보인다. bo-in-da	언제 eon-je 식사했니? sik-sa-hass-ni	앉 아라. anj-a-ra	책을 chaek-eul 읽자. ilk-ja	정말 jeong-mal 반갑구나. ban-gab-gu-na
informal	해요체 hae-yo-che (honorific) -어요, -지요, -네요, -시죠, -여요, -해요	물이 mul-i 보여요. bo-yeo-yo	언제 eon-je 식사했어요? sik-sa-haess-eo-yo	앉 아요. anj-a-yo	책을 chaek-eul 읽어요. ilk-eo-yo	정말 jeong-mal 반가워요. ban-ga-wo-yo
	해체 hae-che (talk-down) -아, -어, -지, -군, -해	물이 mul-i 보여. bo-yeo	언제 eon-je 식사했어? sik-sa-haess-eo	앉 아. anj-a	책을 chaek-eul 읽어. ilk-eo	정말 jeong-mal 반가워. ban-ga-wo
English		Water is seen.	When did you have your meal?	Sit down.	Read books.	How nice to meet you.

10. Choosing the types of Korean according to the relationships

	relationship	type	relationship
polite	stranger ↔ stranger	해요체 hae-yo-che	not close
	older but lower status → younger but higher status	하십시오체, ha-sib-si-o-che 해요체 hae-yo-che	close or not
	younger but higher status → older but lower status	하십시오체 ha-sib-si-o-che	close or not
	• Talking on the broadcast • Talking in public • Giving a speech in front of the audience • Writing a polite sentence in a book or document		
plain	same age ↔ same age	해라체, hae-ra-che 해체| hae-che	close
	senior → junior	해라체, hae-ra-che 해체| hae-che	close
	junior → senior	형/오빠/엄마/아빠 + 해라체, 해체 hyeong/o-ppa/eom-ma/a-ppa + hae-ra-che, hae-che	close
	• Close ↔ Close • Parent-child relationship　＊not used in conservative families • In most books and documents.		
one-sided talk down	higher status → lower status	해라체, 해체 hae-ra-che, hae-che	close
	older person → younger person	해라체, 해체 hae-ra-che, hae-che	close
	younger but higher status → older but lower status	해라체, 해체 hae-ra-che, hae-che	In places that value class or status, such as the military
one sided honorific	lower status → higher status	하십시오체 ha-sib-si-o-che	close or not
	younger person → older person	하십시오체 ha-sib-si-o-che	not close
	older but lower status → younger but higher status	하십시오체 ha-sib-si-o-che	In places that value class or status, such as the military

11. Honorific Words

plain	honorific	plain	honorific	English
-은/는 eun/neun	-께서는 kke-seo-neun	삼촌은 sam-chon-eun 갔다. gass-da	삼촌께서는 sam-chon-kke-seo-neun 가셨습니다. ga-syeoss-seub-ni-da.	Uncle went.
-다 da	-습니다 seub-ni-da	삼촌은 sam-chon-eun 갔다. gass-da	삼촌께서는 sam-chon-kke-seo-neun 가셨습니다. ga-syeoss-seub-ni-da.	Uncle went.
-이냐? i-nya	-입니까? ib-ni-kka	이거 i-geo 인형이냐? in-hyeong-i-nya	이거 i-geo 인형 입니까? in-hyeong ib-ni-kka	Is this a doll?
-에게 e-ge	-께 kke	삼촌에게 sam-chon-e-ge	삼촌께 sam-chon-kke	to uncle
-이/가 i/ga	-께서 kke-seo	삼촌이 sam-chon-i 온다. on-da.	삼촌께서 sam-chon-kke-seo 오신다. o-sin-da.	Uncle comes.
-이/그/저 사람 i/geu/jeo sa-ram	-이/그/저 분 i/geu/jeo bun	이 사람 i sa-ram	이 분 i bun	this man
-이다 i-da	-입니다 ib-ni-da	그는 geu-neun 시장이다. si-jang-i-da	그는 geu-neun 시장입니다. si-jang-ib-ni-da	He is a mayor.
-어 eo	-어요 eo-yo	이것을 받어. i-geos-eul bad-eo.	이것을 받어요. i-geos-eul bad-eo-yo.	Take this.

* Tips for Korean

Korean-related contents will be uploaded

English	plain	honorific	English	plain	honorific
meal	밥 bab	진지 jin-ji	be	있다 iss-da	계신다 gye-sin-da
name	이름 i-reum	성함 seong-ham		이다 i-da	이시다 i-si-da
		존함 jon-ham	drink	마신다 ma-sin-da	드신다 deu-sin-da
age	나이 na-i	연세 yeon-se	sleep	잔다 jan-da	주무신다 ju-mu-sin-da
		춘추 chun-chu	listen	듣는다 deud-neun-da	들으신다 deul-eu-sin-da
house	집 jib	댁 daek	talk	말한다 mal-han-da	말씀하신다 mal-sseum-ha-sin-da
wife	아내 a-nae	부인 bu-in	bring	데려온다 de-ryeo-on-da	모셔온다 mo-syeo-on-da
birthday	생일 saeng-il	생신 saeng-sin	eat	먹는다 meog-neun-da	잡수신다 jab-su-sin-da
daughter	딸 ttal	따님 tta-nim			드신다 deu-sin-da
word	말 mal	말씀 mal-sseum	ill	아프다 a-peu-da	편찮으시다 pyeon-chanh-eu-si-da
you	너 neo	자네 ja--ne	dead	죽었다 juk-eoss-da	돌아가셨다 dol-a-ga-syeoss-da
older sister	누나 nu-na	누님 nu-nim	give	준다 jun-da	드린다 deu-rin-da
older brother of woman	오빠 o-ppa	오라버니 o-ra-beo-ni			바친다 ba-chin-da
		오라버님 o-ra-beo-nim	ask	묻는다 mud-neun-da	여쭙는다 yeo-jjub-neun-da
older brother of man	형 hyeong	형님 hyeong-nim			여쭌다 yeo-jjun-da
son	아들 a-deul	아드님 a-deu-nim	meet	만난다 man-nan-da	뵌다 boen-da
father	아버지 a-beo-ji	아버님 a-beo-nim			뵙는다 boeb-neun-da
mother	어머니 eo-meo-ni	어머님 eo-meo-nim	see	본다 bon-da	보신다 bo-sin-da
instruction	지시 ji-si	분부 bun-bu	call	부른다 bu-reun-da	부르신다 bu-reu-sin-da
in person	직접 jik-jeob	손수 son-su	write	쓴다 sseun-da	쓰신다 sseu-sin-da
		친히 chin-hi	come	온다 on-da	오신다 o-sin-da
		몸소 mom-so	make	만든다 man-deun-da	만드신다 man-deu-sin-da
read	읽는다 ilk-neun-da	읽으신다 ilk-eu-sin-da	go	간다 gan-da	가신다 ga-sin-da

ㄱ			가볍다	ga-byeob-da	light
가게	ga-ge	shop	가사	ga-sa	lyrics
가구	ga-gu	furniture	가상	ga-sang	imagination
가까워진다	ga-kka-wo-jin-da	closer	가수	ga-su	singer
가까이	ga-kka-i	closely	가스	ga-seu	gas
가꾼다	ga-kkun-da	take care of	가슴속	ga-seum-sog	heart
가난	ga-nan	poverty	가요	ga-yo	song
가난하다	ga-nan-ha-da	poor	가위	ga-wi	scissors
가늘다	ga-neul-da	thin	가이드	ga-i-deu	guide
가능	ga-neung	possibility	가입	ga-ib	join
가능해진다	ga-neung-hae-jin-da	become possible	가입자	ga-ib-ja	subscriber
가득	ga-deug	full	가입한다	ga-ib-han-da	join
가득하다	ga-deug-ha-da	full	가장	ga-jang	most
가득히	ga-deug-hi	chock-full	가정	ga-jeong	home
가라앉는다	ga-ra-anj-neun--da	sink	가정교사	ga-jeong-gyo-sa	tutor
가려진다	ga-ryeo-jin-da	obscured	가져간다	ga-jyeo-gan-da	take away
가령	ga-ryeong	supposing	가져다준다	ga-jyeo-da-jun-da	bring
가로	ga-ro	width	가져온다	ga-jyeo-on-da	bring
가로등	ga-ro-deung	street lamp	가죽	ga-jug	leather
가로막는다	ga-ro-mag-neun-da	obstruct	가짜	ga-jja	false
가로수	ga-ro-su	street trees	가치관	ga-chi-gwan	values
가루	ga-ru	powder	가톨릭	ga-tol-lig	catholic
가른다	ga-reun-da	divide	가하다	ga-ha-da	inflict
가르침	ga-reu-chim	teaching	각각	gag-gag	each
가린다	ga-rin-da	blind	각국	gag-gug	each country
가리킨다	ga-ri-kin-da	point out	각기	gag-gi	each
가만	ga-man	wait	각오	gag-o	resolution
가만히 있다	ga-man-hi iss-da	stand still	각자	gag-ja	each
가만히	ga-man-hi	still	간격	gan-gyeog	interval
가뭄	ga-mum	drought	간단하다	gan-dan-ha-da	simple
가방	ga-bang	bag			

간단히	gan-dan-hi	simply	감소된다	gam-so-doen-da	reduced
간부	gan-bu	cadre	감소한다	gam-so-han-da	diminish
간섭	gan-seob	interference	감수성	gam-su-seong	sensibility
간식	gan-sig	snack	감싼다	gam-ssan-da	cover
간신히	gan-sin-hi	barely	감옥	gam-og	prison
간장	gan-jang	soy sauce	감자	gam-ja	potato
간접	gan-jeob	indirect	감정적	gam-jeong-jeog	emotional
간접적	gan-jeob-jeog	indirect	감춘다	gam-chun-da	hide
간판	gan-pan	sign	감히	gam-hi	dare
간편하다	gan-pyeon-ha-da	easy	갑	gab	the former
간호	gan-ho	nurse	갑작스럽다	gab-jag-seu-reob-da	sudden
간호사	gan-ho-sa	nurse	값	gabs	value
간혹	gan-hog	sometimes	값싸다	gabs-ssa-da	cheap
갇히다	gad-hi-da	confined	강	gang	river
갈다	gal-da	sharpen	강남	gang-nam	Gangnam
갈비	gal-bi	rib	강당	gang-dang	auditorium
갈비탕	gal-bi-tang	galbitang	강도	gang-do	burglar
갈수록	gal-su-rog	increasingly	강력하다	gang-lyeog-ha-da	powerful
갈아입는다	gal-a-ib-neun-da	change	강력히	gang-lyeog-hi	strongly
갈아탄다	gal-a-tan-da	transfer	강렬하다	gang-ryeol-ha-da	intense
갈증	gal-jeung	thirst	강물	gang-mul	river water
감각	gam-gag	sense	강변	gang-byeon	riverside
감기	gam-gi	cold	강북	gang-bug	Gangbuk
감는다	gam-neun-da	reel in	강사	gang-sa	lecturer
감동	gam-dong	impression	강수량	gang-su-ryang	precipitation
감동적	gam-dong-jeog	touching	강아지	gang-a-ji	puppy
감사	gam-sa	thanks	강요한다	gang-yo-han-da	compel
감상	gam-sang	enjoy	강의	gang-ui	lecture
감상한다	gam-sang-han-da	appreciate	강의한다	gang-ui-han-da	lecture
감소	gam-so	decrease	강제	gang-je	compulsion

강조	gang-jo	emphasis		거울	geo-ul	mirror
강화한다	gang-hwa-han-da	reinforce		거절한다	geo-jeol-han-da	refuse
갖가지	gaj-ga-ji	various		거짓	geo-jis	lie
갖는다	gaj-neun-da	have		거짓말	geo-jis-mal	lie
같이한다	gat-i-han-da	together		거칠다	geo-chil-da	wild
갚는다	gap-neun-da	pay back		거품	geo-pum	bubble
개개인	gae-gae-in	individual		걱정	geog-jeong	worry
개국	gae-gug	country		걱정된다	geog-jeong-doen-da	worried about
갠다	gaen-da	fold		걱정스럽다	geog-jeong-seu-reob-da	worried
개발된다	gae-bal-doen-da	developed		걱정한다	geog-jeong-han-da	worry
개발한다	gae-bal-han-da	develop		건	geon	case
개방	gae-bang	opening		건강하다	geon-gang-ha-da	healthy
개방된다	gae-bang-doen-da	open up		건너	geon-neo	across
개방한다	gae-bang-han-da	open		건너간다	geon-neo-gan-da	cross over
개별	gae-byeol	individual		건넌다	geon-neon-da	cross
개선	gae-seon	improvement		건너온다	geon-neo-on-da	cross over
개선된다	gae-seon-doen-da	improved		건너편	geon-neo-pyeon	other side
개선한다	gae-seon-han-da	improve		건넌방	geon-neon-bang	opposite room
개성	gae-seong	individuality		건넨다	geon-nen-da	pass
개인적	gae-in-jeog	personal		건네준다	geon-ne-jun-da	hand over
객관적	gaeg-gwan-jeog	objective		건드린다	geon-deu-rin-da	touch
거꾸로	geo-kku-ro	backwards		건설된다	geon-seol-doen-da	built
거대하다	geo-dae-ha-da	huge		건설한다	geon-seol-han-da	build
거둔다	geo-dun-da	reap		건전하다	geon-jeon-ha-da	sound
거든다	geo-deun-da	assist		건조	geon-jo	dry
거듭	geo-deub	repeatedly		건조한다	geon-jo-han-da	dry
거리	geo-ri	distance		건진다	geon-jin-da	get back
거부한다	geo-bu-han-da	reject		건축	geon-chug	construction
거실	geo-sil	livingroom		걷기	geod-gi	walking
거액	geo-aeg	fortune		걷는다	geod-neun-da	walk

걸어간다	geol-eo-gan-da	walk	경기	gyeong-gi	game
걸어온다	geol-eo-on-da	walk	경기장	gyeong-gi-jang	stadium
걸음	geol-eum	step	경력	gyeong-lyeog	career
검사	geom-sa	test	경비	gyeong-bi	security
검토	geom-to	examine	경영한다	gyeong-yeong-han-da	manage
겁	geob	cowardice	경쟁력	gyeong-jaeng-ryeog	competitiveness
겁난다	geob-nan-da	scared	경제력	gyeong-je-ryeog	economic power
겉	geot	outside	경제적	gyeong-je-jeog	economical
게다가	ge-da-ga	furthermore	경제학	gyeong-je-hag	economics
게시판	ge-si-pan	notice board	경찰서	gyeong-chal-seo	police office
게으르다	ge-eu-reu-da	lazy	경치	gyeong-chi	sight
게임	ge-im	game	경향	gyeong-hyang	tendency
겨우	gyeo-u	barely	경험한다	gyeong-heom-han-da	experience
겨울철	gyeo-ul-cheol	winter	곁	gyeot	beside
겨자	gyeo-ja	mustard	계곡	gye-gog	valley
견딘다	gyeon-din-da	endure	계단	gye-dan	stairs
견해	gyeon-hae	view	계란	gye-ran	egg
결과적	gyeol-gwa-jeog	consequential	계산	gye-san	calculation
결론	gyeol-lon	conclusion	계산기	gye-san-gi	calculator
결석	gyeol-seog	absence	계산한다	gye-san-han-da	calculate
결석한다	gyeol-seog-han-da	absent	계속된다	gye-sog-doen-da	continue
결승	gyeol-seung	finals	계속한다	gye-sog-han-da	continue
결심	gyeol-sim	determination	계신다	gye-sin-da	be there
결심한다	gyeol-sim-han-da	decide	계약	gye-yag	contract
결정	gyeol-jeong	decision	계절	gye-jeol	season
결정된다	gyeol-jeong-doen-da	decided	계좌	gye-jwa	account
결혼한다	gyeol-hon-han-da	marry	계층	gye-cheung	hierarchy
경계	gyeong-gye	boundary	계획한다	gye-hoeg-han-da	plan
경고	gyeong-go	warning	고개	go-gae	head
경고한다	gyeong-go-han-da	warn	고객	go-gaeg	customer

고교	go-gyo	high school		고통스럽다	go-tong-seu-reob-da	painful
고구마	go-gu-ma	sweet potato		고프다	go-peu-da	hungry
고궁	go-gung	ancient palace		고함	go-ham	shout
고급	go-geub	high class		곡	gog	song
고급스럽다	go-geub-seu-reob-da	luxurious		곡식	gog-sig	grain
고기	go-gi	meat		곤란하다	gon-ran-ha-da	difficult
고등학교	go-deung-hag-gyo	high school		곧다	god-da	straight
고등학생	go-deung-hag-saeng	high school student		곧바로	god-ba-ro	right away
고려한다	go-ryeo-han-da	consider		곧이어	god-i-eo	soon after
고른다	go-reun-da	choose		곧잘	god-jal	often
고무신	go-mu-sin	rubber shoes		곧장	god-jang	right away
고민	go-min	worry		골고루	gol-go-ru	evenly
고민한다	go-min-han-da	be in agony		골목	gol-mog	alley
고생	go-saeng	hardship		골목길	gol-mog-gil	alley
고생한다	go-saeng-han-da	suffer		골짜기	gol-jja-gi	valley
고소한다	go-so-han-da	sue		골치	gol-chi	trouble
고속	go-sog	high speed		골프장	gol-peu-jang	golf course
고속도로	go-sog-do-ro	highway		곱다	gob-da	pretty
고속버스	go-sog-beo-seu	express bus		곳곳	gos-gos	everywhere
고양이	go-yang-i	cat		공개	gong-gae	open
고요하다	go-yo-ha-da	quiet		공개한다	gong-gae-han-da	open to the public
고작	go-jag	only		공격	gong-gyeog	attack
고장	go-jang	breakdown		공격한다	gong-gyeog-han-da	attack
고전	go-jeon	classic		공공	gong-gong	public
고집	go-jib	stubbornness		공군	gong-gun	air force
고집한다	go-jib-han-da	insist on		공급	gong-geub	supply
고추	go-chu	pepper		공기	gong-gi	air
고추장	go-chu-jang	chili pepper paste		공무원	gong-mu-won	official
고춧가루	go-chus-ga-ru	chili powder		공사	gong-sa	construction
고친다	go-chin-da	fix		공식	gong-sig	formula

공식적으로	gong-sig-jeog-eu-ro	officially		과학자	gwa-hag-ja	scientist
공업	gong-eob	industry		과학적	gwa-hag-jeog	scientific
공연	gong-yeon	show		관객	gwan-gaeg	audience
공연된다	gong-yeon-doen-da	performed		관계된다	gwan-gye-doen-da	concerned
공연장	gong-yeon-jang	concert hall		관계없이	gwan-gye-eobs-i	regardless
공연한다	gong-yeon-han-da	perform		관계자	gwan-gye-ja	officials
공연히	gong-yeon-hi	vainly		관광	gwan-gwang	tourism
공원	gong-won	park		관광객	gwan-gwang-gaeg	tourist
공주	gong-ju	princess		관광버스	gwan-gwang-beo-seu	tour bus
공중전화	gong-jung-jeon-hwa	payphone		관광지	gwan-gwang-ji	tourist destination
공짜	gong-jja	free		관념	gwan-nyeom	notion
공책	gong-chaeg	notebook		관람	gwan-lam	viewing
공통	gong-tong	common		관람객	gwan-lam-gaeg	audience
공통된다	gong-tong-doen-da	common		관련된다	gwan-lyeon-doen-da	related
공통적	gong-tong-jeog	common		관련있다	gwan-lyeon-iss-da	relate
공통점	gong-tong-jeom	commonality		관리	gwan-li	management
공포	gong-po	fear		관리한다	gwan-li-han-da	manage
공항	gong-hang	airport		관습	gwan-seub	custom
공항버스	gong-hang-beo-seu	airport bus		관심사	gwan-sim-sa	interest
공해	gong-hae	pollution		관찰	gwan-chal	observation
공휴일	gong-hyu-il	holiday		관찰한다	gwan-chal-han-da	observe
과	gwa	class		광경	gwang-gyeong	scene
과거	gwa-geo	past		광장	gwang-jang	plaza
과목	gwa-mog	subject		괜히	gwaen-hi	in vain
과외	gwa-oe	tutoring		괴로움	goe-ro-um	suffering
과일	gwa-il	fruit		괴로워한다	goe-ro-wo-han-da	suffer
과자	gwa-ja	snack		괴롭다	goe-rob-da	painful
과장	gwa-jang	exaggeration		괴롭힌다	goe-rob-hin-da	bother
과정	gwa-jeong	process		굉장하다	goeng-jang-ha-da	amazing
과제	gwa-je	assignment		굉장히	goeng-jang-hi	greatly

교과서	gyo-gwa-seo	textbook		구별된다	gu-byeol-doen-da	set apart
교내	gyo-nae	on campus		구별한다	gu-byeol-han-da	distinguish
교대	gyo-dae	rotation		구분	gu-bun	division
교류	gyo-ryu	interchange		구분된다	gu-bun-doen-da	separate
교문	gyo-mun	school gate		구분한다	gu-bun-han-da	divide
교복	gyo-bog	uniform		구석	gu-seog	corner
교시	gyo-si	period		구석구석	gu-seog-gu-seog	every nook and cranny
교실	gyo-sil	classroom		구성된다	gu-seong-doen-da	consist of
교양	gyo-yang	culture		구성한다	gu-seong-han-da	make up
교외	gyo-oe	suburbs		구속	gu-sog	restriction
교육비	gyo-yug-bi	education expenses		구속된다	gu-sog-doen-da	restricted
교육자	gyo-yug-ja	educator		구속한다	gu-sog-han-da	bind
교장	gyo-jang	principal		구역	gu-yeog	area
교재	gyo-jae	textbook		구입	gu-ib	purchase
교직	gyo-jig	teaching profession		구입한다	gu-ib-han-da	buy
교체	gyo-che	substitution		구청	gu-cheong	ward office
교통	gyo-tong	traffic		구한다	gu-han-da	save
교통사고	gyo-tong-sa-go	traffic accident		국	gug	soup
교포	gyo-po	overseas Korean		국가적	gug-ga-jeog	national
교환	gyo-hwan	exchange		국기	gug-gi	flag
교환한다	gyo-hwan-han-da	exchange		국내선	gug-nae-seon	domestic flight
교회	gyo-hoe	church		국내외	gug-nae-oe	domestic and foreign
교훈	gyo-hun	lesson		국립	gug-lib	national
구경	gu-gyeong	sightseeing		국물	gug-mul	soup
구경한다	gu-gyeong-han-da	take a look		국민적	gug-min-jeog	national
구두	gu-du	shoes		국사	gug-sa	national history
구른다	gu-reun-da	roll		국산	gug-san	domestic
구름	gu-reum	cloud		국수	gug-su	noodle
구멍	gu-meong	hole		국어	gug-eo	Korean
구별	gu-byeol	distinction		국왕	gug-wang	king

국적	gug-jeog	nationality	귀엽다	gwi-yeob-da	cute
국제선	gug-je-seon	international	귀중하다	gwi-jung-ha-da	precious
국제적	gug-je-jeog	international	귀찮다	gwi-chanh-da	annoying
국제화	gug-je-hwa	internationalization	귀하다	gwi-ha-da	precious
국회	gug-hoe	congress	귓속	gwis-sog	in the ear
국회의원	gug-hoe-ui-won	member of congress	규정	gyu-jeong	rule
군	gun	army	규칙	gyu-chig	rule
군대	gun-dae	military	규칙적	gyu-chig-jeog	regular
군데	gun-de	place	균형	gyun-hyeong	balance
군사	gun-sa	military	그	geu	that
군인	gun-in	soldier	그간	geu-gan	so far
굳다	gud-da	harden	그나마	geu-na-ma	by the way
굳어진다	gud-eo-jin-da	harden	그놈	geu-nom	that guy
굳이	gud-i	dare	그늘	geu-neul	shade
굳힌다	gud-hin-da	harden	그다음	geu-da-eum	next
굵다	gulg-da	thick	그다지	geu-da-ji	not very
굶는다	gulm-neun-da	starve	그대	geu-dae	you
굽는다	gub-neun-da	bake	그때그때	geu-ttae-geu-ttae	from time to time
굽힌다	gub-hin-da	bend	그래	geu-rae	yes
궁극적	gung-geug-jeog	ultimate	그래서	geu-rae-seo	therefore
궁금하다	gung-geum-ha-da	curious	그래야	geu-rae-ya	so that
권	gwon	volume	그래픽	geu-rae-pig	graphic
권리	gwon-li	right	그램	geu-raem	gram
권위	gwon-wi	authority	그러므로	geu-reo-meu-ro	therefore
권한다	gwon-han-da	recommend	그런대로	geu-reon-dae-ro	enough
귀가	gwi-ga	homecoming	그럴듯하다	geu-reol-deus-ha-da	plausible
귀가한다	gwi-ga-han-da	go home	그럼	geu-reom	then
귀국	gwi-gug	return	그렇지	geu-reoh-ji	yes
귀국한다	gwi-gug-han-da	return home	그렇지만	geu-reoh-ji-man	but
귀신	gwi-sin	ghost	그려진다	geu-ryeo-jin-da	painted

그루	geu-ru	tree		극장	geug-jang	theater
그릇	geu-reus	bowl		극히	geug-hi	like mad
그리	geu-ri	so		근거	geun-geo	evidence
그리로	geu-ri-ro	there		근거한다	geun-geo-han-da	based
그리움	geu-ri-um	longing		근교	geun-gyo	suburb
그리워한다	geu-ri-wo-han-da	miss		근래	geun-lae	lately
그리하여	geu-ri-ha-yeo	therefore		근로	geun-lo	work
그림자	geu-rim-ja	shadow		근로자	geun-lo-ja	employee
그립다	geu-rib-da	miss		근무	geun-mu	work
그만둔다	geu-man-dun-da	quit		근무한다	geun-mu-han-da	work
그만큼	geu-man-keum	that much		근본	geun-bon	fundamental
그만한다	geu-man-han-da	stop		근본적	geun-bon-jeog	fundamental
그분	geu-bun	him		근원	geun-won	source
그사이	geu-sa-i	in between		근육	geun-yug	muscle
그야말로	geu-ya-mal-lo	truly		근처	geun-cheo	around
그이	geu-i	him		글쎄	geul-sse	well
그저	geu-jeo	just		글쎄요	geul-sse-yo	I don't know.
그저께	geu-jeo-kke	day before yesterday		글쓰기	geul-sseu-gi	writing
그전	geu-jeon	before that		글씨	geul-ssi	writing
그제서야	geu-je-seo-ya	only then		글자	geul-ja	letter
그제야	geu-je-ya	just then		긁다	geulg-da	scratch
그중	geu-jung	among them		금	geum	gold
그쪽	geu-jjog	that		금고	geum-go	safe
그친다	geu-chin-da	stop		금년	geum-nyeon	this year
그토록	geu-to-rog	so		금메달	geum-me-dal	gold medal
그해	geu-hae	that year		금방	geum-bang	soon
극	geug	pole		금세	geum-se	soon
극복	geug-bog	conquest		금액	geum-aeg	amount
극복한다	geug-bog-han-da	overcome		금연	geum-yeon	no smoking
극작가	geug-jag-ga	playwright		금지	geum-ji	prohibition

금지된다	geum-ji-doen-da	forbidden	기록한다	gi-rog-han-da	record
금지한다	geum-ji-han-da	prohibit	기름	gi-reum	oil
금한다	geum-han-da	forbid	기막히다	gi-mag-hi-da	amazing
급	geub	grade	기법	gi-beob	technique
급격히	geub-gyeog-hi	rapidly	기본적	gi-bon-jeog	basic
급속히	geub-sog-hi	rapidly	기뻐한다	gi-bbeo-han-da	happy
급증한다	geub-jeung-han-da	soar	기쁘다	gi-bbeu-da	pleased
급하다	geub-ha-da	in a hurry	기쁨	gi-bbeum	pleasure
급히	geub-hi	in haste	기사	gi-sa	article
긋다	geus-da	draw	기성	gi-seong	ready-made
긍정적	geung-jeong-jeog	positive	기성세대	gi-seong-se-dae	older generation
기	gi	energy	기숙사	gi-sug-sa	dormitory
기구	gi-gu	instrument	기술자	gi-sul-ja	technician
기기	gi-gi	device	기술한다	gi-sul-han-da	describe
기념	gi-nyeom	commemoration	기억난다	gi-eog-nan-da	remember
기념일	gi-nyeom-il	anniversary	기억된다	gi-eog-doen-da	remembered
기념품	gi-nyeom-pum	souvenir	기억한다	gi-eog-han-da	remember
기념한다	gi-nyeom-han-da	celebrate	기업인	gi-eob-in	businessmen
기능	gi-neung	function	기여	gi-yeo	contribution
긴다	gin-da	crawl	기여한다	gi-yeo-han-da	contribute
기대	gi-dae	expectation	기온	gi-on	temperatures
기댄다	gi-daen-da	lean	기운	gi-un	strength
기대된다	gi-dae-doen-da	look forward to	기운다	gi-un-da	slant
기대한다	gi-dae-han-da	expect	기울인다	gi-ul-in-da	incline
기도	gi-do	prayer	기원	gi-won	origin
기도한다	gi-do-han-da	pray	기원전	gi-won-jeon	B.C.
기독교	gi-dog-gyo	Christian	기적	gi-jeog	miracle
기둥	gi-dung	pillar	기차	gi-cha	train
기록	gi-rog	record	기초	gi-cho	foundation
기록된다	gi-rog-doen-da	recorded	기초적	gi-cho-jeog	basic

기초한다	gi-cho-han-da	base	깜짝	kkam-jjag	surprise
기침	gi-chim	cough	깡패	kkang-pae	bully
기타	gi-ta	other	깨끗이	kkae-kkeus-i	clean
기호	gi-ho	sign	깨끗하다	kkae-kkeus-ha-da	clean
기혼	gi-hon	married	깨끗해진다	kkae-kkeus-hae-jin-da	become clean
기획	gi-hoeg	plan	깬다	kkaen-da	wake up
기후	gi-hu	climate	깨닫는다	kkae-dad-neun-da	realize
긴급	gin-geub	emergency	깨달음	kkae-dal-eum	enlightenment
긴장	gin-jang	tension	깨뜨린다	kkae-tteu-rin-da	break
긴장감	gin-jang-gam	tension	깨소금	kkae-so-geum	sesame salt
긴장된다	gin-jang-doen-da	nervous	깨어난다	kkae-eo-nan-da	wake up
긴장한다	gin-jang-han-da	nervous	깨어진다	kkae-eo-jin-da	break up
길가	gil-ga	roadside	깨운다	kkae-un-da	wake up
길거리	gil-geo-ri	street	깨진다	kkae-jin-da	be broken
길어진다	gil-eo-jin-da	lengthen	꺼진다	kkeo-jin-da	go out
길이	gil-i	length	꺾는다	kkeokk-neun-da	break
김	gim	seaweed	껍질	kkeob-jil	skin
김밥	gim-bab	gimbab	꼬리	kko-ri	tail
김치	gim-chi	kimchi	꼬마	kko-ma	little
김치찌개	gim-chi-jji-gae	kimchi soup	꼭	kkog	please
깊숙이	gip-sug-i	deeply	꼭대기	kkog-dae-gi	top
깊이	gip-i	depth	꼴	kkol	form
깐다	kkan-da	peel	꼼꼼하다	kkom-kkom-ha-da	meticulous
까맣다	kka-mah-da	black	꼼짝	kkom-jjag	freeze
까먹는다	kka-meog-neun-da	forget	꼽힌다	kkob-hin-da	be counted
깎는다	kkakk-neun-da	cut	꽂는다	kkoj-neun-da	stick
깔끔하다	kkal-kkeum-ha-da	clean	꽃씨	kkocc-ssi	flower seed
깔다	kkal-da	lay	꽃잎	kkocc-ip	petal
깔린다	kkal-lin-da	lay down	꽉	kkwag	closely
깜빡	kkam-ppag	flash	꽤	kkwae	fairly

꾸린다	kku-rin-da	manage	나누어진다	na-nu-eo-jin-da	divided
꾸민다	kku-min-da	decorate	나뉜다	na-nwin-da	split
꾸준하다	kku-jun-ha-da	steady	나들이	na-deul-i	picnic
꾸준히	kku-jun-hi	steadily	나란히	na-ran-hi	side by side
꾸중	kku-jung	rebuke	나른다	na-reun-da	tote
꾼다	kkun-da	borrow	나름	na-reum	depending on
꿀	kkul	honey	나머지	na-meo-ji	remaining
꿈꾼다	kkum-kkun-da	dream	나물	na-mul	herbs
꿈속	kkum-sog	in a dream	나뭇가지	na-mus-ga-ji	branch
끈다	kkeun-da	turn off	나뭇잎	na-mus-ip	leaf
끄덕인다	kkeu-deog-in-da	nod	나빠진다	na-ppa-jin-da	get worse
끈	kkeun	string	나아진다	na-a-jin-da	get better
끊긴다	kkeunh-gin-da	cut off	나침반	na-chim-ban	compass
끊는다	kkeunh-neun-da	quit	나흘	na-heul	four days
끊어진다	kkeunh-eo-jin-da	cut off	낚시	nakk-si	fishing
끊임없다	kkeunh-im-eobs-da	incessant	낚시꾼	nakk-si-kkun	angler
끊임없이	kkeunh-im-eobs-i	endlessly	낚싯대	nakk-sis-dae	fishing rod
끌린다	kkeul-lin-da	be drawn	난리	nan-li	riot
끌어당긴다	kkeul-eo-dang-gin-da	pull	난방	nan-bang	heating
끓는다	kkeulh-neun-da	boil	날개	nal-gae	wing
끓인다	kkeulh-in-da	boil	난다	nan-da	fly
끝내	kkeut-nae	finally	날린다	nal-lin-da	fly
끝낸다	kkeut-naen-da	finish	날씨	nal-ssi	weather
끝없다	kkeut-eobs-da	endless	날아간다	nal-a-gan-da	fly away
끝없이	kkeut-eobs-i	eternally	날아다닌다	nal-a-da-nin-da	fly
끼	kki	talent	날아온다	nal-a-on-da	fly
끼어든다	kki-eo-deun-da	interrupt	날짜	nal-jja	date
끼운다	kki-un-da	insert	날카롭다	nal-ka-rob-da	sharp
낀다	kkin-da	put on	낡았다	nalg-ass-da	old
			남	nam	other
ㄴ			남긴다	nam-gin-da	leave

남녀	nam-nyeo	male and female		내적	nae-jeog	inner
남동생	nam-dong-saeng	brother		내준다	nae-jun-da	let
남매	nam-mae	siblings		내지	nae-ji	or
남부	nam-bu	southern		내후년	nae-hu-nyeon	three years from now
남학생	nam-hag-saeng	boy		냄비	naem-bi	pot
납득한다	nab-deug-han-da	convinced		냄새	naem-sae	smell
낫다	nas-da	better		냇물	naes-mul	stream
낭비	nang-bi	waste		냉동	naeng-dong	frozen
낮	naj	afternoon		냉면	naeng-myeon	cold noodles
낮다	naj-da	low		냉방	naeng-bang	cooling
낮아진다	naj-a-jin-da	lower		냉장고	naeng-jang-go	refrigerator
낮춘다	naj-chun-da	lower		너머	neo-meo	beyond
낯설다	nach-seol-da	strange		너무나	neo-mu-na	too
낱말	nat-mal	word		너희	neo-hui	you guys
내과	nae-gwa	internal medicine		넉	neog	four
내내	nae-nae	all the time		넉넉하다	neog-neog-ha-da	plentiful
내년	nae-nyeon	next year		널리	neol-li	extensively
내놓는다	nae-noh-neun-da	put out		넓어진다	neolb-eo-jin-da	widen
내다본다	nae-da-bon-da	look out		넓힌다	neolb-hin-da	widen
내달	nae-dal	next month		넘겨준다	neom-gyeo-jun-da	hand over
내려놓는다	nae-ryeo-noh-neun-da	put down		넘긴다	neom-gin-da	pass over
내려다본다	nae-ryeo -da-bon-da	look down		넘어간다	neom-eo-gan-da	skip
내려진다	nae-ryeo-jin-da	be taken down		넘어뜨린다	neom-eo-tteu-rin-da	knock down
내민다	nae-min-da	hold out		넘어선다	neom-eo-seon-da	go beyond
내버린다	nae-beo-rin-da	throw away		넘어온다	neom-eo-on-da	come across
내보낸다	nae-bo-naen-da	send out		넘어진다	neom-eo-jin-da	fall down
내부	nae-bu	inside		넘친다	neom-chin-da	spill over
내쉰다	nae-swin-da	exhale		네	ne	yeah
내외	nae-oe	inside and outside		네거리	ne-geo-ri	crossroads
내용물	nae-yong-mul	contents		넥타이	neg-ta-i	necktie

넷째	nes-jjae	fourth	농사	nong-sa	farming
녀석	nyeo-seog	guy	농사일	nong-sa-il	farm work
년도	nyeon-do	year	농사짓는다	nong-sa-jis-neun-da	farm
년생	nyeon-saeng	born	농산물	nong-san-mul	agricultural products
노랗다	no-rah-da	yellow	농장	nong-jang	farm
노래방	no-rae-bang	karaoke	농촌	nong-chon	rural
노래한다	no-rae-han-da	sing	높아진다	nop-a-jin-da	rise
노랫소리	no-raes-so-ri	singing	높이	nop-i	height
노선	no-seon	route	높인다	nop-in-da	heighten
노인	no-in	old man	놓아둔다	noh-a-dun-da	let go
노트	no-teu	note	놓인다	noh-in-da	be put in
녹는다	nog-neun-da	melt	놓친다	noh-chin-da	let go
녹음	nog-eum	record	놔둔다	nwa-dun-da	let go
녹음한다	nog-eum-han-da	record	뇌	noe	brain
녹인다	nog-in-da	melt	누른다	nu-reun-da	press down
녹차	nog-cha	green tea	눈	nun	eye
녹화	nog-hwa	recording	눈가	nun-ga	eye area
논	non	rice paddy	눈감는다	nun-gam-neun-da	close eyes
논리	non-li	logic	눈길	nun-gil	line of vision
논리적	non-li-jeog	logical	눈동자	nun-dong-ja	pupil
논문	non-mun	thesis	눈뜬다	nun-tteun-da	wake up
논의한다	non-ui-han-da	discuss	눈병	nun-byeong	eye disease
논쟁	non-jaeng	argument	눈부시다	nun-bu-si-da	dazzle
논한다	non-han-da	reason	눈빛	nun-bicc	a look
놀랍다	nol-lab-da	surprising	눈앞	nun-ap	before one's eyes
놀린다	nol-lin-da	badinage	느리다	neu-ri-da	slow
놀이	nol-i	play	늘다	neul-da	gain
놀이터	nol-i-teo	playground	늘린다	neul-lin-da	increase
농담	nong-dam	joke	늘어놓는다	neul-eo-noh-neun-da	arrange
농부	nong-bu	farmer	늘어선다	neul-eo-seon-da	line up

늘어진다	neul-eo-jin-da	sag	다행히	da-haeng-hi	fortunately
늙었다	neulg-eoss-da	old	닥친다	dag-chin-da	befall
능동적	neung-dong-jeog	active	단	dan	only
늦가을	neuj-ga-eul	late autumn	단골	dan-gol	frequenter
늦는다	neuj-neun-da	late	단단하다	dan-dan-ha-da	hard
늦어진다	neuj-eo-jin-da	be late	단독	dan-dog	single

ㄷ			단맛	dan-mas	sweetness
다	da	all	단순	dan-sun	simple
다가간다	da-ga-gan-da	go closer	단순하다	dan-sun-ha-da	simple
다가선다	da-ga-seon-da	approach	단순히	dan-sun-hi	simply
다가온다	da-ga-on-da	come closer	단어	dan-eo	word
다녀간다	da-nyeo-gan-da	go to	단위	dan-wi	unit
다녀온다	da-nyeo-on-da	go to	단점	dan-jeom	disadvantages
다듬는다	da-deum-neun-da	trim	단추	dan-chu	button
다룬다	da-run-da	handle	단편	dan-pyeon	snippet
다름없다	da-reum-eobs-da	no different	닫는다	dad-neun-da	close
다리	da-ri	leg	닫힌다	dad-hin-da	shut
다방	da-bang	coffee house	달걀	dal-gyal	egg
다소	da-so	a little	달다	dal-da	sweet
다수	da-su	many	달랜다	dal-laen-da	lull
다양성	da-yang-seong	diversity	달러	dal-leo	dollar
다양해진다	da-yang-hae-jin-da	diversified	달려간다	dal-lyeo-gan-da	run
다이어트	da-i-eo-teu	diet	달려든다	dal-lyeo-deun-da	rush
다정하다	da-jeong-ha-da	considerate	달려온다	dal-lyeo-on-da	run
다진다	da-jin-da	mince	달력	dal-lyeog	calendar
다짐한다	da-jim-han-da	pledge	달리기	dal-li-gi	running
다친다	da-chin-da	get hurt	달린다	dal-lin-da	run
다툰다	da-tun-da	contend	달리한다	dal-li-han-da	change
다툼	da-tum	conflict	달빛	dal-bicc	moonlight
다한다	da-han-da	fulfill	달아난다	dal-a-nan-da	run away
다행	da-haeng	relief			

닭고기	dalg-go-gi	chicken	대기	dae-gi	atmosphere
닮았다	dalm-ass-da	resemble	대기업	dae-gi-eob	major company
담	dam	wall	대기한다	dae-gi-han-da	wait
담근다	dam-geun-da	dip	대낮	dae-naj	midday
담긴다	dam-gin-da	put in	대다수	dae-da-su	plurality
담당	dam-dang	charge	대단하다	dae-dan-ha-da	awesome
담당자	dam-dang-ja	manager	대단히	dae-dan-hi	very
담당한다	dam-dang-han-da	responsible for	대답	dae-dab	answer
담요	dam-yo	blanket	대답한다	dae-dab-han-da	answer
담임	dam-im	homeroom teacher	대도시	dae-do-si	big city
답	dab	answer	대략	dae-ryag	approximately
답답하다	dab-dab-ha-da	frustrated	대량	dae-ryang	large amount
답변	dab-byeon	answer	대륙	dae-ryug	continent
답장	dab-jang	reply	대문	dae-mun	main door
답한다	dab-han-da	answer	대비	dae-bi	preparation
닷새	das-sae	five days	대비한다	dae-bi-han-da	be ready
당근	dang-geun	carrot	대사	dae-sa	script
당긴다	dang-gin-da	pull	대사관	dae-sa-gwan	embassy
당당하다	dang-dang-ha-da	confident	대상자	dae-sang-ja	subject
당분간	dang-bun-gan	for now	대여섯	dae-yeo-seos	five or six
당연하다	dang-yeon-ha-da	of course	대응	dae-eung	action
당연히	dang-yeon-hi	of course	대응한다	dae-eung-han-da	deal with
당장	dang-jang	right now	대입	dae-ib	college admission
당황한다	dang-hwang-han-da	panic	대접	dae-jeob	hospitality
닿는다	dah-neun-da	reach	대접한다	dae-jeob-han-da	entertain
대	dae	big	대중교통	dae-jung-gyo-tong	public transport
대가	dae-ga	cost	대중문화	dae-jung-mun-hwa	popular culture
대강	dae-gang	outline	대중적	dae-jung-jeog	popular
대개	dae-gae	mostly	대처한다	dae-cheo-han-da	cope
대규모	dae-gyu-mo	large-scale	대체	dae-che	how

대체로	dae-che-ro	generally	덮는다	deop-neun-da	cover
대출	dae-chul	loan	덮인다	deop-in-da	covered
대충	dae-chung	roughly	데려간다	de-ryeo-gan-da	take
대표적	dae-pyo-jeog	typical	데려온다	de-ryeo-on-da	bring
대표한다	dae-pyo-han-da	represent	데운다	de-un-da	warm up
대학교	dae-hag-gyo	university	데이트	de-i-teu	date
대학교수	dae-hag-gyo-su	university professor	도구	do-gu	tool
대학생	dae-hag-saeng	college student	도달한다	do-dal-han-da	reach
대학원	dae-hag-won	graduate school	도대체	do-dae-che	why
대합실	dae-hab-sil	waiting room	도덕	do-deog	moral
대형	dae-hyeong	large	도둑	do-dug	thief
대화한다	dae-hwa-han-da	converse with	도로	do-ro	road
댁	daeg	home	도리어	do-ri-eo	on the contrary
댐	daem	dam	도마	do-ma	cutting board
더구나	deo-gu-na	moreover	도망	do-mang	escape
더더욱	deo-deo-ug	even more	도망간다	do-mang-gan-da	run away
더러워진다	deo-reo-wo-jin-da	get dirty	도망친다	do-mang-chin-da	run away
더럽다	deo-reob-da	dirty	도서관	do-seo-gwan	library
더불어	deo-bul-eo	together	도시락	do-si-rag	lunch box
더욱더	deo-ug-deo	more and more	도심	do-sim	downtown
더욱이	deo-ug-i	furthermore	도와준다	do-wa-jun-da	help
더위	deo-wi	heat	도움말	do-um-mal	help
더한다	deo-han-da	add	도입	do-ib	introduction
덕	deog	virtue	도자기	do-ja-gi	ceramic
덕분	deog-bun	thanks to	도장	do-jang	stamp
덜	deol	less	도저히	do-jeo-hi	absolutely
던다	deon-da	subtract	도전	do-jeon	challenge
덥다	deob-da	hot	도중	do-jung	en route
덧붙인다	deos-but-in-da	add	도착	do-chag	arrival
덩어리	deong-eo-ri	lump	도착한다	do-chag-han-da	arrive

독감	dog-gam	flu	동일하다	dong-il-ha-da	same
독립	dog-lib	independence	동작	dong-jag	movement
독립한다	dog-lib-han-da	independent	동전	dong-jeon	coin
독서	dog-seo	reading	동창	dong-chang	alumni
독일어	dog-il-eo	German	동포	dong-po	compatriots
독창적	dog-chang-jeog	original	동행	dong-haeng	accompany
독특하다	dog-teug-ha-da	special	동화	dong-hwa	fairy tale
독하다	dog-ha-da	strong	동화책	dong-hwa-chaeg	fairy tale book
돌	dol	rock	돼지고기	dwae-ji-go-gi	pork
돌려준다	dol-lyeo-jun-da	give back	되게	doe-ge	very
돌멩이	dol-meng-i	stone	되돌린다	doe-dol-lin-da	get back
돌본다	dol-bon-da	take care	되돌아간다	doe-dol-a-gan-da	go back
돌아다닌다	dol-a-da-nin-da	roam	되돌아본다	doe-dol-a-bon-da	look back
돌아본다	dol-a-bon-da	look back	되돌아온다	doe-dol-a-on-da	come back
돌아선다	dol-a-seon-da	turn around	되살린다	doe-sal-lin-da	revive
돕는다	dob-neun-da	help	되찾는다	doe-chaj-neun-da	get back
동거	dong-geo	cohabitation	되풀이된다	doe-pul-i-doen-da	repeat
동그라미	dong-geu-ra-mi	circle	되풀이한다	doe-pul-i-han-da	repeat
동그랗다	dong-geu-rah-da	round	된장	doen-jang	miso
동기	dong-gi	motivation	된장찌개	doen-jang-jji-gae	soybean paste stew
동료	dong-lyo	colleague	두껍다	du-kkeob-da	thick
동물	dong-mul	animal	두께	du-kke	thickness
동물원	dong-mul-won	zoo	두뇌	du-noe	brains
동부	dong-bu	eastern	두드러진다	du-deu-reo-jin-da	stand out
동서남북	dong-seo-nam-bug	east west south north	두드린다	du-deu-rin-da	knock
동아리	dong-a-ri	club	두려움	du-ryeo-um	fear
동양	dong-yang	eastern	두려워한다	du-ryeo-wo-han-da	afraid of
동양인	dong-yang-in	an Asian	두렵다	du-ryeob-da	afraid
동의	dong-ui	agreement	두른다	du-reun-da	wear
동의한다	dong-ui-han-da	agree	두리번거린다	du-ri-beon-geo-rin-da	look around

두부	du-bu	tofu	들여놓는다	deul-yeo-noh-neun-da	bring in
두세	du-se	two or three	들여다본다	deul-yeo-da-bon-da	look into
두어	du-eo	two or three	들인다	deul-in-da	admit
두통	du-tong	headache	들이마신다	deul-i-ma-sin-da	inhale
둘러본다	dul-leo-bon-da	look around	들이킨다	deul-i-kin-da	inhale
둘러싼다	dul-leo-ssan-da	surround	듯싶다	deus-sip-da	seems like
둘러싸인다	dul-leo-ssa-in-da	be surrounded	등등	deung-deung	etc
둘째	dul-jjae	second	등록	deung-log	registration
둥글다	dung-geul-da	round	등록금	deung-log-geum	tuition
둥지	dung-ji	nest	등록증	deung-log-jeung	registration
뒤늦는다	dwi-neuj--neun-da	be late	등록한다	deung-log-han-da	register
뒤따른다	dwi-tta-reun-da	follow	등산	deung-san	mountain climbing
뒤진다	dwi-jin-da	fall behind	등산로	deung-san-lo	hiking trail
뒤집는다	dwi-jib-neun-da	reverse	등장	deung-jang	appearance
뒤쪽	dwi-jjog	behind	디스크	di-seu-keu	disk
뒤편	dwi-pyeon	backside	디자이너	di-ja-i-neo	designer
뒷골목	dwis-gol-mog	back street	디자인	di-ja-in	design
뒷모습	dwis-mo-seub	back	따님	tta-nim	daughter
뒷문	dwis-mun	back door	따뜻하다	tta-tteus-ha-da	warm
뒷산	dwis-san	back mountain	따라간다	tta-ra-gan-da	follow
드디어	deu-di-eo	at last	따라다닌다	tta-ra-da-nin-da	follow
드라마	deu-ra-ma	drama	따라온다	tta-ra-on-da	follow
드린다	deu-rin-da	give	따로	tta-ro	separately
드물다	deu-mul-da	rare	따로따로	tta-ro-tta-ro	separately
들	deul	field	따른다	tta-reun-da	follow
든다	deun-da	lift	따스하다	tta-seu-ha-da	warm
들려온다	deul-lyeo-on-da	hear	딱	ttag	perfect
들려준다	deul-lyeo-jun-da	tell	딱딱하다	ttag-ttag-ha-da	hard
들른다	deul-leun-da	drop in at	딴	ttan	different
들어준다	deul-eo-jun-da	carry	딴다	ttan-da	pick

딸아이	ttal-a-i	daughter	뚫는다	ttulh-neun-da	pierce
땀	ttam	sweat	뚱뚱하다	ttung-ttung-ha-da	fat
땅바닥	ttang-ba-dag	ground floor	뛰논다	ttwi-non-da	run around
땅속	ttang-sog	underground	뛴다	ttwin-da	run
땅콩	ttang-kong	peanut	뛰어간다	ttwi-eo-gan-da	run
때	ttae	the time	뛰어나간다	ttwi-eo-na-gan-da	run out
때때로	ttae-ttae-ro	sometimes	뛰어나다	ttwi-eo-na-da	outstanding
때로	ttae-ro	sometimes	뛰어나온다	ttwi-eo-na-on-da	jump out
때린다	ttae-rin-da	hit	뛰어내린다	ttwi-eo-nae-rin-da	jump off
땜	ttaem	tinkering	뛰어넘는다	ttwi-eo-neom-neun-da	jump over
떠나간다	tteo-na-gan-da	leave	뛰어논다	ttwi-eo-non-da	run around
떠나온다	tteo-na-on-da	leave	뛰어다닌다	ttwi-eo-da-nin-da	run around
떠든다	tteo-deun-da	chatter	뛰어든다	ttwi-eo-deun-da	dive in
떠들썩하다	tteo-deul-sseog-ha-da	bustle	뛰어온다	ttwi-eo-on-da	come running
떠오른다	tteo-o-reun-da	come to mind	뛰어오른다	ttwi-eo-o-reun-da	jump up
떠올린다	tteo-ol-lin-da	recall	뜨겁다	tteu-geob-da	hot
떡	tteog	rice cake	뜬다	tteun-da	rise
떡국	tteog-gug	rice cake soup	뜯는다	tteud-neun-da	tear off
떡볶이	tteog-bokk-i	tteokbokki (Stir-fried Rice Cake)	뜰	tteul	garden
떤다	tteon-da	shiver	뜻대로	tteus-dae-ro	at will
떨린다	tteol-lin-da	nervous	뜻밖	tteus-bakk	unexpected
떨어뜨린다	tteol-eo-tteu-rin-da	drop	뜻밖에	tteus-bakk-e	unexpectedly
떼	tte	group	뜻한다	tteus-han-da	mean
뗀다	tten-da	cut	띈다	ttuin-da	stand out
또다시	tto-da-si	again	띄운다	ttui-un-da	float
똑같다	ttog-gat-da	same	ㄹ		
똑같이	ttog-gat-i	same	라디오	ra-di-o	radio
똑똑하다	ttog-ttog-ha-da	smart	라면	ra-myeon	ramen
똑바로	ttog-ba-ro	upright	라이벌	ra-i-beol	rival
뚜껑	ttu-kkeong	lid	라이터	la-i-teo	lighter
			라켓	ra-kes	racket

레몬	le-mon	lemon	마이크	ma-i-keu	mic
레스토랑	re-seu-to-rang	restaurant	마주	ma-ju	facing
레이저	le-i-jeo	laser	마주친다	ma-ju-chin-da	come across
레저	le-jeo	leisure	마중	ma-jung	picking up
렌즈	len-jeu	lens	마찰	ma-chal	friction
로봇	ro-bos	robot	마침	ma-chim	just in time
로터리	ro-teo-ri	roundabout	마침내	ma-chim-nae	finally
리그	li-geu	league	마크	ma-keu	mark
리듬	ri-deum	rhythm	막	mag	just
리터	li-teo	liter	막걸리	mag-geol-li	makgeolli (raw rice wine)
□			막내	mag-nae	youngest
마구	ma-gu	randomly	막상	mag-sang	really
마누라	ma-nu-ra	wife	막힌다	mag-hin-da	blocked
마늘	ma-neul	garlic	만	man	just
마당	ma-dang	yard	만다	man-da	roll
마땅하다	ma-ttang-ha-da	deserve	만남	man-nam	meeting
마련	ma-ryeon	preparation	만두	man-du	dumpling
마련된다	ma-ryeon-doen-da	be prepared	만들어진다	man-deul-eo-jin-da	created
마루	ma-ru	floor	만만하다	man-man-ha-da	okay
마른다	ma-reun-da	dry	만세	man-se	hurray
마리	ma-ri	number of animals	만약	man-yag	if
마무리	ma-mu-ri	wrap-up	만일	man-il	if
마사지	ma-sa-ji	massage	만점	man-jeom	perfect score
마약	ma-yag	drug	만족	man-jog	satisfaction
마요네즈	ma-yo-ne-jeu	mayonnaise	만족스럽다	man-jog-seu-reob-da	satisfied
마음가짐	ma-eum-ga-jim	mental attitude	만족한다	man-jog-han-da	satisfied
마음껏	ma-eum-kkeos	to your heart's content	만진다	man-jin-da	touch
마음대로	ma-eum-dae-ro	as you please	만화	man-hwa	cartoon
마음먹는다	ma-eum-meog-neun-da	make up one's mind	만화가	man-hwa-ga	cartoonist
마음속	ma-eum-sog	in the heart	많아진다	manh-a-jin-da	increase
마음씨	ma-eum-ssi	nature			

말	mal	word		매장	mae-jang	store
말기	mal-gi	late stage		매주	mae-ju	every week
말린다	mal-lin-da	dry		매체	mae-che	media
말씀하신다	mal-sseum-ha-sin-da	speak		맥주	maeg-ju	beer
말없이	mal-eobs-i	without a word		맨	maen	bare
말투	mal-tu	speech		맨다	maen-da	tie
맑다	malg-da	clear		맵다	maeb-da	spicy
맘	mam	heart		맺는다	maej-neun-da	form
맘대로	mam-dae-ro	at will		머리말	meo-ri-mal	preface
맛본다	mas-bon-da	taste		머리카락	meo-ri-ka-rag	hair
맛없다	mas-eobs-da	not delicious		머리칼	meo-ri-kal	hair
망설인다	mang-seol-in-da	hesitate		머릿속	meo-ris-sog	brain
망원경	mang-won-gyeong	telescope		머무른다	meo-mu-reun-da	stay
망친다	mang-chin-da	ruin		머문다	meo-mun-da	stay
망한다	mang-han-da	fail		먹고산다	meog-go-san-da	make a living
맞다	maj-da	right		먹는다	meog-neun-da	eat
맞선다	maj-seon-da	stand opposite		먹이	meog-i	food
맞은편	maj-eun-pyeon	across		먹인다	meog-in-da	feed
맞이한다	maj-i-han-da	greet		먹힌다	meog-hin-da	get eaten
맡긴다	mat-gin-da	entrust		먼지	meon-ji	dust
맡는다	mat-neun-da	take on		멀어진다	meol-eo-jin-da	get further away
매너	mae-neo	manner		멈춘다	meom-chun-da	stop
매년	mae-nyeon	every year		멋	meos	style
매단다	mae-dan-da	suspend		멋있다	meos-iss-da	cool
매달	mae-dal	every month		멋지다	meos-ji-da	awesome
매달린다	mae-dal-lin-da	hang on		멍멍	meong-meong	woof woof
매력	mae-ryeog	attractiveness		멎는다	meoj-neun-da	stop
매번	mae-beon	every time		메뉴	me-nyu	menu
매스컴	mae-seu-keom	media		메모	me-mo	memo
매일	mae-il	everyday		메시지	me-si-ji	message

메운다	me-un-da	fill up	모자	mo-ja	hat
메일	me-il	mail	모자란다	mo-ja-ran-da	not enough
멘다	men-da	carry	모조리	mo-jo-ri	all
면	myeon	noodle	모집	mo-jib	recruitment
면담	myeon-dam	interview	모집한다	mo-jib-han-da	recruit
면적	myeon-jeog	area	모처럼	mo-cheo-reom	with great effort
면접	myeon-jeob	interview	모퉁이	mo-tung-i	corner
면한다	myeon-han-da	get rid of	목	mog	neck
명단	myeong-dan	list	목걸이	mog-geol-i	necklace
명령	myeong-lyeong	command	목록	mog-log	list
명령어	myeong-lyeong-eo	command	목사	mog-sa	minister
명예	myeong-ye	honor	목숨	mog-sum	life
명의	myeong-ui	name	목욕	mog-yog	bath
명절	myeong-jeol	holiday	목욕탕	mog-yog-tang	bath house
명칭	myeong-ching	designation	몬다	mon-da	drive
명함	myeong-ham	business card	몰래	mol-lae	stealthily
명확하다	myeong-hwag-ha-da	clear	몰려든다	mol-lyeo-deun-da	flock
몇	myeocc	some	몰려온다	mol-lyeo-on-da	flock
몇몇	myeocc-myeocc	some	몸매	mom-mae	body
모	mo	what	몸무게	mom-mu-ge	weight
모금	mo-geum	fundraising	몸살	mom-sal	ache all over
모기	mo-gi	mosquito	몸속	mom-sog	in the body
모니터	mo-ni-teo	monitor	몸짓	mom-jis	gesture
모델	mo-del	model	몸통	mom-tong	body
모래	mo-rae	sand	몹시	mob-si	heavily
모레	mo-re	day after tomorrow	못됐다	mos-doess-da	wicked
모범	mo-beom	model	못생겼다	mos-saeng-gyeoss-da	ugly
모색한다	mo-saeg-han-da	seek	못지않다	mos-ji-anh-da	no less
모신다	mo-sin-da	wait on	못한다	mos-han-da	can't do it
모여든다	mo-yeo-deun-da	gather	묘사	myo-sa	description

묘사한다	myo-sa-han-da	depict	묶인다	mukk-in-da	knot
무	mu	radish	문구	mun-gu	phrases
무겁다	mu-geob-da	heavy	문득	mun-deug	suddenly
무게	mu-ge	weight	문밖	mun-bakk	out the door
무관심	mu-gwan-sim	indifference	문법	mun-beob	grammar
무관심하다	mu-gwan-sim-ha-da	indifferent	문서	mun-seo	document
무기	mu-gi	weapon	문자	mun-ja	message
무너진다	mu-neo-jin-da	fallen	문장	mun-jang	sentence
무늬	mu-nui	pattern	문제된다	mun-je-doen-da	become a problem
무더위	mu-deo-wi	sweltering	문제점	mun-je-jeom	problem
무덤	mu-deom	tomb	문학적	mun-hag-jeog	literary
무덥다	mu-deob-da	it's hot	문화재	mun-hwa-jae	cultural heritage
무려	mu-ryeo	whopping	문화적	mun-hwa-jeog	cultural
무렵	mu-ryeob	around	묻는다	mud-neun-da	ask
무료	mu-ryo	free	묻힌다	mud-hin-da	be buried
무릎	mu-reup	knee	물가	mul-ga	prices
무리다	mu-ri-da	unnatural	물결	mul-gyeol	wave
무리한다	mu-ri-han-da	overwork	물고기	mul-go-gi	fish
무사하다	mu-sa-ha-da	safe	물기	mul-gi	bite
무시한다	mu-si-han-da	ignore	문다	mun-da	bite
무역	mu-yeog	trade	물러난다	mul-leo-nan-da	withdraw
무용	mu-yong	dancing	물론	mul-lon	sure
무용가	mu-yong-ga	dancer	물속	mul-sog	underwater
무의미하다	mu-ui-mi-ha-da	meaningless	물어본다	mul-eo-bon-da	ask
무조건	mu-jo-geon	must	물음	mul-eum	question
무지개	mu-ji-gae	rainbow	물질적	mul-jil-jeog	material
무책임하다	mu-chaeg-im-ha-da	irresponsible	물체	mul-che	object
무척	mu-cheog	very	뭘	mwol	what
묵는다	mug-neun-da	lodge	뭣	mwos	what
묶는다	mukk-neun-da	tie	미끄러진다	mi-kkeu-reo-jin-da	slip

미끄럽다	mi-kkeu-reob-da	slippery	밀리미터	mil-li-mi-teo	millimeter
미니	mi-ni	mini	밀린다	mil-lin-da	get stuck in
미디어	mi-di-eo	media	밀접하다	mil-jeob-ha-da	close
미래	mi-rae	future	밉다	mib-da	hate
미룬다	mi-run-da	postpone	밑바닥	mit-ba-dag	bottom
미리	mi-ri	in advance	**ㅂ**		
미만	mi-man	under	바	ba	bar
미사일	mi-sa-il	missile	바가지	ba-ga-ji	overpriced
미소	mi-so	smile	바구니	ba-gu-ni	basket
미술	mi-sul	art	바깥	ba-kkat	outside
미술관	mi-sul-gwan	art gallery	바깥쪽	ba-kkat-jjog	outside
미스	mi-seu	miss	바늘	ba-neul	needle
미안하다	mi-an-ha-da	sorry	바닥	ba-dag	floor
미용실	mi-yong-sil	salon	바닷가	ba-das-ga	beach
미움	mi-um	hate	바닷물	ba-das-mul	sea water
미워한다	mi-wo-han-da	hate	바람	ba-ram	wind
미인	mi-in	beauty	바람직하다	ba-ram-jig-ha-da	desirable
미처	mi-cheo	not yet	바로잡는다	ba-ro-jab-neun-da	straighten
미친다	mi-chin-da	crazy	바른다	ba-reun-da	spread
미터	mi-teo	meter	바보	ba-bo	fool
미혼	mi-hon	single	바싹	ba-ssag	close
민간	min-gan	civilian	바위	ba-wi	rock
민다	min-da	push	바이러스	ba-i-reo-seu	virus
민속	min-sog	folklore	바지	ba-ji	pants
민주	min-ju	democracy	바친다	ba-chin-da	devote
민주주의	min-ju-ju-ui	democracy	바퀴	ba-kwi	wheel
민주화	min-ju-hwa	democratization	박	bag	gourd
믿어진다	mid-eo-jin-da	be believed	박는다	bag-neun-da	thrust
믿음	mid-eum	trust	박물관	bag-mul-gwan	museum
밀가루	mil-ga-ru	flour	박사	bag-sa	doctor
			박수	bag-su	clap

박스	bag-seu	box	발달된다	bal-dal-doen-da	develop
박힌다	bag-hin-da	hammered	발등	bal-deung	top of the foot
반갑다	ban-gab-da	nice to meet	발레	bal-le	ballet
반긴다	ban-gin-da	welcome	발바닥	bal-ba-dag	sole
반대	ban-dae	opposite	발생한다	bal-saeng-han-da	occur
반대편	ban-dae-pyeon	opposite	발음	bal-eum	pronunciation
반대한다	ban-dae-han-da	oppose	발음한다	bal-eum-han-da	pronounce
반말	ban-mal	talk down	발자국	bal-ja-gug	footprint
반면	ban-myeon	on the other hand	발전	bal-jeon	development
반발	ban-bal	repulsion	발전된다	bal-jeon-doen-da	develop
반복된다	ban-bog-doen-da	repeat	발톱	bal-tob	toenail
반복한다	ban-bog-han-da	repeat	발표	bal-pyo	announce
반성	ban-seong	regret	발표된다	bal-pyo-doen-da	announced
반성한다	ban-seong-han-da	reflect on	발휘한다	bal-hwi-han-da	show off
반영한다	ban-yeong-han-da	reflect	밝다	balg-da	bright
반응	ban-eung	reaction	밝아진다	balg-a-jin-da	brighten
반장	ban-jang	class monitor	밝혀낸다	balg-hyeo-naen-da	uncover
반죽	ban-jug	dough	밝혀진다	balg-hyeo-jin-da	come to light
반지	ban-ji	ring	밟다	balb-da	step on
반짝거린다	ban-jjag-geo-rin-da	twinkle	밤	bam	night
반짝인다	ban-jjag-in-da	twinkle	밤낮	bam-naj	night and day
반찬	ban-chan	side dish	밤늦었다	bam-neuj-eoss-da	late at night
반한다	ban-han-da	fall in love	밤새	bam-sae	overnight
받침	bad-chim	support	밤샌다	bam-saen-da	stay up all night
발걸음	bal-geol-eum	footfall	밤새운다	bam-sae-un-da	stay up all night
발견	bal-gyeon	discovery	밤색	bam-saeg	brown
발견된다	bal-gyeon-doen-da	discovered	밤중	bam-jung	midnight
발길	bal-gil	footsteps	밤하늘	bam-ha-neul	night sky
발끝	bal-kkeut	tiptoe	밥그릇	bab-geu-reus	rice bowl
발달	bal-dal	development	밥맛	bab-mas	appetite

밥상	bab-sang	dining table	백화점	baeg-hwa-jeom	department store
밥솥	bab-sot	rice cooker	뱃사람	baes-sa-ram	seafarer
방금	bang-geum	just now	뱉는다	baet-neun-da	disgorge
방면	bang-myeon	direction	버려진다	beo-ryeo-jin-da	abandoned
방문	bang-mun	visit	버릇	beo-reus	habit
방문한다	bang-mun-han-da	visit	버섯	beo-seos	mushroom
방바닥	bang-ba-dag	floor	버스	beo-seu	bus
방송국	bang-song-gug	broadcast stations	버터	beo-teo	butter
방송사	bang-song-sa	broadcaster	버튼	beo-teun	button
방송한다	bang-song-han-da	broadcast	버틴다	beo-tin-da	withstand
방울	bang-ul	bell	번개	beon-gae	lightning
방지	bang-ji	prevention	번거롭다	beon-geo-rob-da	cumbersome
방지한다	bang-ji-han-da	prevent	번역	beon-yeog	translation
방학	bang-hag	vacation	번역한다	beon-yeog-han-da	translate
방해	bang-hae	hindrance	번지	beon-ji	address
방해한다	bang-hae-han-da	interrupt	번호	beon-ho	number
밭	bat	field	벌	beol	punishment
배경	bae-gyeong	background	벌금	beol-geum	fine
배고프다	bae-go-peu-da	hungry	번다	beon-da	earn
배꼽	bae-kkob	navel	벌떡	beol-tteog	suddenly
배다	bae-da	bear	벌레	beol-le	bug
배달	bae-dal	delivery	벌린다	beol-lin-da	be profitable
배부르다	bae-bu-reu-da	full	벌어진다	beol-eo-jin-da	break up
배우	bae-u	actor	범위	beom-wi	range
배우자	bae-u-ja	spouse	범인	beom-in	criminal
배추	bae-chu	napa cabbage	범죄	beom-joe	crime
배추김치	bae-chu-gim-chi	napa cabbage kimchi	법	beob	law
배치	bae-chi	arrangement	법률	beob-lyul	law
백성	baeg-seong	the people	법원	beob-won	court
백인	baeg-in	white	법적	beob-jeog	legal

법칙	beob-chig	rule	보내온다	bo-nae-on-da	send
벗긴다	beos-gin-da	peel	보너스	bo-neo-seu	bonus
벗는다	beos-neun-da	take off	보도	bo-do	sidewalk
베개	be-gae	pillow	보도된다	bo-do-doen-da	reported
벤다	ben-da	mow	보도한다	bo-do-han-da	report
벤치	ben-chi	bench	보람	bo-ram	reward
벨트	bel-teu	belt	보름	bo-reum	fifteen days
벼	byeo	rice	보리	bo-ri	barley
벽	byeog	wall	보살핀다	bo-sal-pin-da	take care of
변경	byeon-gyeong	change	보상	bo-sang	reward
변동	byeon-dong	variance	보수	bo-su	repair
변명	byeon-myeong	excuse	보수적	bo-su-jeog	conservative
변신	byeon-sin	transform	보안	bo-an	security
변호사	byeon-ho-sa	lawyer	보완한다	bo-wan-han-da	redeem
변화된다	byeon-hwa-doen-da	change	보자기	bo-ja-gi	wrapping cloth
변화한다	byeon-hwa-han-da	change	보장	bo-jang	guarantee
별	byeol	star	보장된다	bo-jang-doen-da	guaranteed
별다르다	byeol-da-reu-da	different	보장한다	bo-jang-han-da	vouch
별도	byeol-do	separately	보전	bo-jeon	integrity
별명	byeol-myeong	nickname	보조	bo-jo	assistant
별일	byeol-il	special day	보존	bo-jon	preservation
병	byeong	disease	보존한다	bo-jon-han-da	preserve
병든다	byeong-deun-da	get sick	보충한다	bo-chung-han-da	to make up
병실	byeong-sil	ward	보통	bo-tong	common
병아리	byeong-a-ri	chick	보편적	bo-pyeon-jeog	universal
보고	bo-go	report	보험	bo-heom	insurance
보고서	bo-go-seo	report	보호된다	bo-ho-doen-da	be protected
보고한다	bo-go-han-da	make a report	보호한다	bo-ho-han-da	protect
보관	bo-gwan	keep	복	bog	luck
보관한다	bo-gwan-han-da	store	복도	bog-do	corridor

복사	bog-sa	copy	부대	bu-dae	army unit
복사기	bog-sa-gi	copy machine	부동산	bu-dong-san	real estate
복사한다	bog-sa-han-da	copy	부드럽다	bu-deu-reob-da	soft
복습	bog-seub	review	부딪친다	bu-dij-chin-da	bump into
복습한다	bog-seub-han-da	review	부딪힌다	bu-dij-hin-da	get hit
복잡하다	bog-jab-ha-da	complex	부러워한다	bu-reo-wo-han-da	envy
볶는다	bokk-neun-da	fry	부러진다	bu-reo-jin-da	break
볶음	bokk-eum	stir-fry	부럽다	bu-reob-da	envious
볶음밥	bokk-eum-bab	fried rice	부른다	bu-reun-da	call
본	bon	original	부모님	bu-mo-nim	parents
본격적	bon-gyeog-jeog	full-fledged	부문	bu-mun	sector
본래	bon-lae	originally	부분적	bu-bun-jeog	partial
본부	bon-bu	headquarters	부상	bu-sang	injury
본사	bon-sa	head office	부서	bu-seo	department
본성	bon-seong	original nature	부서진다	bu-seo-jin-da	break
본인	bon-in	person concerned	부엌	bu-eok	kitchen
본질	bon-jil	nature	부위	bu-wi	part
볼일	bol-il	chores	부인	bu-in	wife
봉사	bong-sa	volunteering	부자	bu-ja	wealthy
봉사한다	bong-sa-han-da	serve	부작용	bu-jag-yong	side effect
봉지	bong-ji	bag	부잣집	bu-jas-jib	rich house
봉투	bong-tu	envelope	부장	bu-jang	director
뵌다	boen-da	see you	부재	bu-jae	absence
뵙는다	boeb-neun-da	meet	부정	bu-jeong	denial
부	bu	wealth	부정적	bu-jeong-jeog	negative
부근	bu-geun	vicinity	부정한다	bu-jeong-han-da	deny
부끄러움	bu-kkeu-reo-um	shame	부족	bu-jog	lack
부끄럽다	bu-kkeu-reob-da	embarrassed	부족하다	bu-jog-ha-da	lack
부담	bu-dam	burden	부지런하다	bu-ji-reon-ha-da	diligent
부담한다	bu-dam-han-da	bear	부지런히	bu-ji-reon-hi	industriously

부채	bu-chae	debt	불다	bul-da	blow
부처	bu-cheo	Buddha	불러일으킨다	bul-leo-il-eu-kin-da	arouse
부친다	bu-chin-da	send	불린다	bul-lin-da	be called
부친	bu-chin	father	불리하다	bul-li-ha-da	disadvantage
부탁	bu-tag	ask	불만	bul-man	dissatisfaction
부탁한다	bu-tag-han-da	beg	불법	bul-beob	illegal
부품	bu-pum	part	불빛	bul-bicc	fire
부피	bu-pi	volume	불쌍하다	bul-ssang-ha-da	poor
부회장	bu-hoe-jang	vice-chairman	불안	bul-an	unrest
북	bug	drum	불안하다	bul-an-ha-da	unstable
북부	bug-bu	northern	불어온다	bul-eo-on-da	blow
분노	bun-no	anger	불완전하다	bul-wan-jeon-ha-da	incomplete
분량	bun-lyang	amount	불이익	bul-i-ig	disadvantage
분리	bun-ly	separation	불편	bul-pyeon	inconvenience
분리된다	bun-ly-doen-da	separate	불편하다	bul-pyeon-ha-da	uncomfortable
분리한다	bun-ly-han-da	disunite	불평	bul-pyeong	complain
분명	bun-myeong	for sure	불평등하다	bul-pyeong-deung-ha-da	unequal
분명해진다	bun-myeong-hae-jin-da	become clear	불필요하다	bul-pil-yo-ha-da	unnecessary
분명히	bun-myeong-hi	clearly	불행	bul-haeng	unhappiness
분석한다	bun-seog-han-da	analyze	불행하다	bul-haeng-ha-da	unhappy
분주하다	bun-ju-ha-da	busy	불확실하다	bul-hwag-sil-ha-da	uncertain
분포한다	bun-po-han-da	distribute	붉다	bulg-da	red
분필	bun-pil	chalk	붐빈다	bum-bin-da	bustle
분홍색	bun-hong-saeg	pink	붓는다	bus-neun-da	pour
불가능하다	bul-ga-neung-ha-da	impossible	붙든다	but-deun-da	seize
불가피하다	bul-ga-pi-ha-da	inevitable	붙잡는다	but-jab-neun-da	seize
불고기	bul-go-gi	bulgogi	붙잡힌다	but-jab-hin-da	caught
불과	bul-gwa	only	브랜드	beu-raen-deu	brand
불과하다	hul-gwa-ha-da	mere	블라우스	beul-la-u-seu	blouse
불꽃	bul-kkocc	flame	비	bi	rain

비교	bi-gyo	comparison	비판	bi-pan	criticism
비교적	bi-gyo-jeog	comparative	비판적	bi-pan-jeog	critical
비교한다	bi-gyo-han-da	compare	비판한다	bi-pan-han-da	criticize
비극	bi-geug	tragedy	비행	bi-haeng	flight
비긴다	bi-gin-da	draw with	비행기	bi-haeng-gi	airplane
비난	bi-nan	criticism	비행장	bi-haeng-jang	airfield
비누	bi-nu	soap	빈다	bin-da	beg
비닐	bi-nil	vinyl	빌딩	bil-ding	building
비닐봉지	bi-nil-bong-ji	plastic bag	빌린다	bil-lin-da	borrow
비디오	bi-di-o	video	빗	bis	comb
비로소	bi-ro-so	for the first time	빗물	bis-mul	rainwater
비롯된다	bi-ros-doen-da	come from	빗방울	bis-bang-ul	raindrop
비만	bi-man	obesity	빗줄기	bis-jul-gi	raindrops
비명	bi-myeong	scream	빚	bij	debt
비밀	bi-mil	secret	빛깔	bicc-kkal	color
비바람	bi-ba-ram	rainstorm	빛난다	bicc-nan-da	shine
비빈다	bi-bin-da	rub	빠뜨린다	ppa-tteu-rin-da	miss out
비빔밥	bi-bim-bab	bibimbap	빠져나간다	ppa-jyeo-na-gan-da	get out
비상	bi-sang	emergency	빠져나온다	ppa-jyeo-na-on-da	get out
비서	bi-seo	secretary	빠진다	ppa-jin-da	fall in
비싸다	bi-ssa-da	expensive	빨갛다	ppal-gah-da	red
비용	bi-yong	cost	빤다	ppan-da	suck
비운다	bi-un-da	vacate	빨래	ppal-lae	wash
비웃는다	bi-us-neun-da	make fun of	빵	ppang	bread
비율	bi-yul	ratio	빼놓는다	ppae-noh-neun-da	leave out
비중	bi-jung	importance	빼앗긴다	ppae-as-gin-da	to be taken away
비춘다	bi-chun-da	irradiate	빼앗는다	ppae-as-neun-da	steal
비친다	bi-chin-da	hint	뺏는다	ppaes-neun-da	take away
비킨다	bi-kin-da	get away	뺨	ppyam	cheek
비타민	bi-ta-min	vitamin	뻔하다	ppeon-ha-da	obvious

뻗는다	ppeod-neun-da	stretch		사설	sa-seol	editorial
뼈	ppyeo	bone		사소하다	sa-so-ha-da	trivial
뽑는다	ppob-neun-da	select		사실상	sa-sil-sang	virtually
뽑힌다	ppob-hin-da	be elected		사업가	sa-eob-ga	entrepreneur
뿌리	ppu-ri	root		사업자	sa-eob-ja	businessman
뿌린다	ppu-rin-da	spread		사용된다	sa-yong-doen-da	be used
뿌리친다	ppu-ri-chin-da	reject		사용자	sa-yong-ja	user
ㅅ				사원	sa-won	employee
사	sa	buy		사이사이	sa-i-sa-i	in spare moments
사계절	sa-gye-jeol	four seasons		사이좋다	sa-i-joh-da	get along
사고	sa-go	accident		사장	sa-jang	CEO
사과한다	sa-gwa-han-da	apologize		사전	sa-jeon	dictionary
사귄다	sa-gwin-da	make friends with		사정	sa-jeong	circumstances
사기	sa-gi	fraud		사진기	sa-jin-gi	camera
사나이	sa-na-i	man		사촌	sa-chon	cousin
사냥	sa-nyang	hunt		사춘기	sa-chun-gi	puberty
사들인다	sa-deul-in-da	buy		사투리	sa-tu-ri	dialect
사랑스럽다	sa-rang-seu-reob-da	lovely		사표	sa-pyo	resignation
사례	sa-rye	case		사회생활	sa-hoe-saeng-hwal	social life
사립	sa-rib	private		사회자	sa-hoe-ja	moderator
사망	sa-mang	dead		사회적	sa-hoe-jeog	social
사망한다	sa-mang-han-da	die		사회주의	sa-hoe-ju-ui	socialism
사모님	sa-mo-nim	Mrs		사회학	sa-hoe-hag	sociology
사무	sa-mu	affairs		사흘	sa-heul	three days
사무소	sa-mu-so	office		산길	san-gil	mountain path
사무실	sa-mu-sil	office		산부인과	san-bu-in-gwa	obstetrics and gynecology
사무직	sa-mu-jig	office worker		산소	san-so	oxygen
사물	sa-mul	objects		산속	san-sog	in the mountains
사방	sa-bang	everywhere		산책	san-chaeg	walk
사상	sa-sang	thought		살	sal	fat
사생활	sa-saeng-hwal	privacy				

살린다	sal-lin-da	save	상상	sang-sang	imagination
살림	sal-lim	livelihood	상상력	sang-sang-lyeog	imagination
살아간다	sal-a-gan-da	live	상상한다	sang-sang-han-da	imagine
살아난다	sal-a-nan-da	come alive	상식	sang-sig	common sense
살아남는다	sal-a-nam-neun-da	survive	상업	sang-eob	commerce
살아온다	sal-a-on-da	come alive	상인	sang-in	merchant
살인	sal-in	murder	상점	sang-jeom	shop
살짝	sal-jjag	a little	상징적	sang-jing-jeog	symbolic
살핀다	sal-pin-da	watch	상징한다	sang-jing-han-da	symbolize
삶는다	salm-neun-da	boil	상처	sang-cheo	wound
삼가한다	sam-ga-han-da	forbear	상추	sang-chu	lettuce
삼계탕	sam-gye-tang	samgyetang (chicken soup with ginseng)	상쾌하다	sang-kwae-ha-da	refreshing
삼킨다	sam-kin-da	gulp down	상표	sang-pyo	brand
상	sang	award	상한다	sang-han-da	rot
상관	sang-gwan	relation	새긴다	sae-gin-da	carve
상관없다	sang-gwan-eobs-da	does not matter	새끼	sae-kki	young
상관없이	sang-gwan-eobs-i	regardless of	샌다	saen-da	leak
상금	sang-geum	reward	새로	sae-ro	new
상담	sang-dam	consulting	새로이	sae-ro-i	freshly
상당	sang-dang	equivalent	새소리	sae-so-ri	birdsong
상당수	sang-dang-su	quite a lot	새운다	sae-un-da	stay up
상당하다	sang-dang-ha-da	considerable	새해	sae-hae	new year
상당히	sang-dang-hi	very	색	saeg	color
상대	sang-dae	opponent	색깔	saeg-kkal	color
상대방	sang-dae-bang	opponent	색다르다	saeg-da-reu-da	different
상대성	sang-dae-seong	relativity	색연필	saeg-yeon-pil	color pencil
상대적	sang-dae-jeog	relative	샌드위치	saen-deu-wi-chi	sandwich
상대편	sang-dae-pyeon	the other side	생	saeng	raw
상류	sang-lyu	upstream	생각난다	saeng-gag-nan-da	remember
상반기	sang-ban-gi	the first half	생각된다	saeng-gag-doen-da	think

생겨난다	saeng-gyeo-nan-da	arise		서양인	seo-yang-in	westerner
생기	saeng-gi	vigor		서적	seo-jeog	books
생방송	saeng-bang-song	live broadcast		서점	seo-jeom	bookstore
생산된다	saeng-san-doen-da	be produced		서클	seo-keul	circle
생산력	saeng-san-lyeog	productivity		서투르다	seo-tu-reu-da	clumsy
생산자	saeng-san-ja	producer		서툴다	seo-tul-da	clumsy
생산한다	saeng-san-han-da	produce		석	seog	three
생선	saeng-seon	fish		석사	seog-sa	master
생신	saeng-sin	birthday		석유	seog-yu	oil
생일	saeng-il	birthday		섞다	seokk-da	mix
생활비	saeng-hwal-bi	living expenses		섞인다	seokk-in-da	be mixed
생활수준	saeng-hwal-su-jun	standard of living		선명하다	seon-myeong-ha-da	clear
생활용품	saeng-hwal-yong-pum	household goods		선물	seon-mul	gift
생활한다	saeng-hwal-han-da	live		선물한다	seon-mul-han-da	present
생활환경	saeng-hwal-hwan-gyeong	living environment		선배	seon-bae	elder
샤워	sya-wo	shower		선생	seon-saeng	teacher
서구	seo-gu	western		선언한다	seon-eon-han-da	declare
서너	seo-neo	three or four		선원	seon-won	sailor
서늘하다	seo-neul-ha-da	cool		선장	seon-jang	captain
서두른다	seo-du-reun-da	hurry		선전	seon-jeon	propaganda
서랍	seo-rab	a drawer		선정한다	seon-jeong-han-da	select
서로	seo-ro	each other		선진	seon-jin	advanced
서류	seo-ryu	document		선진국	seon-jin-gug	developed countries
서명	seo-myeong	signature		선택	seon-taeg	selection
서명한다	seo-myeong-han-da	sign		선택한다	seon-taeg-han-da	choose
서민	seo-min	people		선풍기	seon-pung-gi	fan
서부	seo-bu	west		선호한다	seon-ho-han-da	prefer
서비스	seo-bi-seu	service		설거지	seol-geo-ji	washing dishes
서서히	seo-seo-hi	slowly		설날	seol-nal	new year
서양	seo-yang	western		설득한다	seol-deug-han-da	persuade

설렁탕	seol-leong-tang	sullungtang (Ox Bone Soup)	세계관	se-gye-gwan	world-view
설립한다	seol-lib-han-da	establish	세계적	se-gye-jeog	worldwide
설명된다	seol-myeong-doen-da	explained	세금	se-geum	tax
설문	seol-mun	survey	세대	se-dae	generation
설사	seol-sa	diarrhea	세련돼있다	se-ryeon-dwai-iss-da	stylish
설치	seol-chi	installation	세로	se-ro	length
설치된다	seol-chi-doen-da	be installed	세미나	se-mi-na	seminar
설치한다	seol-chi-han-da	install	세상에	se-sang-e	oh my gosh
설탕	seol-tang	sugar	세수	se-su	washing face
섬	seom	island	세워진다	se-wo-jin-da	be built
섭섭하다	seob-seob-ha-da	feel disappointed	세월	se-wol	time
섭씨	seob-ssi	Celsius	세제	se-je	detergent
성	seong	last name	세탁	se-tag	laundry
성경	seong-gyeong	bible	세탁기	se-tag-gi	washing machine
성공	seong-gong	success	세탁소	se-tag-so	laundry
성공적	seong-gong-jeog	successful	세트	se-teu	set
성공한다	seong-gong-han-da	succeed	섹시하다	seg-si-ha-da	sexy
성당	seong-dang	Catholic church	센다	sen-da	count
성립된다	seong-lib-doen-da	be established	센터	sen-teo	center
성립한다	seong-lib-han-da	come true	센티미터	sen-ti-mi-teo	centimeter
성명	seong-myeong	name	셋째	ses-jjae	third
성별	seong-byeol	gender	소개	so-gae	introduction
성숙하다	seong-sug-ha-da	mature	소개된다	so-gae-doen-da	introduced
성실하다	seong-sil-ha-da	be sincere	소개한다	so-gae-han-da	introduce
성인	seong-in	adult	소규모	so-gyu-mo	small
성장한다	seong-jang-han-da	grow up	소극적	so-geug-jeog	passive
성적	seong-jeog	sexual	소금	so-geum	salt
성적	seong-jeog	grade	소나기	so-na-gi	shower
성질	seong-jil	temper	소년	so-nyeon	boy
성함	seong-ham	name	소득	so-deug	income
세 가지	se ga-ji	three kinds			

소리친다	so-ri-chin-da	yell		소파	so-pa	sofa
소망	so-mang	hope		소포	so-po	package
소매	so-mae	sleeve		소풍	so-pung	picnic
소문	so-mun	rumor		소프트웨어	so-peu-teu-we-eo	software
소문난다	so-mun-nan-da	rumored		소형	so-hyeong	small type
소박하다	so-bag-ha-da	simple		소홀히	so-hol-hi	carelessly
소비	so-bi	consumption		소화	so-hwa	digestion
소비한다	so-bi-han-da	spend		소화한다	so-hwa-han-da	digest
소설가	so-seol-ga	novelist		속담	sog-dam	proverb
소속	so-sog	belongings		속도	sog-do	speed
소수	so-su	minority		속마음	sog-ma-eum	heart
소스	so-seu	sauce		속삭인다	sog-sag-in-da	whisper
소시지	so-si-ji	sausage		속상하다	sog-sang-ha-da	upset
소식	so-sig	the news		속옷	sog-os	underwear
소아과	so-a-gwa	pediatrics		속인다	sog-in-da	cheat
소요된다	so-yo-doen-da	take up		속한다	sog-han-da	belong
소용	so-yong	use		손가락	son-ga-lag	finger
소용없다	so-yong-eobs-da	no use		손길	son-gil	hand
소원	so-won	wish		손등	son-deung	back of the hand
소위	so-wi	so called		손목	son-mog	wrist
소유	so-yu	possession		손바닥	son-ba-dag	palm
소유자	so-yu-ja	owner		손발	son-bal	hands and feet
소유한다	so-yu-han-da	own		손뼉	son-ppyeog	clapping
소음	so-eum	noise		손수	son-su	handmade
소재	so-jae	material		손수건	son-su-geon	handkerchief
소주	so-ju	soju		손쉽다	son-swib-da	easy
소중하다	so-jung-ha-da	precious		손실	son-sil	loss
소중히	so-jung-hi	preciously		손자	son-ja	grandson
소지품	so-ji-pum	belongings		손잡는다	son-jab-neun-da	hand in hand
소질	so-jil	talent		손잡이	son-jab-i	handle

손질	son-jil	trim	수박	su-bag	watermelon
손질한다	son-jil-han-da	groom	수백	su-baeg	hundreds
손해	son-hae	loss	수상	su-sang	awards
솔직하다	sol-jig-ha-da	honest	수석	su-seog	top
솔직히	sol-jig-hi	to be honest	수술	su-sul	operation
솜	som	cotton	수시로	su-si-ro	frequently
솜씨	som-ssi	workmanship	수십	su-sib	dozens
솟는다	sos-neun-da	tower	수업	su-eob	class
송아지	song-a-ji	calf	수없이	su-eobs-i	countless
송이	song-i	cluster	수염	su-yeom	mustache
송편	song-pyeon	songpyeon (Half-moon Rice Cake)	수영	su-yeong	swimming
쇠	soe	iron	수영장	su-yeong-jang	swimming pool
쇠고기	soe-go-gi	beef	수요	su-yo	demand
쇼	syo	show	수입	su-ib	income
쇼핑	syo-ping	shopping	수입된다	su-ib-doen-da	imported
수건	su-geon	towel	수입품	su-ib-pum	imports
수고	su-go	effort	수입한다	su-ib-han-da	import
수고한다	su-go-han-da	keep the good work	수저	su-jeo	spoon
수년	su-nyeon	many years	수집	su-jib	collection
수단	su-dan	method	수집한다	su-jib-han-da	collect
수도	su-do	capital	수천	su-cheon	thousands
수도권	su-do-gwon	metropolitan area	수출	su-chul	export
수도꼭지	su-do-kkog-ji	water tap	수출한다	su-chul-han-da	export
수돗물	su-dos-mul	tap water	수컷	su-keos	cock
수동적	su-dong-jeog	passive	수표	su-pyo	check
수리한다	su-ri-han-da	repair	수필	su-pil	essay
수만	su-man	tens of thousands	수행한다	su-haeng-han-da	conduct
수많은	su-manh-eun	numerous	수험생	su-heom-saeng	student
수면	su-myeon	sleep	수화기	su-hwa-gi	receiver
수명	su-myeong	life span	숙녀	sug-nyeo	lady

숙소	sug-so	lodging	스타	seu-ta	star
숙인다	sug-in-da	bow down	스타일	seu-ta-il	style
순간적	sun-gan-jeog	momentary	스튜디오	seu-tyu-di-o	studio
순서	sun-seo	order	스트레스	seu-teu-re-seu	stress
순수	sun-su	purity	스포츠	seu-po-cheu	sports
순수하다	sun-su-ha-da	pure	슬그머니	seul-geu-meo-ni	sneakily
순식간	sun-sig-gan	a moment	슬쩍	seul-jjeog	stealthily
순위	sun-wi	ranking	슬퍼한다	seul-peo-han-da	be sad
순진하다	sun-jin-ha-da	naive	슬프다	seul-peu-da	sad
순하다	sun-ha-da	gentle	슬픔	seul-peum	sadness
술병	sul-byeong	wine bottle	습관	seub-gwan	habit
술자리	sul-ja-ri	drinking party	습기	seub-gi	humidity
술잔	sul-jan	glass	승객	seung-gaeg	passenger
술집	sul-jib	bar	승리	seung-li	victory
숨	sum	breath	승리한다	seung-li-han-da	win
숨긴다	sum-gin-da	hide	승부	seung-bu	match
숨다	sum-da	hide	승용차	seung-yong-cha	car
숨진다	sum-jin-da	die	승진	seung-jin	promotion
숫자	sus-ja	number	시	si	city
쉬다	swi-da	rest	시각	si-gag	standpoint
슈퍼마켓	syu-peo-ma-kes	supermarket	시계	si-gye	clock
스님	seu-nim	monk	시골	si-gol	country
스무	seu-mu	twenty	시금치	si-geum-chi	spinach
스스로	seu-seu-ro	self	시기	si-gi	period
스승	seu-seung	teacher	시끄럽다	si-kkeu-reob-da	noisy
스웨터	seu-we-teo	sweater	시나리오	si-na-rio	scenario
스위치	seu-wi-chi	switch	시내	si-nae	downtown
스친다	seu-chin-da	flash across	시내버스	si-nae-beo-seu	city bus
스케줄	seu-ke-jul	schedule	시대적	si-dae-jeog	historical
스키장	seu-ki-jang	ski resort	시댁	si-daeg	father-in-law's house

시도	si-do	try	식빵	sig-bbang	bread
시도한다	si-do-han-da	attempt	식사한다	sig-sa-han-da	have a meal
시든다	si-deun-da	wither	식생활	sig-saeng-hwal	eating habits
시디	si-di	cd	식욕	sig-yog	appetite
시디롬	si-di-rom	CD-ROM	식용유	sig-yong-yu	cooking oil
시리즈	si-ri-jeu	series	식초	sig-cho	vinegar
시멘트	si-men-teu	cement	식탁	sig-tag	table
시스템	si-seu-tem	system	식품	sig-pum	food
시야	si-ya	eyesight	식품점	sig-pum-jeom	grocery store
시외	si-oe	out of town	식힌다	sig-hin-da	cool down
시외버스	si-oe-beo-seu	intercity bus	신	sin	god
시원하다	si-won-ha-da	cool	신고	sin-go	declaration
시위	si-wi	demonstration	신고한다	sin-go-han-da	report
시일	si-il	time	신규	sin-gyu	new
시작	si-jag	start	신기하다	sin-gi-ha-da	amazing
시점	si-jeom	point in time	신념	sin-nyeom	belief
시즌	si-jeun	season	신는다	sin-neun-da	put on
시집	si-jib	book of poetry	신랑	sin-lang	groom
시집간다	si-jib-gan-da	get married	신문사	sin-mun-sa	newspaper
시청	si-cheong	city hall	신문지	sin-mun-ji	newspaper
시청률	si-cheong-ryul	rating	신발	sin-bal	shoes
시청자	si-cheong-ja	viewers	신부	sin-bu	bride
시합	si-hab	match	신분	sin-bun	identity
식구	sig-gu	family	신비	sin-bi	mystery
식기	sig-gi	tableware	신사	sin-sa	gentleman
식는다	sig-neun-da	cool down	신선하다	sin-seon-ha-da	fresh
식당	sig-dang	restaurant	신설	sin-seol	newly open
식량	sig-lyang	food	신세	sin-se	indebtedness
식료품	sig-lyo-pum	grocery	신세대	sin-se-dae	new generation
식물	sig-mul	plant	신속하다	sin-sog-ha-da	quick

신용	sin-yong	credit	실시된다	sil-si-doen-da	carried out
신인	sin-in	new man	실은	sil-eun	actually
신입생	sin-ib-saeng	freshman	실장	sil-jang	head of a department
신제품	sin-je-pum	new product	실정	sil-jeong	actual circumstances
신중하다	sin-jung-ha-da	careful	실제	sil-je	real
신청	sin-cheong	application	실질적	sil-jil-jeog	practical
신청서	sin-cheong-seo	application form	실천한다	sil-cheon-han-da	practice
신청한다	sin-cheong-han-da	put in for	실체	sil-che	substance
신체	sin-che	body	실컷	sil-keos	heartily
신체적	sin-che-jeog	physical	실태	sil-tae	the actual situation
신호	sin-ho	signal	실패	sil-pae	failure
신호등	sin-ho-deung	traffic light	실패한다	sil-pae-han-da	fail
신혼부부	sin-hon-bu-bu	newly married couple	실험	sil-heom	experiment
신혼여행	sin-hon-yeo-haeng	honeymoon	실현	sil-hyeon	realization
신화	sin-hwa	mythology	실현된다	sil-hyeon-doen-da	come true
싣는다	sid-neun-da	load	실현한다	sil-hyeon-han-da	realize
실	sil	thread	싫어진다	silh-eo-jin-da	hate
실감	sil-gam	realism	싫어한다	silh-eo-han-da	dislike
실내	sil-nae	inside	심각하다	sim-gag-ha-da	serious
실력	sil-lyeog	skill	심각해진다	sim-gag-hae-jin-da	get serious
실례	sil-lye	excuse	심는다	sim-neun-da	plant
실례한다	sil-lye-han-da	excuse me	심리	sim-li	mentality
실로	sil-lo	indeed	심리적	sim-li-jeog	psychological
실린다	sil-lin-da	be put on	심부름	sim-bu-reum	errand
실망	sil-mang	disappointment	심사	sim-sa	judge
실망한다	sil-mang-han-da	disappointed	심심하다	sim-sim-ha-da	bored
실수	sil-su	mistake	심장	sim-jang	heart
실수한다	sil-su-han-da	make a mistake	심정	sim-jeong	heart
실습	sil-seub	training	심판	sim-pan	referee
실시	sil-si	practice	심해진다	sim-hae-jin-da	get worse

싱겁다	sing-geob-da	bland	씨	ssi	seed
싱싱하다	sing-sing-ha-da	fresh	씨앗	ssi-as	seed
싫어진다	sip-eo-jin-da	want to	씩씩하다	ssig-ssig-ha-da	brave
싸구려	ssa-gu-ryeo	cheapie	씹다	ssib-da	chew
싸다	ssa-da	cheap	씻긴다	ssis-gin-da	wash
싸움	ssa-um	fight		ㅇ	
싹	ssag	bud	아가씨	a-ga-ssi	miss
싼값	ssan-gabs	cheap	아까	a-kka	earlier
쌍	ssang	pair	아깝다	a-kkab-da	what a waste
쌍둥이	ssang-dung-i	twins	아낀다	a-kkin-da	economize
쌓다	ssah-da	stack	아나운서	a-na-un-seo	announcer
쌓인다	ssah-in-da	stack up	아냐	a-nya	nope
썩	sseog	very	아뇨	a-nyo	no
썩는다	sseog-neun-da	rot	아니야	a-ni-ya	no
썬다	sseon-da	chop	아니요	a-ni-yo	no
썰렁하다	sseol-leong-ha-da	corny	아니하다	a-ni-ha-da	no
쏜다	sson-da	shot	아드님	a-deu-nim	son
쏟는다	ssod-neun-da	pour out	아래쪽	a-rae-jjog	down
쏟아진다	ssod-a-jin-da	pour out	아래층	a-rae-cheung	downstairs
쓰다듬는다	sseu-da-deum-neun-da	stroke	아랫사람	a-raes-sa-ram	subordinate
쓰러진다	sseu-reo-jin-da	fall down	아르바이트	a-reu-ba-i-teu	part time job
쓰레기통	sseu-re-gi-tong	trash can	아마도	a-ma-do	maybe
쓰인다	sseu-in-da	be used	아무개	a-mu-gae	so and so
쓴다	sseun-da	write	아무것	a-mu-geos	anything
쓴다	sseun-da	sweep	아무래도	a-mu-rae-do	probably
쓴맛	sseun-mas	bitterness	아무렇지 않다	a-mu-reoh-ji-anh-da	nothing
쓸데없다	sseul-de-eobs-da	useless	아무튼	a-mu-teun	anyway
쓸데없이	sseul-de-eobs-i	needlessly	아버님	a-beo-nim	father
쓸쓸하다	sseul-sseul-ha-da	lonely	아쉬움	a-swi-um	regret
씌운다	ssui-un-da	sheathe	아쉽다	a-swib-da	it's a shame
			아스팔트	a-seu-pal-teu	asphalt

아아	a-a	Oh oh!	안전	an-jeon	safety
아예	a-ye	at all	안전하다	an-jeon-ha-da	safe
아울러	a-ul-leo	together	안정	an-jeong	stability
아유	a-yu	aw	안정된다	an-jeong-doen-da	be stable
아이	a-i	child	안주	an-ju	snack
아이고	a-i-go	gosh	안쪽	an-jjog	inside
아이디어	a-i-di-eo	idea	안타깝다	an-ta-kkab-da	regretful
아이스크림	a-i-seu-keu-rim	ice cream	안팎	an-pakk	inside and outside
아주머니	a-ju-meo-ni	old lady	앉힌다	anj-hin-da	seat
아줌마	a-jum-ma	madame	않다	anh-da	not
아파트	a-pa-teu	apartment	알	al	egg
아픔	a-peum	pain	알루미늄	al-lu-mi-nyum	aluminum
아하	a-ha	aha	알맞다	al-maj-da	fit
악기	ag-gi	instrument	알아낸다	al-a-naen-da	to find out
악몽	ag-mong	nightmare	알아듣는다	al-a-deud-neun-da	understand
악수	ag-su	handshake	알아준다	al-a-jun-da	get to know
안	an	not	알코올	al-ko-ol	alcohol
안개	an-gae	fog	앓는다	alh-neun-da	be ill
안경	an-gyeong	glasses	암	am	cancer
안과	an-gwa	ophthalmology	암시	am-si	suggestion
안긴다	an-gin-da	embrace	암컷	am-keos	female
안내	an-nae	guidance	압력	ab-lyeog	pressure
안내한다	an-nae-han-da	guide	앞길	ap-gil	road ahead
안녕	an-nyeong	hi	앞날	ap-nal	future
안녕하다	an-nyeong-ha-da	peaceful	앞두고 있다	ap-du-go iss-da	ahead
안녕히	an-nyeong-hi	bye	앞뒤	ap-dwi	back and forth
안된다	an-doen-da	no	앞문	ap-mun	front door
안방	an-bang	inner room	앞바다	ap-ba-da	offshore
안부	an-bu	safety	앞서	ap-seo	previously
안심한다	an-sim-han-da	feel easy	앞선다	ap-seon-da	precede

앞세운다	ap-se-un-da	put ahead		얇다	yalb-da	thin
앞장선다	ap-jang-seon-da	take the lead		양	yang	amount
앞쪽	ap-jjog	front		양국	yang-gug	both countries
애	ae	baby		양념	yang-nyeom	seasoning
애쓴다	ae-sseun-da	try hard		양력	yang-lyeog	solar calendar
애인	ae-in	lover		양말	yang-mal	socks
애정	ae-jeong	affection		양배추	yang-bae-chu	cabbage
애초	ae-cho	in the first place		양보	yang-bo	concession
액세서리	aeg-se-seo-ri	accessory		양보한다	yang-bo-han-da	yield
액수	aeg-su	amount		양복	yang-bog	suit
앨범	ael-beom	album		양상추	yang-sang-chu	lettuce
야간	ya-gan	nighttime		양식	yang-sig	form
야단	ya-dan	scold		양심	yang-sim	conscience
야옹	ya-ong	meow		양옆	yang-yeop	both sides
야외	ya-oe	outdoor		양주	yang-ju	liquor
야채	ya-chae	vegetable		양쪽	yang-jjog	both sides
야하다	ya-ha-da	naughty		양파	yang-pa	onion
약	yag	approximately		얕다	yat-da	shallow
약간	yag-gan	a little		얘	yae	boy
약국	yag-gug	pharmacy		어긴다	eo-gin-da	violate
약속	yag-sog	promise		어느덧	eo-neu-deos	sooner or later
약속한다	yag-sog-han-da	promise		어느새	eo-neu-sae	suddenly
약수	yag-su	mineral water		어두워진다	eo-du-wo-jin-da	darken
약점	yag-jeom	weakness		어둠	eo-dum	darkness
약품	yag-pum	medicine		어둡다	eo-dub-da	dark
약하다	yag-ha-da	weak		어디	eo-di	where
약해진다	yag-hae-jin-da	weaken		어때	eo-ttae	What do you think?
약혼녀	yag-hon-nyeo	fiancee		어떠니	eo-tteo-ni	How about?
약혼자	yag-hon-ja	fiance		어떡하니	eo-tteog-ha-ni	what to do
얄밉다	yal-mib-da	stupid		어려움	eo-ryeo-um	difficulty

어려워진다	eo-ryeo-wo-jin-da	become difficult	얼른	eol-leun	hurry
어리다	eo-ri-da	young	얼린다	eol-lin-da	freeze
어리석다	eo-ri-seog-da	stupid	얼마간	eol-ma-gan	somewhat
어린아이	eo-rin-a-i	young kid	얼음	eol-eum	ice
어린애	eo-rin-ae	child	얼핏	eol-pis	at a glance
어린이날	eo-rin-i-nal	Children's Day	엄격하다	eom-gyeog-ha-da	strict
어머	eo-meo	oh	엄숙하다	eom-sug-ha-da	solemn
어머님	eo-meo-nim	mother	엄청나다	eom-cheong-na-da	tremendous
어색하다	eo-saeg-ha-da	awkward	업다	eob-da	carry
어서	eo-seo	hurry	업무	eob-mu	task
어저께	eo-jeo-kke	yesterday	업종	eob-jong	sectors
어제	eo-je	yesterday	업체	eob-che	company
어젯밤	eo-jes-bam	yesternight	없앤다	eobs-aen-da	delete
어지럽다	eo-ji-reob-da	dizzy	엇갈린다	eos-gal-lin-da	stagger
어째서	eo-jjae-seo	why	엉덩이	eong-deong-i	hip
어쨌든	eo-jjaess-deun	anyway	엉뚱하다	eong-ttung-ha-da	wrong
어쩌다	eo-jjeo-da	occasionally	엉망	eong-mang	mess
어쩌다가	eo-jjeo-da-ga	how come	엉터리	eong-teo-ri	nonsense
어쩌면	eo-jjeo-myeon	perhaps	엊그제	eoj-geu-je	a day or two ago
어쩐지	eo-jjeon-ji	no wonder	엎드린다	eop-deu-rin-da	kneel down
어쩜	eo-jjeom	how	에	e	to
어찌	eo-jji	how	에너지	e-neo-ji	energy
어찌나	eo-jji-na	how much	에어컨	e-eo-keon	air conditioner
어찌한다	eo-jji-han-da	what to do	엔진	en-jin	engine
억울하다	eog-ul-ha-da	It is unfair	엘리베이터	el-li-be-i-teo	elevator
언다	eon-da	freeze	여	yeo	female
언덕	eon-deog	hill	여가	yeo-ga	leisure
언젠가	eon-jen-ga	someday	여간	yeo-gan	little by little
얹는다	eonj-neun-da	put on	여건	yeo-geon	conditions
얻어먹는다	eod-eo-meog-neun-da	get eaten	여겨진다	yeo-gyeo-jin-da	be considered

여고생	yeo-go-saeng	high school girl	연결	yeon-gyeol	connection
여관	yeo-gwan	motel	연결된다	yeon-gyeol-doen-da	be connected
여군	yeo-gun	female soldier	연결한다	yeon-gyeol-han-da	interlink
여권	yeo-gwon	passport	연관	yeon-gwan	relation
여기저기	yeo-gi-jeo-gi	here and there	연구소	yeon-gu-so	laboratory
여긴다	yeo-gin-da	consider	연구실	yeon-gu-sil	lab
여대생	yeo-dae-saeng	college girl	연구원	yeon-gu-won	researcher
여동생	yeo-dong-saeng	younger sister	연구자	yeon-gu-ja	researcher
여든	yeo-deun	eighty	연구한다	yeon-gu-han-da	research
여러분	yeo-reo-bun	everyone	연기	yeon-gi	acting
여럿	yeo-reos	many	연기되었다	yeon-gi-doe-eoss-da	postponed
여론	yeo-ron	public opinion	연기자	yeon-gi-ja	actor
여름철	yeo-reum-cheol	summertime	연기한다	yeon-gi-han-da	adjourn
여보	yeo-bo	honey	연락	yeon-lag	communication
여보세요	yeo-bo-se-yo	hello	연락처	yeon-lag-cheo	contact
여왕	yeo-wang	queen	연락한다	yeon-lag-han-da	contact
여유	yeo-yu	relaxation	연령	yeon-lyeong	age
여인	yeo-in	woman	연말	yeon-mal	year-end
여전하다	yeo-jeon-ha-da	still	연상한다	yeon-sang-han-da	recall
여직원	yeo-jig-won	female employee	연설	yeon-seol	speech
여쭌다	yeo-jjun-da	ask	연세	yeon-se	age
여학생	yeo-hag-saeng	female student	연속	yeon-sog	continuity
여행사	yeo-haeng-sa	travel agency	연습	yeon-seub	practice
여행한다	yeo-haeng-han-da	travel	연습한다	yeon-seub-han-da	practice
역	yeog	station	연애	yeon-ae	romantic relationship
역사가	yeog-sa-ga	historian	연예인	yeon-ye-in	celebrity
역사상	yeog-sa-sang	in history	연인	yeon-in	couple
역사적	yeog-sa-jeog	historic	연장	yeon-jang	extension
역사학	yeog-sa-hag	history	연주	yeon-ju	play
연간	yeon-gan	yearly	연출	yeon-chul	production

연출한다	yeon-chul-han-da	direct	영화관	yeong-hwa-gwan	cinema
연하다	yeon-ha-da	soft	영화배우	yeong-hwa-bae-u	actor
연합	yeon-hab	union	영화제	yeong-hwa-je	film festival
연휴	yeon-hyu	holidays	옆구리	yeop-gu-ri	side
열	yeol	heat	옆방	yeop-bang	next door
열기	yeol-gi	heat	옆집	yeop-jib	next door
열린다	yeol-lin-da	open	예감	ye-gam	presentiment
열매	yeol-mae	fruit	예고한다	ye-go-han-da	foretell
열쇠	yeol-soe	key	예금	ye-geum	deposit
열정	yeol-jeong	enthusiasm	예매한다	ye-mae-han-da	reserve
열중한다	yeol-jung-han-da	be engrossed	예방	ye-bang	prevention
열차	yeol-cha	train	예방한다	ye-bang-han-da	prevent
열흘	yeol-heul	ten days	예보	ye-bo	forecast
엷다	yeolb-da	thin	예비	ye-bi	spare
염려	yeom-lyeo	worry	예산	ye-san	budget
염려한다	yeom-lyeo-han-da	concerned	예상	ye-sang	prediction
엽서	yeob-seo	postcard	예상된다	ye-sang-doen-da	expected
엿본다	yeos-bon-da	watch for	예상한다	ye-sang-han-da	expect
영	yeong	totally	예선	ye-seon	tryout
영남	yeong-nam	Gyeongsang-do	예술가	ye-sul-ga	artist
영상	yeong-sang	video	예술적	ye-sul-jeog	artistic
영양	yeong-yang	nutrition	예습	ye-seub	preview
영업	yeong-eob	sales	예습한다	ye-seub-han-da	study
영역	yeong-yeog	area	예식장	ye-sig-jang	wedding hall
영웅	yeong-ung	hero	예약	ye-yag	reservation
영원하다	yeong-won-ha-da	forever	예약한다	ye-yag-han-da	make a reservation
영원히	yeong-won-hi	forever	예외	ye-oe	exception
영하	yeong-ha	sub-zero	예의	ye-ui	courtesy
영향력	ycong-hyang-lycog	influence	예전	ye-jeon	previous
영혼	yeong-hon	soul	예절	ye-jeol	etiquette

예정된다	ye-jeong-doen-da	scheduled	온갖	on-gaj	all kinds of
예측한다	ye-cheug-han-da	predict	온도	on-do	temperature
예컨대	ye-keon-dae	for example	온돌	on-dol	on-dol
옛	yes	ancient	온라인	on-la-in	online
옛날이야기	yes-nal-i-ya-gi	old story	온몸	on-mom	whole body
오간다	o-gan-da	come and go	온종일	on-jong-il	all day
오락	o-rag	game	온통	on-tong	all
오래간만	o-rae-gan-man	long time no see	올	ol	this year
오래도록	o-rae-do-rog	for a long time	올가을	ol-ga-eul	this fall
오래되었다	o-rae-doe-eoss-da	longtime	올라선다	ol-la-seon-da	stand up
오래전	o-rae-jeon	lang syne	올라온다	ol-la-on-da	come up
오랜	o-raen	long-time	올라탄다	ol-la-tan-da	get on
오랜만	o-raen-man	long time no see	올려놓는다	ol-lyeo-noh-neun-da	put on
오랫동안	o-laes-dong-an	for a long time	올려다본다	ol-lyeo-da-bon-da	look up
오로지	o-ro-ji	only	올림픽	ol-lim-pig	Olympic
오르내린다	o-reu-nae-rin-da	go up and down	올바르다	ol-ba-reu-da	correct
오른발	o-reun-bal	right foot	올여름	ol-yeo-reum	this summer
오른손	o-reun-son	right hand	옳다	olh-da	right
오른쪽	o-reun-jjog	right	옷차림	os-cha-rim	getup
오븐	o-beun	oven	와	wa	wow
오염	o-yeom	pollution	와이셔츠	wa-i-syeo-cheu	shirt
오염된다	o-yeom-doen-da	be polluted	와인	wa-in	wine
오전	o-jeon	morning	완벽하다	wan-byeog-ha-da	perfect
오직	o-jig	only	완성	wan-seong	completion
오페라	o-pe-ra	opera	완성된다	wan-seong-doen-da	be completed
오피스텔	o-pi-seu-tel	officetels	완성한다	wan-seong-han-da	to complete
오해	o-hae	misunderstanding	완전	wan-jeon	very
옥상	og-sang	rooftop	완전하다	wan-jeon-ha-da	complete
옥수수	og-su-su	corn	왕	wang	king
온	on	all	왕비	wang-bi	queen

왕자	wang-ja	prince	요새	yo-sae	these days
왜냐하면	wae-nya-ha-myeon	because	요약한다	yo-yag-han-da	summarize
왠지	waen-ji	somehow	요일	yo-il	day of the week
외갓집	oe-gas-jib	mother's house	요즈음	yo-jeu-eum	these days
외과	oe-gwa	surgery	요청	yo-cheong	request
외교	oe-gyo	diplomacy	요청한다	yo-cheong-han-da	request
외교관	oe-gyo-gwan	diplomat	욕	yog	swear word
외국인	oe-gug-in	foreigner	욕실	yog-sil	bathroom
외로움	oe-ro-um	loneliness	욕심	yog-sim	greed
외롭다	oe-rob-da	lonely	욕한다	yog-han-da	swear
외면한다	oe-myeon-han-da	turn away	용	yong	dragon
외모	oe-mo	appearance	용감하다	yong-gam-ha-da	brave
외부	oe-bu	out	용기	yong-gi	courage
외아들	oe-a-deul	only son	용도	yong-do	purpose
외운다	oe-un-da	memorize	용돈	yong-don	pin money
외제	oe-je	foreign	용서	yong-seo	forgiveness
외출	oe-chul	outing	용서한다	yong-seo-han-da	forgive
외출한다	oe-chul-han-da	go out	용어	yong-eo	terms
외친다	oe-chin-da	shout out	우려	u-ryeo	concern
외침	oe-chim	shout	우리말	u-ri-mal	native language
외할머니	oe-hal-meo-ni	maternal grandmother	우산	u-san	umbrella
왼다	oen-da	memorize	우수하다	u-su-ha-da	great
왼발	oen-bal	left foot	우습다	u-seub-da	funny
왼손	oen-son	left hand	우승	u-seung	championship
왼쪽	oen-jjog	left	우승한다	u-seung-han-da	win
요구된다	yo-gu-doen-da	requested	우아하다	u-a-ha-da	elegant
요금	yo-geum	fee	우연히	u-yeon-hi	by chance
요리	yo-ri	dish	우울하다	u-ul-ha-da	depressed
요리사	yo-ri-sa	cook	우유	u-yu	milk
요리한다	yo-ri-han-da	cook	우정	u-jeong	friendship

우체국	u-che-gug	post office	원피스	won-pi-seu	(one-piece) dress
우편	u-pyeon	post	월	wol	month
우표	u-pyo	stamp	월급	wol-geub	salary
운	un	luck	월드컵	wol-deu-keob	World Cup
운동복	un-dong-bog	sportswear	월세	wol-se	monthly rent
운동장	un-dong-jang	playground	웨이터	we-i-teo	waiter
운동한다	un-dong-han-da	work out	웬만하다	wen-man-ha-da	tolerable
운동화	un-dong-hwa	running shoes	웬일	wen-il	for some reason
운명	un-myeong	fate	위기	wi-gi	crisis
운반	un-ban	carrying	위대하다	wi-dae-ha-da	great
운영한다	un-yeong-han-da	operate	위로	wi-ro	consolation
운전	un-jeon	driving	위로한다	wi-ro-han-da	console
운전기사	un-jeon-gi-sa	driver	위반	wi-ban	violation
운전사	un-jeon-sa	driver	위반한다	wi-ban-han-da	violate
운전자	un-jeon-ja	operator	위법	wi-beob	illegality
운전한다	un-jeon-han-da	drive	위성	wi-seong	satellite
운행	un-haeng	run	위아래	wi-a-rae	up and down
울린다	ul-lin-da	make cry	위원	wi-won	commissioner
울음	ul-eum	weeping	위원장	wi-won-jang	chairperson
울음소리	ul-eum-so-ri	crying sound	위주	wi-ju	mainly
움직임	um-jig-im	movement	위쪽	wi-jjog	topside
웃긴다	us-gin-da	funny	위층	wi-cheung	upstairs
웃어른	us-eo-reun	grown-up	위치한다	wi-chi-han-da	to be placed
웃음소리	us-eum-so-ri	laughter	위험	wi-heom	danger
워낙	wo-nag	so much	위험성	wi-heom-seong	risks
원	won	original	위험하다	wi-heom-ha-da	dangerous
원고	won-go	manuscript	위협	wi-hyeob	threat
원래	won-lae	originally	윗몸	wis-mom	upper body
원서	won-seo	application	윗사람	wis-sa-ram	superior
원장	won-jang	director	유교	yu-gyo	Confucianism

유난히	yu-nan-hi	exceptionally		음료수	eum-lyo-su	drink
유능하다	yu-neung-ha-da	competent		음반	eum-ban	record
유리	yu-ri	glass		음성	eum-seong	voice
유리창	yu-ri-chang	window		음식물	eum-sig-mul	food and drink
유리하다	yu-ri-ha-da	advantageous		음식점	eum-sig-jeom	restaurant
유머	yu-meo	humor		음악가	eum-ag-ga	musician
유명	yu-myeong	famous		음주	eum-ju	drinking
유명하다	yu-myeong-ha-da	famous		응	eung	yes
유물	yu-mul	relics		응답한다	eung-dab-han-da	to respond
유발한다	yu-bal-han-da	cause		의논	ui-non	discussion
유사하다	yu-sa-ha-da	similar		의논한다	ui-non-han-da	discuss
유산	yu-san	legacy		의도	ui-do	intent
유의한다	yu-ui-han-da	take note		의도적	ui-do-jeog	intentionally
유적	yu-jeog	ruins		의류	ui-ryu	clothing
유적지	yu-jeog-ji	historic sites		의무	ui-mu	duty
유지된다	yu-ji-doen-da	be maintained		의문	ui-mun	question
유치원	yu-chi-won	kindergarden		의미한다	ui-mi-han-da	mean
유학	yu-hag	study abroad		의복	ui-bog	cloth
유학생	yu-hag-saeng	foreign student		의사	ui-sa	doctor
유행	yu-haeng	trend		의식	ui-sig	consciousness
유행한다	yu-haeng-han-da	popular		의식한다	ui-sig-han-da	be conscious
유형	yu-hyeong	category		의심	ui-sim	doubt
육체	yug-che	flesh		의심한다	ui-sim-han-da	doubt
육체적	yug-che-jeog	physical		의외로	ui-oe-ro	surprisingly
으레	eu-re	usually		의욕	ui-yog	will
으응	eu-eung	yes		의원	ui-won	lawmaker
은	eun	silver		의자	ui-ja	chair
은은하다	eun-eun-ha-da	soft		의존한다	ui-jon-han-da	be dependent
음력	eum-lyeog	lunar		의지한다	ui-ji-han-da	rely
음료	eum-lyo	beverage		이	i	this

이같이	i-gat-i	like this		이발소	i-bal-so	barbershop
이것저것	i-geos-jeo-geos	this and that		이별	i-byeol	farewell
이곳저곳	i-gos-jeo-gos	all over the place		이분	i-bun	this man
이긴다	i-gin-da	win		이불	i-bul	bedding
이끈다	i-kkeun-da	lead		이빨	i-ppal	teeth
이념	i-nyeom	ideology		이사	i-sa	move
이놈	i-nom	this guy		이사장	i-sa-jang	chairman
이다음	i-da-eum	next		이사한다	i-sa-han-da	move house
이달	i-dal	this month		이상	i-sang	more than
이대로	i-dae-ro	like this		이상적	i-sang-jeog	ideal
이데올로기	i-de-ol-lo-gi	ideology		이성	i-seong	reason
이동	i-dong	move		이슬	i-seul	dew
이동한다	i-dong-han-da	move		이어	i-eo	following
이따가	i-tta-ga	later		이어서	i-eo-seo	next
이따금	i-tta-geum	sometimes		이외	i-oe	other than
이래	i-rae	since		이용	i-yong	use
이래서	i-rae-seo	for this reason		이용된다	i-yong-doen-da	be used
이러다	i-reo-da	like this		이용자	i-yong-ja	user
이런저런	i-reon-jeo-reon	this or that		이웃집	i-us-jib	next door
이력서	i-ryeog-seo	resume		이월	i-wol	carried over to
이론적	i-ron-jeog	theoretical		이윽고	i-eug-go	finally
이롭다	i-rob-da	beneficial		이익	i-ig	profit
이룩한다	i-rug-han-da	achieve		이자	i-ja	interest
이뤄진다	i-rwo-jin-da	come true		이제야	i-je-ya	now
이르다	i-reu-da	early		이중	i-jung	double
이리	i-ri	wolf		이쪽	i-jjog	this way
이리저리	i-ri-jeo-ri	back and forth		이튿날	i-teud-nal	the next day
이마	i-ma	forehead		이하	i-ha	below
이미지	i-mi-ji	image		이해	i-hae	understanding
이민	i-min	immigrant		이해관계	i-hae-gwan-gye	interest

이해된다	i-hae-doen-da	understand	인제	in-je	now
이혼	i-hon	divorce	인종	in-jong	race
이혼한다	i-hon-han-da	divorce	인체	in-che	anatomy
익다	ig-da	ripe	인터넷	in-teo-nes	internet
익숙하다	ig-sug-ha-da	be used to	인터뷰	in-teo-byu	interview
익숙해진다	ig-sug-hae-jin-da	accustomed	인하	in-ha	cut
익힌다	ig-hin-da	cook	인형	in-hyeong	doll
인간관계	in-gan-gwan-gye	relationships	일기	il-gi	diary
인간성	in-gan-seong	humanity	일대	il-dae	the whole area
인간적	in-gan-jeog	human	일등	il-deung	first class
인격	in-gyeog	personality	일반인	il-ban-in	public
인공	in-gong	being artificial	일반적인	il-ban-jeog-in	in general
인구	in-gu	population	일본어	il-bon-eo	Japanese
인근	in-geun	vicinity	일부러	il-bu-reo	intentionally
인도	in-do	pavement	일상	il-sang	daily life
인분	in-bun	servings	일상생활	il-sang-saeng-hwal	everyday life
인사	in-sa	greetings	일상적	il-sang-jeog	routine
인사말	in-sa-mal	greetings	일생	il-saeng	lifetime
인사한다	in-sa-han-da	greet	일손	il-son	worker
인삼	in-sam	ginseng	일시적	il-si-jeog	temporary
인삼차	in-sam-cha	ginseng tea	일식	il-sig	solar eclipse
인상	in-sang	impression	일쑤	il-ssu	occasionally
인상적	in-sang-jeog	impressive	일어선다	il-eo-seon-da	get up
인쇄	in-swae	print	일일이	il-il-i	one by one
인식한다	in-sig-han-da	recognize	일자리	il-ja-ri	job
인연	in-yeon	destiny	일정	il-jeong	schedule
인원	in-won	personnel	일정하다	il-jeong-ha-da	constant
인재	in-jae	human resources	일종	il-jong	kind
인정된다	in-jeong-doen-da	be recognized	일주일	il-ju-il	one week
인정받는다	in-jeong-bad-neun-da	receive approval	일찍	il-jjig	early

일찍이	il-jjig-i	early		잇따른다	is-tta-reun-da	successive
일체	il-che	entire		잊어버린다	ij-eo-beo-rin-da	forget
일치	il-chi	same		잊혀진다	ij-hyeo-jin-da	be forgotten
일치한다	il-chi-han-da	coincide		**ㅈ**		
일행	il-haeng	party		자가용	ja-ga-yong	own car
일회용	il-hoe-yong	disposable		자격	ja-gyeog	qualification
일회용품	il-hoe-yong-pum	disposable		자격증	ja-gyeog-jeung	certificate
읽힌다	ilg-hin-da	be read		자극	ja-geug	stimulus
잃어버린다	ilh-eo-beo-rin-da	lose		자극한다	ja-geug-han-da	stimulate
임금	im-geum	wage		자꾸	ja-kku	repeatedly
임무	im-mu	mission		자꾸만	ja-kku-man	again and again
임시	im-si	temporary		자네	ja-ne	you
임신	im-sin	pregnant		자녀	ja-nyeo	children
임신부	im-sin-bu	pregnant woman		자동	ja-dong	automatic
임신한다	im-sin-han-da	get pregnant		자라난다	ja-ra-nan-da	grow up
입구	ib-gu	entrance		자랑	ja-rang	boast
입국	ib-gug	entrance		자랑스럽다	ja-rang-seu-reob-da	proud
입대	ib-dae	enlistment		자랑한다	ja-rang-han-da	boast
입력	ib-lyeog	input		자른다	ja-reun-da	cut
입력한다	ib-lyeog-han-da	enter		자리	ja-ri	seat
입맛	ib-mas	taste		자매	ja-mae	sisters
입사	ib-sa	joining a company		자부심	ja-bu-sim	pride
입사한다	ib-sa-han-da	join a company		자살	ja-sal	suicide
입술	ib-sul	lip		자살한다	ja-sal-han-da	commit suicide
입시	ib-si	entrance exam		자세하다	ja-se-ha-da	detailed
입원	ib-won	admission		자세히	ja-se-hi	in detail
입원한다	ib-won-han-da	hospitalize		자신	ja-sin	self
입학	ib-hag	admission		자신감	ja-sin-gam	confidence
입학한다	ib-hag-han-da	enter a school		자연적	ja-yeon-jeog	natural
입힌다	ib-hin-da	plate		자연현상	ja-yeon-hyeon-sang	natural phenomenon
				자연환경	ja-yeon-hwan-gyeong	natural environment

자연히	ja-yeon-hi	naturally	잠긴다	jam-gin-da	sink
자원	ja-won	resource	잠깐	jam-kkan	for a moment
자유롭다	ja-yu-rob-da	free	잠든다	jam-deun-da	fall asleep
자율	ja-yul	autonomy	잠바	jam-ba	jacket
자장면	ja-jang-myeon	jajangmyeon	잠수함	jam-su-ham	submarine
자전거	ja-jeon-geo	bicycle	잠시	jam-si	for a moment
자정	ja-jeong	midnight	잠옷	jam-os	pajamas
자존심	ja-jon-sim	pride	잠자리	jam-ja-ri	dragonfly
자취	ja-chwi	trace	잠잔다	jam-jan-da	sleep
자판	ja-pan	keyboard	잡수신다	jab-su-sin-da	eat
자판기	ja-pan-gi	vending machine	잡순다	jab-sun-da	eat
작성	jag-seong	write	잡아당긴다	jab-a-dang-gin-da	pull
작성한다	jag-seong-han-da	draw up	잡아먹는다	jab-a-meog-neun-da	eat
작아진다	jag-a-jin-da	get smaller	잡지	jab-ji	magazine
작용	jag-yong	action	잡힌다	jab-hin-da	be caught
작용한다	jag-yong-han-da	act	장	jang	sheet
작은아들	jag-eun-a-deul	little son	장가	jang-ga	marry
잔디	jan-di	grass	장군	jang-gun	general
잔디밭	jan-di-bat	lawn	장기간	jang-gi-gan	long term
잔뜩	jan-tteug	loads	장기적	jang-gi-jeog	long term
잔치	jan-chi	party	장난	jang-nan	joke
잘났다	jal-nass-da	good job	장난감	jang-nan-gam	toy
잘된다	jal-doen-da	go well	장남	jang-nam	eldest son
잘린다	jal-lin-da	cut	장래	jang-lae	future
잘못	jal-mos	mistake	장례	jang-lye	funeral
잘못된다	jal-mos-doen-da	go wrong	장례식	jang-lye-sig	funeral
잘못한다	jal-mos-han-da	do wrong	장르	jang-reu	genre
잘산다	jal-san-da	live well	장마	jang-ma	the rainy season
잘생겼다	jal-saeng-gyeoss-da	handsome	장면	jang-myeon	scene
잠근다	jam-geun-da	lock	장비	jang-bi	equipment

장사	jang-sa	business	저것	jeo-geos	that
장사꾼	jang-sa-kkun	merchant	저고리	jeo-go-ri	jeogori
장소	jang-so	location	저곳	jeo-gos	over there
장수	jang-su	long live	저기요	jeo-gi-yo	excuse me
장식	jang-sig	decoration	저녁때	jeo-nyeog-ttae	evening
장애인	jang-ae-in	disabled	저러다	jeo-reo-da	like that
장점	jang-jeom	advantages	저런	jeo-reon	like that
장차	jang-cha	future	저렇다	jeo-reoh-da	like that
장학금	jang-hag-geum	scholarship	저리로	jeo-ri-ro	there
잦다	jaj-da	often	저마다	jeo-ma-da	each
재능	jae-neung	talent	저번	jeo-beon	last time
재다	jae-da	measure	저울	jeo-ul	scale
재미	jae-mi	fun	저자	jeo-ja	author
재미없다	jae-mi-eobs-da	not funny	저절로	jeo-jeol-lo	by itself
재밌다	jae-miss-da	fun	저지른다	jeo-ji-reun-da	commit
재빨리	jae-bbal-li	quickly	저쪽	jeo-jjog	there
재생	jae-saeng	recycling	저축	jeo-chug	saving
재수	jae-su	luck	저편	jeo-pyeon	the other side
재운다	jae-un-da	put sb to sleep	저희	jeo-hui	we
재작년	jae-jag-nyeon	the year before last	적	jeog	enemy
재정	jae-jeong	finance	적극	jeog-geug	actively
재주	jae-ju	skill	적극적	jeog-geug-jeog	active
재즈	jae-jeu	jazz	적다	jeog-da	little
재채기	jae-chae-gi	sneeze	적당하다	jeog-dang-ha-da	suitable
재판	jae-pan	trial	적당히	jeog-dang-hi	moderately
재학	jae-hag	attending	적성	jeog-seong	aptitude
재활용	jae-hwal-yong	recycle	적어도	jeog-eo-do	at least
재활용품	jae-hwal-yong-pum	recyclables	적어진다	jeog-eo-jin-da	become less
저	jeo	um	적용	jeog-yong	application
저거	jeo-geo	that	적용된다	jeog-yong-doen-da	applied

적용한다	jeog-yong-han-da	apply		전세	jeon-se	charter
적응	jeog-eung	adaptation		전시	jeon-si	exhibition
적응한다	jeog-eung-han-da	adapt		전시된다	jeon-si-doen-da	be exhibited
적절하다	jeog-jeol-ha-da	appropriate		전시장	jeon-si-jang	showroom
적합하다	jeog-hab-ha-da	suitable		전시한다	jeon-si-han-da	display
적힌다	jeog-hin-da	write down		전시회	jeon-si-hoe	exhibition
전개	jeon-gae	deployment		전용	jeon-yong	private
전개된다	jeon-gae-doen-da	unfold		전자	jeon-ja	electronic
전개한다	jeon-gae-han-da	unfold		전철	jeon-cheol	subway
전공	jeon-gong	major		전체적	jeon-che-jeog	overall
전공한다	jeon-gong-han-da	specialize		전통문화	jeon-tong-mun-hwa	traditional culture
전구	jeon-gu	bulb		전통적	jeon-tong-jeog	traditional
전국적	jeon-gug-jeog	nationwide		전해진다	jeon-hae-jin-da	transmitted
전기	jeon-gi	electric		전화기	jeon-hwa-gi	cellphone
전기밥솥	jeon-gi-bab-sot	electric rice cooker		전화번호	jeon-hwa-beon-ho	phone number
전날	jeon-nal	eve		전화한다	jeon-hwa-han-da	make a phone call
전달	jeon-dal	relay		전환	jeon-hwan	transform
전달된다	jeon-dal-doen-da	delivered		전환한다	jeon-hwan-han-da	switch
전달한다	jeon-dal-han-da	deliver		전후	jeon-hu	sequence
전망	jeon-mang	view		절대	jeol-dae	absolutely
전망한다	jeon-mang-han-da	view		절대로	jeol-dae-ro	absolutely
전문가	jeon-mun-ga	expert		절대적	jeol-dae-jeog	absolute
전문적	jeon-mun-jeog	professional		절망	jeol-mang	despair
전문점	jeon-mun-jeom	specialty store		절반	jeol-ban	half
전문직	jeon-mun-jig	profession		절약	jeol-yag	saving
전반	jeon-ban	first half		절약한다	jeol-yag-han-da	retrench
전반적	jeon-ban-jeog	overall		절차	jeol-cha	step
전부	jeon-bu	entire		젊은이	jeolm-eun-i	young people
전선	jeon-seon	wire		젊음	jeolm-eum	youth
전설	jeon-seol	legend		점	jeom	dot

점검	jeom-geom	check	정문	jeong-mun	front door
점수	jeom-su	score	정반대	jeong-ban-dae	contrary
점심	jeom-sim	lunch	정보화	jeong-bo-hwa	informatization
점심때	jeom-sim-ttae	at lunch	정비	jeong-bi	maintenance
점심시간	jeom-sim-si-gan	lunch hour	정상	jeong-sang	normal
점원	jeom-won	clerk	정상적	jeong-sang-jeog	normal
점잖다	jeom-janh-da	be gentle	정성	jeong-seong	sincerity
점점	jeom-jeom	increasingly	정식	jeong-sig	formal
점차	jeom-cha	gradually	정신과	jeong-sin-gwa	psychiatry
접근	jeob-geun	access	정신없이	jeong-sin-eobs-i	crazy
접근한다	jeob-geun-han-da	draw close	정신적	jeong-sin-jeog	mental
접는다	jeob-neun-da	fold	정오	jeong-o	noon
접시	jeob-si	dish	정원	jeong-won	garden
접촉	jeob-chog	contact	정장	jeong-jang	suit
접한다	jeob-han-da	meet	정지	jeong-ji	stop
젓가락	jeos-ga-rag	chopsticks	정직하다	jeong-jig-ha-da	be honest
젓다	jeos-da	row	정치권	jeong-chi-gwon	political circles
정	jeong	affection	정치인	jeong-chi-in	politician
정거장	jeong-geo-jang	station	정치적	jeong-chi-jeog	political
정기	jeong-gi	routine	정치학	jeong-chi-hag	politics
정기적	jeong-gi-jeog	regularly	정해진다	jeong-hae-jin-da	destined
정답	jeong-dab	answer	정확히	jeong-hwag-hi	exactly
정당	jeong-dang	party	젖	jeoj	milk
정류장	jeong-ryu-jang	station	젖다	jeoj-da	get wet
정리	jeong-li	organize	제거한다	je-geo-han-da	remove
정리된다	jeong-li-doen-da	tidy up	제공	je-gong	offer
정리한다	jeong-li-han-da	straighten out	제공한다	je-gong-han-da	offer
정말	jeong-mal	really	제과점	je-gwa-jeom	bakery
정말로	jeong-mal-lo	really	제대한다	je-dae-han-da	be discharged
정면	jeong-myeon	face	제도적	je-do-jeog	institutional

제목	je-mog	title	조깅	jo-ging	jogging
제발	je-bal	please	조른다	jo-reun-da	tease
제법	je-beob	quite	조명	jo-myeong	light
제비	je-bi	swallow	조미료	jo-mi-ryo	condiment
제사	je-sa	ancestral rites	조상	jo-sang	ancestor
제삿날	je-sas-nal	memorial day	조심스럽다	jo-sim-seu-reob-da	be careful
제시	je-si	proposal	조용하다	jo-yong-ha-da	silent
제시된다	je-si-doen-da	presented	조용히	jo-yong-hi	quietly
제안	je-an	proposal	조절	jo-jeol	control
제안한다	je-an-han-da	propose	조절한다	jo-jeol-han-da	modulate
제약	je-yag	restrictions	조정	jo-jeong	adjustment
제외된다	je-oe-doen-da	excluded	조정한다	jo-jeong-han-da	mediate
제외한다	je-oe-han-da	except	조화된다	jo-hwa-doen-da	harmonize
제의	je-ui	suggest	존경한다	jon-gyeong-han-da	respect
제의한다	je-ui-han-da	offer	존다	jon-da	snooze
제자	je-ja	student	존댓말	jon-daes-mal	polite word
제자리	je-ja-ri	place	존중한다	jon-jung-han-da	respect
제작	je-jag	produce	졸리다	jol-li-da	sleepy
제작한다	je-jag-han-da	produce	졸업	jol-eob	graduation
제출	je-chul	submission	졸업생	jol-eob-saeng	graduate
제출한다	je-chul-han-da	submit	졸업한다	jol-eob-han-da	graduate
제한	je-han	limit	졸음	jol-eum	drowsiness
제한된다	je-han-doen-da	be limited	좁다	job-da	narrow
제한한다	je-han-han-da	limit	좁힌다	job-hin-da	make narrow
조	jo	article	종	jong	bell
조각	jo-gag	piece	종교적	jong-gyo-jeog	religious
조그마하다	jo-geu-ma-ha-da	small	종소리	jong-so-ri	knell
조그맣다	jo-geu-mah-da	small	종업원	jong-eob-won	employee
조금씩	jo-geum-ssig	gradually	종이	jong-i	paper
조기	jo-gi	early	종이컵	jong-i-keob	paper cup

종일	jong-il	all day	주어진다	ju-eo-jin-da	be given
종종	jong-jong	often	주요	ju-yo	main
종합	jong-hab	synthesis	주요하다	ju-yo-ha-da	major
종합한다	jong-hab-han-da	put together	주의	ju-ui	caution
좋아	joh-a	great	주의한다	ju-ui-han-da	pay heed to
좋아진다	joh-a-jin-da	get better	주인공	ju-in-gong	hero
좌석	jwa-seog	seat	주일	ju-il	weekend
좌우	jwa-u	right and left	주저앉는다	ju-jeo-anj-neun-da	sit down
죄	joe	crime	주차	ju-cha	parking
죄송하다	joe-song-ha-da	sorry	주차한다	ju-cha-han-da	park
죄인	joe-in	sinner	주택	ju-taeg	housing
주	ju	main	주한	ju-han	Korea
주거	ju-geo	dwelling	죽	jug	porridge
주고받는다	ju-go-bad-neun-da	give and take	죽는다	jug-neun-da	die
주관적	ju-gwan-jeog	subjective	죽은 척	jug-eun cheog	playing dead
주년	ju-nyeon	anniversary	죽인다	jug-in-da	kill
주름	ju-reum	wrinkle	준다	jun-da	shrink
주름살	ju-reum-sal	wrinkles	준비	jun-bi	preparation
주말	ju-mal	weekend	준비되었다	jun-bi-doe-eoss-da	be ready
주머니	ju-meo-ni	pocket	준비물	jun-bi-mul	materials
주먹	ju-meog	fist	준비한다	jun-bi-han-da	prepare
주무신다	ju-mu-sin-da	sleep	줄	jul	line
주문	ju-mun	order	줄거리	jul-geo-ri	summary
주문한다	ju-mun-han-da	order	줄곧	jul-god	all the way
주방	ju-bang	kitchen	줄기	jul-gi	stem
주부	ju-bu	housewife	줄무늬	jul-mu-nui	stripe
주사	ju-sa	injection	줄어든다	jul-eo-deun-da	decrease
주소	ju-so	address	줍는다	jub-neun-da	pick up
주스	ju-seu	juice	중간	jung-gan	middle
주식	ju-sig	stock	중계방송	jung-gye-bang-song	broadcast

중국어	jung-gug-eo	Chinese		증명한다	jeung-myeong-han-da	prove
중국집	jung-gug-jib	Chinese restaurant		증상	jeung-sang	symptom
중년	jung-nyeon	middle-age		증세	jeung-se	symptom
중단	jung-dan	stop		지각	ji-gag	tardy
중단된다	jung-dan-doen-da	stop		지갑	ji-gab	wallet
중단한다	jung-dan-han-da	stop		지겹다	ji-gyeob-da	boring
중대하다	jung-dae-ha-da	great		지경	ji-gyeong	situation
중독	jung-dog	addiction		지극히	ji-geug-hi	extremely
중반	jung-ban	mid		지금껏	ji-geum-kkeos	so far
중부	jung-bu	central		지급	ji-geub	payments
중세	jung-se	middle ages		지급한다	ji-geub-han-da	pay
중소기업	jung-so-gi-eob	small business		지나친다	ji-na-chin-da	go too far
중순	jung-sun	mid		지난날	ji-nan-nal	last day
중식	jung-sig	Chinese food		지난달	ji-nan-dal	last month
중심지	jung-sim-ji	center		지난번	ji-nan-beon	last time
중얼거린다	jung-eol-geo-rin-da	murmur		지난주	ji-nan-ju	last week
중요	jung-yo	important		지능	ji-neung	intellect
중요성	jung-yo-seong	importance		지대	ji-dae	belt
중요시한다	jung-yo-si-han-da	give importance		지도	ji-do	map
중학생	jung-hag-saeng	middle schooler		지도자	ji-do-ja	leader
쥔다	jwin-da	hold		지도한다	ji-do-han-da	lead
즉석	jeug-seog	instant		지루하다	ji-ru-ha-da	bored
즉시	jeug-si	immediately		지른다	ji-reun-da	kick
즐거움	jeul-geo-um	joy		지름길	ji-reum-gil	shortcut
즐거워한다	jeul-geo-wo-han-da	have fun		지방	ji-bang	province
증가	jeung-ga	increase		지배한다	ji-bae-han-da	rule
증가한다	jeung-ga-han-da	increase		지불한다	ji-bul-han-da	pay
증거	jeung-geo	evidence		지붕	ji-bung	roof
증권	jeung-gwon	stock		지속된다	ji-sog-doen-da	continue
증권사	jeung-gwon-sa	brokerage		지속적	ji-sog-jeog	constant

지시	ji-si	instruction	진급	jin-geub	promotion
지시한다	ji-si-han-da	instruct	진다	jin-da	lose
지식인	ji-sig-in	intellectual	진단	jin-dan	diagnosis
지우개	ji-u-gae	eraser	진단한다	jin-dan-han-da	diagnose
지운다	ji-un-da	erase	진동	jin-dong	vibration
지워진다	ji-wo-jin-da	be erased	진로	jin-lo	course
지원한다	ji-won-han-da	apply	진료	jin-lyo	diagnosis
지위	ji-wi	status	진리	jin-li	truth
지저분하다	ji-jeo-bun-ha-da	dirty	진실	jin-sil	truth
지적	ji-jeog	point out	진실로	jin-sil-lo	truly
지적된다	ji-jeog-doen-da	pointed out	진심	jin-sim	sincerity
지점	ji-jeom	point	진지하다	jin-ji-ha-da	serious
지지	ji-ji	support	진짜	jin-jja	really
지진	ji-jin	earthquake	진찰	jin-chal	examination
지출	ji-chul	expenditure	진출	jin-chul	debouchment
지친다	ji-chin-da	exhausted	진출한다	jin-chul-han-da	advance
지켜본다	ji-kyeo-bon-da	watch	진통	jin-tong	throes
지폐	ji-pye	paper money	진하다	jin-ha-da	thick
지하	ji-ha	underground	진행	jin-haeng	progress
지하도	ji-ha-do	underpass	진행된다	jin-haeng-doen-da	proceed
지하철	ji-ha-cheol	subway	진행자	jin-haeng-ja	MC
지혜	ji-hye	wisdom	진행한다	jin-haeng-han-da	progress
직선	jig-seon	straight	질	jil	quality
직업	jig-eob	job	질문	jil-mun	question
직원	jig-won	employee	질문한다	jil-mun-han-da	ask a question
직장인	jig-jang-in	office workers	질병	jil-byeong	disease
직전	jig-jeon	just before	질적	jil-jeog	qualitative
직접	jig-jeob	directly	짐	jim	load
직접적	jig-jeob-jeog	direct	짐작	jim-jag	guesswork
직후	jig-hu	immediately after	짐작한다	jim-jag-han-da	guess

				ㅊ	
집다	jib-da	pick up	차갑다	cha-gab-da	cold
집단적	jib-dan-jeog	collective	차남	cha-nam	second son
집안	jib-an	house management	차다	cha-da	cold
집안일	jib-an-il	housework	차라리	cha-ra-ri	rather
집어넣는다	jib-eo-neoh-neun-da	put in	차량	cha-ryang	vehicle
집중	jib-jung	concentration	차린다	cha-rin-da	set up
집중된다	jib-jung-doen-da	be focused	차림	cha-rim	outfit
집중적	jib-jung-jeog	intensive	차마	cha-ma	for the world
집중한다	jib-jung-han-da	concentrate upon	차별	cha-byeol	discrimination
짓	jis	act	차선	cha-seon	lane
짙다	jit-da	thick	차이점	cha-i-jeom	difference
짚는다	jip-neun-da	point out	차차	cha-cha	gradually
짜다	jja-da	salty	차창	cha-chang	car window
짜증	jja-jeung	petulance	차츰	cha-cheum	gradually
짜증스럽다	jja-jeung-seu-reob-da	annoying	착각	chag-gag	illusion
짝	jjag	match	착각한다	chag-gag-han-da	be mistaken
짧아진다	jjalb-a-jin-da	shorten	착하다	chag-ha-da	be good
쩔쩔맨다	jjeol-jjeol-maen-da	be embarrassed	찬물	chan-mul	cold water
쪽	jjog	side	찬성	chan-seong	consent
쫓겨난다	jjoch-gyeo-nan-da	kicked out	찬성한다	chan-seong-han-da	agree
쫓긴다	jjoch-gin-da	be chased	참	cham	alas
쫓는다	jjoch-neun-da	run	참가	cham-ga	participation
쭉	jjug	all the way	참가한다	cham-ga-han-da	participate
찌개	jji-gae	stew	참고한다	cham-go-han-da	refer to
찌꺼기	jji-kkeo-gi	leftover	참기름	cham-gi-reum	sesame oil
찐다	jjin-da	steam	참는다	cham-neun-da	suppress
찌른다	jji-reun-da	stab	참된다	cham-doen-da	be true
찍는다	jjig-neun-da	stamp	참새	cham-sae	sparrow
찍힌다	jjig-hin-da	take a picture	참석	cham-seog	attendance
찢는다	jjij-neun-da	tear			
찢어진다	jjij-eo-jin-da	torn			

참석자	cham-seog-ja	attendee	책방	chaeg-bang	bookstore
참석한다	cham-seog-han-da	attend	책상	chaeg-sang	table
참여	cham-yeo	participation	책임감	chaeg-im-gam	responsibility
참여한다	cham-yeo-han-da	participate	책임자	chaeg-im-ja	person in charge
참외	cham-oe	melon	책임진다	chaeg-im-jin-da	be in charge
참으로	cham-eu-ro	indeed	챔피언	chaem-pi-eon	champion
참조	cham-jo	reference	챙긴다	chaeng-gin-da	take
찻잔	chas-jan	teacup	처녀	cheo-nyeo	virgin
창	chang	window	처리	cheo-ri	process
창가	chang-ga	window	처벌	cheo-beol	punishment
창고	chang-go	warehouse	처지	cheo-ji	situation
창구	chang-gu	window	척	cheog	as if
창문	chang-mun	window	척한다	cheog-han-da	pretend
창밖	chang-bakk	out the window	천	cheon	cloth
창작	chang-jag	creation	천국	cheon-gug	heaven
창조	chang-jo	creation	천둥	cheon-dung	thunder
창조적	chang-jo-jeog	creative	천장	cheon-jang	ceiling
창조한다	chang-jo-han-da	create	천재	cheon-jae	genius
창피하다	chang-pi-ha-da	embarrassing	천천히	cheon-cheon-hi	slowly
찾아간다	chaj-a-gan-da	go look for	철	cheol	steel
찾아낸다	chaj-a-naen-da	find out	철도	cheol-do	railroad
찾아다닌다	chaj-a-da-nin-da	look for	철저하다	cheol-jeo-ha-da	thorough
찾아본다	chaj-a-bon-da	look for	철저히	cheol-jeo-hi	thoroughly
찾아온다	chaj-a-on-da	come	철학	cheol-hag	philosophy
채	chae	stick	철학자	cheol-hag-ja	philosopher
채널	chae-neol	channel	철학적	cheol-hag-jeog	philosophical
채소	chae-so	vegetable	첫날	cheos-nal	first day
채운다	chae-un-da	fill	첫째	cheos-jjae	first
채점	chae-jeom	grading	청년	cheong-nyeon	youth
책가방	chaeg-ga-bang	school bag	청바지	cheong-ba-ji	jeans

청소	cheong-so	clean	초저녁	cho-jeo-nyeog	early evening
청소기	cheong-so-gi	vacuum cleaner	초점	cho-jeom	focus
청소년	cheong-so-nyeon	teenager	초조하다	cho-jo-ha-da	be nervous
청소한다	cheong-so-han-da	clean	초청	cho-cheong	invitation
청춘	cheong-chun	youth	초청장	cho-cheong-jang	invitation
청한다	cheong-han-da	ask	초청한다	cho-cheong-han-da	invite
체계적	che-gye-jeog	systematic	초콜릿	cho-kol-lis	chocolate
체력	che-ryeog	health	촌스럽다	chon-seu-reob-da	rustic
체온	che-on	temperature	촛불	chos-bul	candlelight
체육	che-yug	athletic	총	chong	gun
체육관	che-yug-gwan	gym	총각	chong-gag	bachelor
체중	che-jung	weight	총리	chong-li	prime minister
체한다	che-han-da	pretend	총장	chong-jang	president
체험	che-heom	experience	촬영	chwal-yeong	filming
체험한다	che-heom-han-da	experience	최고급	choe-go-geub	top quality
쳐다본다	chyeo-da-bon-da	look at	최대	choe-dae	maximum
초	cho	candle	최대한	choe-dae-han	most
초대	cho-dae	invitation	최상	choe-sang	the best
초대한다	cho-dae-han-da	invite	최선	choe-seon	best
초등학교	cho-deung-hag-gyo	elementary school	최소	choe-so	least
초등학생	cho-deung-hag-saeng	elementary student	최소한	choe-so-han	at least
초록색	cho-rog-saeg	green	최신	choe-sin	new
초반	cho-ban	early	최악	choe-ag	worst
초밥	cho-bab	sushi	최저	choe-jeo	lowest
초보	cho-bo	beginner	최종	choe-jong	final
초보자	cho-bo-ja	beginner	최초	choe-cho	the first
초상화	cho-sang-hwa	portrait	최후	choe-hu	last
초순	cho-sun	early in	추가	chu-ga	addition
초여름	cho-yeo-reum	early summer	추가된다	chu-ga-doen-da	added
초원	cho-won	grassland	추가한다	chu-ga-han-da	add

추석	chu-seog	thanksgiving	출장	chul-jang	business trip
추억	chu-eog	memories	출퇴근	chul-toe-geun	commute
추위	chu-wi	cold	출판	chul-pan	publishing
추진	chu-jin	pushing ahead	출판사	chul-pan-sa	publisher
추진한다	chu-jin-han-da	carry forward	출현한다	chul-hyeon-han-da	emerge
추천	chu-cheon	suggestion	춤	chum	dance
추천한다	chu-cheon-han-da	recommend	춤춘다	chum-chun-da	dance
추측	chu-cheug	guess	춥다	chub-da	cold
축구공	chug-gu-gong	soccer ball	충격	chung-gyeog	shock
축구장	chug-gu-jang	soccer field	충격적	chung-gyeog-jeog	shocking
축소	chug-so	reduction	충고	chung-go	advice
축제	chug-je	festival	충돌	chung-dol	crash
축하	chug-ha	congrats	충돌한다	chung-dol-han-da	collide
축하한다	chug-ha-han-da	celebrate	충분하다	chung-bun-ha-da	suffice
춘다	chun-da	dance	충분히	chung-bun-hi	enough
출구	chul-gu	exit	취미	chwi-mi	hobby
출국	chul-gug	departure	취소	chwi-so	cancellation
출근	chul-geun	go to work	취소한다	chwi-so-han-da	cancel
출근한다	chul-geun-han-da	go to work	취업	chwi-eob	get a job
출발	chul-bal	start	취재	chwi-jae	gathering news
출발점	chul-bal-jeom	starting point	취직	chwi-jig	getting a job
출발한다	chul-bal-han-da	depart	취한다	chwi-han-da	get drunk
출산	chul-san	delivery	취향	chwi-hyang	taste
출석한다	chul-seog-han-da	attend	치과	chi-gwa	dentist
출신	chul-sin	native	치료	chi-ryo	cure
출연	chul-yeon	appearance	치료법	chi-ryo-beob	cure
출연한다	chul-yeon-han-da	appear	치료한다	chi-ryo-han-da	treat
출입	chul-ib	coming and going	치른다	chi-reun-da	pay
출입국	chul-ib-gug	immigration	치마	chi-ma	skirt
출입문	chul-ib-mun	entrance door	치아	chi-a	teeth

치약	chi-yag	toothpaste	캠페인	kaem-pe-in	campaign
치운다	chi-un-da	clean up	커진다	keo-jin-da	grow big
치즈	chi-jeu	cheese	커튼	keo-teun	curtain
친다	chin-da	hit	컨디션	keon-di-syeon	condition
친절	chin-jeol	kindness	컬러	keol-leo	color
친절하다	chin-jeol-ha-da	nice	케첩	ke-cheob	ketchup
친정	chin-jeong	married woman's parent' home	켜진다	kyeo-jin-da	turn on
친척	chin-cheog	relative	켠다	kyeon-da	turn on
친하다	chin-ha-da	close	코끝	ko-kkeut	tip of nose
친해진다	chin-hae-jin-da	become friendly	코너	ko-neo	corner
칠판	chil-pan	blackboard	코드	ko-deu	code
칠한다	chil-han-da	paint	코미디	ko-mi-di	comedy
침	chim	saliva	코스	ko-seu	course
침대	chim-dae	bed	코치	ko-chi	coach
침묵	chim-mug	silence	코트	ko-teu	coat
침실	chim-sil	bedroom	코피	ko-pi	nosebleed
침착하다	chim-chag-ha-da	keep calm	콘서트	kon-seo-teu	concert
칭찬	ching-chan	compliment	콜라	kol-la	cola
칭찬한다	ching-chan-han-da	praise	콤플렉스	kom-peul-leg-seu	complex
ㅋ			콩	kong	bean
카드	ka-deu	card	콩나물	kong-na-mul	bean sprouts
카레	ka-re	curry	쾌감	kwae-gam	pleasure
카메라	ka-me-ra	camera	쿠데타	ku-de-ta	coup d'etat
카운터	ka-un-teo	counter	크기	keu-gi	size
카페	ka-pe	cafe	크다	keu-da	big
칸	kan	space	크리스마스	keu-ri-seu-ma-seu	Christmas
칼	kal	knife	크림	keu-rim	cream
칼국수	kal-gug-su	chopped noodles	큰길	keun-gil	main street
캄캄하다	kam-kam-ha-da	it's dark	큰딸	keun-ttal	eldest daughter
캐릭터	kae-rig-teo	characters	큰소리	keun-so-ri	loud
캠퍼스	kaem-peo-seu	campus			

큰아들	keun-a-deul	eldest son	터널	teo-neol	tunnel
큰일	keun-il	big deal	터뜨린다	teo-tteu-rin-da	burst
큰절	keun-jeol	big bow	터미널	teo-mi-neol	terminal
클래식	keul-lae-sig	classic	터진다	teo-jin-da	explode
클럽	keul-leob	club	턱	teog	chin
키	ki	key	턴다	teon-da	dust off
키스	ki-seu	kiss	털	teol	hair
킬로	kil-lo	kilo	텅빈	teong bin	empty
킬로그램	kil-lo-geu-raem	kilogram	테니스	te-ni-seu	tennis
킬로미터	kil-lo-mi-teo	kilometer	테러	te-reo	terror
E			테스트	te-seu-teu	test
타고난다	ta-go-nan-da	innate	테이블	te-i-beul	table
타락	ta-rag	corruption	테이프	te-i-peu	tape
타오른다	ta-o-reun-da	burn	텍스트	teg-seu-teu	text
타입	ta-ib	type	텔레비전	tel-le-bi-jeon	television
타자기	ta-ja-gi	typewriter	토끼	to-kki	rabbit
탁	tag	bump	토대	to-dae	foundation
탁월하다	tag-wol-ha-da	excellent	토론	to-ron	debate
탁자	tag-ja	table	토론자	to-ron-ja	panelist
탄다	tan-da	ride	토론한다	to-ron-han-da	have a discussion
탄생	tan-saeng	birth	토론회	to-ron-hoe	debate
탄생한다	tan-saeng-han-da	be born	토마토	to-ma-to	tomato
탈출한다	tal-chul-han-da	escape	토한다	to-han-da	vomit
탑	tab	tower	톤	ton	ton
탓	tas	fault	통	tong	container
태아	tae-a	fetus	통계	tong-gye	statistics
태양	tae-yang	sun	통과	tong-gwa	pass
태운다	tae-un-da	burn	통과한다	tong-gwa-han-da	pass
택시	taeg-si	taxi	통로	tong-lo	passage
택한다	taeg-han-da	select	통역	tong-yeog	translation
탤런트	tael-leon-teu	talent			

통일한다	tong-il-han-da	unify		튼튼히	teun-teun-hi	firmly
통장	tong-jang	bank book		틀	teul	frame
통제	tong-je	control		틀렸다	teul-lyeoss-da	wrong
통증	tong-jeung	ache		틀림없다	teul-lim-eobs-da	no doubt
통합	tong-hab	integration		틀림없이	teul-lim-eobs-i	no doubt
통화	tong-hwa	call		틈	teum	crevice
퇴근	toe-geun	leave work		티브이	ti-beu-i	TV
퇴근한다	toe-geun-han-da	leave work		티셔츠	ti-syeo-cheu	T-shirt
퇴원	toe-won	discharge		팀	tim	team
퇴원한다	toe-won-han-da	discharge		**ㅍ**		
퇴직금	toe-jig-geum	severance pay		파	pa	green onion
투명하다	tu-myeong-ha-da	transparent		파괴한다	pa-goe-han-da	destroy
투표	tu-pyo	vote		파도	pa-do	wave
튀긴다	twi-gin-da	fry		파랗다	pa-rah-da	blue
튀김	twi-gim	fried food		파리	pa-ri	fly
튀어나온다	twi-eo-na-on-da	pop up		파일	pa-il	file
튄다	twin-da	splatter		파출소	pa-chul-so	police box
트럭	teu-reog	truck		파티	pa-ti	party
트인다	teu-in-da	open up		판	pan	board
특급	teug-geub	express		판결	pan-gyeol	verdict
특별	teug-byeol	special		판다	pan-da	dig
특별하다	teug-byeol-ha-da	special		판단	pan-dan	judgment
특별히	teug-byeol-hi	especially		판단한다	pan-dan-han-da	judge
특성	teug-seong	characteristic		판매	pan-mae	sale
특수	teug-su	special		판매된다	pan-mae-doen-da	be sold
특수성	teug-su-seong	distinctiveness		판매한다	pan-mae-han-da	sell
특이하다	teug-i-ha-da	strange		판사	pan-sa	judge
특정한다	teug-jeong-han-da	be specific		팔	pal	arm
튼다	teun-da	turn on		팔린다	pal-lin-da	sell
튼튼하다	teun-teun-ha-da	strong		팝송	pab-song	pop song
				패션	pae-syeon	fashion

팩	paeg	pack	포근하다	po-geun-ha-da	comfy
팩스	paeg-seu	fax	포기한다	po-gi-han-da	give up
팩시밀리	paeg-si-mil-li	fax	포도주	po-do-ju	wine
팬	paen	fan	포스터	po-seu-teo	poster
팬티	paen-ti	panties	포인트	po-in-teu	point
퍼센트	peo-sen-teu	percent	포장	po-jang	packing
퍼진다	peo-jin-da	spread	포장마차	po-jang-ma-cha	snack cart
퍽	peog	very	포크	po-keu	fork
페인트	pe-in-teu	paint	포함	po-ham	including
펴낸다	pyeo-naen-da	publish	포함된다	po-ham-doen-da	to be included
편	pyeon	side	포함한다	po-ham-han-da	include
편견	pyeon-gyeon	prejudice	폭	pog	width
편리하다	pyeon-li-ha-da	convenient	폭넓다	pog-neolb-da	wide
편안하다	pyeon-an-ha-da	comfortable	폭력	pog-lyeog	violence
편의	pyeon-ui	convenience	표	pyo	graph
편하다	pyeon-ha-da	comfortable	표면	pyo-myeon	surface
편히	pyeon-hi	at ease	표시	pyo-si	mark
펼쳐진다	pyeol-chyeo-jin-da	unfold	표시한다	pyo-si-han-da	denote
평	pyeong	3.3058m2	표준	pyo-jun	standard
평가된다	pyeong-ga-doen-da	be evaluated	표현된다	pyo-hyeon-doen-da	be expressed
평가한다	pyeong-ga-han-da	evaluate	푸르다	pu-reu-da	blue
평균	pyeong-gyun	average	푹	pug	good
평범하다	pyeong-beom-ha-da	normal	푼다	pun-da	scoop out
평상시	pyeong-sang-si	normally	풀	pul	grass
평생	pyeong-saeng	forever	풀린다	pul-lin-da	untied
평소	pyeong-so	usually	풀어진다	pul-eo-jin-da	be released
평일	pyeong-il	weekday	품	pum	width
평화	pyeong-hwa	peace	품는다	pum-neun-da	incubate
평화롭다	pyeong-hwa-rob-da	peaceful	품목	pum-mog	subject
폐지	pye-ji	abolition	품질	pum-jil	quality

풍경	pung-gyeong	sight	하나하나	ha-na-ha-na	one by one
풍부하다	pung-bu-ha-da	abundant	하느님	ha-neu-nim	God
풍속	pung-sog	wind speed	하드웨어	ha-deu-we-eo	hardware
풍습	pung-seub	custom	하룻밤	ha-rus-bam	overnight
프로	peu-ro	pro	하반기	ha-ban-gi	second half
프린터	peu-rin-teo	printer	하숙집	ha-sug-jib	boarding house
플라스틱	peul-la-seu-tig	plastic	하순	ha-sun	late
피	pi	blood	하얗다	ha-yah-da	white
피곤	pi-gon	tired	하여튼	ha-yeo-teun	anyway
피곤하다	pi-gon-ha-da	tired	하천	ha-cheon	river
피디	pi-di	PD	하품	ha-pum	yawn
피로	pi-ro	fatigue	하필	ha-pil	of all
피로하다	pi-ro-ha-da	tired	하하	ha-ha	haha
피망	pi-mang	pimento	학과	hag-gwa	department
피부	pi-bu	skin	학교생활	hag-gyo-saeng-hwal	school life
피운다	pi-un-da	smoke	학급	hag-geub	class
피자	pi-ja	pizza	학기	hag-gi	semester
피해자	pi-hae-ja	victim	학력	hag-lyeog	education
핀다	pin-da	blossom	학번	hag-beon	student ID
필름	pil-leum	film	학부모	hag-bu-mo	parents
필수	pil-su	necessary	학비	hag-bi	school expenses
필수적	pil-su-jeog	essential	학생증	hag-saeng-jeung	student ID
필연적	pil-yeon-jeog	inevitable	학술	hag-sul	academic
필요성	pil-yo-seong	necessity	학습	hag-seub	learning
필자	pil-ja	writer	학원	hag-won	academy
필통	pil-tong	pencil case	학위	hag-wi	degree
핑계	ping-gye	excuse	학자	hag-ja	scholar
ㅎ			학점	hag-jeom	grades
하	ha	under	한	han	one
하긴	ha-gin	but	한가운데	han-ga-un-de	midst
하나님	ha-na-nim	God			

한가하다	han-ga-ha-da	idle	한쪽	han-jjog	pair
한겨울	han-gyeo-ul	midwinter	한참	han-cham	long time
한결	han-gyeol	more	한창	han-chang	in full swing
한구석	han-gu-seog	one corner	한층	han-cheung	even
한국말	han-gug-mal	Korean	한평생	han-pyeong-saeng	a lifetime
한국어	han-gug-eo	Korean	한한다	han-han-da	limit
한국적	han-gug-jeog	Korean	할인	hal-in	discount
한글	han-geul	Hangul	함께한다	ham-kke-han-da	together
한글날	han-geul-nal	Hangul Day	함부로	ham-bu-ro	thoughtlessly
한꺼번에	han-kkeo-beon-e	at the same time	합격	hab-gyeog	pass
한낮	han-naj	midday	합격한다	hab-gyeog-han-da	pass an examination
한눈	han-nun	glance	합리적	hab-li-jeog	rational
한데	han-de	together	합친다	hab-chin-da	combine
한동안	han-dong-an	for a while	합한다	hab-han-da	fit
한두	han-du	one or two	항공	hang-gong	airline
한둘	han-dul	one or two	항공기	hang-gong-gi	aircraft
한때	han-ttae	one time	항구	hang-gu	harbor
한마디	han-ma-di	a word	항의	hang-ui	protest
한문	han-mun	Chinese	해결	hae-gyeol	solution
한밤중	han-bam-jung	midnight	해결된다	hae-gyeol-doen-da	solved
한복	han-bog	han bok	해결한다	hae-gyeol-han-da	settle
한순간	han-sun-gan	for a moment	해낸다	hae-naen-da	accomplish
한숨	han-sum	sigh	해답	hae-dab	solution
한식	han-sig	Korean	해당	hae-dang	corresponding
한여름	han-yeo-reum	midsummer	해당된다	hae-dang-doen-da	applicable
한자	han-ja	Chinese character	해당한다	hae-dang-han-da	applicable
한잔	han-jan	a drink	해롭다	hae-rob-da	harmful
한잔한다	han-jan-han-da	have a drink	해마다	hae-ma-da	year after year
한정된다	han-jeong-doen-da	be limited	해물	hae-mul	seafood
한정한다	han-jeong-han-da	limit	해석	hae-seog	translation

해석한다	hae-seog-han-da	interpret	허용	heo-yong	permit
해설	hae-seol	commentary	허용된다	heo-yong-doen-da	allowed
해소	hae-so	solution	허용한다	heo-yong-han-da	permit
해소한다	hae-so-han-da	release	허허	heo-heo	haha
해수욕장	hae-su-yog-jang	beach	헌	heon	old
해안	hae-an	coast	헤맨다	he-maen-da	wander about
해외	hae-oe	overseas	헤아린다	he-a-rin-da	count
해외여행	hae-oe-yeo-haeng	overseas travel	헤어진다	he-eo-jin-da	say goodbye
핵심	haeg-sim	main point	헬기	hel-gi	helicopter
핸드백	haen-deu-baeg	handbag	혀	hyeo	tongue
핸드폰	haen-deu-pon	cell phone	현	hyeon	present
햄버거	haem-beo-geo	hamburger	현관	hyeon-gwan	entrance
햇볕	haes-byeot	sunshine	현관문	hyeon-gwan-mun	main door
햇빛	haes-bicc	sunshine	현금	hyeon-geum	cash
햇살	haes-sal	sunlight	현대인	hyeon-dae-in	modern
행동한다	haeng-dong-han-da	act	현대적	hyeon-dae-jeog	modern
행복	haeng-bog	happiness	현실적	hyeon-sil-jeog	realistic
행복하다	haeng-bog-ha-da	happy	현지	hyeon-ji	local
행사	haeng-sa	event	혈액	hyeol-aeg	blood
행운	haeng-un	luck	협력	hyeob-lyeog	cooperation
행한다	haeng-han-da	do	형사	hyeong-sa	detective
행해진다	haeng-hae-jin-da	done	형성	hyeong-seong	formation
향	hyang	incense	형성된다	hyeong-seong-doen-da	formed
향기	hyang-gi	scent	형성한다	hyeong-seong-han-da	form
향상	hyang-sang	improving	형식적	hyeong-sig-jeog	formal
향상된다	hyang-sang-doen-da	improve	형제	hyeong-je	sibling
향수	hyang-su	perfume	형편	hyeong-pyeon	circumstances
허가	heo-ga	permission	혜택	hye-taeg	benefits
허락	heo-rag	permission	호기심	ho-gi-sim	curiosity
허락한다	heo-rag-han-da	permit	호남	ho-nam	Jeonrado

호박	ho--bag	pumpkin		확대된다	hwag-dae-doen-da	enlarge
호선	ho-seon	line		확대한다	hwag-dae-han-da	enlarge
호수	ho-su	lake		확립한다	hwag-lib-han-da	establish
호실	ho-sil	room		확보	hwag-bo	secure
호주머니	ho-ju-meo-ni	pocket		확산된다	hwag-san-doen-da	spread
호텔	ho-tel	hotel		확신	hwag-sin	assurance
호흡	ho-heub	breath		확신한다	hwag-sin-han-da	convinced
혹시	hog-si	if		확실하다	hwag-sil-ha-da	certainly
혼난다	hon-nan-da	get scolded		확실히	hwag-sil-hi	surely
혼잣말	hon-jas-mal	soliloquy		확인	hwag-in	confirmation
홀로	hol-lo	alone		확인된다	hwag-in-doen-da	confirmed
홈페이지	hom-pe-i-ji	home page		확장	hwag-jang	expansion
홍보	hong-bo	promotion		확정	hwag-jeong	confirmed
홍수	hong-su	flood		환갑	hwan-gab	60th birthday
홍차	hong-cha	black tea		환경오염	hwan-gyeong-o-yeom	pollution
화	hwa	fury		환영	hwan-yeong	illusion
화가	hwa-ga	artist		환영한다	hwan-yeong-han-da	welcome
화난다	hwa-nan-da	angry		환율	hwan-yul	exchange rate
화려하다	hwa-ryeo-ha-da	gorgeous		환하다	hwan-ha-da	clear
화면	hwa-myeon	screen		활기	hwal-gi	vigor
화분	hwa-bun	flowerpot		활동한다	hwal-dong-han-da	act
화살	hwa-sal	arrow		활발하다	hwal-bal-ha-da	be actively
화장	hwa-jang	makeup		활발해진다	hwal-bal-hae-jin-da	become active
화장실	hwa-jang-sil	restroom		활발히	hwal-bal-hi	actively
화장지	hwa-jang-ji	paper towel		활용	hwal-yong	uses
화장품	hwa-jang-pum	cosmetics		활용한다	hwal-yong-han-da	utilize
화재	hwa-jae	fire		활짝	hwal-jjag	wide open
화제	hwa-je	issue		회견	hoe-gyeon	interview
화학	hwa-hag	chemistry		회관	hoe-gwan	hall
확	hwag	sudden		회복	hoe-bog	recovery

회복된다	hoe-bog-doen-da	recover	흐름	heu-reum	flow
회복한다	hoe-bog-han-da	to recover	흐리다	heu-ri-da	cloudy
회원	hoe-won	member	흑백	heug-baeg	black and white
회의	hoe-ui	conference	흑인	heug-in	black
회전	hoe-jeon	rotation	흔든다	heun-deun-da	shake
회화	hoe-hwa	conversation	흔들린다	heun-deul-lin-da	oscillate
횟수	hoes-su	number	흔적	heun-jeog	trace
횡단보도	hoeng-dan-bo-do	crosswalk	흔하다	heun-ha-da	common
효과적	hyo-gwa-jeog	effective	흘러간다	heul-leo-gan-da	flow
효도	hyo-do	filial piety	흘러나온다	heul-leo-na-on-da	flow out
효도한다	hyo-do-han-da	be filial	흘러내린다	heul-leo-nae-rin-da	run down
효율적	hyo-yul-jeog	efficient	흘린다	heul-lin-da	spill
효자	hyo-ja	filial piety	흙	heulg	soil
후기	hu-gi	review	흥미	heung-mi	interest
후반	hu-ban	second half	흥미롭다	heung-mi-rob-da	interesting
후배	hu-bae	junior	흥분	heung-bun	excitement
후보	hu-bo	candidate	흥분한다	heung-bun-han-da	excited
후춧가루	hu-chus-ga-ru	pepper powder	흩어진다	heut-eo-jin-da	scatter
후회	hu-hoe	regret	희곡	hui-gog	drama
후회한다	hu-hoe-han-da	regret	희다	hui-da	white
훈련	hun-lyeon	training	희망	hui-mang	hope
훌륭하다	hul-lyung-ha-da	excellent	희망한다	hui-mang-han-da	hope
훔친다	hum-chin-da	steal	희생	hui-saeng	sacrifice
휴가	hyu-ga	vacation	희생한다	hui-saeng-han-da	sacrifice
휴식	hyu-sig	rest	힘겹다	him-gyeob-da	it's hard
휴일	hyu-il	day off	힘껏	him-kkeos	amain
휴지	hyu-ji	tissue	힘들어한다	him-deul-eo-han-da	have a hard time
휴지통	hyu-ji-tong	trash can	힘쓴다	him-sseun-da	work hard
흉내	hyung-nae	mimicry	힘없이	him-eobs-i	helplessly
흐려진다	heu-ryeo-jin-da	become cloudy	힘차다	him-cha-da	be strong

MEMO